Axel Theodor Goës

On the reticularian Rhizopoda of the Caribbean Sea

Axel Theodor Goës

On the reticularian Rhizopoda of the Caribbean Sea

ISBN/EAN: 9783743319981

Manufactured in Europe, USA, Canada, Australia, Japa

Cover: Foto ©ninafisch / pixelio.de

Manufactured and distributed by brebook publishing software (www.brebook.com)

Axel Theodor Goës

On the reticularian Rhizopoda of the Caribbean Sea

Among the Lesser Antilles steep banks slope down to considerable depths either directly from the shores, or from the edges of the supporting basis, sunk plateaus of varying extent, usually in forty fathoms water. These banks exhibit within a limited area a remarkable diversity in the conditions offered to animal life, resulting chiefly from the rapid sinking of the temperature from the surface downwards. For, while the littoral zone enjoys an average temperature of $+26°$ C., the bottom at 300 fathoms has $+14°$ C., and at 600 fathoms the reading of the thermometer is not more than about $+5°$ C.

Thus within a very restricted space a bottom is found, which exhibits in great variety representatives of the different areas. Of course, these areas cannot be defined by exact boundary lines. Many of the inhabitants of the cold zone have their outposts high up in the temperate regions and *vice versa*. The denizens of the warm zone however seem to confine themselves to a limited range not reaching lower than 100 fathoms. In profusion of animal life this zone equals or even surpasses localities in other seas which in this respect have become famous. Every spot is teeming with organisms, from masses of Corallines invading and destroying all the vacant shells and calcareous skeletons of every description, and transforming them into amorphous lumps and rocks, to the powerful reef-building Madreporaria with their associated forests of Alcyonaria, and their immense crowds of lodgers and parasites of Crustacea, Annelida, Mollusca, Echinodermata and Protozoa. But it should be borne in mind, that the common dredge seldom affords proof of this abundance, which is hidden in the crevices and tunnels of hard, dead coral-stems and incrustations of Corallines. When however a more muddy and loose bottom is met with, the dredge often becomes choked to the jaws with masses of specimens, particularly clusters of byssiferous Mollusca: Arca, Spondylus etc. sheltering an innumerable host of other Evertebrates.

Already at from 90 to 150 fathoms a fauna begins to appear, the elements of which are different from those of the littoral zone. Here the kingdom of brightly coloured Spongiæ displays its splendour of yellow, orange, red and brown, imparting to most of their cohabitants a higher glow than is generally acquired even in the zone above. This Spongia-zone is very narrow, often disappearing at 200 fathoms, sometimes earlier, particularly where the bottom slopes more gradually and affords more favourable conditions for the deposition of chalk-ooze, which appears in some way to prejudice the growth of the coloured Spongiæ.

The next and third zone may appropriately be designated as the region of Rhizopods, or the real chalk bottom, as nowhere else in this sea this class becomes more prevalent and conspicuous in high development of forms and abundance of specimens than here. It usually commences at from 200 to 300 fathoms. Here many denizens of the deep cold area already present themselves, and it is very probable, that a painstaking and prolonged investigation even in this shallow water would bring to light most of the members of the abyssal fauna.

The constituents of this bottom deposit are chiefly:

1. Very fine amorphous chalk-ooze together with fragments of various exuviæ in great abundance, forming the bulk of the deposit and causing it to be peculiarly heavy and tough.

2. A large quantity of small (0,25 mm.) ovoid-shaped bodies, whose surface is slightly impressed with coarse reticulation. These are composed of tightly compressed or agglutinated chalk-ooze and are of a darker gray hue than the rest of the ooze. Unquestionably they have been formed in the intestines of some lower organisms and represent in a small way the coprolites of the cretaceous strata.

3. Shells of pigmy and young reticularian Rhizopods presenting themselves in great quantity and belonging chiefly to Planorbulina, Pulvinulina, Textularia-formed Buliminæ, Orbiculina, Cornuspira, Miliolina etc.

4. Larger reticularian Rhizopods often in great abundance, chiefly Nodosarinæ, Globigerinæ, Pulvinulinæ, Planorbulinæ, Textulariæ, Amphistegina, Valvulinæ and Litnolinæ.

5. Exuviæ of Molluscs of many descriptions, particularly of the pelagic Pteropoda: Creseis, Hyalea, Cuvieria etc., besides a number of the inhabitants of the ooze.

6. Spongia-spicules, but in very limited quantity, as also a few skeletons of radiolarian Rhizopods and of Diatomaceæ; silicious substances being, in general, very scarce.

There is also another sort of bottom with Rhizopods met with on the very declivities of the banks, where the deposit seemingly consists of an aggregation of dead corallines, calcareous skeletons and worms-nests, all transformed into rough masses and lumps resembling old hardened mortar and gravel. This bottom yields a quantity of shell-sand abounding in large and fine Rhizopods. A nearly similar formation, but on a more level bottom, was met with by Count DE POURTALÈS off Florida and was called after its eminent explorer *Pourtales' Plateau* (Report by L. AGASSIZ; Bullet. Mus. Harv. College I. p. 367). This kind of bottom I have provisionally distinguished as Coralline-gravel.

The high development of the reticularian Rhizopods both on this bottom and in the real ooze is remarkable, not being surpassed even by the same forms which are so much admired in the cretaceous and tertiary strata. *Nodosarina communis* D'ORB. attains here a length of 20 mm.; *Nod. complanata* DEFR. the size of a small fingernail, while *Orbiculina*, *Cornuspira* and *Miliolina*, *Discorbina*, *Pulvinulina* attain a size far superior to those of the littoral zone. *Textularia trochus* D'ORB. assumes a labyrinthic structure and becomes compressed nearly in the same way as a *Cuneolina* D'ORB. Large *bigenerine Textulariæ* associated with very large *nodosarine Lituolinæ*, *Valvulinæ* and *Uvigerinæ* present themselves in great abundance. The *Nummulinidæ* are represented by strongly developed *Amphisteginæ*.

Polymorphina, *Rotalina*, *Orbitolites*, *Operculina* are strikingly absent; *Polystomella* is scanty and stunted.

The want of silicious sand in the ooze may account for the fact, that agglutinating forms, which in other places generally construct their shells of such matter, on this sea-bed usually build them up of *calcareous* fragments. Some species seem to choose for their building-materials the finest mud, which imparts to the shell a fine grain and a certain degree of smoothness. As a substitute for silicious sand others again make use of available sponge-needles intermixing them with calcareous debris. Only a few forms succeed in conglutinating their shells entirely of silicious sand-grains.

It is however somewhat surprising to meet with Lituolina- and Valvulina-forms constructed of such sand, and associated with them their nearest kindred or even the same species incased in calcareous sand and greatly differing in outward shape.

This association on a bottom so deficient in silicious sand, and the apparently decided predilection for that material found among these *silicious* forms, as well as their difference in shape from their calcareous congeners, leave the systematist in some suspense as to the true relation that one set bears to the other. For the present I am inclined to consider their differences to be but of varietal importance.

Some twenty years ago Professor v. REUSS assigned to the agglutinating reticularian Rhizopods a separate place in his system by establishing the suborder *arenaceosilicious*. To this group were referred by its author both those genera the forms of which are not invariably arenaceous, as Valvulina, Bulimina, Textularia, and those genera which are considered as constantly agglutinating, as Lituolina, Trochammina etc. Of these agglutinating genera Lituolina, Trochammina and Valvulina only were at the same period, or rather somewhat before, placed by CARPENTER in the »arenaceous» sub-order, (Introduct. p. 140.) Thus the two authors differ widely as to the compass of this group. Besides, the German naturalist seems not to have recognised other agglutinating forms than »silicious», whilst the English authors state that at least some forms of this sub-order construct their tests of foreign materials of any description — both silicious and calcareous, (CARP., Introd. p. 143; BRADY, Carbonif. and Perm. Foramf., Palæont. Soc. 30, p. 9.)

The impropriety of splitting up such genera as Textularia, Bulimina etc. in order to get their agglutinating forms ranged within the silicious group, is manifest; and as an illustration of the impropriety of the character itself — »silicious» — may serve not only the Lituolinæ and Valvulinæ just mentioned, from my own dredgings, but also the bigenerine multiserial forms of Textularia, which all were referred to this sub-order by its author, but which often have been found »calcareous». TERQUEM also states, that he met with Verneuilina from the Oolitic strata both of calcareous and of silicious construction. (Les Foramf. du Syst. oolit.; Bullet. Soc. hist. nat. Département de la Moselle, 1868, 11, p. 39.)

Consequently, since Prof. v. Reuss' definition of this group has proved to be misleading, the limitation of the »arenaceous« suborder laid down by the British naturalists, particularly by CARPENTER and BRADY, must provisionally be adopted as more or less consistent with nature. Still it should not be overlooked, that of late some few evidences have been adduced, which tend to weaken the confidence in the stability of those prominent characteristics, on which the two sub-orders: »arenaceous« and »vitreous« have been established. Thus, when a whole assemblage of arenaceous species are met with, each assuming the identical shape with that of the corresponding form in the vitreous group, the suggestion is easy, that in as much as a species of Textularia or Bulimina is considered likely to appear in the two conditions, the same sort of identity may also exist in other cases, where a similar kind of dimorphism has been met with. At present science is acquainted with not a few forms amongst the vitreous group, which have their corresponding isomorphs within the arenaceous. Nodosarina, Globigerina, Rotalina, besides the forms just mentioned, afford a fair illustration of this isomorphism. It would therefore be but just to give some credit to the suggestions of several able observers, such as DAWSON[1], WALLICH[2]) and SOLLAS[3]), in regard to the near relation between and even the identity of many arenaceous and vitreous forms, which have been hitherto kept far asunder.

Rash and unphilosophical differentiation of varieties, which have specific unity, as also generic distinctions based on trifling and not even constant characters, is an evil long complained of to descriptive biology in general, and, as to this class in particular, the trespassing in this respect — begun by the founder of systematic Rhizopodology and continued up to this very day — has passed beyond the boundaries of logic and common sense.

Those who have been engaged in the laborious task of throwing light upon the nomenclature of this class, may in many instances have been struck at finding their lists of synonyms swelled to hundreds by different names having been conferred on forms without even varietal distinction, founded upon quite accidental or individual diversity or on no differentiating characters whatever. In this way names have been heaped upon names for one and the same thing, rendering any attempt to arrange all those synonyms the most unremunerative and time-wasting kind of scientific labour. Such proceedings, resulting from want of discernment and judiciousness, would, if not checked by careful and philosophical researches, produce perpetual confusion and render any view of the generic and specific affinity between the forms obscure.

In the midst of this *rudis indigestaque moles* of descriptive biology the scrupulous and ingenious investigations of the eminent and well-known British naturalists: Professors W. C. WILLIAMSON, W. K. PARKER, W. B. CARPENTER and H. BRADY have established a good deal of clearness and systematic order, based on a thorough expe-

---

[1]) Foramf. of St. Lawrence; Canad. Naturalist (n. s.) 5, p. 176; An. M. N. H. (4) 7, p. 86.

[2]) Deep-sea researches on the Biology of Globigerina; Lond. 1876, pp. 62 et seq.

[3]) On the perforated character of the genus Webbina; Geol. Mag. dec. 2, 4 p. 105. (Those »Webbinæ« seem to be irregular Planorbulinæ).

rience of the value of the different characters afforded by this class. It has been objected that the trinomial nomenclature introduced by some of these authors, according to which most of the forms are ranked as varieties under a few species, would involve some inconvenience in dealing with a systematic arrangement of the forms, and on this account it has been of late recommended to return to the method of D'ORBIGNY, v. REUSS and others, which claims a separate designation of specific value for the slightest modification of characters — even when accidental — a method quite out of classical custom and not consistent with ontogenetic biology, the aim of which is to attain a delineation of the origin, descent and affinity of the forms, as true and natural as possible. With this end in view the true notion of »species«, that is to say certain eminent points or landmarks within the masses of modifications, should not be given up.

The amount of difference between forms that warrants their establishment as »species« must always be liable to a more or less arbitrary determination; but it may reasonably be asked of careful observers, who cannot but be interested in keeping the system free from the encumbrance of overcrowding with insignificant distinctions, that they should use some discrimination in valuing the characters for specific distinction.

If a model plan of arrangement for this and other classes of organisms were to be ventured on, it ought to take the shape of a somewhat regular network, where the nodes would indicate the »species«, the nearly equal amount of diversity between which and relation to one another would be marked by the converging and diverging internodes, while the more conspicuous varieties were to be placed on short lines radiating from the nodes. It would then be disturbing to ones sense of natural order, if a form of minor and inconstant divergence should be placed on a node.

Thus I am fully convinced of the propriety of the plan introduced into descriptive biology by LINNÆUS and to a larger extent than ever re-established by those before mentioned English philosophers, considering it a most valuable and suggestive step forward. As for the »varieties« or modifications of minor deviation, the more conspicuous only should be designated in the usual Linnæan way, and those which present merely an individual or accidental difference should not be allowed to become an encumbrance to the system, but mentioned only *en passant*.

In a system founded on true morphological characters it must be quite improper to distinguish one stage of growth by one appellation and institute a new genus for another stage of the same species. Such names should be discarded as generic and used merely to indicate a certain plan of growth. As such illegitimate genera must be regarded: *Clavulina*, *Bigenerina*, *Dimorphina*, *Sagrina* etc., as has been fully demonstrated by PARKER and JONES.

As for the synonyms appended to most of the species in this paper, the list is so far incomplete as merely those created and used by D'ORBIGNY and his successors are referred to, while those of his predecessors, with a few exceptions, are passed over, their nomenclature having been so thoroughly treated of by the unsurpassed investigations of PARKER and JONES, that, for the present at least, it lies beyond my purpose and even power again to review that part of Rhizopodology. Although in arranging these synonymic lists the shrewd and expert indications of those authors have in great measure been consulted, still a great deal of incorrectness and incompleteness may be found by further criticism, for if oftentimes it becomes almost impossible to identify stunted and deformed specimens of this class, it is a still more arduous task to recognize more or less defective delineations of them. Other designations of species besides those represented by figures are not touched upon, as those which are merely recorded, usually lie beyond the limits of scientific jurisdiction. This review is intended to give a synopsis of the principal varieties and at the same time a statement of the range of their geographical and geological distribution.

Not many years ago the Caribbean sea-bed was little more than a *terra incognita* to biological science. While staying for a few years in the Island of St. Bartholomew, one of the Lesser Antilles, I took the opportunity during 1866 and 1869 to make several dredging excursions. But being provided with only a very scanty and primitive equipment I was not able to explore greater depths than 400 fathoms. The principal stations were between St. Bartholomew and St. Eustatius; to the leeward of St. Martin and Anguilla; and windward off the eastern keys of the Virgin Islands. The bottom-deposit designated as Globigerina- or Chalk-ooze was met with between 250 and 400 fathoms chiefly at the second station, the rough Coralline gravel at the first and third stations in 300 fathoms.

In 1868 the United States began to extend their coast-survey into the Caribbean sea and on several occasions since have renewed their exploring expeditions on a large scale combined with researches on the fauna of the sea-bed. The beautiful results of these explorations, for which we are indebted chiefly to the unremitting exertions of the lamented eminent American naturalist Count de POURTALÈS, have been made known during the last decade principally through the Catalogue and Bulletin of the Museum of Comparative Zoology, Harvard College, Cambridge Massachusetts.

The »Challenger's» famous expedition has also largely contributed to our knowledge of these localities.

My own more modest collections have been partly reviewed by Professor S. LOVÉN, Professor G. LINDSTRÖM, Dr. A. LJUNGMAN and Professor G. O. SARS.

The following are the more important papers dealing with this local fauna:

1870—71: *Crustacea* by W. STIMPSON: Bulletin Mus. compar. zool. Harvard College. 2. p. 109.

1871: *Deep-sea Corals* by DE POURTALÈS. Illustr. Catalogue Mus. compar. zool. Harvard College, N:o 4.

» *Brachiopoda* by W. H. DALL: Bullet. Mus. compar. zool. Harv. Coll, 3. p. 1.
» *Ophiuridea* by A. LJUNGMAN: Öfversigt af Kgl. Vet. Ak. Handlingar p. 615.
» *Cumacea* by G. O. SARS, ibid. p. 803.
» *Bryozoa* by F. A. SMITT: Kgl. Vet. Ak. Handl. (n. s.) 10, N:o 11; 11, N:o 4.

1874: Etudes sur les *Echinoïdées* par S. LOVÉN: Kgl. Vet. Ak. Handl. (n. s.) 11, N:o 7.

» *Echini, Crinoids, Corals* by AL. AGASSIZ and DE POURTALÈS: Illustr. Catal. Mus. comp. zool. Harv. Coll. N:o 8. 1.

1875: *Ophiuridæ, Astrophytidæ* by LYMAN. Illustr. Catalogue Mus. compar. zool. Harvard College N:o 8. ›.
1876: *Actinology* of the Atlantic Ocean by G. LINDSTRÖM. Kgl. Vet. Ak. Handlingar (N. S.) 14, N:o 6.
1877: *Hydroida* by GEORGE ALLMAN: Mem. Mus. comp. zool. Harvard Coll. 5, N:o 2.
1878: *Echini* by AGASSIZ, *Corals* and *Crinoidea* by POURTALÈS, *Ophiuridæ* by LYMAN: Bull. Mus. comp. zool. Harvard College 5, N:o 9.
1879: *Hydroida* by S. F. CLARKE: Bull. Mus. comp. zool. Harvard College 5, N:o 10.

In 1868 Professor FR. A. SMITT and Dr. A. LJUNGMAN were fortunate enough to be authorized to accompany as naturalists His Swed. Majesty's ship »Josephine» on her cruise in the Atlantic. At several stations, particularly off the Azores, they succeeded, with their most simple apparatus and without steam, in touching the bottom with the dredge at from 700 to 900 fathoms. Their extensive collection incorporated with that of the State Museum at Stockholm contains a great many interesting and highly developed Reticularian Rhizopods. I have availed myself of this collection in studying the Caribbean forms.

To acknowledge my great obligations to a few gentlemen for their assistance in the preparation of this paper is to me only a pleasant duty.

To Professor S. LOVÉN I am greatly indebted for the liberality, with which he placed the collections of the State Museum at my disposal for examination as also for his generous, instructive and encouraging support throughout the course of the work.

Thanks to the able and disinterested painstaking of my esteemed friend Professor G. LINDSTRÖM I have obtained ample information concerning much of the multifarious and scattered literature on the subject.

To my learned and sensible friend J. A. AHLSTRAND, Custos of the library of the Royal Academy of Sciences, it is but due that I should render thanks for his obliging and unwearied assistance in amply furnishing me with such papers and books as were required.

Lagenæ

are but scantily represented on our localities. As the more remarkable forms I have noted:

L. lævis MONTAG. (L. vulgaris WILL.) appears in two forms, one highly developed with a long neck, and another stunted, starved and with a short neck or with a thick-edged mouth, nearly without neck; such pigmy forms are often somewhat compressed and sometimes two-chambered;

L. lævis var. desmophora RYM. JONES (Java deep-sea Lagenæ; Trans. Lin. Soc. 30, p. 54, t. 19, figg. 23—24). Our form differs in having the chain-like ornamentation wound in a whole spiral from the bottom to the middle of the neck; the Java specimens being furnished with several longitudinal garlands or chains. It is one of the finest forms, well developed, but very scarce, from the ooze;

L. lævis var. marginata WALK & JAC; it is of the same shape as *Entosolenia marginata var. lagenoides* WILL. (Brit. rec. Formf. p. 11, fig. 25), *L. lagenoides* RSS. (Lagenoid: Wien. Ak. S. Ber. l. 46, p. 324, t. 2, figg. 27—28) and *L. vulgaris var. alatomarginata* RYM. JONES (loc. cit. p. 60, t. 19, fig. 44); it occurs in the ooze, scarce and in a pigmy state;

L. lævis var. tetragona PARK. & JONES (Phil. Trans. 155, 1. t. 18, fig. 14), pretty well developed, but scantily represented in the ooze.

L. squamosa MONTAG., scarce and starved.

L. distoma polita PARK. & JONES (N. Atl. and Arct. Oc.; Phil. Trans. 155, I. p. 357, t. 13, fig. 21). It may be considered as a variety of L. lævis; is found in the ooze well developed but scarce;

The insignificant part that the Lagenæ seem to take in the formation of the chalk-ooze and our scanty supply of specimens may sufficiently excuse my passing over their synonymy, for which, *in amplissima forma*, I refer the student to Messrs PARKERS', JONES' and BRADY's admirable treatise on the Crag-Foraminifera (Palæont. Soc. 19).

Nodosarina radicula LIN.
Tab. I, fig. 1—2.

If **Nod. radicula** L. and **Nod. scalaris** BATSCH, both having the same simple plan of growth — their chief difference being the smoothness or striation of the shell — are to be considered as the original types of this genus, two series of forms would be derived from them. Each of these series would then comprise:

1. a **Nodosarina** type = *apertura rotundata, testa recta, teres vel subteres, cameris in seriem dispositis:* Nod. radicula Lin. + Nod. scalaris Batsch.
2. a **Dentalina** type = *apertura rotunda, testa arcuata, teres, cameris in seriem dispositis:* Nod. communis d'Orb. + Nod. obliqua Lin.
3. a **Orthocerina** type (**Rhabdogonium** Rss.) = *apertura rotundata, testa tri-tetragona:* Nod. quadrilatera d'Orb. + O.
4. a **Vaginulina** type = *apertura rotundata, testa plus minusve compressa, plerumque arcuata, cameris in seriem plerumque dispositis:* Nod. legumen Lin. + Nod linearis Mont.
5. a **Cristellaria** type = *apertura rotundata vel trigona, testa plus minusve helicoidea:* Nod. calcar Lin. + Nod. costata Ficht. & Moll.
6. a **Glandulina** type = *apertura rotundata, testa recta, teres, cameris equitantibus vel amplectentibus:* Nod. lævigata d'Orb. - Nod. glans d'Orb.
7. a **Frondicularia** type = *apertura plerumque rotundata, testa compressa, cameris equitantibus:* Nod. complanata Defr. + Nod. striata d'Orb.
8. a **Lingulina** type = *apertura rimæformis, testa plerumque recta, compressa, cameris in seriem plerumque dispositis:* Nod. (Lingulina) carinata d'Orb. + Nod. (Lingulina) costata d'Orb.

Such would be a sketch of this genus in a systematic and descriptive sense. But we must be prepared to find, that this mode of arrangement answers but imperfectly to the natural order of things, for between each of these 15—16 species or types we shall meet with a host of varieties and intermediate forms. For their place in the system many of these depend mostly on the tact and discrimination of the systematist.

The list of synonyms is a fair exhibition of the links, which exist between the typical »species».

In the same way we meet with intermediate links between the smooth species and the corresponding striated ones of both series. And we shall therefore get into no less embarassment, if we look out for specific characters in the condition of the surface of the shell. For every »species» of the *scalaris*-series will sometimes be found to loose its ornamentation by age, the later chambers becoming smooth (= »semistriatæ», »seminudæ»); or the chambers are only partially marked with ribs and lines (= »intermittentes») or very sligthly striated (= »sublæves»). It is for this reason more consistent with the usual conception of »species», and also more agreeing with a philosophical and less confusing method of arrangement, after all, to consider the striated and ribbed Nodosarinæ as too closely allied with their corresponding smooth forms for to rank them as distinct species. In this respect we readily accept the method followed by Professor Williamson in his classical treatise »*On the recent Foraminifera of Great Britain*».

Between *Nod. radicula* Lin. and *Nod. monile* Sold. there seems at the first glance to be a wide interval of difference and yet it will be found impossible to claim for the latter the rank of species. Neither can N. radicula be well distinguished from *Nod.*

(*Glandulina*) *lævigata* d'ORB., nor from *Nod.* (*Lingulina*) *carinata* d'ORB. We meet also with the strongest affinities to *Nod.* (*Dentalina*) *communis* d'ORB., *Nod. legumen* LIN. och *Nod.* (*Cristellaria*) *crepidula* FICHT. & MOLL.

Some forms of *Frondicularia* (= *Nodos. complanata* DEFR.), which have been described as such, are but slightly compressed varieties of Nod. radicula.

Nod. semistriata d'ORB. shows its near relation to *Nod. scalaris*.

Our form is not commonly met with in the chalk-ooze; the pigmy form is not seldom more or less compressed.

Fig. 1: The typical form of *N. radicula* LIN. or *Nod. humilis* RÖM. It is a pigmy form, not common in the chalk-ooze. 1 b: The same more magnified.

Fig. 2: has enclosed narrow necks, which are transversely rippled, showing its affinity to *N. scalaris*. Were it not for its smooth surface and stout growth, it would have been placed with the latter.

Syn.	Nautilius	radicula	MONTAGU 1803, Test. Britann. p. 197, t. 6, fig. 4.
	Nodosaria	humilis	ROEM. 1841, Verstein. nordd. Kreidegebirg. p. 95, t. 15, f. 6.
	»	»	JONES & PARKER 1860, For. fr. Chellaston. Quart. Journ. geol. Soc. 16, p. 453, t. 19, f. 6.
	»	aspera	REUSS 1845, Böhm. Kreide 1, p. 26, t. 13, figg. 14—15 (spinosa).
	»	conferta	REUSS ibid. p. 26, t. 13, f. 10.
	»	radicula	PARKER & JONES 1865, Northatl. and Arct. Oceans; Phil. Transact. 155, 1, p. 341, t. 13, figg. 2—7.
	»	radicula var. Jonesi	BRADY 1866, Carbon. and Perm. Foram.; Pal. Society 30, p. 126, t. 10, fig. 13.
	Glandulina	mutabilis	REUSS 1862, Nordd. Hils u. Gault, Wien. Ak. Sitz. Ber. 1, 46, p. 58, t. 5, fgg. 7—11.
	»	aperta	STACHE 1865, Tert. Mergel d. Whaingaroa Haf; Nov. Reise. geol. 1, 2, p. 188, t. 22, fig. 11.
	»	erecta	STACHE ibid. p. 189, t. 22, fig. 12.
	»	immutabilis	SCHWAG. 1865, Jurass. Sch.; Würtemb. Nat. Verein Jhreshaft. 21, p. 114, t. 6, figg. 13—14, 18.
	»	cylindrica	ALTH, 1849, Umgeb. Lemberg, Haid. Nat. Abh. 3, 2, p. 271, t. 13, fig. 30.
	»	discreta	REUSS 1849, neue For. Osterr. tert. Beck.; Wien. Ak. Dkschr. 1. 1, p. 366, t. 46, fig. 3.
	»	cylindracea	REUSS, 1845, Böhm. Kreidef. 1, p. 25, t. 13, figg. 1—2; 1850, Kreidemerg. Lemberg: Haid. Nat. Abh. 4. 1, p. 23, t. 1, fig. 5.
	Nodosaria	Kingi	RICHT., 1861, Geinitz' Dyas, p. 124, t. 20, fig. 29.
	»	radicula var. Kingi	BRADY, 1876, Carbonif. and Perm. foramf.; Pal. Soc. 30, t. 10, fig. 12.
	Vaginulina	clavata	COSTA, 1855, Marna terz. Messina, Mem. Nap. 2, p. 145, t. 2, fig. 18.
	Nodosaria	subulata	REUSS., 1845, Böhm. Kreidef. 1, p. 26, t. 13, fig. 11.
	»	clava	CORNUEL, 1848, nouv. foss. microscop.; Mém. Soc. géol. France (2) 3, p. 250, t. 1, figg. 16—17.
	»	Kirkbyi	RICHT. 1861, Geinitz' Dyas p. 124, t. 20, fig. 30.
	»	Kirkbyi	SCHMID 1867, Kleine organische Form. Zechsteinkalk d. Selters Wetterau; Leonh. und Broan Jhb. 1867, p. 586, t. 6, fig. 55.
	»	radicula var. Kirkbyi	BRADY, 1876, Carbonif. and Perm. foramf.; Pal. Soc. 30, p. 126, t. 10, fig. 11.
	»	oblonga	COSTA, 1854, Pal. Nap. 2, t. 13, fig. 13. (N. communi propinqua).
	»	Naumanni	REUSS, 1873, Geinitz' Elbthal. Geb. Sachsen. 2, p. 82, t. II. 20, fig. 11.
	»	radicula	BRAD. 1876, Carb. and Perm. foram.; Pal. Society 30, p. 124, t. 10, figg. 7—10.
	»	Geinitzi	REUSS, 1854—55, Jahresb. Wetterau Gesellsch. 1, p. 77, fig. 12.
	»	»	RICHT., Ztschr. deutsch. geol. Gesellsch. 1855, 7, p. 532, t. 26, fig. 26.
	»	»	RICHT. 1861, Geinitz' Dyas p. 124, t. 20, fig. 28.

Syn. Nodosaria radicula var. Geinitzi BRADY, 1876, Carb. and Perm. foramf., Pal. Soc. 30, p. 124, t. 10, fig. 6.
» Neugeboreni HANTK., 1875, Clav. Szab. Sch. t. 2, fig. 5.
» pupa KARRER 1878, Foram. Luzon; Bolet. Comis. Mapa geol. Esp. 7, 2, p. 16, t. E, fig. 9.

Dent. subrecta, Nod. lepida, concinna REUSS, 1859, Westph. Kr.; Wien. Ak. Sitz.-Ber. 40, p. 182, t. 1, figg. 10, 2, 3.

Glandulina elongata REUSS, 1859, Westph. Kr., ibid. p. 190, t. 4, fig. 2.
» elegans, Reussi, Nod. incerta, Nod. Beyrichi, Nod. ambigua NEUGEB., For. Stichost. Ob. Lapugy; Wien. Ak. Dkschr. 1, 12, 2, t. 1, figg. 5—11, figg. 13—16.

Nodosaria tornata SCHW., 1866, For. Kar-Nikobar; Nov. Reise, geol. 2, 2, p. 223, t. 5, fig. 51.
» insolita SCHW., ibid. p. 230, t. 6, fig. 63.
» glandigena SCHW., ibid. p. 219, t. 5, fig. 46.
» tuberosa SCHW., 1863, Jurass. Sch.; Würtemb. Nat. Verein. Jhrshft. 21, p. 97, t. 4, fig. 19.

Glandulina pupiformis GÜMB. 1869, For. Cassian-Raibler Sch.; Österr. geol. Reichsanst. Jhb. 19, p. 177, t. 5, figg. 7—8.

Lingulina intumescens GÜMB., ibid. p. 182, t. 6, fig. 27.

Nodosaria radicula JONES & PARK. 1860, For. fr. Chellaston; Quart. Journ. geol. Soc. 16, p. 455, t. 19, figg. 1—5.

Dent. spec. indet. HANTK., For. Clav. Szab. Sch. p. 34, t. 12, fig. 18.

Nodosaria cylindracea, N. clava COSTA, 1854, Pal. Nap. 2, p. 146, 147, t. 12, figg. 12—14, t. 13, figg. 6, 7.

Dentalina Loubeana GÜMB., 1871, Ulmer Cem. Merg; Münch. Ak. Sitz.-Ber. 1, p. 64, t. 1, fig. 5.

Nodosaria marginata MARSS., 1877, Rüg. Schreibckr.; Greifsw. Nat. Verein. Mittheil. 1877—78, p. 126, t. 1, fig. 5.

Lingulina rimosa STACHE, 1865, tert. Mergel. Whaingar. Haf.; Novara Reise, geol. 1, 2, p. 192, t. 22, fig. 16.

Gland. inæqualis, candela EGG., 1857, Mioc. Ortenburg; Leonh. u. Bronn. Jhrb. 1857, p. 304, 305, t. 15, fig. 26—27; 28—29.

b) in Nodosarinam lævigatam (Glandulinam) d'ORB. transgredions:

Glandulina strobilus RSS., 1865, Sept. Thon.; Wien. Ak. Dkschr. 1, 25, p. 136, t. 2, fig. 24.
» parallela MARSS., 1877, Rüg. Schreibckr.; Greifsw. Nat. Verein. Mtth 1877—78, p. 124, t. 1, fig. 4.
» nummularia GÜMB., 1868, Nordalp. Eoc.; K. Bayr. Ak. Wiss. 1, 10, 2, p. 628, t. 1, fig. 50.
» pigmæa SCHWAG., 1863, Jurass. Sch.; Würtemb. Nat. Verein. Jahressh. 21, p. 115, t. 4, fig. 12.
» subconica ALTH., 1849, Umgeb. Lemberg; Haid. Nat. Abh. 3, 2, p. 270, t. 13, fig. 32.
» manifesta RSS., 1850, Kreidein. Lemberg; Haid. Nat. Abh. 4, 1, p. 23, t. 1, fig. 4.
» elliptica RSS., 1863, Sept. Thon. Offenbach; Wien. Ak. Sitz.-Ber. 1, 48, p. 47, t. 3, fig. 29—31.
» æqualis RSS., 1863, ibid. p. 48, t. 3, fig. 28; Steinsalzablag. Wieliczka, Wien. Ak. Sitz.-Ber. 1, 55, p. 83, t. 3, fig. 4.
» gracilis RSS., 1865, deut. Sept. Thon; Wien. Ak. Dkschr. 1, 25, 1, p. 137, t. 2, figg. 25—27.
» oblonga COSTA, 1855, Marna terz. Messina; Mem. Nap. 2, p. 141, t. 2, fig. 1.
» discreta RSS., 1849, neue For. österr. tert. Beck.; Wien. Ak. Dkschr. 1, 1, p. 366, t. 46, fig. 3.
» discreta HANTK., 1775, For. Clav. Szab. Sch. p. 4, t. 13, fig. 16.
» solita SCHWAG., 1866, For. Kar Nikob.; Nov. Reise, geol. 2, 2, p. 237, t. 6, fig. 78.
» Haidingerana, mammilla, incisa, lævigata NEUGEB., 1852, 1856, Siebenbürg. Verein. Mittheil. 1850—52, t. 1, figg. 2, 3, 7; Wien. Ak. Dkschr. 1, 12, 2, p. 67, t. 1, figg. 3—4.

c) in Nodosarinam carinatam (Lingulinam) transiens:

Syn. **Lingulina rotundata** D'ORB., 1846, Bass. tert. Vienne, p. 61, t. 2, figg. 48—51 (Lituolinæ similis).
» **nodosaria** RSS., 1862, Nordd. Hils u. Gault; Wien. Ak. Sitz.-Ber. 1. 46, p. 59, t. 5, fig. 12.
» **tuberosa** GÜMB., 1868, Nordalp. Eoc.; K. Bayr. Ak. Wiss. Abh. 1. 10. 2, p. 629, t. 1, fig. 52.
» **papillosa** NEUGEB., 1856, For. Stichosteg. Ob. Lapug.; Wien. Ak. Dkschr. 1. 12. 2, p. 97, t. 5, fig. 6.
» **bohemica** RSS., 1845, Böhm. Kreidef. 2, p. 108, t. 43, fig. 10.
» **ovalis** SCHWAG., 1865, Jurass. Sch.; Würtemb. Nat. Verein. Jhft. 21, p. 116, t. 4, figg. 21—24.
» **olisa** SCHWAG., ibid. p. 115, t. 4, fig. 20.
» **propinqua** STACHE, 1865, tert. Merg. Whaingar. Haf.; Nov. Reise, geol. 1. 2. p. 191, t. 22, fig. 15.

d) in Nodosarinam complanatam (Frondiculariam) transiens:

Frondicularia peregrina RSS., 1845, Böhm. Kreide 2. p. 108, t. 24, fig. 45.
» **bicuspidata** RSS., ibid. 1. p. 32, t. 13, fig. 46.
» **pupa** D'ORB., 1826, Tab. meth., Acad. Sc. Nat. 7, p. 256, N:o 4.
» **digitata** D'ORB., ibid. p. 256, N:o 6.
» **venusta** NEUGEB., 1856, For. Stichost. Ob. Lapug.; Wien. Ak. Dkschr. 1. 12. 2, p. 94, t. 5, fig. 5.
» **laevis** MARSS., 1876, Rüg. Schreibkr.; Greifsw. Nat. Verein. Mitth. 1877—78, p. 136, t. 2, fig. 16.
» **Stachei** KARR., 1870, Kreide. Leitzerdorf; Oesterr. geol. Reichsanst. Jhb. 20, t. 11, fig. 2.
» **spathulata** BRAD., 1879, Notes on Ret. Rhizop.; Qu Journ. Micr. Sc. (n. Ser.) 75, p. 270, t. 8, figg. 5 a b.

Appendix.

Forma »Rhabdogonii» sive »Orthocerinæ» REUSS, D'ORB.

Rhabdogon. acutangulum, articulatum, insigne, Strombecki, Martensi RSS., 1862, Nordd. Hils u. Gault; Wien. Ak. Sitz.-Ber. 1. 46, p. 55, 56; t. 4, fig. 14; t. 5, figg. 1—4.
» **excavatum** RSS., ibid. p. 91; t. 12, fig. 8.
» **Römeri, anomalum** RSS., 1859, Westph. Kreide, Wien. Ak. Sitz.-Ber. 40, p. 201, t. 6, fig. 7, t. 7, fig. 1.
» **dobile** GÜMB., 1871, Ulm. Cem. Merg.; Münch. Ak. Sitz.-Ber. 1. 1, p. 66, t. 1, fig. 8.
» **budense** HANTK., 1875, Clav. Szab. Sch. p. 42, t. 13, fig. 12.
Triplasia Murchisonii RSS., 1854, Kreide Ostalp.; Wien. Ak. Dkschr. 1. 7, t. 25, figg. 1—3.
Rhabdogon. minutum RSS., 1867, Steinsalzablag. Wieliczka; Wien. Ak. Sitz.-Ber. 1. 55, p. 84, t. 5, figg. 4—5.
» **hæringense** GÜMB., 1868, Nordalp. Eoc.; K. Bayr. Ak. Wiss. Abh. 1. 10. 2, p. 631, t. 1, fig. 55.
Orthocerina quadrilatera D'ORB., 1839, Cuba, p. 18, t. 1, figg. 11—12; Bass. tert. Vienne p. 41, t. 21, figg. 3—4.

Nodosarina radicula Lin. var. monile Sold.
Tab. I, fig. 3—7.

The shape of the chambers varies from globular and ovoid to cylindrical, sometimes produced and extenuated nearly to the same diameter as the necks. In such cases the limits of them and the chambers become nearly effaced and the shell becomes cane-shaped with slight impressions at the joints.

By some intermediate varieties, on which many names have been bestowed by different authors — as *Nod. limbata* d'Orb., *Nod. grandis* Rss., *Nod. insecta* Schw., *Nod. subnodosa* Rss., *Nod. globifera* Rss., *Nod. punctata, glabra, rugosa* d'Orb. etc., all provided with more or less globular, short-necked, tightly joined chambers — N. monile passes over in its type N. radicula.

On the other hand the straw- or cane-shaped varieties — as *N. longiscata, ovicula* d'Orb., *N. Ewaldi, trichostoma* Rss., *N. arundinacea* Schwag., *N. Cizechiana* Neuger. — link N. monile very closely to the slender forms of *Nod. communis* d'Orb. — that is to say: *Dental. Roemana, consobrina, Lorneiana* d'Orb. — which are scarcely distinguishable from these forms of N. monile.

Nod. inflexa Rss., *N. guttifera* d'Orb. and some others with globular chambers and somewhat constricted joints are also such intermediate forms between N. monile and N. communis.

The length of the visible necks between the chambers is of no specific value; for in the same shell we often meet with the chambers of the first stage closely connected, but those which come last are often separated by long necks. The shape of the neck and its being inclosed more or less by a subsequent chamber occasion the the greatest inconstancy in the shape of this variety.

Such specimens as are covered with spines, prickles or short bristles, should not be distinguished by particular names — as has been done by some authors. The production of these appendages is probably quite occasional, and in most cases they are broken off remains of pseudopodial tubes, their generation and preservation having been promoted by the locality and the mode of life of the animals. A pelagic life seems to be favourable to the growth of such a development of shell-substance.

Fig. 3 represents a variety near to *Dent. soluta* Rss.

Fig. 4 is the same as *Nod. inversa* Neuger.

Fig. 5 is *Nod. stipitata* Rss. or *N. semirugosa* d'Orb.

Fig. 6 belongs to the same variety, coming very near to the straw-shaped Nod. monile.

Fig. 7 represents an aulostomas form. The chambers are compressed, vial-shaped, somewhat triangular in the vertical section and set alternately, the broad diameter of one chamber being placed at right angle to the same diameter of the next.

Like other aulostomas-monstrosities — not uncommon in Nodosarinæ and Polymorphinæ and sometimes also in Planorbulinæ and Globigerinæ (in Carpenteria it is nearly the rule) — its chambers in their upper part are provided with a few short, wide tubes. It is not improbable, that such forms have given rise to Rup. Jones' genus *Ramulina*. See Wright's »List of the cretac. Microzoa of the North of Ireland«, Rep. and Proc. of Belfast Nat. Field Club 1873—74, Append. p. 88, t. 3, figg. 19—20; compare also: *Ramulina globulifera* Brady: »Notes on some of the Retic. Rhizop. of the Challenger Exped.; Quart. Journ. Micr. Science 1879 (n. ser.) 75, p. 272, t. 8, figg. 32—33).

a) » radicula typica vix distinguenda:

Syn.	Nodosaria	Radicula	d'Orb. 1826, Tabl. method.; Ann. Sc. Nat. 7, p. 252, N:o 3, Mod. 1.
»	»	rugosa	d'Orb., 1839, Cuba, p. 13, t. 1, figg. 2—3 (aspera).
»	»	verruculosa	Neugeb., 1852, Foram. Ober. Lapugy; Mittheil. Siebenbürg. Verein 1852, t. 1 fig. 43.
»	»	brevicula	Schwag., 1866, Foss. Foramf. Kar.-Nikobar; Nov. Reise, geol. Th. 2. 2, p. 234, t. 6, fig. 71.
»	»	calomorpha	Rss., 1866, deutsch. Septarienthon; Wien. Ak. Dkschr. 1. 25. 1, p. 129, t. 1, figg. 15—19.
»	»	Geinitziana	Neugeb., 1852, For. Ob. Lapug.; Mittheil. Siebenbürg. Verein. 1852, t. 1, fig. 1.
»	»	glandulinoides	Neugeb., 1852, ibid. t. 1, fig. 2.
»	»	glabra	d'Orb., 1826, Tabl. meth.; Ann. Sc. Nat. 7, p. 253, N:o 12.
»	»	punctata	d'Orb., 1839, Cuba, p. 14, t. 1, figg. 4—5.
»	»	spec. indet.	Costa, 1855, Marna terz. Messina; Mem. Nap. 2, t. 1, fig. 5.
	Frondicularia	nodosaria	Ehrenb., 1854, Microgeol. t. 25, fig. 7.
	Nodosaria	Jonesi	Rss., 1862, Nordd. Hils u. Gault; Wien. Ak. Sitz.-Ber. 1. 46, p. 89, t. 12, fig. 6.
»	»	Koina	Schwag., 1866, For. Kar.-Nikobar; Novara Reise, geol. Th. 2. 2, p. 220, t. 5, fig. 47.
»	»	conica	Neugeb., 1852, For. Ob. Lapug.; Mitth. Siebenb. Verein. 1852, t. 1, fig. 4 (scabriuscula).
»	»	fistuca	Schwag., 1866, Foss. For. Kar.-Nikob.; Novara Reise, geol. Th. 2. 2, p. 216, t. 5, figg. 36—37 (hispida).
»	»	granulata	Karr., 1878, Foramf. Luzon.; Bolet. Comis. Mapa geol. del España 7. 2, t. E, fig. 10.
»	»	subtertenuata	Schwag., 1866, Foss. For. Kar.-Nikob.; Novara Reise, geol. Th. 2. 2, p. 235, t. 6, fig. 74.
	Dentalina	oligosphaerica	Rss., 1864, deutsche Oberoligoc.; Wien. Ak. Sitz.-Ber. 1. 50, p. 454, t. 4, fig. 9 (N. communi propinqua).
»	»	subnodosa	Rss., 1850, Kreidemerg. Lemberg; Haid. Nat. Abh. 4, 1, p. 24, t. 1, fig. 9.
	Nodosaria	praegnans	Rss., 1865, Kreide Kanara See bey Küstendsche; Wien. Ak. Sitz.-Ber. 52, p. 450, fig. 4.
»	»	tumidiuscula	Gümb., 1868, For. nordalp. Eocän.; K. Bayr. Ak. Wiss. 1. 10. 2, p. 610, t. 1, fig. 14.
»	»	insecta	Schwag., 1866, For. Kar.-Nikobar; Novara Reise, geol. Th. 2. 2, p. 224, figg. 53—54.
»	»	monile	Hagenow, 1842, Rügens Kreidevers.; Leonh. u. Bronns, Jhrb. 1842, p. 568.
	Dentalina	monile	Alth, 1849, Umgeb. Lembergs; Haid. Nat. Abh. 3. 2, p. 269, t. 13, fig. 28.
	Nod. granitocalcarea,	pycnostyla	Gümb., 1868, Nordalp. Eocän.; K. Bayr. Ak. Wiss. Abh. 1. 10. 2, p. 615, t. 1, figg. 19—20.
	Dentalina	piluligera	Schwag., 1863, Juras. Schicht.; Würtemb. Nat. Verein. Jhhft. 21, p. 107, t. 3, figg. 14—15.
»		dolioligera	Schwag., 1863, ibid. p. 109, t. 3, figg. 26, 32.
	Nodosaria	anomala	Rss., 1865, deutsch. Septarienthon; Wien. Ak. Dkschr. 1. 25. 1, p. 129, t. 1, figg. 20—22.
»		grandis	Rss., 1865, ibid. p. 131, t. 1, figg. 26—28.
»		culminiformis	Gümb., 1868, Nordalp. Eocän.; K. Bayr. Ak. Wiss. 1. 10. 2, p. 614, t. 1, fig. 23.

Syn. Nodosaria	conferta	SCHMID, Zechsteinkalk von Selters Wetterau, Leonh. u. Bronn., Jhrb. 1867, p. 585, t. 6, fig. 49.
»	radicula var. conferta	BRAD., 1876, Carbonif. a. Perm. For.; Pal. Soc. 30, p. 126, t. 10, fig. 14.
»	citriformis	SCHMID, l. cit. p. 586, t. 6, figg. 52—53.
»	radicula var. citriformis	BRAD., 1876, l. c. p. 126, t. 10, fig. 16,
»	ovalis	SCHMID, l. cit., p. 585, t. 6, figg. 50—51.
»	radicula var. ovalis	BRAD., 1876, l. cit. p. 126, t. 10, fig. 14.
»	duplicans	RICHT., 1861, Geinitz' Dyas, p. 120, t. 20, fig. 26.
»	tumescens	EHRENB., 1854, Microg., t. 24, fig. 7.
»	acus	EHRENB., ibid., t. 32, fig. 3; N. lævis, subulata, turgescens EHRENB., ibid., t. 25, figg. 4, 5, 6.
Nautilus	spinulosus	MONTAGU, 1808, Testac. Brit. Suppl., p. 86, t. 19, fig. 5.
Dentalina	spinescens	BORNEM., 1855, Septaricnthon. Hermsdorf; Ztschr. deutsch. geol. Ges. 7, p. 324, t. 13, fig. 5.
Nodosaria	filiformis	D'ORB., 1826, Tabl. meth., Ann. Sc. Nat. 7, p. 253, N:o 14.
»	ovicula	D'ORB., 1826, ibid. p. 252, N:o 6.
»	antennula	COSTA, 1854, Pal. Nap. 2, p. 140, t. 16, fig. 3; t. 12, fig. 25 sup.
»	spec. indet.	COSTA, 1855, Marna terr. Messina, Mem. Nap. 2, t. 1, figg. 15, 19, 20.
Dentalina	retrorsa	REUSS, 1863, Septarienthon. Offenbach; Wien. Ak. Sitz.-Ber. 1. 48, p. 46, t. 3, fig. 27 (spinescens).
»	globuligera	NEUGEB., 1856, For. Stichost. Ob. Lapug.; Wien. Ak. Dkschr. 1. 12. 2, p. 81, t. 2, fig. 10.
»	Cassiana	GÜMB., 1869, For. etc. Cassian und Raibler Sch.; Österr. geol. Reichsanst. Jhrb. 19, p. 177, t. 5, fig. 16.
Nodosaria	deformis	COSTA, 1854, Pal. Nap. 2, p. 161, t. 13, fig. 19.
»	oligostegia	REUSS, 1845, Böhm. Kreide 1, p. 27, t. 13, figg. 19—20; 1850, Kreidem. Lemberg; Haid. Nat. Abh. 4. 1, p. 25, t. 1, fig. 10.
»	»	COSTA, 1854, Pal. Nap. 2, p. 145, t. 16, fig. 6 (hispida).
»	dubiosa	STACHE, 1865, tert. Mergel Whaingar. Hafen, Novara Reise, geol. Theil, 1. 2, p. 202, t. 22, fig. 27.
Dentalina	Lilli	REUSS, 1850, Kreidemergel Lemberg; Haid. Nat. Abh. 4. 1, p. 25, t. 1, fig. 11.
Nodosaria	gramen	COSTA, 1855, For. Marna blu d. Vaticano; Mem. Nap. 2, p. 117, t. 1, fig. 3.
»	interrupta	D'ORB., 1826, Tabl. meth.; An. Sc. Nat. 7, p. 252, N:o 11.
»	limbata	D'ORB., 1839, Craie blanche Paris; Mem. Soc. geol. Fr. (1) 4, t. 1, fig. 1.
»	»	COSTA, 1854, Pal. Nap. 2, p. 136, t. 12, fig. 25 (inf.).
»	antipodum	STACHE, 1865, tert. Mergel d. Whaingar. Hafen; Novara Reise, geol. Th. 1. 2, p. 194, t. 22, fig. 19.
»	pumilis, N. Krossenbergensis	GÜMB., 1868, Nordalp. Eocän.; K. Bayr. Ak. Wiss. Abh. 1. 10. 2, p. 608, t. 1, figg. 11—12.
»	ovularis	COSTA, 1855, Marna tert. Messina, Mem. Nap. 2, p. 141, t. 1, figg. 8—9.
»	spec. indet.	COSTA, 1855, ibid. t. 1, fig. 11.
Glandulina	cylindracea	REUSS, 1859, Westph. Kreide.; Wien. Ak. Sitz.-Ber. 40, p. 190, t. 4, fig. 1.
Dentalina	abbreviata	NEUGEB., 1856, For. Stich. Felsö Lapug.; Wien. Ak. Dkschr. 1. 12. 2, p. 86. t. 3, fig. 18.
Nodosaria	adspersa	REUSS, 1863, Sept Thon. Offenbach; Wien. Ak. Sitz.-Ber. 1. 48, p. 43, t. 2. fig. 13.
»	subinflata	COSTA, 1854, Pal. Nap. 2, p. 27, figg. 6—7.
»	maculata	SCHWAG., 1866, For. Kar-Nikob.; Novara Reise, geol. Th. 2. 2, p. 214, t. 5, fig. 33.
»	alpigena	GÜMB., 1868, For. Nordalp. Eocän.; K. Bayr. Ak. Wiss. Abh. 1. 10. 2, p. 610, t. 1, fig. 13.
»	Flurli	GÜMB., 1868, ibid. p. 614, t. 1, fig. 22; N. resupinata GÜMB., ibid. t. 1, fig. 24.
»	monile	EHRENB., 1854, Microgeol., t. 19, fig. 81.
Margin.	armata	REUSS, 1859, Westph. Kreide; Wien. Ak. Sitz.-Ber. 40, p. 209, t. 7, fig. 7.
Dentalina	setosa	HKEN., 1875, For. Clavel. Száb. Sch., p. 39, t. 13, fig. 9 (Nod. communem approximans).

Syn. **Nodosaria conspurcata** Rss., 1851, Sept. Thon Berlin; Zeitschr. deutsch. geol. Gesellsch. 3, p. 59, t. 3, fig. 3; 1863, Sept. Thon v. Offenbach, Wien. Ak. Sitz.-Ber. 1, 48, p. 43, t. 2, figg. 10—12.
» **setosa** Schwag., 1866, For. Kar-Nikob.; Novara Reise, geol. Th. 2. 2, p. 218, t. 5, fig. 40.
» **triloculata** Karr., 1867, For. fauna Österr.; Wien. Ak. Sitz.-Ber. 1. 55, p. 367, t. 3, fig. 9.
» **holosericea** Schwag., 1866, For. Kar-Nikob.; Novara Reise, geol. Th. 2. 2, p. 221, t 5, fig. 49.
» **aculeata** d'Orb., 1846, For. tert. Vienne, p. 35, t. 1, figg. 26—27.
» **verruculosa** Neugeb., 1852, For. Stich. Felsö Lapug.; Siebenburg. Ver. Mittheil. 1852, t. 1, fig. 43.

b) magis constricta vel stipitata:

Dentalina soluta Rss., 1851, Sept. Thon Berlin; Ztschr. deutsch. geol. Gesellsch. 3, p. 60, t. 3, fig. 4.
»   »   Stache, 1865, tert. Mergel Whaingar. Hafen; Novara Reise, geol. Th. 1. 2, p. 203, t. 22, fig. 29.
»   »   Hken., 1875, Clav. Szab. Sch., p. 29, t. 3, figg. 2, 14.
Nodosaria soluta Rss., 1866, For. deutsch. Sept. Thon; Wien. Ak. Dkschr. 1. 25. 1, p. 131, t. 2, figg. 4—8.
»   »   Borneman, 1855, Sept. Thon Hermsdorff; Ztschr. deutsch. geol. Gesellsch. 7, p. 322, t. 12, fig. 12.
» **appendiculata** Costa, 1854, Pal. Nap. 2, p. 142, t. 12, fig. 22.
» **Fichteliana, asperula**, Neugeb., 1852, For. Felsö Lapugy; Siebenb. Verein. Mittheil. 1852, t. 1, figg. 39—41.
» **pyrula** d'Orb., 1826, Tabl. meth., Ann. Sc. Nat. 7, p. 253, Nro 13.
Dentalina peregrina Rss., 1860, Crag. Antwerp.; Wien. Ak. Sitz.-Ber. 42, p. 356, t. 1, fig. 6 (N. communi propinqua.)
Nodosaria rudis d'Orb., 1846, For. tert. Vienne, p. 33, t. 1, figg. 17—19.
» **monile** Ehrenb., 1854, Microgeol., t. 24, fig. 6.
» **hirsuta** d'Orb., 1826, Tabl. meth., Ann. Sc. Nat. 7, p. 252, Nro 7.
Dentalina floscula d'Orb., 1846, For. tert. Vienne, p. 50, t. 2, figg. 16—17.
Nodosaria siphonostoma Rss., 1867, Steinsalzablager. Wieliczka; Wien. Ak. Sitz.-Ber. 1. 55, p. 81, t. 3, fig. 3.
» **spec. indet.** Costa, 1855, Marna terz. Messina; Mem. Nap. 2, t. 1, fig. 14 et 30.
» **lepidula** Schwag., 1866, For. Kar-Nikob.; Novara Reise, geol. Th. 2. 2, p. 210, t. 5, figg. 27—28 (spinescens).
» **hispida** d'Orb., 1846, For. tert. Vienne, p. 35, t. 1, figg. 24—25.
»   »   Costa, 1854, Marna terz. Messina; Mem. Nap. 2, p. 140, t. 1, fig. 10; Pal. Nap., p. 151, t. 11, figg. 27—40 (partim).
» **Marim** d'Orb., 1846, For. tert. Vienne, p. 33, t. 1, figg. 15—16.
» **stipitata** Rss., 1849, Neue Foramf. Osterreich. tert. Becken; Wien. Ak. Dkschr. 1. 1, p. 366, t. 46, fig. 4; Sept. Thon Kreuznach, Wien. Ak. Sitz.-Ber. 1. 48, p. 65, t. 7, fig. 88.
» **semirugosa** d'Orb., 1846, For. tert. Vienne, p. 34, t. 1, figg. 20—23 (cameris semilineatis).
Dentalina expansa Rss., 1859, Westph. Kreidef.; Wien. Ak. Sitz.-Ber. 40, p. 188, t. 3, fig. 4.
Nodosaria pyrula Williams, 1858, Brit. rec. For. p. 17, fig. 39.
»   »   Schwag., 1866, For. Kar-Nikob.; Novara Reise, geol. Th. 2. 2, p. 217, t. 5, fig. 38.
» **intertenuata** Schwag., 1866, ibid. p. 226, t. 6, fig. 58.
» **resupinata, hectica** Gümb., 1868, Nordalp. Eocän., K. Bayr. Wiss. Abh. 1. 10. 2, p. 615, t. 1, figg. 24—25.
» **dacrydium** Rss., 1865, deutsch. Sept. Thon; Wien. Ak. Dkschr. 1 25, p. 128, t. 1, figg. 13—14.

Syn. Dentalina spec. indet.   Stache, Mergel d. Whaingar. Hafen; Novara Reise, geol. Th. 1. 2, p. 204, t. 22, fig. 30.
Nodosaria recta   Schwag., 1866, ibid. 2. 2, p. 216, t. 5, fig. 35.
» inversa, Haueriana, lagonifera, Bruckenthaliana, Orbignyana Neugeb., 1852. For. Felsö Lapugy; Siebenbürg. Verein. Mittheil. 1852, t. 1, figg. 5—15.
Lagena ulmensis   Gümb., 1871, Ulmer Cement. Mergel, Münch. Ak. Sitz.-Ber. 1, p. 65, t. 1, fig. 7.
Nodosaria Cziscekiana, Haidingeriana, Bronniana, Bielziana Neugeb., 1. cit. t. 1, figg. 30—37 (ad usu potius pertinet).
Dentalina verticalis   Stache, 1865, tert. Mergel Whaingar. Hafen; Novara Reise, geol. Th. 1. 2, p. 202, t. 22, fig. 28 (ad usu potius pertinent).
Dentalina Benningseni   Rss., 1863, Sept. Thon Offenbach, Wien. Ak. Sitz.-Ber. 1. 48, p. 44, t. 2, fig. 14.
Nodosaria pygmæa   Rss., deut. Sept. Thon; Wien. Ak. Dkschr. 1. 25. 1, p. 133, t. 2, fig. 9.
» Kuhnitziana Karr., 1877, Hochquell-Wasserleit., Osterr. geol. Reichsanst. Abh. 9, p. 379, t. 16, fig. 22.

c) culmiformis:

Nodosaria longiscata   d'Orb., 1846, For. tert. Vienne, p. 32, t. 1, figg. 10—12.
» arundinea   Schwag., 1866, For. Kar.-Nikob.; Novara Reise, geol. Th. 2. 2, p. 211, t. 5, figg. 43—45.
» irregularis   d'Orb., 1846, For. tert. Vienne, p. 32, t. 1, figg. 13—14.
» Buchiana, Ackneriana, Römeriana, nodifera, capillaris, exilis, gracilis, claviformis Neugeb., 1852, Siebenb. Verein. Mittheil. 1852, t. 1, figg. 16—29, fig. 38.
» exilis   Rss., 1865, deutsch. Sept. Thon; Wien. Ak. Dkschr. 1. 25. 1, p. 130, t. 2, fig. 17.
» spec. indet.   Costa, 1855, Mare. terz. Messina; Mem. Nap. 2, t. 1, figg. 25—26; ibid. t. 2, fig. 10.
» Ewaldi   Rss., 1851, Sept. Thon Berlin; Ztschr. deutsch. geol. Gesellsch. 3, p. 58, t. 3, fig. 2; Wien. Ak. Dkschr. 1. 25. 1, p. 129, t. 2, fig. 18.
» »   Bornemann, 1855, Sept. Thon Hermsdorff; Ztschr. deutsch. geol. Ges. 7, p. 321, t. 12, fig. 10.
» gracillima   Costa, 1854, Pal. Nap. 2, t. 16, fig. 22.
» tympanoplectriformis Schwag., 1866, For. Kar.-Nikob.; Novara Reise, geol. Th. 2. 2, p. 215, t. 5, fig. 34.
» polystoma   Schwag., N. exilis Schwag., ibid. p. 217, 223, t. 5, figg. 39, 52 (uso approximato).
» myrmecoides   Costa, 1854, Pal. Nap. 2, p. 160, t. 13, fig. 18.
» marsupifera, Nod. toranta, Dent. spec. indet. Schwag., 1863, Jurass. Sch.; Würtemb. Nat. Verein. Jhrshft. 21, p. 96—112; t. 2, fig. 9; tt. 3, 4, figg. 27, 7. 9; t. 4, figg. 2—5 (ad usu potius pertinent).
» culmon   Costa, 1854, Pal. Nap. 2, p. 158, t. 13, fig. 15.
Dentalina rudiuscula   Costa, ibid., p. 170, t. 12, fig. 13.
Nodosaria cannæformis   Rss., 1860, For. Diegel. Westphal. (miocän.); Wien. Ak. Sitz.-Ber. 42, p. 364, t. 1, fig. 2.
» siphunculus   Costa, 1854, Pal. Nap. 2, p. 143, t. 12, fig. 11.
» internodifera   Gümb., 1868, Nordalp. Eocän.; K. Bayr. Ak. Wiss. 1. 10. 2, p. 611, t. 1, fig. 15.

d) in Nod. communem transiens:

Dentalina acuticauda   Gümb., 1868, Nordalp. Eocän.; K. Bayr. Ak. Wiss. 1. 10. 2, p 624, t. 1, fig. 40.
» gliricauda   Gümb., ibid. p. 624, t. 1, fig. 41.
» globulicauda   Gümb., ibid. p. 623, t. 1, fig. 38.
» annulifera   Gümb., ibid. p. 614, t. 1, fig. 21.

Syn. Dentalina annulata		Rss., 1845, Böhm. Kreide, p. 27, t. 13, fig. 21; t. 8, figg. 4 et 67.
» »		Alth., 1849, Umgeb. Lemberg; Haid. Nat. Abh. 3. 2, p. 269, t. 13, fg. 29.
Nodosaria scabriuscula		Costa, 1854, Pal. Nap. 2, p. 140, t. 16, fig. 1.
Dentalina scabra		Reuss., 1849, Neue For. österr. tert. Beck.; Wien. Ak. Dkschr. 1. 1, p. 367, t. 46, figg. 7—8 (hispida).
Nodosaria monile		Rss., 1845, Böhm. Kreide 1, p. 27, t. 8, fig. 7.
Dentalina spinoscens		Rss., 1851, Sept. Thon Berlin; Ztschr. deutsch. geol. Ges. 3, p. 62, t. 3, fig. 10.
»	globifera	Rss., 1855, tert. Sch. nordl. u. mittl. Deutschl.; Wien. Ak. Sitz.-Ber. 1. 18, p. 223, t. 1, fig. 3.
»	permiana	Jones, Richt. 1855, Thür. Zechstein.; Zeitschr. deutsch. geol. Ges. 7, p. 532, t. 26, fig. 27.
»	laxa	Rss., 1865, deut. Sept. Thon; Wien. Ak. Dkschr. 1. 25. 1, p. 132, t. 2, fgg. 2—3.
Nodosaria distorta		Costa, 1854, Pal. Nap. 2, p. 173, t. 16, fig. 17.
»	hispida	Schwag., 1866, For. Kar.-Nikobar.; Novara Reise, geol. Th. 2. 2, p. 231, t. 6, fig. 65.
»	alternans	Costa, 1854, Pal. Nap. 2, p. 139, t. 13, fig. 16 (hispida, costulata).
Dentalina pauperata		Hke., 1875, For. Clav. Szab. Sch., p. 31, t. 3, fig. 6.
»	trichostoma	Rss., 1849, Neue For. österr. tert. Beck.; Wien. Ak. Dkschr. 1. 1, p. 367, t. 46, fig. 6.
»	monile	Cornuel, 1849, nouv. foss. microsc.; Mem. Soc. geol. France (2), 3, p. 250, t. 1, fig 18.
»	elongata	Costa, 1854, Pal. Nap. 2, t. 16, fig. 19.
»	spec. indet.	Hke., 1875, For. Clav. Szab. Sch., p. 34, t. 3, fig. 11.
»	aculeata	d'Orb., 1839, For. Craie bl. Paris; Mem. Soc. geol. France 4, p. 13, t. 4, fig. 2 (hispida).
Nodosaria aculeata		Reuss., 1845, Böhm. Kreide 1, p. 28, t. 12, fig. 29 (hispida).
»	inflexa	Rss., 1865, deutsch. Sept. Thon; Wien. Ak. Dkschr. 1. 25. 1, p. 131, t. 2, fig. 1.
Dentalina guttifera		d'Orb., 1846, For. tert. Vienne, p. 49, t. 2, figg. 11—13.
»	guttifera	Park. and Jones, 1865, For. N. Atl. and Arct. Oceans; Phil. Transact. 155. I, p. 343, t. 13, fig. 11.
»	communis	Park. and Jones, 1857, For. Coast. of Norway; Ann. Mag. Nat. Hist. (2) 19, p. 282, t. 10, figg. 3—4.
Dentalina Adolphina		d'Orb., 1846, For. tert. Vienne, p. 51, t. 2, figg. 18—20.
»	»	Gümb., 1868, Nordalp. Eocän.; K. Bayr. Ak. Wiss. Abh. 1. 10. 2, p. 623, t. 1, fig. 39.
Nodosaria »		Schwag., 1866, For. Kar.-Nikobar.; Novara Reise, geol. Th. 2. 2, p. 235, t. 6, fig. 72.
Dentalina subspinosa		Neugeb., 1856, For. Stichosteg.; Wien. Ak. Dkschr. 1. 12. 2, p. 88, t. 4, fig. 7.

Nodosarina radicula Lin. var. raphanus Lin.

Tab. 1, fig. 9—10.

Our form comes pretty near to *Nod. multicosta* Neugeb., *Nod. striata* Stache etc. The long and narrow forms are by some authors designated as *Nod. raphanistrum*, but it is in vain to distinguish these forms from one another.

It has been found only on the coralline-gravel bottom.

Nodosarina radicula Lin. var. scalaris Batsch.

Tab. I, fig. 8.

Is the pigmy-form of the preceeding and too closely related to that, to attain the rank of species. Such forms as *Nod. inflata* Rss., *Nod. nana* Reuss, *Nod. badenensis* d'Orb., *Nod. tenuicostata* Costa, etc. have the character of both.

Its characteristic distinguishing feature should be the thinness of the shell and the prolongation and slenderness of the chamber-necks. But such marks are no longer recognised as being of any distinctive importance in this class, where each species seems to have its dwarfish, tiny forms, which during their whole life remain in a sort of juvenile stage.

It has been stated above, that the shape of the necks cannot be of any specific importance.

This form occurs both on the chalkbottom and in the coralline-gravel. It attains seldom more than 1—1,5 mm. in length.

Nodosarina radicula var. Raphanus.

Syn.	Nodosaria	lamellosa	d'Orb., 1826, Tabl. meth.; Ann. Sc. Nat. 7, p. 253, N:o 17, t. 10, figg. 4—6.
	»	scalaris	d'Orb., ibid., p. 253, N.o 18.
	»	badenensis	Park. and Jones, 1860, For. Chellast.; Qu. Journ. geol. Soc. 16, p. 453, t. 19, figg. 8—9.
	»	tenuicostata	Costa 1854, Pal. Nap. 2, p. 156, t. 12, fig. 5; t. 16, figg. 8—13.
	Dentalina	bifurcata	Hkr., 1875, Clav. Szab. Sch. p. 35, t. 3, figg. 18, 21.
	Nodosaria	pachycephala, latejugata	Gümb., 1868, Nordalp. Foc.; K. Bayr. Ak. Wiss. Abh. 1. 10. 2, p. 616, 619, t. 1, figg. 27, 32.
	»	Raibliana	Gümb., 1869, For. Cassino u. Raibler Sch.; Osterr. geol. Reichsanst. Jhrb 19, p. 181, t. 6, fig. 28.
	»	Vásárhelyii, latejugata	Hkr., 1875, Clav. Szab. Schicht., p. 36, t 4, fg. 4; t. 2, fgg 6 a. b. c.
	Amphimorphina striata		Rss., 1862, Nordd. Hils u. Gault; Wien. Ak. Sitz.-Ber. 1. 46, p. 57, t. 5. fg. 5.
	Nodosaria	multicosta	Neugeb., 1856, For. Stichosteg. ob. Lapug.; Wien. Ak. Dkschr. 1. 12. 2, p. 78, t. 1, fig. 12.
	»	subradicula	Schwag., ibid. p. 322, t. 5, fig. 50 (ad N. scalarem vergens).
	»	columella	Karr., 1877, Hochqu. Wasserl.; Osterr. geol. Reichsanst. Abh. 9, p. 379, t. 16, figg. 21—22.
	»	annulata, spinulosa	Costa, 1855, Mars. terz. Messina; Mem. Nap. 2, p. 139, t. 1, fgg. 16, 28.
	»	Ludwigi	Rss., 1865, Sept. Thon Deutschl.; Wien. Ak. Dkschr. 1. 25. 1, p. 135, t. 2, fig. 23.
	Nodosarina-Nodosaria	Rhaphanus	Parker and Jones, 1866, Crag. For.; Pal. Soc. 19, p. 49, t. 1, figg. 4, 5, 22, 23.
	Crist. somituberculata		Karr., 1867, For. Faun. Österr.; Wien. Ak. Sitz.-Ber. 1. 55, p. 355, t. 1, fig. 7.
	Nodosaria	semicostata	Costa, 1854, Pal. Nap. t. 27, figg. 8, 10.
	»	manubrium	Schwag., 1863, Jurass. Sch.; Würtemb. Nat. Wiss. Verein. Jhrb. 21, p. 99, t. 2, fig. 14.
	»	Raphanus	Park. and Jones, 1860, For. Chellast.; Qu. Journ. geol. Soc. 16, p. 453, t. 19. fig. 10.

Syn. Dentalina crassula Rss., 1850, Kreidemerg. Lemberg; Haid. Nat Abh. 4. 1, p. 24, t. 1, fig 8.
  Nodosaria inops Rss., ibid. p. 24, t. 1, fig. 7.
  » proboscidea Rss., ibid. p. 23, t. 1, fig. 6.
  » crassa Hke., 1875, Clav. Szab. Sch., t. 13. fig. 4.
  » inflata Costa, 1855, Marn. terz. Messina; Mem. Nap. 2, p. 139, t. 1, fig. 18.
  » inflata, intermedia Costa, 1854. Pal. Nap. 2, p. 153, 154, t. 13, fig. 4; t. 16, fig. 1.
  » striatissima Stache, 1865. Tert. Mergel Whainger. Hafen; Novara Reise, geol. Th. 1. 2, p. 199, t. 22, fig. 25; p. 208, t. 22, fig. 38.
  » Rapa d'Orb., 1826, Tabl. meth., Ann. Sc. Nat. 7, p. 253, N:o 27.
  » obscura Rss., 1845, Böhm. Kreide 1, p. 26, t. 13, figg. 7—9.
  » » Reuss, 1873, Gein., Elbthalgeb. Sachs. 2, p. 81, t. 11, 20, fig. 1—4.
  » obsolescens Reuss, ibid. p. 83, t. 11. 20, fig. 14.
  » undecimcostata, septemcostata Gein., 1839, Sachs. Kreidegeb. p. 69, t. 17, figg. 19—20.
  Nautilus costatus Montagu, 1803, Test. Brit. p. 199, t. 14, fig. 5; 1808, ibid. Supplem. p. 83, t. 19, fig. 2.
  Nodosaria raphanistrum Parr. and Jones, 1866, Crag. For.; Pal. Soc. 19, p. 50, t. 1, figg. 6—8.
  » pentecostata Costa, 1854. Pal. Nap. 2, p. 161, t. 16, fig. 15.
  » mutabilis, propinqua, turgidula, Rhogina, Dentalina irregularis var. Costa, ibid., t. 13, figg. 1—3; t. 27, figg. 9, 11, 15.
  » mutabilis, sulcata Costa, 1855, Marna terz. Messina; Mem. Nap. 2, p. 134, 140, t. 1, figg. 1—2; t. 1, fig. 29.
  » affinis, bacillum d'Orb., 1846, For. terl. Vienne, p. 39, 40; t. 1, figg. 36—47.
  » tenuicosta, affinis Rss., 1845, Böhm. Kreidef. 1. p. 25, 26, t. 13, figg. 5—6, 16.
  » affinis Rss., 1873, Gein. Elbthalgeb. Sachs. 2, p. 83, t. 11. 20, fig. 12.
  » Paueri, subalpina, eocaena, Holli, bacillum, sceptriformis, capitata, flssicostata Gümb., 1868, Nordalp. Eocaen.; K. Bayr. Ak. Wiss. Abh. 1. 10. 2, p. 612—626, t. 1, figg. 18, 26, 28, 29, 30, 33, 42, 46.
  » Maximiliana, nummulina Gümb., ibid. p. 619, 626; t. 1, figg. 31, 45.
  » bacilloides, budensis Hke., 1875, Clav. Szab, Sch., t. 2, figg. 8, 10.
  » bacillum var. minor, acuminata Hke., ibid. p. 26, t. 2, figg. 7, 9; t. 13, fig. 5.
  » Hochstetteri Schwag., 1866, For. Kas.-Nikob.; Novara Reise, geol. Th. 2. 2, p. 214, t. 5, fig. 32.
  » perversa, deceptoria, inconstans, gomphiformis, crassitesta, Skobina Schwag., 1866, For. Kas.-Nikob.; Novara Reise, geol. Th. 2. 2, p. 212, t. 5, figg. 29—31; p. 220—224, t. 5, figg. 48, 55, 56.
  » subsimilis, substrigata, callosa, obliquecostata, striatissima, scarificata Stache, 1865, tert. Merg. Whaingar. Hafen; Novara Reise, geol. Th. 1. 1, p. 195—197, 208, t. 22, figg. 21—24, 38, 40.
  » clugypha, turbiformis Schwag., 1863, Jerass. Sch.; Würtemberg. Nat. Verein. Jhrbft. 21, p. 96, 98, t. 2, figg. 8, 13.
  » bacillum, contracta, dehiscens, excentrica, spec. indet. Costa, 1855, Marna terz. Messina; Mem. Nap. 2, p 134—137, t. 1, figg. 1, 3, 6, 21; t. 2, fig. 14.
  » plicata, cylindrum Costa, 1854. Pal. Nap. 2, p. 152, t. 12, fig. 4; t. 27, fig. 1.
  » paupercula Rss., 1845, Böhm. Kreide. 1, p. 26, t. 12, fig. 12; 1873, Geinitz, Elbthalgeb. Sachsen 2, p. 81, t. 11. 20, figg. 5—7.
  » amphioxus, fusula, oligotoma Rss., 1871, ibid. 1, p. 82, 135, t. 11. 20, figg. 8, 9; t. 33, fig. 16.
  » bactridium Rss., 1865, deutsch. Sept. Thon; Wien. Ak. Dkschr. 1. 25. 1, p. 130, t. 1, figg. 24—25.
  » intercostata, duplicostata, prismatica Rss., 1859, Westphal. Kreidef.; Wien. Ak. Sitz.-Ber. 40, t. 1, figg. 4—5, t. 2, fig. 2.
  » sceptrum, tubifora, bactroides, lamello-costata, prismatica, Dent. inepta, Marg. aequivoca, Marg. acuticostata Rss., 1862, Nordd. Hils u. Gault, Wien. Ak. Sitz.-Ber. 1. 46, p. 37, t. 2, figg. 3—7, 13; t. 5, fig. 17; t. 6, fig. 3.
  » polygona Rss., 1855, Kreidegeb. Meklenb.; Ztschr. deutsch. geol. Ges. 7, p. 265, t. 8, figg. 7—8.
  » majuscula, laticosta, clausa Marss., 1877, Rügen. Schreibekr.; Greifswald. Nat. Verein. Mittheil. 1877—78, p. 130, 131, t. 1, figg. 7—9.

Syn. Nodosaria decemcostata Egg., 1857, Miec. Ortenburg; Leonh. u. Bronn. Jhrb. 1857, p. 306, t. 15,
fgg. 24—25.
» Bolli Rss., 1855, Kreideg. Mcklenb.; Ztschr. deutsch. geol. Ges. 7, p. 265, t. 8,
fig. 6.
» tetragona Rss., 1859, Westph. Kreidef.; Wien. Ak. Sitz.-Ber. 40, t. 2, fig. 1.
» orthopleura Rss., 1862, Nordd. Hils u. Gault; Wien. Ak. Sitz.-Ber. 1. 46, p. 89, t. 12,
fig. 5.
» tetragona Costa, 1855, Marna blu Vaticano; Mem. Nap. 2, p. 116, t. 1, fig. 1.
» compressiuscula, Dent. carinata Neugeb., 1856, For. Stichost. Ob. Lapugy; Wien. Ak.
Dkschr. 1. 12. 2, p. 79, 91, t. 2, 4, figg. 1—7; 17.

b) moniliformis:

Nodosaria nitida d'Orb., 1826, Tabl. meth., Ann. Sc. Nat. 7, p. 254, N:o 33.
» Boueana d'Orb., 1846, For. tert. Vienne, p. 37, t. 1, figg. 30—31.
» quadrata, Lingulina mutabilis d'Orb., ibid. p. 36, 61, t. 1, fig. 28; t. 2, fig. 52.
» subrhombica Stache, 1865, Tert. Merg. Whainger. Hafen, Novara Reise, geol. Th. 1. 2,
p. 201, t. 22, fig. 26.
» Zippei Rss., 1845, Böhm. Kreide 1, p. 25, 26; t. 8, figg. 2—3.
» distans Rss., 1855, Kreideg. Mcklenburg; Ztschr. deutsch. geol. Ges. 7, p. 264, t. 8,
fig. 5.
» coarctata Rkk., 1875, Clav. Szab. Sch., t. 12, fig. 15.
» coccoptycha Gümb., 1868, Nordalp. Eocän.; K. Bayr. Ak. Wiss. Abh. 1. 10. 2, p. 611,
t. 1, fig. 16 (verrucosa).

c) semistriata:

Nodosaria semistriata, Soldanii d'Orb., 1826, Ann. Sc. Nat. 7, p. 252, 254, N:ris 9, 30 (an N.
scalaris).
» tholigera Schwag., 1866, Kar.-Nikobar.; Novara Reise, geol. Th. 2. 2, p. 218, t. 5,
fig. 41.
? » ambigua Costa, 1854, Pal. Nap. 2, p. 137, t. 12, figg. 9—10.

d) compressa: in Nodos. (Frondicul.) complanatam Defr. var. striatam d'Orb. transiens:

Amphimorphina Haueriana Neugeb., 1850, For. Felsö Lapug.; Siebenb. Ver. Mittheil. 1850, p. 127,
t. 4, figg. 13—14 (vide Nod. compressiuscula Neugeb. p. 23).
» » Karrer, 1864, Leythakalk Wien. Beck.; Wien. Ak. Sitz.-Ber. 1. 50, p.
705, t. 1, fig. 6.
» » Fuchs, Modell, N:o 51.
Frond. digitalis, affinis, Bielzana, rostrata, semicostata, diversicostata, tenuicostata, cultrata, irregularis, Acknoriana, pulchella, lapugyensis Neugeb.,
1850, For. Felsö Lapug.; Siebenb. Ver. Mittheil. 1850, p. 119, 120,
t. 3, figg. 3—10; t. 4, figg. 11—12; t. 3, figg. 1—2.
» bicostata Karrer, 1878, Foram. Luzon; Bolet. Comis. Mapa geol. del España, 7. 2,
p. 17, t. E, fig. 13.
» mucronata Karr., 1867, For. Faun. Österr.; Wien. Ak. Sitz.-Ber. 1. 55, p. 354, t. 1,
fig. 6.

e α) Frondicul. Archiaciana d'Orb. quæ inter Nod. radiculam frondiculariæformem et
Raphanum tenet medium, camera primordiali solum costata, (additis paucis
Nod. (Frond.) striatæ d'Orb. proximis):

Frond. Archiaciana, ornata, angulosa d'Orb., 1839, For. Craie blanc. Par.; Mem. Soc. geol. Fr. 4,
p. 20—22, t. 1, figg. 31—39.
» Archiacina Rss., 1845, Böhm. Kreide 1, p. 31, t. 13, fig. 39.

Syn. Frond. Archiaciana   WILLIAMS., 1858, Brit. ree. For. p. 24, fig. 51.
» angulosa   Rss., 1845, Böhm. Kreide 1, p. 31, t. 13, fig. 40; 2, p. 107, t. 24, fig. 42.
» tenuis   Rss., ibid. 1, p. 30, t. 8, fig. 25; 1873, Gein., Elbthalgeb. Sachsen, 2, p. 94, t. II. 20, fig. 3.
» turgida   Rss., ibid. 2, p. 107, t. 24, figg. 41—44; 1873, Gein., Elbthalgeb. Sachs. 2, p. 97, t. II. 21, figg. 17—18.
» marginata, canaliculata   Rss., 1845, Böhm. Kreide 1, 2, p. 30, 107; t. 12, fig. 9; t. 24, fig. 39; t. 8, figg. 20—21.
» Decheni, apiculata, marginata, canaliculata, Marg. ornatissima   Rss., 1859, Westphäl. Kreide; Wien. Ak. Sitz.-Ber. 40, p. 191—209, t. 4, fig. 3; t. 5, figg. 2—3; t. 6, fig. 1; t. 7, fig. 2.
» elegans, Vernouiliana   D'ORB., 1839, Craie bl. Paris; Mem. Soc. geol. Fr. 4, p. 19, 20, t. 1, figg. 29—30, 32—33.
» Ungeri   Rss., 1862, Nordd. Hils u. Gault; Wien. Ak. Sitz.-Ber. 1. 46, p. 54, t. 4, fig. 11.
» Sedgvicki   Rss., 1854, Kreide. Ostalpen; Wien. Ak. Sitz.-Ber. 7, p. 66, t. 25, fig. 4.
» angusta   Rss., 1845, Böhm. Kreide 1, t. 8, fig. 14.

e β) magis expansa:

Frond. Fuchsii   KARR., 1870, Kreide Leitzendorf; Jhrb. k. k. geol. Reichsanst. 20, p. 174, t. 11, fig. 1. (Pr. Stachei KARR., p. 15, huc potius referenda).
» Goldfussi, microdisca, gaultina   Rss., 1859, Westphäl. Kreide; Wien. Ak. Sitz.-Ber. 40, p. 192—195, t. 4, fig. 7; t. 5, fig. 4; t. 5, fig. 5.
» Speyeri   Rss., 1864, Oberoligoc.; Wien. Ak. Sitz.-Ber. 1. 50, p. 458, t. 4, fig. 8.
» Althii, pyrum   KARR., 1870, Kreidef. Leitzendorf; Jahrb. k. geol. Reichsanst. 20, p. 172, 175, t. 10, fig. 1, t. 11, fig. 4.
» denticulata, dentic. var. spinosa   COSTA, 1855, Marna terz. Messina; Mem. Nap. 2, p. 371, t. 2, figg. 20, 22—23; t. 3, fig. 4 (in Nod. striatam D'ORB. transiens).

f) tricarinata (Rhabdogonii forma):

Vaginul. tricarinata   D'ORB., 1826, Tabl. meth.; Ann. Sc. Nat. 7, p. 258, No 4, Mod. 4 (ad Nod. linearem vel legumen vergens).
Rhabdogonium pyramidale   KARR., 1861, Marin. Tegel; Wien. Ak. Sitz.-Ber. 1. 44, p. 444, t. 1, fig. 5.
Frond. tricarinata   D'ORB., 1839, For. Craie bl. Par.; Mem. Soc. geol. Fr. 4, p. 21, t. 2, figg. 1—3.
» amoena   Rss., 1850, Kreidem. Lemberg; Haid. Nat. Abh. 4. 1, p. 29, t. 1, fig. 21.
Dentalina trigona   SCHWAG., 1863, Jurass. Sch.: Wurtemb. Nat. Verein. Jhrhft. 21, p. 114, t. 3, fig. 31.
Dentalinopsis subtriquetra   Rss., 1862, Nordd. Hils u. Gault; Wien. Ak. Sitz.-Ber. 1. 46, p. 57, t. 5, fig. 5; Fric's Modell. N:o 52.

g) in Nod. obliquam transgrediens:

Dentalina Münsteri   GÜMB., 1968, Nordalp. Eocän.; K. Bayr. Ak. Wiss. I. 10. 2, p. 624, t. 1, fig. 43.
Nodosaria tosta   SCHWAG., 1866, Kar.-Nikobar; Novara Reise, geol. Th. 2, 2, p. 219, t. 5, fig. 42.
» equisetiformis   SCHWAG., ibid. p. 231, t. 6, fig. 66.
» spec. indet.   COSTA, 1855, Marna terz. Messina; Mem. Nap. 2, t. 1, figg. 23, 34.
» conspurcata   Rss., 186 , For. deutsch. Sept. Thon; Wien. Ak. Dksehr. 1. 25, t. 2, figg. 19—21 (seminuda).

g a) intermittens:

Syn. **Nodosaria intermittens** Römer, 1838, Nordd. tert. Meeress.; Leonh. u. Bronn. Jhrb. 1838, p. 382, t. 3, fig. 2.
Dentalina cylindrella, capitata, Sandbergeri, Girardana Reuss, 1855, Tert. Sch. nördl. u. mittl. Deutschl.; Wien. Ak. Sitz.-Ber. 1. 18, p. 222—224, t. 1, figg. 2, 4, 5, 6.
Nodosaria capitata Bott., 1846, Ostseeländ. p. 177, t. 2, fig. 13.
» » Reuss, 1864, Oligocän.; Wien. Ak. Sitz. Ber. 1. 50, p. 450, t. 1, figg. 8—10.
» » Hkr., 1875, Clav. Szab. Sch., p. 55, t. 3, fig. 16.
Dentalina Philippi, Buchi Rss., 1851, Sept. Thon. Berlin; Ztschr. deutsch. geol. Ges. 3, p. 60, t. 3, figg. 5—6.
» **antennula** d'Orb., 1846, For. tert. Vienne, p. 53, t. 2, figg. 29—30.
Nodosaria multilineata Mauss., Rügen Schreibekr., Greifswald. Nat. Verein. Mittheil. 1877—78, p. 131, t. 1, fig. 10.

h) papillosa:

Glandulina ornatissima Karr., 1878, For. Luzon; Bolet. Comis. Mapa geol. d. España 7. 2, p. 17, t. E, fig. 12.

Nodosarina radicula var. scalaris.

Syn. **Nodosaria sulcata**, longicauda d'Orb., 1826, Tabl. meth. Ann. Sc. Nat. 7, p. 253, 254, N:o 21, 28.
» **Candei**, Catesbyi d'Orb., 1839, Cuba p. 15, 16, t. 1, figg. 6—9.
» **striaticollis** d'Orb., 1844, Iles Canaries, p. 124, t. 1, figg. 3—4.
» **spinicosta** d'Orb., 1846, For. tert. Vienne, p. 37, t. 1, figg. 32—33 (an N. radicula var. Raphanus).
» **scalaris** Park. and Jones, 1865, N. atl and aret. Oc., Phil. Trans. 155. 1, p. 340, t. 16, fig. 2.
Nodosarina-Nodosaria scalaris Park. and Jones, 1866, Crag. For., Pal. Soc. 19, p. 52, t. 4, fig. 8.
Nodosaria radicula Will., 1858, Brit. rec. For., p. 15, figg. 36—38.
» **Roussiana**, variabilis, Ehrenbergiana, elegans Neugeb., 1852, For. Felsö Lapug., Siebenb. Nat. Verein. Mitth. 1850—52; t. 1, figg. 46—53
» **inflata** Rss., 1845, Böhm. Kreidef. 1, p. 25, t. 13, figg. 3—4; 1855, Kreide. Meklenb.; Ztschr. deutsch. geol. Ges. 7, p. 263, t. 8, figg. 2, 3, 4.
» **venusta** Rss., 1849, Neue For. österr. tert. Beck.; Wien. Ak. Dkschr. 1. 1, p. 367, t. 46, fig. 5.
» » Hkr., 1875, Clav. Szab. Sch. t. 12, fig. 14.
? » **nana** Rss., 1859, Westph. Kreide, Wien. Ak. Sitz.-Ber. 40, t. 1, fg. 6.
» **badenensis** d'Orb., 1846, For. tert. Vienne, p. 38, t. 1, figg. 34—35.
?**Dentalina urnula** d'Orb. ibid. p. 54, t. 2, figg. 31—32.
?**Nodosaria badenensis** var. Eocka, 1857, Mioc. Orteub.; Leonh. u. Bronn. Jhrb. 1857, p. 305, t. 15, figg. 17—21.
» **Roussii** Costa, 1854, Paleont. Nap. 2, p. 155, t. 16, fig. 5.

b) semistriata:

Nodosaria semiornata Karrer, 1878, Foraminf. Luzon, Bolet. Comis. Mapa geolog. del España 7. 2, p. 15, t. E, fig. 8.

Nodosarina communis D'ORB.
Tab. I, figg. 11—16.

This wide-spread species has been aptly arranged by PARKER and JONES in four sub-types of varieties. The difference between them is, as usual, much too slight and inconstant to justify their being distinguished as species with a nomenclature of their own.

a) *crassa, septis horizontalibus.* Nod. radiculæ proxima, (= *Dental. brevis* D'ORB.).

b) *longa, tenuis, septis horizontalibus.* Nod. radiculæ var. monili propinqua (= *Dent. communis, elegans, Lorneiana, Boueana* etc. D'ORB.).

c) *crassa, septis obliquis.* Nod. legumini LIN. valde propinqua (= *Dent. obliqua* D'ORB. [non LIN.], *Dent. nana* REUSS.).

d) *longa tenuis, septis obliquis;* etiam Nod. legumini quam maxime affinis (= *Dent. communis, inornata, badenensis* etc. D'ORB.).

The great affinity between N. communis D'ORB. and N. legumen LIN. makes it hardly possible to dispose fairly their many names in their resp. lists of synonyms. It is also on reasonable grounds that Professor WILLIAMSON has not kept N. communis distinct from N. legumen.

It is very commonly met with both among the Coralline-gravel and in the Chalk-ooze; its slender, graceful form, its often pearly lustre and its great size (15 mm. and more in length) distinguish this species as one of attractive beauty.

Fig. 11 is a pygmean form near to *Dent. brevis* D'ORB. It is exactly the same as *Dent. linearis* RÖM., *Dent. inermis* CZJZ. etc., from the Chalk-ooze.

Fig. 12, 12 b comes near to *Dent. Lorneiana* D'ORB. or *Dent. consobrina* D'ORB., it is a pigmy from the Chalkbottom.

Fig. 13—14 are near to *Dent. Boueana et aliis* D'ORB. Both are from the Coralline gravel and the Chalk-ooze.

Fig. 15 represents a highly developed *Nod. communis* from the Coralline-gravel.

Fig. 16 comes nearest to *Dent. badenensis* D'ORB., from the Chalk-ooze.

a) crassa: septis horizontalibus; N. radiculæ propinqua.

Syn. **Nodosaria nuda**	RSS., 1862, Nordd. Hils u. Gault; Wien. Ak. Sitz.-Ber. 1. 46, p. 38, t. 2, figg. 8—9.
Dentalina brevis	D'ORB., 1846, For. tert. Vienne, p. 48, t. 2, figg. 9—10.
" "	PARK. and JONES, 1860, For. Chellast. Qu. Journ. geol. Soc. 16, p. 453, t. 19, fig. 23.
Nodosarina radicula, Dentalina communis subvar. **brevis** PARK. and JONES, 1866, *Crag. Foram.*; Palæogr. Soc. 19, p. 63, t. 4, fig. 10.
Dent. pseudochrysalis	RSS., 1862, Nordd. Hils u. Gault; Wien. Ak. Sitz.-Ber. 1. 46, p. 40, t. 2, fig. 12.
Dentalina chrysalina	CORN., 1848, Nouv. foss. microsc. cret.; Mem. Soc. geol. Fr. (2) 3, p. 251, t. 1, fig. 21.

Syn. Dent. megalopolitana	Rss., 1855, Kreide. Mekleuburg; Ztschr. deutsch. geol. Ges. 7, p. 267, t. 8, fig. 10.	
» nitens	Costa, 1854, Pal. Nap. 2, p. 165, t. 12, fig. 26 (infer.).	
» obesa	Costa, 1854, Pal. Nap. t. 27, fig. 13.	
» fusiformis, torulosa	Schwag., 1863, Jurass. Sch., Würtemb. Nat. Ver. Jhrhft. 21, p. 99—100, t. 2, figg. 16—17 (a N. radicula vix distincta).	
» siliqua, Hilsoana, cylindroides	Rss., 1862, Nordd. Hils u. Gault, Wien. Ak. Sitz.-Ber. 1. 46, p. 41, t. 2, figg. 11, 14, 16.	
» cylindroides, cognata, D. distincta, strangulata, catenula, discrepans	Rss., 1859; Westphäl. Kreide; Wien. Ak. Sitz.-Ber. 40, p. 184—185, t. 1, fig. 8; t. 1, fig. 9; t. 2, fig. 5; t. 3, figg. 6—7.	
Nautilus rectus	Montag, 1803, Test. Britann. p. 197; Supplem. p. 82, t. 19, figg. 4—7.	
Nodosaria radicularis	Münst., Röm. 1838, Nordd. tert. Meeressand, Leonh. n. Bronn. Jhrb. 1838, p. 382, t. 3, fig. 3.	
Dentalina punctata	d'Orb., 1846, For. tert. Vienne, p. 49, t. 2, figg. 14—15.	
» inermis	Czjz., 1847, For. Wien. Beck.; Haid. Nat. Abh. 2, 1, p. 139, t. 12, figg. 3—7.	
Marginul. contraria	Czjz., 1847, ibid. p. 140, t. 12, figg. 17—20 (Nod. legumini approxim.).	
Nodosaria linearis	Röm., 1842, Verst. nordd. Kreidegeb. p. 95, t. 15, fig. 5.	
Dentalina linearis	Rss., 1862, Nordd. Hils u. Gault; Wien. Ak. Sitz.-Ber. 1. 46, p. 42, t. 2, fig. 15.	
» »	Gümb., 1868, Nordalp. Eocän., K. Bayr. Ak. Wiss. Abh. 1. 10. 2, p. 622, t. 1, figg. 36.	
Nodosaria pupiformis	Karr., 1867, For. Fauna Österreich.; Wien. Ak. Sitz.-Ber. 1. 55, p. 354, t. 1, fig. 5.	
Dentalina Vernouilli	Bornemann, 1855, Sept. Thon. Hermsdorf; Ztschr. d. geol. Ges. 7, p. 324, t. 13, fig. 8.	
» corniculum	Costa, 1854, Pal. Nap. t. 27, fig. 14.	
» intermedia	Corn., 1848, Nouv. foss. microse. cret.; Mem. Soc. geol. Fr. (2) 3. p. 251, t. 1, fig. 20.	
Nodosaria tauricornis	Schwag., 1866, For. Kar.-Nikobar.; Novara Reise, geol. Th. 2. 2, p. 228, t. 6, fig. 61.	
Dentalina transmontana	Gümb., 1862, For. St. Cassian u. Raibl.; Österr. geol. Reichsanst. Jhrb. 19, p. 177, t. 5, fig. 17.	
Dentalina gomphoides	Costa, 1854, Pal. Nap. 2, t. 27, figg. 24—25.	
» acuminata	Rss., 1859, Westph. Kreide, Wien. Ak. Sitz.-Ber. 40, p. 181, t. 1, fig. 7.	
» tenuicaudata	Rss., 1859, ibid. p. 182, t. 2, fig. 3.	
» commutata	Rss., 1859, ibid. p. 183, t. 2, fig. 4.	
» Vernouillii	d'Orb., 1846, For. tert. Vienne, p. 48, t. 2, figg. 7—8.	
» rotundata	Stache, 1865, Tert. Merg. Whaingar. Hafen; Novara Reise, geol. Th. 1. 2, p. 205, t. 22, fig. 33.	
» pomuligera	Stache, 1865, ibid. p. 204, t. 22, fig. 31.	
» vagina	Stache, 1865, ibid. p. 206, t. 22, fig. 34.	
» deformis	Stache, 1865, ibid. p. 205, t. 22, fig. 32.	
» Haidingeri	Neuger., 1856, For. Stichosteg. Felsö Lapug.; Wien. Ak. Dkschr. 1. 12. 2, p. 85, t. 3, fig. 12.	
» aequalis	Karr., 1865, For. Grünsandstein N. Zeeland; Novara Reise, geol. Th. 1. 2 p. 74, t. 16, fig. 1.	
» ahercules	Gümb., 1868, Nordalp. Eocän.; K. Bayr. Ak. Abh. 1. 10. 2, p. 621, t. 1, fig. 34.	
Marginul. torulosa	Costa, 1854, Pal. Nap. 2, p. 185, t. 12, fig. 15.	
Dentalina Hörnesi	Hkr., 1875, For. Clav. Száb. Schichten p. 37, t. 4, fig. 2 (au Uvigerina).	
Spec. indet.	Costa, 1855, Marna terz. Messina, Mem. Nap. 2, t. 1, fig. 36.	
Spec. indet.	Schwag., 1863, Jurass. Sch.; Würtemb. Nat. Vereiu. Jhrhft. 21, t. 4, fig. 31.	
Dentalina pusilla, bullata, Fraasi	Schwag., ibid. p. 104, 107, 110, t. 3, figg. 3, 23, 24.	
Nodosaria pauperata	Park. and Jones, 1865, Nordatl. and Aert. Oceans; Phil. Trans. 155, p. 342, t. 13, fig. 8—9.	

b) magis extenuata; septis horizontalibus:

Syn. **Nodosaria vermiculum**		Rss., 1865, For. deutsch. Sept. Thon; Wien. Ak. Dkschr. 1. 25. 1, p. 133, t. 2, figg. 14—15.
Dentalina fasciata		Seg., 1862, Rhizopod. d. Catania, Acad. Gioenia Atti (2), 18, p. 12, t. 1, fig. 1.
»	mutabilis	Bailey, 1850, Examin. of Soundings; Smithson. Contrib. of knowledge 2, Art. 3, p. 10, fig. 7.
»	gigantea	Hke., 1875, Clav. Szàb. Sch. p. 34, t. 3, fig. 15.
Nodosaria contorta		Costa, 1856, Pal. Nap. 2. t. 16, fig. 2.
Dentalina consobrina		Bornemann, 1855, Sept. Thon Hermsdorf; Ztschr. deutsch. geol. Ges. 7, p. 323, t. 13, figg. 1—4 (ad monile vergens).
»	obtusata	Rss., 1851, Tert. Sch. Oberschlesien; Zeitschr. deutsch. geol. Ges. p. 151, t. 8, fig. 1.
»	indifferens	Rss., 1863, Sept. Thon Offenbach. Wien. Ak. Sitz.-Ber. 1. 48, p. 44, t. 2, figg. 15—16.
»	communis	Park. and Jones, 1860, For. Chellast.; Qu. Journ. geol. Soc. 16, p. 453, t. 19, fig. 25.
»	perversa	Neugeb., 1856, For. Stichost. Ob. Lapug.; Wien. Ak. Dkschr. 1. 12. 2, p. 80, t. 2, fig. 8.
Marginul. tenuis		Bornem., 1855, Sept. Thon Hermsdorf; Ztschr. deutsch. geol. Ges. 7, p. 326, t. 13, fig. 14.
Dentalina antenna		Cornu., 1848, Nouv. foss. microse.; Mem. Soc. geol. France (2) 3, p. 250, t. 1, fig. 19.
»	tenuicollis	Rss., 1855, Kreidegeb. Meklenburg; Zeitschr. deutsch. geol. Ges. 7, p. 267, t. 8, fig. 11; 1865, Kreide am Kanara See; Wien. Ak. Sitz.-Ber. 52, p. 452, fig. 6.
»	Zsigmondyi	Hke., 1875, Clav. Szàb. Sch., p. 32, t. 12, fig. 17.
»	Reitzi	Hke., ibid. p. 33, t. 13, fig. 6.
»	glandulifera	Gumb., 1868, Nordalp. Eocän.; K. Bayr. Ak. Wiss. Abh. 1. 10. 2, p. 622, t. 1, fig. 37.
»	pugiunculus	Rss., 1859, Westphäl. Kreide, Wien. Ak. Sitz.-Ber. 40, p. 183, t. 3, fig. 9,
»	»	Schwag., 1863, Jurass. Sch., Wurtemb. Nat. Ver. Jhrhft. 21, p. 111, t. 4, fig. 1.
»	filiformis	Rss., 1859, Westphal. Kreide; Wien. Ak. Sitz.-Ber. 40, p. 188, t. 3, fig. 8.
»	perscripta	Egg., 1857, Miocän. Ortenburg; Leonh. u. Bronn Jhrb. 1857, p. 307, t. 15. figg 30—31.
»	pauperata	Park. and Jones, 1860, For. Chellast.; Qu. Journ geol. Soc. 16, p. 453, t. 19, fig. 22.
»	fusiformis	Gumb., 1868, Nordalp. Eocän.; K. Bayr. Ak. Wiss. Abh. 1. 10. 2, p. 621, t. 1, fig. 35.
Nautilus subarcuatus		Montag., 1803, Test. Britan. p. 198, t. 6, fig. 5.
Dentalina farcimen		(Sold.) Rss., 1863, For. Crag. d'Anvers, Bull. Ac. Belg. (2). 15. p. 146, t. 1, fig. 18.
»	communis	d'Orb., 1826, Tabl. meth. Ac. Sc. Nat 7, p. 254, N.o 35.
»	»	Park. and Jones, 1866, Crag For.; Pal. Soc. 19, p. 58, t. 1, figg. 15—17.
»	?legumen	Rss., 1845, Böhm. Kreide 1. p. 28, t. 13, figg. 23—24; Kreide. Lemberg. Haid. Nat. Abh. 4. 1, p. 36, t. 1, fig. 14 (in N. legumen vergens).
»	elegans	d'Orb., 1846, For. tert. Vienne p. 45, t. 1, figg. 52—56.
»	»	Schwag., 1865, For. Kar.-Nikobar.; Novara Reise, geol. Th. 2. 2., p. 233, t. 6, fig. 68.
»	»	Hke., 1875, Clav. Szàb. Sch. p 30, t. 3, fig. 7.
»	scripta	d'Orb., 1846, For. tert. Vienne p. 51, t. 2, figg. 21—23.
»	intermedia	Hke., 1875, For. Clav. Szàb. Sch. p. 30, t. 3, figg. 4, 8.
»	Verneuilii	Hke., 1875, ibid. p. 32, t. 3, fig. 9.
»	Gümbeli	Schwag., 1863, Jurass. Sch.; Württemb. Nat. Verein. Jhrhft. 21, p. 101, t. 2, fig. 20.
»	emaciata	Rss., 1851, Sept. Thon von Berlin; Zeitschr. deutsch. geol. Ges. 3, p. 63, t. 3, fig. 9.

KONGL. SV. VET. AKADEMIENS HANDLINGAR. BAND. 19. N:O 4. 29

Syn. Dentalina Reussi		Neugeb., 1856, For. Stichosteg. Ob. Lapug.; Wien. Ak. Dkschr. 1. 12. 2, p. 85, t. 3, figg. 6—7; 17.
»	Scharbergana	Neugeb., 1856, ibid. p. 87, t. 4, figg. 1—4.
»	nodosa	d'Orb., 1839, For. Craie bl. Paris; Mem. Soc. geol. France (2) 4, p. 14, t. 1, figg. 6—7.
Nodosaria nodosa		Rss., 1845, Böhm. Kreide 1, p. 28, t. 13, fig. 22.
Dentalina nodosa		Costa, 1854, Pal. Nap. 2, p. 164, t. 12, fig. 8.
»	praelonga	Costa, 1854, ibid. p. 163, t. 12, fig. 21.
»	abbreviata	Costa, 1854, ibid. t. 27, fig. 21.
»	adunca	Costa, 1855, For. Marna blu' Vaticano; Mem. Nap. 2, p. 117, t. 1, fig. 1.
»	nopos	Costa, 1855, ibid. p. 117, t. 1, fig. 2".
»	subtilis	Hke., 1875, For. Clav. Szab. Sch. p. 33, t. 3, fig. 13.
»	gracilis	d'Orb., 1839, For. Craie bl. Paris; Mem. Soc. geol. France (2) 4. p. 14, t. 1, fig. 5.
»	»	Alth., 1849, Umgeb. Lemb.; Haid. Nat. Abh. 3. 2, p. 269, t. 13, fig. 27.
»	spec. indet.	Costa, Pal. Nap. 2, t. 12, fig. 28.
Nodosaria gracilis		Rss., 1845, Böhm. Kreide 1, p. 27, t. 8, fig. 6.
Dentalina acuticauda		Rss., 1851, Sept. Thon von Berlin; Zeitschr. deutsch. geol. Ges. 3, p. 62, t. 3, fig. 8.
»	»	Rss., 1863, Sept. Thon Offenbach; Wien. Ak. Sitz.-Ber. 1. 48, p. 45, t. 3, fig. 26.
Nodosaria peracuta		Rss., 1873, Geinitz, Elbthalgeb. Sachsen 2, p. 86, t. II. 20, fig. 21.
Dentalina annulata		Rss., 1850, Kreide Lemberg; Haid. Nat. Abh. 4. 1, p. 26, t. 1, fig. 13.
Nodosaria	»	Rss., 1875, Geinitz Elbthalgeb. Sachsen 2, p. 85, t. II. 20, figg. 19—20.
»	Costai	Schwag., 1866, For. Kar-Nikobar; Novara Reise, geol. Th. 2. 2, p. 229, t. 6. fig. 62.
»	stimulea	Schwag., 1866, ibid. t. 6, fig. 57.
»	fustiformis	Schwag., 1866, ibid. p. 228, t. 6, fig. 60.
»	inarticulata	Rss., 1865, Kreide am Kanara See; Wien. Ak. Sitz.-Ber. 52, p. 454, fig. 5.
»	laevigata	Nilss., 1827, Petrificata Sveeana p. 8, t. 9, fig. 2.
Dentalina pauperata		d'Orb., 1846, For. tert. Vienne, p. 46, t. 1, figg. 57—58.
»	communis	subvar. pauperata Park. and Jones, 1866, Crag. For.; Pal. Soc. 19, p. 58, t. 1, figg. 13, 20.
Dentalina pauperata		Bornem., 1855, Sept. Thon Hermsdorf; Zeitschr. deutsch. geol. Ges. 7, p. 324, t. 13, fig. 7.
Nodosaria approximata		Rss., 1865, deutsch. Sept. Thon, Wien. Ak. Dkschr. 1. 25. 1, p. 134, t. 2. fig. 22.
»	»	Hke., 1875, Clav. Szab. Sch. p. 31, t. 3, fig. 5.
Nodosaria clava		Karrer, 1878, Foram. Luzon; Bolet. Comis. Mapa geol. del España, 7. 2, p. 16, t. 1, fig. 11.
Dentalina plebeja		Rss., 1855, Kreidegeb. Meklenburg; Zeitschr. deutsch. geol. Ges. 7, p. 267, t. 8, fig. 9.
»	Lorneiana	d'Orb., 1831, For. Craie bl. Paris; Mem. Soc. geol. France (2) 4. p. 14, t. 1, figg. 8—9.
»	»	Reuss, 1845, Böhm Kreidef. 1, p. 27, t. 8, fig. 5 (ad N. monile vergens).
»	Boueana	d'Orb., 1846, For. tert. Vienne p. 47, t. 2, figg. 4—6.
»	»	Hke., 1875, For. Clav. Szab. Sch. p. 31, t. 12, figg. 11, 19 (ad N. monile vergens).
»	consobrina	d'Orb., 1846, For. tert. Vienne, p. 46, t. 2, figg. 1—3 (ad Nod. monile vergens).
»	»	Reuss, 1863, Sept. Thon Offenbach; Wien. Ak. Sitz.-Ber. 1. 48, p. 45, t. 2, figg. 19—23.
»	»	Neugeb., 1856, For. Stichost. Ob. Lapug.; Wien. Ak. Dkschr. 1. 12. 2, p. 86, t. 3, fig. 15.
»	»	Park. and Jones, 1865, North. Atl. and Arct. Oc.; Phil. Trans. 155, 1, p. 342, t. 16, fig. 3.
»	»	Hke., 1875, For. Clav. Szab. Sch. p. 30, t. 3, figg. 3, 10.
»	affinis communi Gümb., Ulmer Cementmerg.; Münch. Ak. Sitz.-Ber. 1, p. 65, t. 1, fig. 6.	
»	spinigera, tenuis Neugb., 1856, For. Stichost. Ob. Lapug.; Wien. Ak. Dkschr. 1. 12. 2, p. 84, 86, t. 3, figg. 16, 14.	

c) crassa, oblique septata:

Syn. Dentalina declivis, turgida, conferta, mutabilis, cylindrica, abolета, Quenstedti, crenata, filocincta, aequabilis Schwag., 1863, Jurass. Sch.; Würtemberg. Nat. Ver. Jhrbft. 21, t. 3. fig. 1; t. 1, figg 6, 11; t. 2, fig. 19; t. 5, fig. 9; t. 2, fig. 24; t. 3, fig. 28; t 3, fig. 5; t. 3, fig. 22; t. 3, fig. 25; t. 3, fig. 13; t. 4, fig. 6.
» abnormis Rss., 1863, Sept. Thon Offenbach; Wien. Ak. Sitz.-Ber. 1. 48, p. 46, t. 2, fig. 24.
Marginul. elongata Rss., 1850, Kreidemerg. Lemberg; Haid. Nat. Abh. 4. 1, p. 28, t. 1, fig. 17.
Dentalina debilis Hrv., 1875, For. Clav. Szab. Sch. p. 33, t. 13, fig. 10
» hamulifera, nana Rss., 1862, Nordd Hils u. Gault; Wien. Ak. Sitz.-Ber. 1. 46, p. 42, 39, t. 2, figg. 17, 10—18.
» contracta, tarentina, phiala Costa, 1854, Pal. Nap. 2, t. 27, fig. 12; t. 13, figg. 12, 20—21.
» spec. indet. Costa, 1855, Marna terz Messina; Mem. Nap. 2, t. 1, fig. 35; t. 2, fig. 3.
» obliquesutura Stache, 1865, Tert. Mergel Whaingar. Hafen, Novara Reise geol. Th. 1. 2, p. 207, t. 22, fig. 36.
» colligata Rxuss, 1861, Grünsand, N. Jers.; Wien. Ak. Sitz.-Ber. 1. 44, p. 334, t. 7, fig. 4.
» Korynophora Gumb., 1869, For. St. Cassian u. Räibl. Sch.; österr. geol. Reichsanst. Jhrb. 19, p. 176, t. 5, fig. 1.
Marginul. duracina Stache, 1865, Tert. Mergel Whaingar. Hafen; Novara Reise geol. Th. 1. 2, p. 211, t. 22, fig. 42.
» inversa Costa, 1854, Pal. Nap. 2, p. 139, t. 12, fig. 16.
» nuda Schwag., 1863, Jurass. Sch.; Würtemb. Nat. Verein. Jhrbft. 21, p. 119, t. 5, fig. 2 (Nod. legumini propinqua).
Dentalina conferta, Roemeri, Orbignyana, mucronata Neugeb., 1856, For. Stichost. Ob. Lapugy; Wien. Ak. Dkschr. 1. 12. 2, p. 81, t. 2, fig. 11; t. 2, figg. 13 – 17; t. 3, figg. 1—3; t. 3, figg. 8—11.
Marginul. apiculata Rss., 1850, Kreidemerg. Lemberg; Haid. Nat. Abh. 4. 1, p. 28, t. 1, fig. 18.
Dentalina obliqua, arcuata d'Orb., 1826, Tabl. Meth.; Ann. Sc. Nat. 7, p. 254, N:ris 36, 38; mod. 5.
» intermedia Rss., 1859, Westph. Kreide; Wien. Ak. Dkschr. 40, p. 186, t. 2, fig. 8.

d) angusta, septis obliquis:

Dentalina carinata d'Orb., 1826, Tabl. Meth.; Ann. Sc. Nat. 7, p. 255, N:o 39.
» communis d'Orb., 1839, Craie bl. Paris; Mem. Soc. geol. France (2) 4, p. 13, t. 1, fig. 4.
Nodosaria » Reuss, 1845, Böhm. Kreide 1, p. 28, t. 12, fig. 21.
» communis Park. and Jones, 1865, North. Atl. and Arct. Oceans; Phil. Trans. 155. 1, p. 342, t. 13, fig. 10.
Dentalina communis Brad., 1876, Carbonif. and Perm. foramf.; Pal. Soc. 30, p. 127, t. 10, figg. 17–18.
» spec. indet. Costa, 1854; Pal. Nap. 2, p. 171, t. 16, fig. 23.
» Forstliana Czjz., 1847, Foramf. Wien. Beck.; Haid. Nat. Abh. 2. 1, p. 140, t. 12, figg. 10—13.
» badenensis d'Orb., 1846, For. tert. Vienne, p. 44, t. 1, figg. 48—49.
» » Costa, 1854, Pal. Nap. 2, p. 171, t. 16, fig. 23.
» spec. indet. Costa, 1855, Marna terz. Messina; Mem. Nap. 2, t. 1, figg. 32—33.
» cingulata Czjz., 1847, Foramf. Wien. Beck.; Haid. Nat. Abh. 2. 1, p. 139, t. 12, figg. 8—9.
» inornata d'Orb., 1846, For. tert. Vienne, p. 44, t. 1, figg. 50—51.
» » Reuss, 1865, Sept. Thon Offenbach; Wien. Ak. Sitz.-Ber. 1. 48, p. 45, t. 2, fig. 18.
» gracilis Costa, 1854, Pal. Nap. 2, t. 12, fig. 26 sup.

Syn Dentalina elegans		Bornem., 1855, Sept. Thon Hermsdorf; Ztschr. deutsch. geol. Ges. 7, p. 323, t. 13, fig. 6.
»	Böttcheri, obliquata	Reuss, 1863, Sept. Thon Offenbach; Wien. Ak. Sitz.-Ber. 1. 48, p. 44, 46, t. 2, figg. 17, 25.
»	budensis, simplex	Hkr., 1875, For. Clav. Szab. Sch., p. 33, 34, t. 3, 13, figg. 12, 7.
»	xiphioides, deflexa	Rss., 1862, Nordd. Hils u. Gault; Wien. Ak. Sitz.-Ber. 1. 48, p. 43, t. 3, fig. 1; t. 2, fig. 19.
»	acus	Rss., 1850, Kreidemergel Lemberg; Haid. Nat. Abh. 4. 1, p. 27, t. 1, fig. 15. (an N. legumen).
»	pygmaea, subtilis, Partschi, subulata	Neugeb., 1856, For. Stichost. Ob. Lapug.; Wien. Ak. Dkschr. I. 12, 2, p. 80, t. 2, fig. 9; t. 3, figg. 4, 5, 13.
»	funiculus, extensa, lutigena, sublinearis, imbecilla, geniculosa, Oppelii, Marginul. procera	Schwag., 1863, Jurass. Sch.; Württemb. Nat. Ver. Jhrhft. 24, p. 109—118, t. 2, figg. 18, 21, 22, 25, 26, 27; t. 3, figg. 16·17; t. 5, fig. 1.
Nodosaria Neugeboreni, graciloscens		Schwag., 1866, For. Kar-Nikobar; Novara Reise, geol. Th. 2. 2, p. 232, 234, t. 6, figg. 67, 70. (an N. legumen).

Nodosarina communis d'Orb. var. obliqua Lin.

Tab. I. figg. 17—19.

The line of distinction between *Nod. obliqua* and *raphanus* is just as faint and untraceable as it is between *Nod. communis* and *radicula*.

Slender varieties of Nod. raphanus are not distinguishable from N. obliqua but by its bended axis.

Figg. 17—19 come near to *Dent. sulcata* and *acuta* d'Orb., *Dent. polyphragma*, *Zippei* (part.) Reuss, *Nod. stiliformis* Schwag. etc.

The strength, distance and number of the ridges, which like finished sculpture adorn the shell, are subject to many degrees of variation. It has some propensity to become quite smooth by age as if returning to Nod. communis. Sometimes again it becomes very slightly striated. It is not scarce either on the coralline- or on the chalk-bottom and attains a length of 22 mm.

Fig. 19 represents a more finely ridged or rather finely wrinkled form with globular chambers. It resembles most *Nod. Zippei* (part.) Reuss, from the Bohemian chalk. Those wrinkles become sometime very faint.

a) crassa, var. Raphano proxima:

Syn. Nodosaria	substriata, Dentalina cornicula	d'Orb., 1826, Tabl. Meth.; Ann. Sc. Nat. 7, p. 255, N:ris 46—47.
	Dentalina multicostata	d'Orb., 1839, For. Craie bl. Paris; Mem. Soc. geol. Fr. (2) 4, p. 16, t. 1, figg. 14—15.
»	»	Brady, 1876, Carb. and Perm. foramf.; Pal. Soc. 30, p. 129, t. 10, fig. 19.
»	Kingi	Jones, 1850, Kings monogr. perm. foss. p. 17, t. 6, figg. 2—3. (ser. Brady.)
»	»	Richt., 1861, Geinitz Dyas, p. 122, t. 20, fig. 33. (see. Brady.)
»	irregularis	Costa, 1854, Pal. Nap. 2, p. 166, t. 12, figg. 23, 27.
»	bifurcata	d'Orb., 1846, For. tert. Vienne p. 56, t. 2, figg. 38—39.
»	»	Reuss, 1848, Neue Forf. Österr.; Wien. Ak. Dkschr. I. 1, p. 367, t. 46, fig. 10.
»	»	Costa, 1854, Pal. Nap. 2, p. 162, t. 12, fig. 27.
»	Marcki	Rss., 1859, Westph. Kreide; Wien. Ak. Sitz.-Ber. 40, p. 188, t. 2, fig. 7.

b) **obliqua vera:**

Syn.	Nautilus jugosus	Montag., 1803, Test. Brit. p. 198, t. 14, fig. 4.
	Nodosaria raphanus	var. Dentalina obliqua Park. and Jones, 1866, Crag. For.; Pal. Soc. 19, t. 1, fig. 9.
	» lineolata	Reuss, 1845, Böhm. Kreide 1, p. 27, t. 8, fig. 8.
	Dentalina lineolata	Park. and Jones, 1860, For. Chellast.; Qu. Journ. geol. Soc. 16, p. 453, t. 19, figg. 11—12.
	» pulchra	Gabb, 1859, Am. tert. and cret. foss.; Journ. Philad. Ac. Sc. (2), 4, p. 402, t. 69, figg. 40 41.
	Nodosaria nodosa	d'Orb., 1826, Tabl. Meth.; An. Sc. Nat. 7, p. 254, Nio 31.
	Dentalina elegantissima	d'Orb., 1846, For. tert. Vienne p. 55, t. 2, figg. 33—35.
	Nodosaria acicula	Phil., 1843, Tert. Versteiner. nordw. Deut-chl. t. 1, fig. 33
	Dentalina Konincki	Rss., 1860, Crag. Antwerp.; Wien. Ak. Sitz.-Ber. 42, p. 356, t. 1, fig. 3.
	» microptycha, arcuata	Rss., 1860, Dingd., Westphal.; ibid. p. 364, 365, t. 1, figg. 4—5.
	Modosaria costellata,	Zippei (partim) Rss., Böhm. Kreidef. 1, p. 27, 28, t. 13, fig. 18; t. 8, fig. 1.
	Dentalina baltica	Rss., 1855, Kreide Mecklenb.; Zeitschr. deutsch. geol. Ges. 7, p. 269, t. 8, fig. 15.
	» Hörnesi, Beyrichana, Lamarcki	Neugeb., 1856, For. Stichost. Ob. Lapugy; Wien. Ak. Dksehr. 1. 12. 2, p. 89, 91; t. 4, figg. 10—11, 16.
	Nodosaria acuticosta	Rss., 1849, Neue For. Österr.; Wien. Ak. Dksehr. 1. 1, p. 368, t. 46, fig. 11.
	» acuticosta, bifurcata	Hornem., 1855, Sept. Thou Hermsdorf; Zeitschr. deutsch. geol. Ges. 7, p. 325, t. 13, figg. 9—11.
	Nodosaria hircicornis	Schwag., 1866, For. Kar-Nikobar; Novara Reise, geol. Th. 2, 2, p. 230, t. 6, fig. 64.
	» eximia	Karr., 1868, Mioc. For. Kostey; Wien. Ak. Sitz.-Ber. 1. 58, p. 164, t. 4, fig. 1
	» sulcata	Nilsson, 1825, Mängrummiga snäckor i kritformat. i Sverige; K. Vet. Ak. Handl. 1825, p. 344; 1827, Petref. svecana p. 8, t. 9, fig. 19.
	» »	Reuss, 1845, Böhm. Kreidef. 1, p. 26, t. 13, fig. 17.
	» »	d'Orb., 1839, Craie bl. Paris; Mem. Soc. geol. Fr. (2) 4, p. 45, t. 1, figg. 10—13.
	Dentalina multilineata	Hornem., 1855, Sept. Thou Hermsdorf; Zeitschr. deutsch. geol. Ges. 7, p. 325, t. 13, fig. 12.
	» »	Rss., 1873, Geim. Elbthalgeb. Sachsen 2, p. 83, t. II. 20, fig. 13.
	» pungens	Rss., 1851, Sept. Thou Berlin, Zeitschr. deutsch. geol. Ges. 3, p. 61, t. 3, fig. 13.
	» »	Hkr., 1875, For. Clav. Szab. Sch. p. 36, t. 4, fig. 3.
	» »	Gümb., 1868, Nordalp. Eoc.; K. Bayr. Ak. Wissensch. Abh. 1. 10, 2, p. 625, t. 1, fig. 44.
	» acicularis	Costa, 1854, Pal. Nap. 2, p. 166, t. 12, fig. 21.
	» acutissima	Rss., 1855, Kreidef. Mecklenb.; Zischr. deutsch. geol. Ges. 7, p. 268, t. 8, fig. 13.
	» Steenstrupi	Rss., 1855, Kreidef. Mecklenb.; Zischr. deutsch. geol. Ges. 7, p. 268, t. 8, fig. 14 a.
	» longicauda	Rss., 1855. ibid. p. 267, t. 8, fig. 12.
	» polyphragma	Reuss, 1859, Westphäl. Kreide; Wien. Ak. Sitz.-Ber. 40, p. 189, t. 3, fig. 1.
	Nodosaria equisetiformis, acuta, Dentalina Ehrenbergana, fissicostata, Gümbeli, contorta, semilaevis	Hkr., 1875, For. Clav. Szab. Sch. p. 36 -39; t. 2, fig. 11; t. 3, figg. 17, 19, 20; t. 4, figg. 1, 5, 6; t. 12, fig. 13.
	Dentalina acuta	d'Orb., 1846, For. tert. Vienne p. 56, t. 2, figg. 40—43.
	Nodosaria siphunculoides	Costa, 1855, Marna terz. Messina; Mem. Nap. 2, p. 135, t. 2, fig. 27.
	» stiliformis	Schwag., 1866, For. Kar-Nikobar; Novara Reise, geol. Th. 2, 2, p. 233, t. 6, fig. 59.
	Dentalina obscura	Stache, 1865, Tert. Mergel Whaingar. Hafen; Novara Reise, geol. Th. 1, 2, p. 208, t. 22, fig. 37.
	» paucicostata	Costa, 1854, Pal. Nap. t. 27, fig. 20.
	Nodosaria elegans	v. Münster, 1838; Römer, Leonh. u. Bronn Jhrb. 1838, p. 382, t. 3, fig. 1.
	Dentalina Münsteri	Rss., 1855, Tert. Sch. nordl. u. mittl. Deutschl.; Wien. Ak. Sitz.-Ber. 1. 18, p. 224, t. 1, fig. 8.

Syn. Dentalina Schwartzii	Karr., 1864, Leythakalk Wien. Beck.; Wien. Ak. Sitz.-Ber. 1. 50, p. 705, t. 1, fig. 5.
» confluens	Rss., 1861, Grünsand N. Jersey; Wien. Ak. Sitz.-Ber. 1. 44, p. 335. t. 7, fig. 5.
» Ehrenbergana, crebricosta Neugeb., 1856, For. Stiehost. Ob. Lapugy; Wien. Ak. Dkschr. 1. 12. 2, p. 90, t. 4, figg. 12—14.
» truncana	Gümb., 1868, Nordalp. Eoc.; K. Bayr. Ak. Wiss. Abh. 1. 10. 2, p. 627, t. 1, fig. 47.
Nodosaria grossecostata	Costa, 1854, Pal. Nap. 2, p. 148, t. 12, figg. 1—3.
Dentalina Cuvieri	d'Orb., 1826, Tabl. Meth.; An. Sc. Nat. 7, p. 255, N:o 45.
» spinosa	d'Orb., 1846, For. tert. Vienne p. 55, t. 2, figg. 36—37.

c) obliquestriata:

Dentalina obliquestriata	Rss. (partim) 1851, Sept. Thon Berlin; Zeitschr. deutsch. geol. Ges. 3, p. 63, t. 3, fig. 12.
» strigosa	Costa, 1854, Pal. Nap. 2, p. 168, t. 12, fig. 6.
» Geinitzana	Neugeb., 1856, For. Stiehost. Lapug.; Wien. Ak. Dkschr. 1. 12. 2, p. 91, t. 4, fig. 15.
» divergens	Rss., 1864, Oberoligocän.; Wien. Ak. Sitz.-Ber. 1. 50, p. 456, t. 4, fig. 10.
Nodosarina-Dentalina obliquestriata	Park. and Jones, 1866, Crag. For.; Pal. Soc. 19, p. 56, t. 1, fig. 19.

d) seminuda:

Nodosaria seminuda	Rss., 1849, Neue For. Österr.; Wien. Ak. Dkschr. 1. 1, p. 367, t. 46, fig. 9.
Dentalina semilaevis	Hag., 1875, For. Clav. Szab Seh. p. 39, t. 12, fig. 13.
» Konincki	Rss., 1863, For. Crag. d'Anvers; Bull. Ac. Belg. (2) 15, p. 146, t. 1, fig. 12.
Marginul. corniculum	Costa, 1854, Pal. Nap. 2, p. 186, t. 13, fig. 14.

e) intermittens:

Dentalina aciculata	d'Orb., 1826, Tabl. Meth.; An. Sc. Nat. 7, p. 255, N:o 41.
» flexuosa	d'Orb., 1826, ibid. p. 254, N:o 32.
» lineata	Rss., 1864, Oligocän.; Wien. Ak. Sitz.-Ber. 1. 50, p. 456, t. 4, fig. 11.
Nodosaria filiformis	Rss., 1845, Böhm. Kreide 1, p. 28, t. 12, fig. 28.
Dentalina intermittens	Rss., 1858, Tert. Sch. nordl. u. mittl. Deutschl.; Wien. Ak. Sitz.-Ber. 1. 18, p. 224, t. 1, fig. 7.
» semiplicata, semicostata d'Orb., 1846, For. tert. Vienne p. 52—53, t. 2, figg. 24—28.
Nodos. subcanaliculata	Neugeb., 1856, For. Stiehost. Ob. Lapugy; Wien. Ak. Dkschr. 1. 12. 2, p. 87, t. 4, figg. 5—6.
Dentalina interlineata	Rss., 1855, Kreidegeb. Meklenburg; Zeitschr. deutsch. geol. Ges. 7, p. 287, t. 11, fig. 2.
» »	Marsson, 1878, Rügen. Schreibkr.; Greifsw. Nat. Verein. Mitth. 1877—78, p. 132, t. 1, fig. 11.
» obliquestriata	Rss., 1851 (partim), Sept. Thon Berlin; Zeitschr. deutsch. geol. Ges. 3, p. 63, t. 3, fig. 11.
» subornata	Rss., 1865, Feuerstein Kreide Kanara See; Wien. Ak. Sitz.-Ber. 52, p. 450, figg. 9—10.
» proteus	Rss., 1864, Kreidestuff Maastricht; Wien. Ak. Sitz.-Ber. 44, p. 306, t. 1, figg. 6—9 (in Nod. raphanum transiens).

f) tenuissime striata:

Nodosaria acicula	Rss., 1873, Grünitz Elbthalgeb Sachs 2, p. 82, t. 11. 20, fig. 10.

Nodosarina legumen Lin.

Tab. II, figg. 20—31.

Through such intermediate forms as *Marginulina bullata* Rss., etc., Nod. legumen becomes closely connected with Nod. radicula. Its great affinity to Nod. communis has been mentioned.

The compression of its shell is often very slight. Sometimes it is quite conspicuous during a less adult stage but gives place to a cylindrical form by age. The inclination of the septa to the shells axis is also very variable. But it will still be necessary to retain this Linnean species, as it must be used as are presentative type of those broader forms, on which D'Orbigny and others have founded their genera *Marginulina* and *Vaginulina*.

Frondicularia lingua Boll. is a connecting link between Nod. legumen and Nod. complanata Defr.

When in the young state the shell is more or less coiled up to a spiral, intermediate forms to Nod. crepidula Ficht. and Moll. are originated.

The pigmy forms of Nod. legumen (0,50—1 mm. in length) are not uncommon in the chalk-ooze; the stouter forms (about 12 mm.) occur in the coralline-gravel.

Figg. 20—21 b is *Vagin. lævigata* Röm. or *Vagin. badenensis* D'Orb.; it is a dwarfish form from the chalk-bottom.

Figg. 22—25: highly developed forms; some with the older chambers compressed and those of later growth cylindrical; some with quite cylindrical chambers through all stages of growth. The shell is thin, nearly transparent and of a silky lustre.

Figg. 26—26 b: peculiar form, approaching *Nod. crepidula*.

Figg. 27—27 b: the same as *Margin. ensis* Reuss and *Margin. lituus* D'Orb. etc. pygmies from the chalk-ooze.

Figg. 28—31: stouter forms from the coralline-gravel.

a) Nod. Bertheloti D'Orb. sive bullata Rss.

Syn. **Margin. bullata**		Rss., 1845, Böhm. Kreide I, p. 29, t. 13, figg. 34—38; 1859, Westphal. Kreide; Wien. Ak. Sitz.-Ber. 40, p. 205, t. 6. figg. 4—6.
Margin. pediformis		Borneman, 1855, Sept. Thon Hermsdorff; Ztschr. deutsch. geol. Gesellsch. 7, p. 326, t. 13, fig. 13.
»	», subbullata	Hantk., 1875, For. Clavul. Szab. Sch., p. 45, t. 4, figg. 12—13; t. 5, figg. 8—9.
»	comma	Röm., 1841, Verstein. Nordd. Kreide, p. 96, t. 15, fig. 15.
»	Bertheloti	D'Orb., 1844, Iles Canaries, p. 125, t. 1, figg. 12—13.
»	aculeata, hispida, pustulosa, affinis, agglutinans, echinata Neugeb., 1851, For. Felső Lapugy; Siebenb. Verein. Mittheil. 1851, p. 142, t. 4, figg. 21—25.	
Crist. (Marg.) spinulosa Karr., 1877, Hochquell-Wasserleit.; Österr. geol. Reichsanst. Abh. 9, p. 382, t. 16, fig. 34.		
Marg. variabilis, Acknoriana, erecta, intermedia Neugeb., 1851, For. Felső Lapug.; Siebenbürg. Verein. Mittheil. 1851, p. 133, t. 5, figg. 10—16; 18—19 (in var. lituum vergens).		
» pauciloculata		Hantk., 1875, For. Clav. Szab. Sch., p. 47, t. 14, fig. 10.

Syn. **Margin. infarcto** Rss., 1863, Septarienthon. Offenbach; Wien. Ak. Sitz.-Ber. 1. 48, p. 48, t. 3, fig. 36—37.
» **elongata** Rss., 1845, Böhm. Kreide 2, p. 107; t. 24, figg. 31—36.
» **deformis**, abbreviata, **Hauerina, Haldingeriana, Czizekiana, inflata** Neuge., 1851, For. Felsö Lapug.; Siebenbürg. Verein. Mittheil. 1851, p. 127, t. 5, figg. 3—7, 9.
» **abbreviata** Karrer, 1861, Marin. Terg. Wien. Beck.; Wien. Ak. Sitz.-Ber. 1. 44, p. 445, t. 1, fig. 7.
Gland. deformis Costa, 1854, Pal. Nap. 2, p. 129, t. 11, figg. 16—18; 26.
Rimulina ventricosa Costa, 1854, ibid., p. 177, t. 13, fig. 11.
Margin. pachygaster Gümb., 1868, Nordalp. Eocän.; K. Bayr. Ak. Wiss. Abh. 1. 10. z, p. 633, t. 1, fig. 60.
» **angistoma** Stache, 1865, tert. Mergel Whaingar. Hafen, Novara Reise, geol. Theil 1. z, p. 213, t. 22, fig. 46.
» **opaca** Stache, 1865, ibid. p. 214, t. 22, fig. 47.
» **mucronatula** Stache, 1865, ibid. p. 215, t. 22, fig. 48.
Crist. spec. indet.; pisiformis, exigua Schwag., 1865, Jurass. Sch; Würtemb. Nat. Verein. Mitth. Jhrshft. 21, t. 5, fig. 17; t. 6, fig. 9.
Cristell. incerta Egg., 1857, Mioc. Ortenburg; Leonh. u. Bronn. Jhrb. 1857, p. 296, t. 14, figg. 31—33.
Margin. subcrassa Schwag., 1866, Kar.-Nikobar.; Novara Reise, geol. Th. 2. z, p. 240, t. 6, fig. 82.
Psecadium ellipticum, simplex Neuge., 1856, For. Stich. Ob. Lapug.; Wien. Ak. Dkschr. 1. 12. z, p. 99, t. 5, figg. 13—14.
» Rss., Prěs Modellen N:o 55.
Gland. elongata, adunca Costa, 1854, Pal. Nap. 2, p. 128, t. 11, figg. 23—24.
Psecadium subovatum Karr., 1864, Leythakalk Wien. Beck.; Wien. Ak. Sitz.-Ber. 1. 50, p. 705, t. 1, fig. 7.
» **Nussdorfense**, Crist. (Margin.) humilis, mirabilis, ampla Karr., 1877, Hochquell. Wasserleit.; Osterr. geol. Reichsanst. Abh. 9, p. 379, 382, t. 16, figg. 23, 33, 35; 36.

b) Nod. lituus D'Orb.

Crist. cephalotes, lituiformis Rss., 1862, Nordd. Hils u. Gault; Wien. Ak. Sitz.-Ber. 1. 46, p. 67, t. 7, figg. 5—6; 1863, Sept. Thon. Offenbach; Wien. Ak. Sitz.-Ber. 1. 48, p. 51, t. 4. fig. 50.
— **Hauerina** D'Orb., 1846, For. tert. Vienne, p. 84, t. 3. figg. 24—25.
Margin. spinulosa Stache, 1865, Tert. Merg. Whaingar. Hafen, Novara Reise, geol. Th. 1. z, p. 216, t. 22, fig. 50.
» **cristellarioides** Czjz., 1847, For. Wien. Beck.; Haid. Nat. Abh. 2. 1, p. 140, t. 12, figg. 14—16.
Crist. gracillima, foeda Rss., 1862, Nordd. Hils u. Gault; Wien. Ak Sitz.-Ber. 1. 46, p. 64, t. 6, figg. 9—10; 11—13.
Margin. lituus D'Orb., 1826, Tabl. meth., Ann. Sc. Nat. 7, p. 259.
» **rhomboidea** Czjz., 1847, For. Wien. Beck.; Haid. Nat. Abh. 2. 1, p. 141, t. 12, figg. 21—23.
» **sublituus** Park. and Jones, 1860, For. Chellaston; Qu. Journ. geol. Soc. 16, t. 20, fig. 37.
» **glabra** Park. and Jones, 1866, Crag. For.; Pal. Soc. 19, p. 69, t. 1, fig. 26.
Crist. Kressenbergensis Gümb., 1868, Nordalp. Eocän.; K. Bayr. Ak. Wiss. Abh. 1. 10. z, p. 638, t. 1, fig. 66 (limbata).
Margin. lituus Park. and Jones, 1865, North. Atl. and Arct. Oc.; Phil. Trans. 155. 1, p. 343, t. 13, fig. 14.
Crist. calcar var. Park. and Jones, 1857, For. Coast of Norway, An. Mag. Nat. Hist. 19, p. 269, t. 10, fig. 1.
Margin. neglecta Karr., 1865, Grünsand, Orakey Bay, N. Zeel.; Novara Reise, geol Th. 1. z, p. 76, t. 16, fig. 4.

Syn Margin. irregularis, Boiorana GöMB., 1862, Streiteub. Schwammlag., Wurtemb. Nat. Verein. Jhrhft. 1862, p. 220, t. 3, figg. 15—18; 20.
» bacillum Rss., 1845, Böhm. Kreide 8, p. 29, t. 1, fig. 11; 1859, Westphal. Kreidei; Wien. Ak. Sitz.-Ber. 46, p. 208, t. 6, fig. 8.
» ensis Rss., 1845, Böhm. Kreide 1, p. 29, t. 12, fig. 13, 26, 27.
» » Rss., 1850, Kreidem. Lemberg; Haid. Nat. Abh. 4. 1, p. 27, t. 1, fig. 16.
» gradata d'Orb., 1839, For. Craie bl. Par.; Mem. Soc. geol. Fr. (2) 4, p. 18, t. 1. figg. 23—24 (limbata).

c) Nod. glabra d'Orb. (a præcedente vix discernenda).

Margin. pedum d'Orb., 1846, For. tert. Vienne, p. 68, t. 3, figg. 13—14.
Cristell. simplex d'Orb., ibid. p. 85, t. 3, figg. 26—29.
» glabra d'Orb., 1826, Tabl. meth.; An. Sc. Nat. 7. p. 259, N:o 6, Mod. N:o 55.
» similis, triangularis d'Orb., 1846, For. tert. Vienne, p. 69, 71; t. 3, figg. 15—16; 22—23
» » Costa, 1851, Pal. Nap. 2, p. 185, t. 16, fig. 18.
» regularis d'Orb., 1846, For. tert. Vienne, p. 68, t. 3, figg. 9—12.
» tumida Rss., 1851, Böttcheri Rss., 1863, Sept. Thon Berlin; Ztschr. deutsch. geol. Ges. 3, p. 64, t. 3, fig. 14; Sept. Thon Offenbach; Wien. Ak. Sitz.-Ber. 1. 48, p. 48, t. 3, figg. 32—35; ibid. p. 49, t. 3, fig. 38—42.
» recta Hken., 1875, For. Clav. Szab. Sch. p. 47, t. 4, fig. 15.
» splendens, indifferens, irregularis, budensis Hken., ibid. t. 4, figg. 11, 14; t. 14, figg. 2—3; 5.
» Bachei Bailey, 1850, Micr. Examin. of Soundings; Smithson. contrib. knowl. 2, Art. 3, p. 10, figg. 2—6.
» tumida Gümb., 1868, Nordalp. Eocän.; K. Bayr. Ak. Wiss. Abh. I. 10. 2, p. 632, t. 1, fig. 59.
» soluta, inæqualis Rss., 1859, Westphäl. Kreide; Wien. Ak. Sitz.-Ber. 1, 40, p. 205, t. 7, fig. 4; t. 7, fig. 3; 1862, Nordd. Hils u. Gault; Wien. Ak. Sitz.-Ber. 1. 46, p. 59, t. 5, fig. 13; t. 6, fig. 8.
» subtrigona Schwag., 1866, For. Kar.-Nikobar; Novara Reise, geol. Th. 2. 2, p. 240, t. 6, fig. 83.
Cristell. mucronata Karr., 1878, Forami Luzon; Bolet. Comis. Mapa del España, 7. 2, p. 19, t. F, fig. 2.
» flaccida, resupinata, megalocephala, deformis, parallela, rasa Schwag., 1865, Jurass. Sch.; Württemberg. Nat. Verein. Jhrhft. 21, pp. 116, 117, 121, 128, t. 4, figg. 27, 28, 29, 30, 34; t. 5, fig. 5; t. 6, fig. 6.
» contracta Costa, 1854, Pal. Nap. 2, p. 186, t. 13, fig. 10.
Crist. Dewalquei Rss., 1863, For. Crag. d'Anvers; Bull. Ac. Belg. (2) 15, p. 149, t. 2, figg. 22—23.
Margin. dubia (et 15 aliæ) Neuges., 1851, For. Felso Lapug; Siebenbürg. Ver. Mittheil. 1851, p. 120, tt. 4—5; figg. 1—19; figg. 1, 8.
» trilobata d'Orb., 1839, For. Craie blanc. Par.; Mem. Soc. geol. Fr. (2) 4, p. 16, t. 1, figg. 16—17.
» Parkeri, Crist. Schlönbachi, exilis, parallela, Rss., 1862, Nordd. Hils u. Gault; Wien. Ak. Sitz.-Ber. 1. 46, p. 59, 64, 66, 67; t. 5, fig. 14; t. 6, figg. 14—15; t. 6, fig. 19; t. 7, figg. 1—2.
» calliopsis Rss., ibid. p. 60, t. 5, fig. 16; Crist. humilis Rss., ibid. t. 6, figg. 16, 17 (limbata).
Crist. Gosæ Rss., 1854, Kreide. Ostalpen; Wien. Ak. Dkschr. 7, p. 67, t. 7, fig. 25 (limbata).
Margin. compressa d'Orb., 1839, Craie bl. Paris; Mem. Soc. geol. Fr. (2) 4, p. 17, t. 1, figg. 18—19.
» gladius Phil., 1843, Tert. Verstein. n. w. Deutschl., t. 1, fig. 37; Rss., 1855, Tert. Schicht. nördl. u. mittl. Deutschl.; Wien. Ak. Sitz.-Ber. 1. 18, p. 232, tt. 2, 3, figg. 31—33; Rss., 1864, Oberoligocän., Wien. Ak. Sitz.-Ber. 1. 50, p. 462, t. 2, figg. 14—17; Hken., 1875, Clav. Szab. Schicht., p. 51, t. 5, fig. 12 (limbata).

Syn. Margin. simplex   KARR., 1861, Marin. Tegel Wien. Beck.; Wien. Ak. Sitz.-Ber. 1. 14, p. 445,
                              t. 1, fig. 6.
      »   modesta   Rss., 1859, Westphal. Kreide; Wien. Ak. Sitz.-Ber. 40, p. 207, t. 7, fig. 5.
      »   crassa, mutabilis, lata CORN., 1848, Nouv. foss. cret.; Mem. Soc. geol. Fr. (2) 3, p. 251,
                              252, t. 1, figg. 22—25, 26—31; 34—37.
      »   lata   Rss., 1859, Westphal. Kreidef., Wien. Ak. Sitz.-Ber. 40, p. 206, t. 5, fig. 7.
    Cristell. lata   KARR., 1879, Hochquell. Wasserleit.; Osterr. geol. Reichsanst. Abh. 9, p. 383,
                              t. 16. fig. 37.
      »   subarcuata   GÜMB., 1868, Nordalp. Eocän; K. Bayr. Ak. Wiss. Abh. 1. 10. 2, p. 637,
                              t. 1, fig. 64.
    Margin. jurassica   GÜMB., 1862, Streitenberg. Schwammlager; Wurtemb. Nat. Wiss. Ver. Jhrbft.
                              1862, p. 222, t. 3, figg. 21—22.
    Cristell. compressa   COSTA, 1854, Pal. Nap. 2, t. 27, fig. 23.
    Vagin. denudata. incompta, plana, protosphæra Rss., 1862, Nordd. Hils u. Gault; Wien. Akad
                              Sitz.-Ber. 1. 46, p. 45, 68, 72; t. 3, fig. 4; t. 3, fig. 5; t. 8, fig. 3,
                              t. 7, fig. 8 (in Vaginulinam s. Planulariam propriam transiens).

d) Vaginulina D'ORB.

Vaginulina Kochi var. lævis RÖM., 1842, Neue Kreidefor., Leonh. u. Bronn. Jhrb. 1842, p. 273,
                              t. 7 B, fig. 1.
    Planularia longa   CORN., 1848, Nouv. foss. microsc. cret; Mem. Soc. geol. Fr. (2) 3, p. 253,
                              t. 1, figg. 38—39.
      »   costata   CORN., ibid. p. 253, t. 2, figg. 5—8.
    Vaginulina elegans   D'ORB., 1826, Tabl. meth.; Ann. Sc. Nat. 7, p. 257, Mod. 54.
      »   marginulinoides, truncata, arguta, recta, corynota, protosphæra (alis) Rss., 1862,
                              Nordd. Hils, u. Gault; Wien. Ak. Sitz.-Ber. 1. 46, p. 44, 47, 48, 90,
                              t. 3, figg. 2, 9, 13—15; t. 12, figg. 9—10.
      »   arguta   Rss., 1859, Westphäl. Kreidef.; Wien. Ak. Sitz.-Ber. 1. 40, p. 202, t. 8,
                              fig. 4.
      »   transversalis, bicostulata Rss., 1859, ibid. t. 8, figg. 3, 5.
      »   ligata   Rss., 1864, Oberoligocän.; Wien. Ak. Sitz.-Ber. 1. 50, p. 457, t. 1, fig. 11.
    Vaginulina Goinitsi   REUSS, 1873, Gräinitz, Elbthalgeb. Sachs. 2, p. 94, t. II. 20, fig. 1.
      »   costulata   Rss., ibid. t. II. 20, fig. 24.
    Margin. costulata   REUSS, 1845, Böhm. Kreide I, p. 28, t. 13, fig. 25.
    Vaginulina costulata   RÖM., 1842, Neue Kreidefor.; Leonh. u. Bronn., Jhrb. 1842, p. 273, t. 7. B,
                              fig. 3, a. b. c. (in N. legumen typicum transgrediens.)
      »   italica   COSTA, 1855, Marna terz. Messina; Mem. Nap. 2, p. 145, t. 2, fig. 15
                              (semistriata).
      »   Bruckenthali NEUGB., 1856, For. Stichosteg. Ob. Lapug.; Wien. Ak. Dkschr. 1. 12. 2,
                              p. 98, t. 5, fig. 10.

e) Nod. legumen propria s. Nod. lævigata RÖM.; elongata D'ORB.

Nautilus legumen   MONTAGU, 1808, Test. Britan. Supplem. p. 82, t. 19, fig. 6.
Dentalina legumen   WILLIAMS., 1858, Rec. For. p. 22, fig. 45.
Vaginulina caudata   D'ORB., 1826, Tabl. meth., Ann. Sc. Nat. 7, p. 258, N:o 8.
    »   badenensis   D'ORB., 1846, For. tert. Vienne, p. 65, t. 3, figg. 6—8.
    »   »   NEUGB., 1856, For. Stichost. Ob. Lapugy; Wien. Ak. Dkschr. 1. 12. 2, p.
                              98, t. 5, figg. 7, 9.
    »   subulata   EHRENB., 1854, Microgeol., t. 24, fig. 10.
    »   lævigata   RÖM., 1838, Leonh. u. Bronn. Jhrb. 1838, p. 383, t. 3, fig. 11.
    »   »   Rss., 1855, Tert. Schicht. nordl. u. mittl. Deutschl., p. 226, t. 1, fig. 9.
Margin. gracilis   CORN., 1848, Nouv. foss. microsc.; Mem. Soc. geol. Fr. (2) 3, p. 252, t. 1,
                              figg. 32—33.
    »   elongata   D'ORB., 1839, Craie bl. Paris; Mem. Soc. geol. Fr. 4, p. 17, t. 1, figg.
                              20—21.

Syn. **Marginulina elongata** Rss., 1845, Böhm. Kreide, 1, p. 29, t. 13, fig. 28—32; 2, p. 107, t. 24, fig. 36.
  Cristell. luna Karr., 1868, Mioc. For. Faun. Kostej; Wien. Ak. Sitz.-Ber. 1. 58, p 171, t. 4, fig. 6.
  Marginulina Römeri Rss., 1845, Böhm. Kreide. 1, p. 28, t. 8, fig. 10.
    » **Beyrichi** Rss., 1855, Tert. Schicht. nordl. u. mittl. Deutschl.; Wien. Ak. Sitz.-Ber. 1. 18, p. 226, t. 1, fig. 10.
  Vaginulina cretæ Ehrenb., 1854, Mikrogeol., t. 24, fig. 8.
    » **bullosa** Ehrenb., ibid. t. 24, fig. 9.
  Cristellaria perprocera Schwag., 1866, For. Kar.-Nikob.; Novara Reise, geol. Th. 2. 2, p. 241, t. 6 fig. 84.
  Marginulina linearis, Cristell. linearis Rss., 1862, Nordd. Hils u. Gault; Wien. Ak. Sitz.-Ber. 1. 46, p. 60, t. 5, fig. 15; t. 12, fig. 1.
  Vaginulina recta Karr., 1865, Tert. Grünsand, Orakey Bay; Novara Reise, geol. Theil 1 2, p. 74, t. 16, fig. 2 (limbata).
  Marginulina obliqua Rss., 1855, Kreidef. Ostalp.; Wien. Ak. Dkschr. 7, p. 65, t. 25, fig. 9 (limbata).
  Vaginulina legumen Parker and Jones, 1860, For. Chellaston; Qu. Journ. geol. Soc. 16, p. 453, t. 19, fig. 26—28.
  Nodosaria legumen Rss., 1845, Böhm. Kreide 1, p. 28, t. 13, fig. 24.
    » » Rss., 1859, Westphäl. Kreide; Wien. Ak. Sitz.-Ber. 40, p. 187, t. 3, fig. 5.
  Vagin. legumen subvar. **lævigata** Park. and Jones, 1866, Crag. Foramf.; Palæont Soc. 19, p 66, t. 4, fig. 9.
  Dentalina marginulinoides Rss., 1850, Kreidem. Lemberg; Haid. Nat. Abh. 4. 1, p. 25, t. 1. fig. 12.
    » **æquivoca** Costa 1854, Pal. Nap. 2, p. 170, t. 13, fig. 8.

f) in Nod. crepidulam transiens:

Cristellaria cœlata Schwag., 1866, For. Kar.-Nikobar.; Novara Reise, geol. Th. 2. 2, p. 244, t. 7, fig. 88.
  » **Kochi** Rss., 1865, Sept. Thon Deutschl.; Wien. Ak. Dkschr. 1. 25. 1, p. 149, t. 2, fig. 35.
  » » Hkkr., 1875, For. Clav. Szab. Sch., p. 53. t. 5, fig. 7.
  » **propinqua** Hantk., ibid. p. 52, t. 5, fig. 1.
Hemicristellaria infrapapillata, verrucosa Stache, Mergel d. Whsingar. Hafen; Novara Reise, geol. Th. 1. 2, p. 224, 226, t. 22, fig. 1; t. 23, fig. 5.
Marginulina Hochstetteri Stache, ibid. p. 221, t. 22, fig. 55.

g) in Nod. complanatam Defr. transiens:

Frondicul. ensiformis Rom., 1838, Norid. tert. Meeressand; Leonh. u. Bronn. Jhrb. 1838, p. 382, t. 3, fig. 8.
  » **lingua** Boll, Bröckner, 1846, Ostseeländern, p. 177, t. 2, fig. 12.

Nodosarina legumen Lin. var. linearis Montagu.

Tab. II, fig. 32—35.

This variety is not generally provided with broad and prominent ribs, but it will be impossible to define it from such forms, represented, as they are, by *Marginulina raphanus* d'Orb. with very few and strong ribs.

It is often quite cylindrical and hardly to be distinguished from *Nod. communis* var. *obliqua*. It has also its *forma obliquestriata*, which has been considered as a feature of specific importance. It has also its *forma seminuda* and *intermittens* with many names, as *Frondicul. seminuda* Rss., *Marg. granitocalcarea* Gümb., *Marg. vaginella* Rss. etc.

Fig. 32 represents a stout, quite cylindrical nicely striated form with a strong affinity to Nod. communis var. obliqua; from the coralline-gravel.

Fig. 33 is near to *Marg. raphanus* d'Orb. but is finer costate than this. Sometimes in our form the costæ are interrupted, becoming like chains of raised dashes. It is somewhat obliquely costulated, which is not uncommonly the case with all striated forms of Nodosarina-genus.

Figg. 34—35 is near to or perhaps identical with *Robulina ariminensis* d'Orb.; which also may be considered as the »raphanus»-form of *Nodosaria calcar* Lin.

a) Nod. Raphano propinqua:

Syn. **Margin. Raphanus, sublituus** d'Orb., 1826, Tabl. meth., Ann. Sc. Nat. 7, p. 255, N:o 1, Mod. N:o 6; t. 10, figg. 7—8, p. 259, N:o 9.
Nautilus costatus Batsch., 1791, Seehs Kupfertaf. t. 1, fig. 1a—1g. (ver. Park. and Jones.)
Marg. rugoso-costata d'Orb., 1846, For. tert. Vienne, p. 70, t. 3, figg. 19—21.
Vaginul. linearis (Montagu) Park. and Jones, 1865, For. N Atl. and Arct Oceans; Phil Transact. 155. 1, p. 343, t. 13, fig. 12—13; t. 16, fig. 1.
Nodosarina raphanus marginuloides Park and Jones, 1866, Crag. For.: Pal. Soc. 19. p. 71, t. 1, fig. 2.
Crist. subarcuatula var. **costata** (partim) Williams., 1858, Brit. rec. For. p. 31, fig. 63.
Margin. tenuissima, Jonesi, Mülleri, striatocostata, dispar, robusta, turgida Rss., 1862, Nordd Hils u. Gault; Wien. Ak. Sitz.-Ber. 1. 46, p. 61—63, t. 5, figg. 18—19; t. 6, figg. 1—2, 4, 7.
Nodosaria lævipes Marss., 1878, Rüg. Schreibekr.; Greifsw. Nat. Verein. Mitth. 1877—78, p. 130, t. 1, fig. 6.
Margin. corticulata, spec. indet., Crist. sculptilis Schwag., 1865, Jurass. Sch., Würtemb. Nat. Verein. Jhrhft. 21, p. 118, 129, t. 4, fig. 32. t. 7, fig. 23; t. 6, fig. 10.
Dentalina gibbosa, Margin. interamniæ Costa, 1854, Pal. Nap. 2, p 167. 184, t. 12, fig. 7; t. 13, fig. 9
Vagin. sulcata Costa, 1855, Marns tert. Messina; Mem. Nap. 2, p. 145, t. 2, fig. 17.
Margin. interrupta, apiculata, pellucida, tricuspis, asprocostulata, elatissima Stache, 1865, tert. Mergel Whaïanger. Hafen; Novara Reise, geol. Th. 1. 2, p. 212, 216—219, t. 22, figg. 45, 49; 51—54.
» **costata, rugosa** Neugeb., 1856, For. Stichosteg., Wien. Ak. Dkschr. 1. 12. v. p. 98, t. 5, fig. 11; 1854; Siebenb, Verein. Mittheil. t. 4, fig. 20.
» **raricosta** d'Orb., 1839, For. Craie blanche Paris; Mem. Soc. geol Fr. 4, p. 51, t. 1, fig. 25.
» **tunicata** Hken., 1875, Clav. Scäb. Sch., p. 48, t. 14, fig. 8.
» **serratocostata** Gümb., 1862, Streitenberg. Schwammlager; Würtemb. Verein. Jhrhft. 17. p. 222, t. 3, fig. 23.
Cristell. crassicosta Karr., 1870, Kreidef. Leitzendorf; Österr. geol. Reichsanst. Jhrb. 20, p. 177, t. 11, fig. 8.

f) obliquestriata:

Syn. **Margin. obliquestriata** Karr., 1861, Mar. Tegel Wien. Beck.; Wien. Ak. Sitz.-Ber. 1. 44, p. 446, t. 1, fig. 8.

γ) crenulato-costata, vel papilluto-limbata:

Nautilus semilituus Montagu, 1808, Testac. Brit. Suppl., p. 80, t. 19, fig. 3.
Cristell. Behmi Rss., 1865, deutsch. Sept. Thon; Wien. Ak. Dkschr. t. 25, p. 138, t. 2, fig. 37. (Margin. hirsuta d'Orb., 1846, For. tert. Vienne, t. 3, figg. 17—18, valde propinqva).
Margin. Behmi, arcuata, fragaria Hken., 1875, Clav. Szab. Sch., p. 48, 51, 53, t. 5, figg. 1 - 2, t. 14, fig. 6; t. 5, fig. 10; t. 6, figg. 1—3.
» rugoso-striata, fragaria, coronata, asperula, cumulicostata Gümb., 1868, Nordalp. Eocän.; K. Bayr. Ak. Wiss. Abh. 1. 10. 2, p. 633—638, t. 1, figg 57 58; 61; 65; 67.

δ) seminuda:

Nautilus linearis Montagu, 1808, Test. Brit. Supplem. p. 87, t. 30, fig. 9.
Dentalina legumen var. **linearis** Williams., 1858, Brit. rec. For. p. 23, figg. 46—48.
Vaginulina lens Costa, 1855, Marna terz. Mess.; Mem. Nap. 2, p. 144, t. 2, fig. 16.
Nodosarina Vaginulina legumen, subv. **linearis** Park. and Jones, 1866, Crag. forf.; Pal. Soc. 19, p. 67, t. 1, figg. 10—12.
Margin. tenuissima var. Rss., 1862, Nordd. Hils u. Gault; Wien. Ak. Sitz.-Ber. 1. 46, p. 92, t. 12 fig. 12.
» **seminotata** Rss., 1859, Westph. Kreidef.; Wien. Ak. Sitz.-Ber. 1. 40, p. 208, t. 5, fig. 6.
» **semicostata** Rss., 1851, Tert. Sch. Ob. Schles.; Ztschr. deutsch. geol. Gesellsch. 3, p. 152. t. 8, fig. 3.
» **vaginella** Rss., 1851, Tert. Sch. Oberschles.; Ztschr. deutsch. geol. Gesellsch. 3, p. 152. t. 8, fig. 2.
» **tonsillaris, granitocalcarea** Gümb., 1868, Nordalp. Eocän., K. Bayr. Ak. Wiss. 1. 10. 2, p. 634, t. 1, figg. 56; 62.
Frond. seminuda Rss., 1851, Sept. Thon Berlin; Ztschr. deutsch geol. Ges. 3, p. 65, t. 3, fig. 15—16.

h) magis complanata (= Vaginulina, Planularia d'Orb.).

Vagin. striata d'Orb., 1826, Tabl. meth., Ann. Sc. Nat. 7, p. 257, N:o 3.
» » Costa, 1854, Pal. Nap. 2, p. 182, t. 16, fig. 17.
» **angustissima** Rss., 1862, Nordd. Hils u. Gault; Wien. Ak. Sitz.-Ber. 1. 46 p. 45, t. 3, fig. 3.
Frond. tricostulata Rss., 1849, Neue For. österr. tert. Beck.; Wurm. Ak. Dkschr. 1. 1, p. 368, t. 46, fig. 12.
Flaboll. striata Hken., 1875, Clav. Szab. Sch., p. 43, t. 13, fig. 13.
» **ensiformis** Rss., 1863, Oberoligocän.; Wien. Ak. Sitz.-Ber. 1. 50, p. 469, t. 5. fig. 2.
Crist. subarcuatula var. **costata** Williams., Brit. rec. Forf.; p. 31, figg. 64—67.
Marg. flabellata Gümb., 1862, Streitenb. Schwammlag. Würtemb. Nat. Verein. Jhrhft. 17. p. 223, t. 3, fig. 24.

Syn. Vagin. eocaena, dilute-striata Güмв., 1868, For. Nordalp. Eocän.; K. Bayr. Ak. Wiss. Abh. 1. 10. 2, p. 632, 639, t. 1, fig. 49; fig. 69.
» harpa Röм., 1842, Verstein. Nordd. Kreidegeb. p. 96, t. 15, fig. 12.
» Dunkeri Косн, Paläontogr. 1. 4, p. 172, t. 24, fig. 3.
Planulina reticulata Cornu., 1848, Nouv. foss. mics. Mem. geol. France (2) 3, p. 253, t. 2, fig. 1—4.
Vagin. striatula Röм., 1842, Neue Kreideforamf.; Leonh. u. Bronn. Jhrb. 1842, p. 273, t. 7 B, fig. 2.
Citharina strigillata Rss., 1845, Böhm. Kreidef. 2, p. 106, t. 24, fig. 29.
Vagin. » Park. and Jones, 1860, For. Chellast., Qu. Journ. geol. Soc. 16, p. 453, t. 19, fig. 29; t. 20, figg. 31—36.
» acuminata, orthonota, cristellaroides Rss., 1862, Nordd. Hils u. Gault; Wien. Ak. Sitz.-Ber. 1. 46, p. 48, 49, t. 4, figg. 1, 3; t. 3, fig. 17.
» discors, intumescens Rss., ibid. t. 3, figg. 10—12; t. 4, fig. 2.
» sparsicostata, harpa, paucicostata, incrassata Rss., ibid., p. 50—52, t. 4, figg. 4—9.
» · notata Rss., 1859, Westph. Kreidef.; Wien. Ak. Sitz.-Ber. 1 40, p. 203, t. 9, fig. 3.

b. β) interlineata:

Vagin. Zeuschneri Rss., 1850, Kreidemergel Lemberg; Haid. Nat. Abh. 4. 1, p. 28, t. 1, fig. 19.
» Schlönbachi, striolata, Strombecki, paucistriata Rss., 1862, Nordd. Hils u. Gault; Wien. Ak. Sitz.-Ber. 1. 46, p. 46—48, t. 3, figg. 6—8; 16.

b. γ) seminada.

Planularia Cymba, Auris, rostrata d'Orb., 1826, Tabl. meth., Ann. Nat. 7, p. 260, N:ris 4, 5, 7, t. 10, fig. 9; Mod. 27 (In N. crepidulam vergens).
Frond. pulchra d'Orb., 1839, For. Craie bl. Paris; Mem. Soc. geol. France 4, p. 25, t. 2, figg. 12—14.
Crist. compressa, lanceolata, semiluna d'Orb., 1846, For. tert. Vienne, p. 86, 89, 90, t. 3, figg. 32—33; 41—44 (in N. crepidulam vergens).
» auricula Rss., 1855, tert. Sch. nordl. u. mittl. Deutschl.; Wien. Ak. Sitz.-Ber. 1. 18, p. 235, t. 3, fig. 38.
Frond. interrupta, longiuscula, typica, lanceolata, angustata, similis, ovata, subangulata, subfalcata, silicula Costa, 1855, Marna terr. Messina, Mem. Nap. 2, p. 372, 373; t. 2, figg. 25—26; t. 3, figg. 5, 7, 9, 11, 12, 14, 16, 17, 19. 20.
Cristoll. vaginata Karrer, 1878, Foramf. Luzon; Bolet. Comis. Mapa geolog. del España 7 2, p. 18, t. F, fig. 1.

c) frondicularioides:

Flabellina ensiformis Rss., 1855, Tert. Sch. nördl. u. mittl. Deutschl.; Wien. Ak. Sitz.-Ber. 1. 18, p. 229, t. 2, figg. 23—24.
» obliqua Rss., (partim) ibid., t. 2, figg. 20—22; 1864, Oberoligocän.; Wien. Akad. Sitz.-Ber. 1. 50, p. 460, t. 2, figg. 5—7.

Appendix.

Nodosarina (Frondicularia) striata d'Orb.

Syn. Frond. angusta, angustissima, lanceola Rss., 1859, Westph. Kreide; Wien. Ak. Sitz.-Ber. 1. 40, p. 196—198, t. 4, figg. 5—6; t. 5, fig. 1.
Flabellina cuneata Rss. 1855, Tert. Sch. nördl. u. mittl. Deutschl.; Wien. Ak. Sitz.-Ber. 1. 18, p. 231, t. 2, fig. 29.
» » Rss., 1864, Oberoligoc.; Wien. Ak. Sitz.-Ber. 1. 50, p. 460, t. 2, fig. 8.
» » Brady, 1881, Notes on retic. Rhizop.; Qu. Journ. micr. Sc. (n. s.) p. 271, t. 8, fig. 7.
Frond. Antonina Karr., 1878, Foramf. Luzon.; Bolet. Comis. Mapa geol. del España 7. 2, p. 17, t. E, fig. 14.
» striata d'Orb., 1826, Tabl. meth.; Ann. Sc. Nat. 7, p. 256, N:o 3.
» angusta Rss., 1845, Böhm. Kreide 1, p. 29, t. 8, figg 13 (non fig. 14).
» trisulca, striatula, apiculata Rss., 1845, Böhm. Kreide 1, p. 30, t. 8, figg. 22—24; t. 43, fig. 11.
» do Rss., 1873, Grin., Elbthalgeb. Sachsen, 2, p. 94. t. II. 20, fig. 2.
» striatula Park. and Jones, 1860, For. Chellast.; Qu. Journ. geol. Soc. 16, t 19. figg. 16—18.
» capillaris Rss., 1850, Kreidemerg. Lemberg; Haid. Nat. Abh. 4. 1, p. 29, t. 1, fig. 20
» pala Karr., 1870, Kreidef Leitzendorf; Jahrb. k. k. österr. geol. Reichsanst. 20, p. 172, t. 10, fig. 11.
» multilineata Rss., 1853, Kreide Ostalp.; Wien. Ak. Dkschr. 7, p. 66, t. 25, fig. 5.
» Reussi, sculpta, badenensis, paupera Karr., 1861, Marin. Tegel Wien. Beck.; Wien. Ak. Sitz. Ber. 1. 44, p. 441, 443, t. 1, fig. 1—4.
» tricuspis Rss., 1849, Neue for. österr. tert. Becken; Wien. Ak. Dkschr. 1. 1, p. 368, t. 46, fig. 13.
» Hörnesi, Lapugyensis, speciosa Neugeb., 1856, For. Stichost. Ob. Lapug.; Wien. Ak. Dkschr. 1. 12. 2. p. 93, t. 5, fig. 1—4.
» inversa Rss., 1873, Grin., Elbthalgeb. Sachs. 2, p. 94, t. II. 21, figg. 5—7.
» concinna Koch, Palæontogr. 1. 4, p. 172, t. 24, fig. 5.
» » Rss., 1862, Nordd. Hils u. Gault; Wien. Ak. Sitz.-Ber. 1. 46, p. 54, t. 4, fig. 13.
» foliola Karr., 1868, Mioc. Forfauna Kostej; Wien. Ak. Sitz.-Ber. 1. 58, p. 167, t. 4, fig. 4.
» interrupta, superba, sculpta Karr., 1877, Hochqu. Wasserl.; österr. geol. Reichsanst. Abh. 9, p. 380, 381, t. 16, fig. 27, 29, 30.
» solea v. Hag., 1842, Rügen. Kreideverst.; Leonh. u. Bronn. Jhrb. 1842, p. 569, t. 9, fig. 20.
» solea, multistriata, linguæformis, affinis Marss., 1877, Rügen. Schreibekr.; Greifswald. Nat. Verein. Mittheil. 1877—78, p. 133—136, t. 2. figg. 12—15.

β) seminuda et interlineata:

Frond. intermittens Rss., 1865, Feuersteinkreide Kanara See; Wien. Ak. Sitz.-Ber. 52, p. 460, fig. 11.
» guestphalica, Becksi, strigillata Rss., 1859, Westphal. Kreidef.; Wien. Ak. Sitz.-Ber. 40, p. 192, 195, t. 6, figg. 2—4.
» semicosta, raricosta Karr. 1877, Hochqu. Wasserleit.: k. k. österr. geol. Reichsanst. Abh. 9. t. 16, figg. 26, 28.
» Dumontana Rss., 1860, Crag. Antwerp; Wien. Ak. Sitz.-Ber. 42, p. 359, t. 1, fig. 7.
» cuneata Röm., 1838, Nordd. tert. Meeress.; Leonh. u. Bronn. Jhrb. 1838, p. 383, t. 3, fig. 10.
» elongata, spatulata Costa, 1855, Marna terz. Messina; Mem. Nap. 2, p. 371, t. 3, fig. 1, t. 2, fig. 19.
» lævigata Karr., 1868, Mioc. Kostej.; Wien. Ak. Sitz.-Ber. 1. 58, p. 167, t. 4, fig 3.
» sulcata Bornem., 1854, Lääsform. Göttingen p. 37, t. 3, fig. 22.

Syn.	Frond. striata	Röm., 1838, Norddt. tert. Meeres.; Leonh. u. Bronn, Jhrb. 1838, p. 382, t. 3, fig. 9.
	Flabell. »	Rss., 1855, Tert. Schicht. nördl. u. mittl. Deutschl.; Wien. Ak. Sitz.-Ber. 1. 18, p. 230, t. 2, figg. 25—28.
	Frond. microsphæra	Rss., 1873, Gein. Elbthalgeb. Sachs. 2, p. 94, t. II. 21, fig. 4.
	Planularia elliptica	Nilss., 1827, Petref. Svec., p. 11, t. 9, fig. 21.
	?Frond. Cordai	Rss., 1845, Böhm. Kreide. 1, t. 8, figg. 26—28; 2, t. 24, fig. 38.
	Frond. Cordai	Rss., ibid. t. 13, fig. 41.
	» »	Rss., 1859, Kreideg. Ostalp.; Wien. Akad. Sitz.-Ber. 7, t. 25, fig. 3, p. 66
	» speciosa	Karr., 1870, Kreidef. Leitzendorf; Jhrb. k. k. österr. geol. Reichsanst. 20, p. 175, t. 11, fig. 6.
	» radiata	d'Orb., 1839, For. Craie bl. Paris; Mem. Soc. géol. France 4, p. 19, t. 1, figg. 36—28.
	» Hosiusi	Rss., 1860, For. Dingden. Westphal.; Wien. Ak. Sitz.-Ber. 42, p. 365. t. 1. figg. 8—9.
	» annularis	d'Orb., 1846, For. tert. Vienne, t. 2, figg. 44—47.

Nodosarina Crepidula Ficht. and Moll.

Tab. II, III, figg. 36—44.

This species constitutes a link between *Nod. legumen* and *Nod. calcar*. Our long list of synonyms shows how steadily and gradually this transformation goes on. It does not attain any high development either on the coralline-gravel or on the chalk-bottom, and remains a dwarf in comparison with the allied *Nod. calcar* from the same localities.

Figg. 36—37 comes near to *Crist. cymbuides* d'Orb., *Crist. nummulitica* Gümb. and others with a very slight helicoid arrangement of the first chambers. It is not possible to distinguish such pigmy forms from some forms of *Nod. complanata* Defr. in their earliest stage of growth.

Fig. 38, more inflated and irregular in growth, is called *Crist. subarcuatula* (Walk.) by Williamson loc. cit.

Fig. 39, stouter with some remaining features of *Nod. legumen*.

Fig. 40 »aulostoma«-form.

Figg. 41—42, pygmies from the chalk-bottom.

Fig. 43, the same with a peculiar arrangement of the first chambers.

Fig. 44, (tab. II) broad carinated form with a strong affinity to *Nod. calcar.*, from the coralline-gravel.

a) Nod. legumini proxima, vix distincta:

Syn.	Margin. vagina	Neugb., 1856, For. Stich. Ob. Lapug.; Wien. Ak. Dkschr. 1. 12. 2, p. 103, t. 5, fig. 12.
	Cristell. recta, limbata	Rss., 1845, Böhm. Kreidef. 1, t. 13, fig. 55, 56.
	» Hagenowi, triplcura, harpa, inepta	Rss., 1859, Westphäl. Kreide; Wien. Ak. Sitz.-Ber. 40. p. 210, 211, t. 9, figg. 5—6; t. 10, figg. 1—2, 4.
	Cristell. Köneni	Rss., 1865, deut. Sept. Thon; Wien. Ak. Dkschr. 1. 25. 1. p. 139, t. 3, fig. 1.
	» vaginalis	Rss., 1863, Sept. Thon. Offenbach; Wien. Ak. Sitz.-Ber. 1. 48, p. 50, t. 4, fig. 49.
	» major, deformis	Bornem., 1854, Liasform. Göttingen p. 40, 41, t. 4, figg. 31, 35.

Syn. Cristell. intermedia   Rss., 1845, Böhm. Kreidef. 1, p. 33, t. 13, figg. 57—58; 2, p. 108, t. 24, figg. 50—51.
»   dilocta   Rss., 1862, Nordd. Hils u. Gault; Wien. Ak. Sitz.-Ber. 1, 46, p. 71, t. 7, fig. 12 (limbata).
Hemicrist. procera, excavata, Hemirob. compressa Stache 1865, Tert. Mergel d. Whaingar. Haf.; Nov. Reise, geol. 1, 2, p. 222, 224, 229, t. 23, fig. 1, 3, 8.
Cristell. æquilata   Rss., 1864, Oberoligocän.; Wien. Ak. Sitz-Ber. 1, 50, p. 462, t. 2, fig. 13.
»   manubrium   Schwag. 1863, Jurass. Sch.; Würtemb. Nat. Verein Jhrsheft. 21, p. 121, t. 5, fig. 6.
Cristell. porvaensis, minuta, elegans Hyken., 1875, For. Clav. Száb. Schicht., p. 50, 88, t. 14, figg. 1, 7, 4.
»   conforta   Rss., 1863, Sept. Thon Offenbach; Wien. Ak. Sitz.-Ber. 1. 48, p. 50, t. 4, fig. 46.
»   inclinata, increscens Rss., 1863, ibid. p. 50 t. 4, figg. 45; 47—48.
»   incurvata, perobliqua Rss., 1862, Nordd. Hils u. Gault; Wien. Ak. Sitz.-Ber. 1. 46, p. 66, 67, t. 6, fig. 18; t. 7, fig. 3.
»   hastata   Karr., 1878, Foramf. Luzon.; Bolet. Comis. Mapa geol. del España 7. 2, p. 20, t. F, fig. 4.

b) magis typica:

Nautilius crepidula   Ficht. and Moll., 1803, Test. micr. p. 107, t. 19, figg. g—i.
Cristell. cymboides   d'Orb., 1846, Bass. tert. Vienne. p. 86, t. 3, figg. 30—31.
»   Hyken., 1875, Clav. Száb. Sch. p. 49, t. 5, fig. 3.
»   nummulitica   Gümb., 1868, Nordalp. Eoc.; K. Bayr. Ak. Wiss. Abh. 1. 10. 2. p. 636, t. 1, fig. 63.
»   Hars., 1875, Clav. Száb. Sch. p. 51, t. 6, fig. 4.
»   dentata   Karr., 1867, For. Faun. Österr.; Wien. Ak. Sitz.-Ber. 1. 55, p. 348, t. 1, fig. 1.
»   insolita   Schwag., 1866, For. Kar-Nikobar; Nov. Reise, geol. Th. 2, 2, p. 242, t. 6, fig. 85.
Vagin. laminæformis   Gümb., 1868, Nordalp. Eoc.; K. Bayr. Ak. Wiss. 1, 10. 2, p. 632, t. 1, fig 48.
Cristell. angusta   Rss., 1850, Kreidem. Lemberg; Haid. Nat. Abh. 4. 1, p. 32, t. 2, fig 7.
Margin. triangularis   Costa, 1855, For. Marna blu d. Vaticano; Mem. Nap. 2, p. 119, t. 1, fig. 9.
Cristell. spongiphila   Gümb., 1862. Streitenb. Schwammlag.; Würtemb. Nat. Verein. Jhrhft. 17, p. 224, t. 3, fig. 26.
Margin. Webbiana   d'Orb., 1844, Iles Canaries, p. 124, t. 1, figg. 7—11.
Cristell. denticulata   Rss., 1845, Böhm. Kreidef. 1, p. 33, t. 8, fig. 12.
»   recta   d'Orb., 1839, Craie bl. Paris; Mem. Soc. geol. Fr. 4, p. 28, t. 2, figg. 23—24.
»   cornucopiæ, ?complanata Schwag., 1863, Jurass. Sch., Würtemb. Nat. Ver. Jhrhft. 21, t. 1. figg. 5—7; t. 5, fig. 8.
Margin. compressa, Cristell. complanata Rss., 1845, Böhm. Kreidef. 1, p. 29, 33, t. 13, figg. 33, 54.
Cristell. complanata   Rss., 1862, Nordd. Hils u. Gault; Wien. Ak Sitz.-Ber. 1. 46, p. 92, t. 12, fig. 13 (limbata).
»   compressiuscula   Marss., 1877, Rüg. Schreibekr.; Greifsw. Nat. Verein. Mittheil. 1877—78, p. 142.
»   crepidulæformis   Gümb., 1871, Ulmer Cem. Mergel; Münch. Ak. Sitz.-Ber. 1, p. 66, t. 1, fig. 11.
»   Fraasi   Schwag., 1863, Jurass. Schicht.; Würtemb. Nat. Verein. Jhrhft. 21, p. 123, t. 5, fig. 10.
»   tensa, subcompressa, spicula, irretita, amygdaloidea, laminosa, inclusa, sorrigibbosa, subscalprata, insecta, impleta, multangulosa, implicata, turgida, subangulata, suprajurassica, lanceolata, Gümbeli, cristata, comptula, Alberti, collarifera Schwag., 1863, ibid. t. 5, figg. 4, 9, 11, 12, 13, 14, 15, 16; t. 6, figg. 1, 2, 3, 5, 7, 11, 12, 13, 14, 18, 19, 20; t. 7, fig. 24.
Planularia crepidularia   Röm., 1842, Neue Kreidef.; Leonh. u. Bronn. Jhrb. 1842, p. 273, t. 7 B, fig. 4 (in N. legumen vergens.)
Cristell. varians   Bornem., 1854, Liasform. Göttingen p. 41, t. 4, figg. 32—34.

Syn. Cristell. Fraasi   Gümb., 1871, Ulm. Cem. Mergel; Münch. Ak. Sitz.-Ber. 1, p. 67, t. 1, fig. 12.
  »   reniformis   d'Orb., 1846, For. tert. Vienne p. 88, t. 3, figg. 59—40.
Nautilus subarcuatulus Montagu, 1808, Test. Brit. Suppl. p. 89, t. 19, fig. 1 (limbata).
Margin. s. potius Planularia spirata, arcuata, compressiuscula, intermedia, semicircularis
                       Phil., 1843, Tert. Verstein. m. w. Deutschl. t. 1, figg. 27—29, figg. 38—39.
Cristell. arcuata, arguta, Nauckana Rss., 1855, Tert. Schicht. nördl. u. mittl. Deutschl.; Wien. Ak.
                       Sitz.-Ber. 1. 18, p. 233, 235, t. 3, figg. 34, 37—40 (limbata).
  »   arcuata   Rss., 1864, deutsche Oberoligoc.; Wien. Ak. Sitz.-Ber. 1. 50, p. 463, t. 2,
                       figg. 9—11.
  »   voluta   Corn., 1848, mouv. foss. microsc. cret.; Mém. Soc. geol. France (2) 3, p. 255,
                       t. 2, figg. 14—16.
  »   Schwageri   Hken., 1875, Clav. Szab. Sch. p. 49, t. 5, fig. 11.
  »   Bertheloti   d'Orb., 1844, Iles Canaries p. 127, t. 1, figg. 14—15 (in Nod. legumen
                       vergens).
  »   lævigata   Rss., 1862, Nordd. Hils u. Gault; Wien. Ak. Sitz.-Ber. 1. 46, p. 92, t. 12,
                       fig. 14 (in N. legumen vergens).
  »   crepidula   d'Orb., 1839, Cuba p. 41, t. 8, figg. 17—19.
  »   crepidularis Rss., 1862, Nordd. Hils u. Gault; Wien, Ak. Sitz.-Ber. 1. 46, p. 69, t. 7,
                       fig. 10 (limbata).
  »   tricarinella Rss., 1862, ibid. p. 68, t. 7, fig. 9; t. 12, figg. 2—4 (limbata).
Planularia orbiculata   Röm., 1842, Neue Kreidefor.; Leonh. u. Bronn. Jhrb. 1842, p. 273, t. 7 B,
                       fig. 6.
Cristell. truncana   Gümb., 1868, For. nordalp. Eocän.; K. Bayr. Ak. Wiss. 1. 10. v, p. 639,
                       t. 1, fig. 68.
  »   subarcuatula Williams, 1859, Brit. rec. Foramf., p. 30, figg. 56—62.
  »   calcar var. oblonga Williams, 1859, ibid. p. 28, fig. 55.
  »   Strombecki, grata Rss., 1862, Nordd. Hils u. Gault, Wien. Ak. Sitz.-Ber. 1, 46, p. 68, 70,
                       t. 7, figg. 7, 14.
  »   intermedia   Alth., 1849, Umgeb. Lemberg; Haid. Nat. Abh. 3. v, p. 267, t. 13, fig. 23.
  »   multiseptata Rss., 1850, Kreidemerg. Lemberg; Haid. Nat. Abh. 4, t, p. 33, t. 2, fig. 9.
  -    Jugleri   Rss., 1851, Ztschr. deutsch. geol. Ges. 3, p. 89, t. 4, fig. 19.
  »   crepidula   Park. and Jones, 1865, N. atl. and Arct. Oc., Phil. Trans. 155. 1, p. 344,
                       t. 13, figg. 15—16; t. 16, fig. 4.
  »   decorata   Rss., 1855, Kreidegeb. Meklenburg; Zeitschr. deutsch. geol. Ges. 7, p. 269,
                       t. 8, fig. 16; t. 9, figg. 1—2 (limbata).
Planularia crepidula d'Orb., Cristell. elongata, bilobata d'Orb., 1826, Tabl. meth. Ann. Sc. Nat. 7,
                       p. 260, N:o 6; p. 292, N:ris 11, 12.
  »   Auris   d'Orb. 1826, Tabl. meth.; Ann. Sc. Nat. 7, p. 260, N:o 5.
Cristell. Soldani   d'Orb., 1826, ibid. p. 291, N:o 4.
  »   plana   Rss., 1862, Nordd. Hils u. Gault 1. 16, p. 72, t. 8, fig. 3.
  »   cassis   d'Orb., 1826, Tabl. meth.; Ann. Sc. Nat. 7, p. 290, N:o 3, Mod. 83; 1846,
                       For. tert. Vicone, p. 91, t. 4, figg. 4—7.
Planularia auricula   v. Münst.; Römer, 1838, Nordd. tert. Meeressande; Leonh. u. Bronn. Jhrb.
                       1838, p. 383. t. 3, fig. 12.
  »   Bronni   Park. and Jones, 1860, For. Chellaston; Qu. Journ. geol. Soc. 16, t. 20,
                       fig. 40.
Cristell. folinoea   Marss., 1877, Rüg. Schreibekr.; Greifsw. Nat. Verein. Mitth. 1877—78, p. 143,
                       t. 2, fig. 18.
  »   Jurassica, alata Gümb., 1862, Streitberg. Schwammlag.; Württemb. Nat. Verein. Jhrhft. 1862,
                       p. 224, t. 3, fig. 25; p. 226, t. 4, fig. 1.
  »   pauporata?   Gümb., 1869, Cassian u. Raibl. Schicht.; Österr. geol. Reichsanst. Jhrb. 19,
                       p. 182, t. 6, figg. 29—30.
Rob. lata   Rss., 1863, Sept. Thon Offenbach, Wien. Ak. Sitz.-Ber. 1. 48, p. 52, t. 5,
                       fig. 57.
Cristell. spinulosa   Rss., 1851, Zeitschr. deutsch. geol. Gesellsch. (2) 4, 1852, p. 17 c. fig.
                       xylograph.

Syn. **Planularia pauperata**   Park and Jones, 1860, For. Chellast.; Qu. Journ. geol. Soc. 16, t. 20, fig. 39.
    Cristell. pauperata   Schwag., 1863, Jurass. Sch.; Würtemb. Nat. Verein. Jhrhft. 21, p. 131, t. 6, fig. 45.
    Planularia nodosa   v. Hagen., 1842, Rügen. Kreide; Leonh. u. Bronn. Jhrb. 1842, p. 569, t. 9, fig. 21

c) frondicularioidea:

Cristell. Gaudryana d'Orb., 1839, **Flab. rugosa, Baudouiniana** Craie bl. Paris; Mém. Soc. geol. Fr. 4, t. 2, 26—27, figg. 4, 5, 7. 8—11.
   Flab. rugosa, Baudouiniana, ornata Rss., 1845, Böhm. Kreide 1, p. 32, 33, t. 8, figg. 31—36, t. 13, figg. 48—52; t. 24, fig. 43; 1873, Geinitz' Elbthalgeb. Sachs. 2, p. 99, t. 11, 21, fig. 1.
   Flab. macrospira   Rss., 1859, Westphäl. Kreide; Wien. Ak. Sitz.-Ber. 1. 40, p. 217, t. 9. fig. 2.
   »   **cristellaroides,** Jonesi Karr., 1877, Hochgn. Wasserheit.; Österr. geol. Reichsanst. Abh. 9, p. 381—382, t. 16, figg. 31—32.
   »   **incrassata**   Rss., 1867, Steinsalzablager. Wicliczka; Wien. Ak. Sitz.-Ber. 1. 55, p. 85. t. 3, fig. 5.
   »   **rugosa**   Jones & Park. 1860, For. fr. Chellaston; Quart. Journ. geol. Soc. 16, t. 19, figg. 20—21.
   »   **simplex**   Rss., 1850, Kreidem. Lemberg; Haid. nat. Abh. 4. 1, p. 31, t. 2, fig. 2.
   »   **budensis**   Hkr., 1875, For. Clav. Szab. Sch., p. 44, t. 4, fig. 17.
   »   **lingula**   Rss., 1861, Kreidef. Rügen; Wien. Ak. Sitz.-Ber. 1. 44, p. 326, t. 5, figg. 6—7.
? »   **cordata**   Rss. (partim), 1845, Böhm. Kreide 1. p. 32, t. 8, figg. 39—46; 1854, Kreide Ostalp.; Wien. Ak. Discbr., p. 67, t. 25, figg. 6—8.
? »   **interpunctata**   Rss., 1859, Westph. Kreide, Wien. Ak. Sitz.-Ber. 40, p. 216, t. 9, fig. 1.
? »   **oblonga**   Rss., 1855, Tert. Schicht. n. ö. m. Deutschl.; Wien. Ak. Sitz.-Ber. 1. 18, p. 226, t. 1, figg. 11—16; t. 2, figg. 17—19 (in Frond. complanatam Defr. transiens).

d) in Nod. calcar transgrediens:

Cristell. obliqua   v. Hag., Kreideverstein. Rügen; Leonh. u. Bronn. Jhrb. 1842, p. 573, t. 9. fig. 25.
   »   **planiuscula**   Rss., 1862, Nordd. Hils u. Gault; Wien. Ak. Sitz-Ber. 1. 46, p. 71, t. 7, fig. 15.
   »   **pulchella, sulcifera,** nuda var. Rss., 1842, ibid. p. 71, 74, 72, t. 8, figg. 1, 8,1,2.
   »   **Wetzleri**   Gümb., 1871, Ulmer Cem. Merg; Müneb. Ak. Sitz.-Ber. 1, p. 67, t. 1, fig. 14.
   »   **franconica**   Gümb., 1862, Streitberg, Schwammlag.; Würtemb. Nat. Verein. Jhrb. 1862, p. 226, t. 3, fig. 27.
   »   **minima, ornata, galeata, Robulina porvaensis** Hkn., 1875, For. Clav. Szab. Sch., p. 54, 58, t. 13, fig. 21; t. 13, 14, figg. 20, 12; t. 18, fig. 19, t. 14, fig. 11 (N. calcari proxima).
   »   **recurrens, spectabilis** Rss., 1865, Deutsch. Septariethon; Wien. Ak. Dkschr. 1. 25. 1, p. 140, t. 2, fig. 36; t. 3, figg. 9—10.
   »   **Gerlachi, simplicissima, concinna** Rss., 1862, Sept. Thon. Offenbach; Wien. Ak. Sitz.-Ber. 1. 48, p. 51, t. 4, fig. 54; t. 5, figg. 55—59; t. 4, figg. 51—53; t. 5, fig. 58.
Rob. deformis   Rss., 1862, ibid. p. 53, t. 5, figg. 60—61.
Cristell. nuda, Williamsoni Rss., 1861, Kreide v. Rügen; Wien. Ak. Sitz.-Ber. 1. 44, p. 327, 328, t. 6, figg. 1, 4.
   »   **auriformis**   Rss., 1851, Tert. Schicht. Oberschlesien; Ztschr. deutsch. geol. Ges. 3, p. 153, t. 8, fig. 4.
Rob. lepida   Rss., 1845, Böhm. Kreide 2, p. 109, t. 24, fig. 46.
Cristell. granulata, minuta, convoluta Bornem., 1854, Lineform, Gött. p. 41, 42, t. 4, fig 36, 38.

Syn. Cristell. convergens, elliptica, excisa, Rob. compressa Bornem., 1855, Sept. Thon Hermsdorf;
  Zeitschr. deutsch. geol. Ges. 7, t. 13, figg. 17, 18, 19—20; t. 15,
  fig. 17.
» pulchella   Costa, 1855, For. Marna blu Vaticano; Mem. Nap. 2, p. 121, t. 1, fig. 8.
» gibba   d'Orb., 1839, Cuba Forf. p. 40, t. 7, figg. 20—21.
» Landgrebeana, Rob. torosa Rss., 1864, Oberoligocæn.; Wien. Ak. Sitz.-Ber. 1. 50, p. 461,
  465, t. 3, figg. 1—2.
»   » , polita Rss., 1855, Tert. Sch. norddl. u. mittl. Deutschl.; Wien. Ak. Sitz.-Ber
  1. 18, p. 237, t. 3, figg. 42, 41.
» truncata   Rss., 1850, Kreidemerg. Lemberg; Haid. Nat. Abh. 4. 1, p. 32, t. 2, fig. 8.
» intermedia var. Rss., 1861, Grünsand, New Jersey; Wien. Ak. Sitz.-Ber. 1. 44, p. 336, t. 8,
  fig. 2.
» rostrata, Russeggeri Rss., 1867, Steinsalzablag. Wieliczka; Wien. Ak. Sitz.-Ber. 1. 55, p. 86,
  t. 3, figg. 6, 7.
» variabilis   Rss. 1849, neue For. Österr. tert. Beck.; Wien. Ak. Dkschr. 1. 1. p. 369,
  t. 46, figg. 15—16.
» galeata   Rss., 1851, Sept. Thon. v. Berlin: Ztschr. deutsch. geol. Ges. 3, p. 66, t. 4,
  fig. 20.
»   »   Hken., 1875, For. Clav. Szab. Sch. p. 54, tt. 13, 14, figg. 20, 12.
» nuda var.   Rss., 1861, Palæont. Beiträge; Wien. Ak. Sitz.-Ber. 1. 44, p. 328, t. 6,
  figg. 1—3.
Anomalina auricula   Römer, 1842, Verstein. Nordd. Kreide p. 98, t. 15, fig. 26.
Cristell. Osnabrugensis Rss., 1855, Tert. Schicht. nordl. u. mittl. Deutschl.; Wien. Ak. Sitz.-Ber.
  1. 18, p. 238, t. 4, figg. 44—45.
Nautilina puteolana   Costa, 1854, Pal. Nap. t. 27, fig. 28.
Cristell. Josephina   d'Orb., 1846, For. teri. Vienne p. 88, t. 3, figg. 37—38.
» acuta   Rss., 1859, Westph. Kreidef.; Wien. Ak. Sitz.-Ber. 40, p. 213, t. 10, fig. 3.
» Larva   Stache, 1865, tert. Mergel. Whaingar. Haf., Novara Reise, geol. 1. 2, p. 232,
  t. 23, fig. 11
Robul. Kressenborgensis Gümb., 1868, Nordalp. Eocän.; K. Bayr. Ak. Wiss. Abh. 1. 10. 2, p. 641,
  t. 1, fig. 71.

c) costata, vel striata:

Robul. elegantissima   Costa, 1855, Pal. Nap. p. 198, t. 19, fig. 4.

Nodosarina crepidula var. italica Defr.

Tab. III, figg. 45—49.

Is a highly inflated Nod. crepidula, which not seldom becomes trigonal and, nearly like an *Orthocerina*, particularly when the first chambers are very slightly or not at all arranged in a helicoid manner. The inclination of the septa to the axis is liable to great variation. Sometimes the shell has the shape of a duplex trigonal pyramid with sharp angles and somewhat excavated sides, the aperture being seemingly central.

Its beautiful pearly shell is met with both on the coralline-gravel and on the chalk-ooze. It attains 3 mm. in height and 2 mm. in breadth.

Fig. 47: The outlines of the septal plan.

Syn. Saraconaria italica   DEFR., 1825, Blainv. DEFR. Dict. Sc. Nat.; planches Conchyl. 71, t. 13, fig. 6.
Cristell. italica   D'ORB., 1826, Tabl. Meth.; An. Sc. Nat. 7, p. 293, N:o 26; Mod. 19 et 185.
»   italica var. cincta, aureola KARR., 1877, Hochquellenwasserleit.; Österr. geol. Reichsanst. Abh. 9, p. 383, t. 16, figg. 38—39.
»   Volpicella, contracta COSTA, 1855, For. Mars. blu' Vatic.; Mem. Nap. 2, p. 120, t. 1, figg. 4—5.
Margin. lobata   D'ORB., 1826, Tabl. meth.; An. Sc. Nat. 7, p. 259, N.o 12.
Cristell. obesa   COSTA, 1855, For. Mars. blu' Vatic.; Mem. Nap. 2, p. 121, t. 1, fig. 7.
»   triquetra   GÜMB., 1862, Streitb. Schwamml.; Württemb. Nat. Ver. Jhrhft. 17, p. 225, t. 3, fig. 28.
»   navicula, triangularis D'ORB., 1839, For. Craie bl. Paris; Mem. Soc. geol. France 4, p. 27, t. 2, figg. 19—22.
»   arcuata   D'ORB., 1846, For. tert. Vienne p. 87, t. 3, figg. 34—36.
»   »   HANT., 1875, For. Clav. Száb. Sch. p. 53, t. 5, fig. 5.
»   triangularis   RSS., 1845, Böhm. Kreide. 1, p. 34, t. 4, fig. 48.
»   pyramidata   RSS., 1862, Nordd. Hils u. Gault; Wien. Ak. Sitz.-Ber. 1. 46, p. 70 (sine icone).
Hemicristellaria corculum, Hemirobul. galeola STACHE, 1865, Tert. Merg. Whainger. Hafen; Novara Reise, geol. Th. 1. 2, p. 223, 228, t. 23, figg. 2, 7.
Cristell. gibbosa   COSTA, 1854, Pal. Nap. 2, p. 191, t. 14, fig. 1; t. 16, fig. 24.
»   subarcuatula var. Scapha WILLIAMS., 1859, Rec. brit. Forf. p. 30, figg. 56—62.
Naut. acutauricularis   FICHT. and MOLL., 1803, Test. micr. p. 102, t. 18, figg. g, h, i.
Hemirobul. arcuatula   STACHE, 1865, tert. Merg. Whainger. Hafen; Novara Reise, geol. Th. 1. 2, p. 227, t. 23, fig. 6.
Cristell. trigonalis   RSS., 1864, Oberoligocän.; Wien. Ak. Sitz.-Ber. 1. 50, p. 461, t. 2, fig. 12.
»   Bronni   RSS., 1862, Nordd. Hils u. Gault; Wien. Ak. Sitz.-Ber. 1. 46, p. 70, t. 7, fig. 13.
»   tetraëdra   BORNEM., 1855, Sept. Thon Hermsdorf; Ztschr. deutsch. geol. Ges. 7, p. 327, t. 13, fig. 15.
»   Escri   GÜMB., 1871, Ulmer Cementmerg.; Münch. Ak. Sitz.-Ber. 1, p. 66, t. 1, fig. 10.
»   paucisepta   RSS., 1851, Zeitschr. deutsch. geol. Ges. (2) 4, p. 17 (xylograph.)
»   brachyspira, pygmæa RSS., 1863, Sept. Thon Offenbach; Wien. Ak. Sitz.-Ber. 1. 48, p. 49, t. 3, 4, figg. 43, 44.
»   Nysti   RSS., 1863, For. Crag. d'Anvers; Bull. Ac. Belg. (2). 15, p. 150, t. 2, fig. 24.
»   minima   KARR., 1864, Leythakalk; Wien. Ak. Sitz.-Ber. 1. 50, p. 707, t. 1, fig. 8.
»   mirabilis   RSS., 1855, Tert. Schicht. nördl. u. mittl. Deutschl.; Wien. Ak. Sitz.-Ber. 1. 18, p. 236, t. 3, fig. 39.
»   obvelata   RSS., 1850, Kreidemerg. Lemberg; Haid. Nat. Abh. 4. 1, p. 33, t. 2, fig. 11.
»   ovalis   RSS., 1845, Böhm. Kreidef. 1, p. 34, t. 8, fig. 49; t. 13, figg. 60—63; t. 12, fig. 19; 1873, Geinitz' Elbthal. Geb. Sachsen. 2, p. 103, t. II. 22, figg. 6—11.

Nodosarina crepidula var. cassis F. & Moll.

Tab. III. figg. 50—51.

Sometimes this variety differs a great deal from the typical *N. crepidula*. It bears the same relation to this as the knobbed and spine-margined variety of *Nod. calcar* to its typical form. It is of course in vain to attempt to make a clear distinction between this variety and even Nod. calcar, as is best understood by d'Orbigny's representation of it in his *For. bass. tert. de Vienne t. 4, fig. 5*, which shows more affinity to Nod. calcar than to our form.

The individuals represented by Ficht. & Moll. are more »cultrated« than our form, which is narrowkeeled.

It is a fine, highly developed form from the coralline-gravel. A more oblong and smaller form occurs in the chalkooze.

Fig. 51 edge-view of the aperture.

Syn.		
Nautilus cassis	Ficht. and Moll., 1803, Test. microscop. p. 95, t. 17, figg. a—b; t. 18, figg. a—c.	
Cristoll. consecta, navicularis, nitida, Rob. marginata	d'Orb., 1826, Tabl. Meth.; Ann. Sc. Nat. 7, p. 290, 291, 288 N:ris 1, 2, 5, 6.	
(**Naut.**) **Cristell. Galea**	Ficht. and Moll., l. cit. p. 100, t. 18, figg. d—f; d'Orb., l. cit. p. 291, N:o 6.	
Cristell. erinacea	Karrer, 1878, Forsm. Luzon; Bolet. Comis. Mapa geol. del España, 7. ? p. 19, t. F, fig. 3.	

Nodosarina calcar Lin.

Tab. III. figg. 52—61.

This species rivals *Nod. legumen* in the abundance of names, which might be shared suitably by *three* or *four* varieties at the most.

The differences consist generally:

1) in the presence or absence of knobs and striæ (*verrucosa* et *lineata*),
2) in somewhat marked and raised septal bands (*limbata*),
3) in strongly curved septa (*vorticalis*).

The varieties called »cultrata» and »aculeata» are more or less accidental forms; those appendages or outgrowths of the shell are of too fickle a character to justify a particular nomination. The number of the chambers in the last whorl varies from 6—15.

Thanks to d'Orbigny's efforts to split up Nod. calcar into two genera, the list of synonyms has been wantonly encumbered.

Nod. calcar becomes highly developed both on the chalkbottom and on the coralline-gravel, and it yields not in size to specimens from the chalk and tertiary formation.

Fig. 52 is a mixed form from Nod. calcar and Nod. legumen. It has been favoured with many names, as *Cristellaria Hildesiensis* Röm.; *Crist. Saulcyi* d'Orb., *Crist. Marcki* Rss., *Crist. inflata* Rss. etc.

Fig. 53 represents a peculiar monstrosity; a full-formed Nod. calcar turning back into Nod. legumen.

Figg. 54—56 are d'Orbigny's *Robulina aculeata* of 1826 and his *Rob. calcar* of 1846. The larger one is from the chalk-bottom, the smaller from the coralline-gravel.

Figg. 57—59 has been named *Crist. inornata*, *austriaca* d'Orb., *Crist. tangentialis* Rss. etc. It is provided with a very thin and broad wing or keel and could also be referred to *Crist. cultrata* Montf.; but this appendage is met with throughout all the varieties and is not peculiar to any of them. From the chalk-bottom.

Figg. 60—61 are monstrosities with luxuriant alar- and umbilical processes. From coralline-gravel.

The regular, typical form, *rotulata* Lmk., is the most abundant and the stoutest of all our forms (3—5 mm.).

a) lævis:

Nautilus lævigatulus	Montagu, 1803, Test. Brit. p. 188; 1808; Suppl. p. 75, t. 18, figg. 7—8.
Lenticulites Comptoni	Nilsson, 1825, Mångrummiga snäckor i kritformat. i Sverige; K. Vet. Ak. Handl. 1825, p. 337; 1827, Petref. svecana p. 7, t. 2, fig. 3.
Cristell. rotulata	d'Orb., 1839, For. craie bl.; Mém. Soc. géol. Fr. 4, p. 26, t. 2, figg. 15—18.
» »	Reuss, 1845, Böhm. Kreide 1, p. 34, t. 8, fig. 50; t. 12, fig. 25; t. 24, figg. 48—49.
» »	Park. and Jones, 1865, N. Atl. and Arct. Oc.; Phil. Trans. 1. 55. 1, p. 345, t. 13, fig. 19.
» **simplex**	d'Orb., 1846, For. tert. Vienne, p. 103. t. 4, figg. 27—28.
» **calcar**	Park. and Jones, 1857, For. Coast. of Norway; Ann. Mag. Nat. Hist. (2). 19, p. 289.
Rob. canariensis	d'Orb., 1844, Iles Canaries, p. 127, t. 3, figg. 3—4.
Cristell. polita	Schwag., 1866, For. Kar-Nikobar; Novara Reise, geol. Th. 2. 2, p. 242. t. 6, fig. 86.
Rob. plicata	d'Orb., 1826, Tab. meth.; An. Sc. N. p. 290, N:o 23.
Cristell. multiseptata	Rss., 1865, For. deutsch. Sept. Thon; Wien. Ak. Dkschr. 1. 25. 1, p. 147, t. 3, figg. 14—15.
Rob. neglecta	Rss., 1851, Sept. Thon Berlin; Zeitschr. deutsch. geol. Ges. 3, p. 63, t. 4, fig. 27.
» **stellifera**	Czjz., 1847, For. Wien. Beck.; Haid. Nat. Abh. 2. 1, p. 142, t. 12, figg. 26—27.
» **dimorpha, incompta**	Rss., 1851, Sept. Thon v. Berlin; Zeitschr. deutsch. geol. Ges. 3, p. 67, 70, figg. 23, 28.
Cristell. macrodisca	Rss., 1862, Nordd. Hils u. Gault, Wien. Ak. Sitz.-Ber. 1. 46, p. 78, t. 9, fig. 5.
Cristell. paupercula	Rss., 1865, deutsch. Sept. Thon; Wien. Ak. Dkschr. 1. 25. 1, p. 141, t. 3, figg. 6—7.
Rob. Gottingensis, nautiloides	Bornem., 1854, Liasform. Göttingen p. 43, t. 4, figg. 40—42.
Rob. trigonostoma, declivis	Bornem., 1855, Sept. Thon Hermsdorf; Ztschr. deutsch. geol. Ges. 7, p. 333—336, t. 15, figg. 8—11.

Syn. Rob. trigonostoma   Rss., 1851, Sept. Thon v. Berlin; Zeitschr. deutsch. geol. Ges. 3, p. 69,
                              t. 4, fig. 26.
  » subnodosa, propinqua, Münst., Röm., 1838, Nordd. tert. Meeressand, Leonh. u. Bronn. Jhrb.
                              1838, p. 391, t. 3, figg. 61, 63.
     Cristell. eximia   Rss., 1865, Sept. Thon Offenbach; Wien. Ak. Sitz.-Ber. 1. 48, p. 52, t. 5,
                              fig. 56.
  »   Oppeli, semiexpleta Schwag., 1863, Jurass. Sch.; Würtemb. Nat. Verein. Jhrhft. 21, p.
                              134, 135, t. 7, figg. 1, 3.
  »   lenticula   Rss., 1849, Neue For. österr. tert. Beck.; Wien. Ak. Dkschr. 1. 1. p. 369,
                              t. 46, fig. 17.
     Rob. arcuata   Karr., 1861, Marin. Tegel Wien. Beck.; Wien. Ak. Sitz.-Ber. 1. 44, p. 446,
                              t. 2, fig. 1.
     Cristell. umbilicata   Rss., 1861, Kreide Rügen; Wien. Ak. Sitz.-Ber. 1. 44, p. 327, t. 6, fig. 6.
     Rob. discrepans, impressa, turgidula, Dunkeri Rss., 1862, Nordd. Hils u. Gault; Wien. Ak. Sitz.-
                              Ber. 1. 46, p. 78, 77, 73, t. 9, figg. 7, 2; t. 8, figg. 4, 6.
     Cristell. deformis   Karr., 1867, For. Fauna Österreich.; Wien. Ak. Sitz.-Ber. 1. 55, p. 349,
                              t. 1, fig. 3.
  »   Spechholzi   Rss., 1850, Kreidemerg. Lemberg; Haid. Nat. Abh. 4. 1, p. 33, t. 2, fig. 10.
  »   convergens, integra, Bornem., 1855, Sept. Thon Hermsdorf; Zeitschr. deutsch. geol. Ges. 7,
                              p. 327, t. 13, fig. 16; p. 334, t. 15, figg. 12—16.
  »   lobata   Rss., 1845, Böhm. Kreidef. 1, p. 34, t. 13, fig. 59; 1873, Geln. Elbthalgeb.
                              Sachsen 2, p. 104, t. II. 22, fig. 12; t. II. 23, fig. 1.
  »   inops   Rss., 1851, Tert. Schicht. Oberschlesien; Zeitschr. deutsch. geol. Ges. 3, p.
                              155, t. 8, fig. 5.
  »   oligostegia   Reuss, 1859, Westphäl. Kreide; Wien. Ak. Sitz.-Ber. 1 40, p. 213, t. 8,
                              fig. 8; 1862, Nordd. Hils u. Gault; Wien. Ak. Sitz.-Ber. 1. 46, p.
                              93, t. 13, fig. 2.
  »   tumida   Karr., 1870, Kreidef. Leitzendorf; Österr. geol. Reichsanst. Jhrb. 20, p. 180,
                              t. 11, fig. 10.
  »   crassa   d'Orb., 1846, For. tert. Vienne, p. 90, t. 4, figg. 1—3.
  »   coarctata, bicornis Costa, 1854; Pal. Nap. 2, p. 192, t. 17, figg. 1. 3.
     Rob. articulata   Rss., 1863, Sept. Thon Offenbach; Wien. Ak. Sitz.-Ber. 1. 48, p. 53, t. 5,
                              fig. 62, t. 6 fig. 63.
     Cristell. obesa   Karr., 1877, Hochqu. Wasserl.; k. k. österr. geol. Reichsanst. Abh. 9, p. 383,
                              t. 16, fig. 40.
  »   depauperata, deformis Rss., 1851, Sept. Thon v. Berlin; Zeitschr. deutsch. geol. Ges. 3,
                              p. 70, t. 4, figg. 29, 30; 1863, Sept. Thon Offenb.; Wien. Ak. Sitz.-
                              Ber. 1. 48 p. 54, t. 6, figg. 67—68, t. 8, fig. 90.
     Rob. deformis, depauperata, incompta Bornem., 1855, Sept. Thon Hermsdorf; Zischr. deutsch. geol.
                              Ges. 7, p. 337, t. 14, figg. 1—3, 11—12.
  »   bullata   Hkr., 1875, Clav. Száb. Sch. p. 58, t. 14, fig. 13.
  »   ambigua   Costa, 1854, Pal. Nap. 2, t. 20, fig. 17.
  »   angulata   Rss., 1851, Tert. Sch. Oberschles.; Zeitschr. deutsch. geol. Ges. 3, p. 154,
                              t. 8, fig. 6.
     Cristell. Cassiana   Gümb. 1869, For. Cassian-Raibler Sch.; Österr. geol. Reichsanst. Jhb. 19,
                              p. 177, t. 5, figg. 2—3.
  »   lactea   Stache, 1865, tert. Mergel Whaingar. Hafen; Novara Reise, geol. Th. 1. 2,
                              p. 235, t. 23, fig. 14.
  »   subangulata   Rss., 1862, Nordd. Hils u. Gault; Wien. Ak. Sitz.-Ber. 1. 46, p. 74, t. 8,
                              fig. 7; 1863, Sept. Thon v. Offenbach; Wien. Ak. Sitz.-Ber. 1. 48,
                              p. 53, t. 6, fig. 64.
     Rob. inornata, austriaca d'Orb., 1846, For. tert. Vienne p. 102, t. 4, figg. 25—26, t. 5, figg. 1—2.
  »   »   Bornem., 1855, Sept. Thon Hermsdorf; Zeitschr. deutsch. geol. Ges. 7, p.
                              334, t. 15, figg. 2—3.
  »   intermedia   d'Orb., 1846, For. tert. Vienne, p. 104, t. 5, figg. 3—4.

Syn. **Rob. nitida** Rss., 1863, Sept. Thon Offenbach; Wien. Ak. Sitz.-Ber. 1. 48, p. 54, t. 6, fig. 66.

Cristell. tangentialis, semiimpressa Rss., 1866, deutsch. Septarienthon; Wien. Ak. Dkschr. 1. 25. 1, p. 143, t. 3, fig. 13.

Rob. umbonata Rss., 1851, Sept. Thon Berlin; Zeitschr. deutsch. geol. Ges. 3, p. 68, t. 4, fig. 24.

» **cultrata** d'Orb., 1826, Tabl. Meth.; Ann. Sc. Nat. 7, p. 287, N:o 1; Mod. 82.
Soldania carinata d'Orb., ibid. p. 281, N:o 1.
Nautilus calcar var. λ Ficht. and Moll., 1803, Test. microsc. p. 78, t. 13, figg. e—g.

Rob. halophora Stache, 1865, Tert. Mergel Whaingar. Hafen; Novara Reise geol. Th. 1. 2, p. 248, t. 23, fig. 28.

Cristell. Grundensis Karr., 1867, For. Faun. Österr.; Wien. Ak. Sitz.-Ber. 1. 55, p. 355, t. 1, fig. 8.

Rob. d'Orbignii Bailey, 1850, Examin. of Soundings; Smithson. Contrib. of knowledge 2, Art. 3, figg. 9—10.

Cristell. cultrata Park. and Jones, 1865, North. Atl. and Arct. Oc.; Phil. Trans. 155, 1, p. 314, t. 13, figg. 17—18; t. 16, fig. 5.

Rob. cultrata β **antipodum** Stache, 1865, Tert. Mergel Whaingar. Hafen; Novara Reise, geol. Th. 1. 2, p. 251, t. 23, fig. 30.

» **nitidissima, galeata** Rss., 1851, Sept. Berlin; Zeitschr. deutsch. geol. Ges. 3, p. 68. t. 4, fig. 25; fig. 21.

Cristell. Gemellarii Seg., 1862, Rhizopod. d. Catania, Acad. Gioenia Atti (2), 18, p. 13, t. 1, fig. 2.

Rob. limbosa Rss., 1863, Sept. Thon Offenbach; Wien. Ak. Sitz.-Ber. 1. 48, p. 55, t. 6, fig. 69.

» **depauperata** β. **callifera** Rss., 1863, Sept. Thon Kreuznach; Wien. Ak. Sitz.-Ber. 1. 48, p. 66, t. 8, fig. 91.

Cristell. Josephina β. **tuberculata** Karr., 1868, Mioc. faun. Kostej; Wien. Ak. Sitz.-Ber. 1. 58, p. 170, t. 4, fig. 7.

» **nikobarensis, peregrina** Schwag., 1866, For. Kar-Nikobar; Novara Reise, geol. Th. 2. 2, p. 243, 245; t. 6, fig. 87; t. 7, fig. 89.

» **hebetata** 1863, Jurass. Sch.; Württemb. Nat. Verein. Jahresh. 21, p. 134, t. 7, fig. 2.

» **moravica, Ruditziana** Karr., 1864, Leythakalk Wien. Beck.; Wien. Ak. Sitz.-Ber. 1, 50, p. 707, 708, t. 2, figg. 9—10.

Rob. Beyrichi Bornem., 1855, Sept. Thon. Hermsdorff; Zeitschr. deutsch. geol. Ges. 7, p. 332, t. 14, fig. 8.

» **Kubinyii** Hntn., 1875, For. Clav. Szab. Sch. p. 56, t. 6, fig. 7.

» **depauperata, princeps, limbosa, budensis** Hntn., ibid. p. 55—58; t. 6, figg. 5—6, 8, 11; t. 7, fig. 1; t. 14, fig. 16.

Cristell. Haasti, rotula, Clio, Rob. oculus Stache, 1865, Tert. Merg. Whaingar. Hafen; Novara Reise, geol. Th. 1. 2, p. 247, t. 23, figg. 10, 12, 13, 27.

Crist. Loubeana, ulmensis Gümb., 1871, Ulmer Cement, Mergel, Münch. Ak. Sitz.-Ber. 1, p. 67, t. 1, figg. 13, 15.

Rob. radiata, limbata, spec. indet. Bornem., 1855, Septarienthon. Hermsdorf; Ztschr. deutsch. geol. Ges. 7, p. 335, 336, t. 15, figg. 1—7.

Rob. radiata Rss., 1863, Sept. Thon Offenbach; Wien. Ak. Sitz.-Ber. 1. 48, p. 54, t. 6, fig. 65.

Cristell. grata Rss., 1866, deutsch. Sept. Thon; Wien. Ak. Dkschr. 1. 25, p. 145.

Rob. rosetta Gümb., 1868, Nordalp. Eocän; K. Bayr. Ak. Wiss. Abh. 1. 10. 2, p. 642, t. 1, fig. 73.

Rob. radiata, pulchella, laevigata, aculeata d'Orb., 1826, Tabl. Meth.; Ann. Sc. Nat. 7, p. 288, 289, N:ris 7, 8, 9, 14.

Syn. **Nautilus calcar**
    var. α
    » β
    » χ
    » μ
                    FICHT. and MOLL., 1803, Test. microsc. p. 71, 76, 73, t. 11, figg. a. b. e;
                       t. 12, figg. i. k; t. 13, figg. c. d. h. i.

Rob. calcar   D'ORB., 1846, For. tert. Vienne, p. 99, t. 2, figg. 18—20.

b) vortex:

Nautilus vortex   FICHT. and MOLL., 1803, Test. microsc. p. 33, t. 2, figg. d—i.
Rob. orbicularis, vortex D'ORB., 1826, Tab. meth.; An. Sc. Nat. 7, p. 288, Nris 2. 4; t. 15, figg.
                             8—9.
» **Soldanii**   D'ORB., ibid. p. 288, N:o 5.
Cristell. falcata   KARR., 1878, For. Luzon; Bolet. Comis. Mapa geol. d. España 7. 2, p. 20,
                       t. F, fig. 5.
Rob. imperatoria   D'ORB., 1846, For. tert. Vienne, p. 104, t. 5, figg. 5—6.
» **obtusa**   RSS., 1849, Neue For. österr. tert. Beck.; Wien. Ak. Dkschr. 1. 1, p. 369,
                       t. 46, fig. 18.
Cristell. Baylei   RSS., 1861, Grünsand N. Jersey; Wien. Ak. Sitz.-Ber. 1. 44, p. 336, t. 7,
                       fig. 7.
Rob. subangulosa, inornata, festonata COVA, 1854, Pal. Nap. 2, p. 229, t. 14, fig. 2; t. 19, fig. 6,
                       t. 19, fig. 1.
» **arcuato-striata**   HKN., 1875, For. Clav. Scäb. Seh. p. 56, t. 7, fig. 2.
» **regina**   KARR., 1865, For. Grünsandstein N. Zeeland; Novara Reise, geol. Th. 1. 2,
                     p. 76, t. 16, fig. 6.
**Cristell. callifera, duracina, bucculenta, glaucina, intermedia, gyroscalprum, Rob. foliata,
       corona lunæ, pseudocalcarata, incrustata** STACHE, Tert. Mergel
       Wischgar. Half.; Novara Reise, geol. Th. 1. 2, p. 236—254, t. 23,
       figg. 15—17, 20—22, 24, 29, 31, 33.
Rob. alato-limbata   GÜMB., 1868, Nordalp. Eoc.; K. Bayr. Ak. Wissensch. Abh. 1. 10. 2, p. 641,
                       t. 1, fig. 70.
» **Cumingii (Michelotti)** BORNEM., 1860, For. Magdeb.; Zeitschr. deutsch. geol. Ges. 12, p. 156,
                       t. 6, fig. 1.
Cristell. microptera   RSS., 1859, Westphäl. Kreidef.; Wien. Ak. Sitz.-Ber. 40, p. 215, t. 8, fig. 7.

c) limbata:

Nautilus calcar   FICHT. and MOLL., 1803, Test. Micros. p. 72, 76, t. 11, figg. d—f, t. 12,
                       figg. d—h.
» **depressulus**   MONTAGU 1803, Test. Britann. p. 190; 1808, Suppl. p. 78, t. 18, fig. 9.
Rob. rotunda   D'ORB., 1826, Tab. meth.; An. Sc. Nat. 7, p. 290, N:o 24.
Lenticulites cristella NILSS., 1827, Petrificata Svecana p. 7, t. 2, fig. 4.
Nautilus calcar   MONTAGU, 1803, Test. Brit. p. 189, t. 15, fig. 4; 1808, Suppl. p. 76.
Rob. cultrata   D'ORB., 1846, For. tert. Vienne, p. 96, t. 4, figg. 10—13.
» **similis, clypeiformis** D'ORB., ibid. p. 98, 101, t. 4, figg. 14—15, 23—24.
Rob. Osnabrügensis, Cristell. subcostata v. MÜNST., RÖM., 1838, Cephalop. tert. Meeress. Nordd.;
                     Leonh. u. Bronn. Jhrb. 1838, p. 391, t. 3, figg. 62, 64.
Cristell. subcostata   RSS., 1855, Tert. Sch. nördl. u. mittl. Deutschl.; Wien. Ak. Sitz.-Ber. 1. 18,
                     p. 237, t. 3, fig. 43.
» **planicosta**   v. HAGENOW, 1842, Rügens Kreideverst.; Leonh. u. Bronns, Jhrb. 1842, p.
                     572, t. 9, fig. 24.
» **exarata**   RSS., 1861, Paläont. Beiträg. Rügen; Wien. Ak. Sitz.-Ber. 1. 44, p. 327,
                     t. 6, fig.
» **orbicula, subalata** RSS., 1854, Kreide Ostalp.; Wien. Ak. Dkschr. 7, p. 68, t. 25, figg.
                     12—13.

Syn. Cristell. rotulata   Rss., 1845, (partim), Böhm. Kreide t. 8, fig. 70.
    Rob. angustimargo   Rss., 1851, Sept. Thon Berlin; Ztschr. deutsch. geol. Ges. 3, p. 67, t. 4,
                               fig. 22.
    »   dimorpha   Rss., ibid. p. 67, t. 4, fig. 23.
    »   polyphragma, princeps, insignis Rss., 1864, Oberoligocän.; Wien. Ak. Sitz.-Ber. 1. 50, p. 465,
                               466, t. 4, fig. 5; t. 5, figg. 3—4.
    »   angustimargo   Bornem., 1855, Sept. Thon Hermsdorf; Ztschr. deutsch. geol. Ges. 7, p. 332,
                               t. 14, figg. 6—7.
    Cristell. falcifer, Rob. lenticula Stache, 1865, Tert. Merg. Whainger. Haf.; Novara Reise, geol. Th.
                               1. 2, p. 240, 246, t. 23, figg. 19, 25.
    »   magna   Costa, 1854, Palæont. Nap. 2, p. 193, t. 19, fig. 2.
    »   austriaca   Costa, 1855, For. Marna blu' d. Vaticano; Mem. Nap. 2, p. 122, t. 1,
                               fig. 10.
    Rob. pterodiscoidea, declivis, radlifera, acutimargo Gümb., 1868, Nordalp. Eocän.; K. Bayr. Ak.
                               Wiss. 1. 10, 2, p. 642, 640; t. 1, fig. 72; t. 2, figg. 76, 76 aa, 76 bb.
    Cristell. Quenstedti   Gümb., 1862, Streitb. Schwammlag.; Würtemb. Nat. Verein Jhrbft. 1862,
                               p. 226, t. 4, fig. 2.
    »   pachynota, Römeri, subalata, Münsteri Rss., 1862, Nordd. Hils u. Gault; Wien. Ak. Sitz.-
                               Ber. 1. 46, p. 69, 75, 76, 77, t. 7, fig. 11; t. 8, fig. 9; t. 9, figg.
                               1, 3, 4.
    »   prominula, megalopolitana Rss., 1855, Kreideg. Mecklenburg; Ztschr. deutsch. geol. Ges. 7,
                               p. 271, t. 9, figg. 3, 5.
    »   secans   Rss., 1859, Westph. Kreide; Wien. Ak. Dkschr. 40, p. 215, t. 9, fig. 7.
    Rob. magdeburgica   Bornemann, 1860, For. Magdeb.; Zeitschr deutsch. geol. Ges. 12, p. 157,
                               t. 6, fig. 2.
    »   spec. indet.   Bornemann, 1855, Sept. Thon. Hermsdorf; Ztschr. d. geol. Ges. 7, p. 333,
                               t. 14, figg. 9—10.
    Cristell. lapugyensis   Karr., 1864, Leythakalk Wien. Beck.; Wien. Ak. Sitz.-Ber. 1. 50, p. 708,
                               t. 2, fig. 11.
    Rob. colorata, loculosa, pusilla Stache, 1865, Tert. Merg. Whainger. Haf.; Novara Reise, geol. Th.
                               1. 2, p. 229, 244, 247, t. 23, fig. 9; t. 23, figg. 23, 26.
    Cristell. fenestrata, subplana Rss., 1865, deutsch. Sept. Thon; Wien. Ak. Dkschr. 1. 25. 1, p. 142,
                               143, t. 3, figg. 11—12.
    Rob. virgata   d'Orb., 1826, Tab. meth.; An. Sc. Nat. 7, p. 290; N:o 17; Mod. N:o 14.
    »   nodosa   Rss., 1862, Nordd. Hils. u. Gault; Wien. Ak. Sitz.-Ber. 1. 46, p. 78, t. 9,
                               fig. 6.
    »   lobata   Costa, 1854, Pal. Nap. 2, t. 20, fig. 14.

   d) papillosa:

Nautilus papillosus   Fight. & Moll., 1803, Test. micr. p. 82, t. 14, figg. a. b. c.
Rob. calcar   d'Orb., 1826, Tab. meth.; An. Sc. Nat. 7, p. 289, N:o 12.
Crist. marginata, tuberculata }
    » aculeata, elegans, papillosa } d'Orb., ibid. p. 291—293, N:o 7, 13, 14, 24, 25.
Rob. echinata   d'Orb., 1846, For. tert. Vienne, p. 100, t. 4, figg. 21—22 (striata).
Nautilus calcar var. γ, δ, ε Figt. and Moll., 1803, Test. micr. t. 11. figg. g, h, i, k; t. 12, figg. a, b, c;
                       t. 13, figg. a, b.
Rob. rosacea   d'Orb., 1826, Tabl. meth.; Ann. Sc. Nat. 7, p. 289, N:o 11.
Bob. trachyomphala   Rss., 1850, Kreidemerg. Lemberg; Haid. Nat. Abh. 4. 1, p. 34, t. 2, fig. 12.
Rob. gutticostata, florigemma Gümb., 1868, Nordalp. Eocän.; K. Bayer. Ak. Wiss. 1. 10. 2, p. 643,
                       644, t. 1, figg. 74—75.
    » jurassofranconica Gümb., 1862, Streitenb. Schwammlag.; Würtemb. Nat. Verein. Jhrbft. 1862,
                       p. 227, t. 4. fig. 3.

Syn. Cristell. mamilligera   KARR., 1865, For. Grünsandst. N. Zeeland; Novara Reise, geol. Th. 1. 2, p. 76, t. 16, fig. 5.
Rob. gutticostata, baconica, granulata HKE., 1875, Clav. Száb. Sch. p. 57, 58; t. 6, fig. 10; t. 14, figg. 9, 15.
Cristell. Bufo   STACHE, 1865, Tert. Merg. Whaingar. Hafen; Novara Reise, geol. Th. 1. 2, p. 239, t. 23, fig. 18.
» Helenæ   KARR., 1877, Hochquellenwasserl.; Österr. geol. Reichsanst. Abh. 9, p. 384, t. 16, fig. 42.
» undulata   KARR., 1867, For. Österr.; Wien. Ak. Sitz.-Ber. 1. 55, p. 348, t. 1, fig. 2.
» inflata   KARR., ibid. p. 355, t. 1, fig. 9.

e) striolata-costata:

Rob. echinata, striolata   CZJZ., 1847, Foramf. Wien. Beck.; Haid. Nat. Abh. 2. 1, p. 141, 142, t. 12, figg. 24—25, 28—29.
» inæqualis, cancellata, semistriata COSTA, 1854, Pal. Nap. 2, p. 328, 230, t. 19, figg. 3, 5, 7.
» signata   RSS., 1855, Kreideg. Meklenb.; Ztschr. deutsch. geol. Ges. 7, p. 272, t. 9, fig. 4.
» tettowatta   STACHE, 1865, Tert. Merg. Whaingar. Hafen; Novara Reise, geol. Th. 1. 2, p. 252, t. 23, fig. 32.
» Vaticana   COSTA, 1855, For. Marna blu' d' Vaticano; Mem. Nap. 2, p. 122, t. 1, fig. 17.
» costata   D'ORB., 1826, An. Sc. Nat. 7, p. 289, N:o 13, Mod. 84.
Nautilus costatus   FICHT. and MOLL., 1803, Tert. micr. p. 47, t. 4, figg. g, h, i.
Rob. ornata   D'ORB., 1846, For. tert. Vienne p. 98, t. 4, figg. 16—17.
» ariminensis   D'ORB., ibid. p. p. 95, t. 4, figg. 8—9.
» Paulæ   KARR., 1877, Hochquell. Wasserl.; geol. Reichsanst. Abh. 9, p. 384, t. 16, fig. 41 (aculeata).

f) forma »Rhabdogonium»:

Rhabdogon. globiferum   RSS., 1859, Westph. Kreide; Wien. Ak. Sitz.-Ber. 40, p. 201, t. 7, fig. 6.
» pygmæum   RSS., 1865, Deutsch. Sept. Thon; Wien. Ak. Dkschr. 1. 25. 1, t. 1, fig. 32.

g) in Nod. legumen rediens:

Cristell. Hildesiensis   RÖM., 1838, Nordd. tert. Meeress.; Leonh. u. Bronn. Jhrb. 1838, p. 391, t. 3, fig. 65.
? » lævigata   D'ORB., 1826, Tab. meth.; An. Sc. Nat. 7, p. 292, N:o 19, Mod. N:o 47.
» Saulcyi   D'ORB., 1844, Iles Canaries p. 126, t. 3, figg. 7—9.
» inflata, Marckl RSS., 1859, Westph. Kreidef.; Wien. Ak. Sitz.-Ber. 40, p. 212, t. 8, fig. 6; t. 9, fig. 4.
» biolivosa, inflata, informis SCHWAG., 1863, Jurass. Sch.; Würtemb. Nat. Verein. Jhrshft. 21, p. 133, t. 6, fig. 21; p. 132, t. 6, fig. 16; p. 128, t. 6, fig. 8.
? » lituola, excentrica CORN., 1848, Nouv. foss. microsc.; Mem. Soc. geol. France (2) 3, p. 254, t. 2, figg. 9—13 (Nod. crepidulæ propinqua).
Spiralina ? Streitbergensis GÜMB., 1861, Streitberg. Schwammlag.; Würtemb. Nat. Verein. Jhrshft. 17, p. 232, t. 4, fig. 7.
Cristell. lituola   RSS., 1845, Böhm. Kreide 2, p. 109, t. 24, fig. 47.

Nodosarina complanata Defr.
Tab. III, figg. 62—64.

It is not without some hesitation that this form should be distinguished as a »species»; for a closer study leads to the conclusion, that it possibly may originate from different species of Nodosarina, thus being descendants, each bearing small marks of variation pointing back to their origin, but all still maintaining in common a feature of essential unity.

1. From *Nod. radicula* some simple forms of »*Frondicularia*» have seemingly their direct origin.

2. Other varieties keep close to *Nod.* (*Glandulina*) *lævigata* D'ORB., as *Frondicularia spathulata* WILLIAMS., *Frond. simplex* Rss., *Frond. folium* ALTH.

3. *Frondicularia ensiformis* RÖM., *Frond. lingua* BOLL. bear the same relation to *Nod. legumen*.

4. All smooth varieties with their earliest chambers arranged in the same way as in Nod. crepidula are, it would seem, immediate offsets of this species. *Cristellaria Gaudryana* D'ORB., *Flabellina macrospira* Rss. etc. are instances of this transition.

In systematising the costate forms of Nod. complanata the same difficulty is met with as in the other Nodosarinæ. Sometimes the primordial chamber only is ribbed, the other parts being quite smooth; at another time the striation of the shell is quite faint and scarce.

When both forms of Nod. complanata (Frondicularia and Flabellina) with their numerous modifications of form are collected from the same localitiy, they certainly create the impression that they all belong to a single species.

This set of Nodosarina gives us a noteworthy hint of, how unsatisfactory must be the result of the attempts of our days to make out the genealogy of a species, for it can scarcely be denied, that sometimes one form may possibly have originated from several different species.

Fig. 62 is next to *Frond. alata* D'ORB., it is taken from a small specimen, but on the chalkbottom it often attains the size of 10 mm. in hight and 8 mm. in breadth.

Fig. 63 the same with the younger state of *crepidula* growth.

Fig. 64 is still nearer Nod. crepidula. Sometimes the primordial chamber is provided with a couple of secondary chambers set at right angles to the ordinary ones. If this plan of growth had continued a four-winged form would have originated.

A stout lanceolate-elliptical form is also met with among the coralline-gravel

Syn. **Frond.** obliqua	v. MÜNST., RÖM., 1838, Nordd. tert. Meeresa.; Leonh. u. Broun. Jahrb. 1838, p. 382, t. 3, fig. 7.	
» oblonga, ovata	RÖM., ibid. t. 3, fig. 4—6.	
» obliqua	ALTH., 1849, Umgeb. Lemberg; Haid. Nat. Abh. 3. 2, p. 268, t. 13, fig. 26.	
» lancea	PUSCH., 1843, Teri. Versteiner. nordw. Deutschl. t. 1, fig. 31.	
» Meyeri	BOLL., 1846, Ostseeländern. p. 177, t. 2, fig. 18.	

Syn. Frond.	Bradyana	KARR., 1877, Hochquellenwasserleit.; Österr. geol. Reichsanst. Abh. 9, p. 380, t. 16, fig. 24.
	Medelingensis	KARR., ibid. p. 380, t. 16, fig. 25.
»	fragilis	KARR., 1870, Kreidef. Leitzendorf; Jhrb. k. k. österr. geol. Reichsanst. 20, p. 175, t. 11, fig. 3.
? »	folia	KARR., ibid. p. 172, t. 10, fig. 9.
»	tenuissima	HKRN., 1875, For. Clav. Szab. Sch. p. 43, t. 13, fig. 11.
»	spathulata	WILL., 1858, Brit. rec. foramf. p. 23, fig. 50.
»	tribus	KARR., Kreidef. in Leitzendorf; Jhrb. k. k. österr. geol. Reichsanst. 20, p. 175, t. 11, fig. 5.
»	foliacea	SCHWAG., 1866, For. Kar.-Nikob.; Novara Reise, geol. Th. 2. 2, p. 236, t. 6, fig. 76.
»	folium	ALTH, 1849, Umgeb. Lemberg; Hald. Nat. Abh. 3. 2, p. 268, t. 13, fig. 25
»	inæqualis, compressa	COSTA, 1855, Marna terz. Messina, Mem. Nap. 2, t. 3, figg. 2—3.
»	Whaingaroica	STACHE, 1865, Tert. Merg. Whaingar. Halen; Novara Reise, geol. Th. 1. 2, p. 210, t. 22, fig. 43.

Frond.	Mandelslohoana	GÜMB., 1871, Ulmer Cem. Merg.; Münch. Ak. Sitz.-Ber. 1, p. 66, t. 1, fig. 9
»	biformis	MARSS., 1879, Rügen. Schreibkr.; Greifsw. Nat. Ver. Mittheil. 1877—78, p. 137, t. 2, fig. 17.
»	compta	BRADY, 1879, Notes on Retic. Rhizop.; Qu. Journ. microsc. Sc. (n. ser.) 75, p. 271, t. 8, fig. 6.
»	amoena	KARR., 1870, Kreidef. Leitzendorf; Jhrb. k. k. österr. geol. Reichsanst. 20, p. 172, t. 10, fig. 10.
»	Leitzendorfensis, pulchella, sarissa, plana KARR., ibid. p. 171—174; t. 10, figg. 7—8, 13—14.
»	lingulæformis	SCHWAG., 1863, Jurass. Sch.; Würtemb. Nat. Verein. Jhrhft. 19, p. 113, t. 4, fig. 11.
»	complanata var.	JONES & PARK. 1860, For. fr. Chellaston; Quart. Journ. geol. Soc. 16, t. 19, fig. 19.
»	monocantha	RSS., 1839, Neue Forf. österr. tert. Beck.; Wien. Ak. Dkschr. 1. 1, p. 368, t. 44, fig. 14.
»	mucronata	RSS., 1845, Böhm. Kreide 1, p. 31, t. 13, fig. 43; Geinitz' Elbthalgeb. Sachs. 2, p. 96, t. 11. 2, figg. 14—16.
»	bicornis	RSS., 1845, Böhm. Kreide 1, p. 32, t. 13. fig. 45; 2, p. 108, t. 24, fig. 37.
»	Parkeri	RSS., 1862, Nordd. Hils u. Gault; Wien. Ak. Sitz.-Ber. 1. 46, p. 91, t. 12, fig. 7.
»	filocincta	RSS., ibid. p. 54, t. 4, fig. 12.
»	rhomboidalis, alata, complanata D'ORB., 1826, Tab. meth.; An. Sc. Nat. 7, p. 256, Nris 1, 2, 5, Mod. 3.
»	spec. indet., parabolica, acuminata, rhombea COSTA, 1855, Marna terz. Messina; Mem. Nap. 2, p. 371, t. 2, figg. 21, 24; t. 3, figg. 10, 13, 15.
»	superba	HRRN., 1875, Clav. Szab. Sch., p. 42, t. 4, fig. 16.
»	hastata	RÖM., 1842, Neue Kreideforamf.; Leonh. u. Bronn. Jhrb. 1842, p. 272, t. 7 B, fig. 5.
»	»	RSS., 1862, Nordd. Hils u. Gault; Wien. Ak. Sitz.-Ber. 1. 46, p. 53, t. 4, fig. 10.
»	inversa	RSS., 1845, Böhm. Kreide 1, p. 31, t. 8, figg. 15—19; t. 13, fig. 42.
»	crassa, simplex	RSS., ibid. t. 8, figg. 29—30.

Syn. **Flaboll. reticulata**   Rss., 1850, Kreidemerg. Lemberg; Haid. Nat. Abh. 7. 1, p. 30, t. 1, fig. 22.
    » **foliacea**   Brady, 1879, Notes on Ret. Rhizop.; Qu. Journ. Sc. (n. ser.) 75, p. 271, t. 8, figg. 8—10 (in sequentem (b) transiens).

b) Nod. crepidulæ propinqua vide: Nod. crepidula (p. 46. c).

Nodosarina carinata d'Orb.
Tab. I, fig. 65—67.

Attains a high development particularly in the coralline-gravel. It is liable to great variation, sometimes being very ventricous and broadly wedge-shaped, and sometimes compressed and more linear. Sometimes it is provided with fine costæ on the flanks; being the first step to the strongly and entirely costate »raphanus« form. Some forms, described as *Frondicularia* and *Lingulinopsis* are more properly referred to this species.

Genus *Fissurina* Rss. who has been ranked with Lagena, seems to be the embryonal or the pigmy-form to Nod. carinata.

Fig. 65—66 is the typical *Lingulina carinata* d'Orb. of large growth.

Fig. 67 has the same shape as *Lingulina costata* d'Orb., and is identical with *Lingulina seminuda* Hken.

Syn. **Lingulina carinata, alata**   d'Orb., 1826, Tab. meth.; An. Sc. Nat. 7, p. 257, N:o 1, 2; Mod. 26.
    »   »   d'Orb., 1839, Cuba p. 20, t. 1, figg. 13—14.
    »   »   d'Orb., 1844, Iles Canaries p. 124, t. 1, figg. 5—6.
    »   »   Costa, 1854, Pal. Nap. 2, t. 16, fig. 25.
    »   »   Parker and Jones, 1860, For. Chellast. Qu. Journ. geol. Soc. 16, t. 19, figg. 13—14.
    »   **glabra**   Hken., 1875, Clav. Száb. Sch. p. 42, t. 13, fig. 14.
    »   **bursæformis**   Gümb., 1868, Nordalp. Eocän-q. K. Bayr. Ak. Abh. 1. 10. 2, p. 628, t. 1, fig. 51.
?**Frond. granulata, lucida**   Schwag., 1863, Jurass. Schicht.; Würtemb. Nat. Ver. Jhrhft. 21, p. 113, t. 4, figg. 25—26 (apertura rotundata; ad (d) p. 14 potius pertinet.).
Lingulina pygmæa   Rss., 1873, Grinitz' Elbthalgeb. Sachsen 2, p. 90, t. II. 20, fig. 23.
Frond. Nysti   Rss., 1863, Crag. d'Anvers; Bull. Ac. Belg. (2) 15, p. 148, t. 2, fig. 20.
    »   **linearis**   Phil., 1843, Tert. Versteiner. n. w. Deutschl. t. 1, fig. 32.

b) costata l. semicostata:

Lingulina costata   d'Orb., 1846, For. tert. Vienne, p. 62, t. 3, figg. 1—5.
    »   **multicostata**   Costa, 1855, Marna terz. Messina; Mem. Nap. 2, p. 146, t. 2, fig. 6.
    »   **costata** var. **seminuda** Hken., 1875, Clav. Száb. Sch. p. 41, t. 4, fig. 8.
    »   **carinata** var. **striata** Parker and Jones, 1860, For. Chellast.; Qu. Journ. geol. Soc. 16, t. 19, fig. 15.

Uvigerina pygmæa d'Orb.
Tab. IV, figg. 68—70.

This handsome species becomes pretty well developed on both the coralline-gravel and the chalk-ooze.

The neck of our form is nearly always provided with a lamina, like a screwthread twisted a half or whole turn round it, also a mark of its intimate relation to certain Nodosarinæ. It is not common.

Uvigerina Raphanus Park. and Jones is probably its »Sagrina»-development.

Figg. 68—69: the typical form.

Fig. 70: a very young, 3-chambered specimen.

a) costata:

Syn.	Uvigerina pygmæa	d'Orb., 1826, Tab. meth.; Acad. Sc. Nat. 7, p. 269, t. 12, figg. 8—9; Mod. 67.
»	nodosa	d'Orb., ibid. p. 269, N:o 3.
»	pygmæa	d'Orb., 1846, Bass. tert. Vienne, p. 190, t. 11, figg. 25—26.
»	bifurcata	d'Orb., 1839, Voy. Amer. 5, t. 7. fig. 17.
»	striata	Costa, 1854, Pal. Nap. 2, p. 266, t. 15, fig. 3.
»	pygmæa	Williams., 1858, Brit. rec. forf. p. 66, figg. 138—139.
»	»	Parker and Jones, 1857, For. Coast. of Norway; A. M. N. H. (2) 19. p. 297, t. 11, figg. 41—43 (forma emaciata).
»	»	Hke., 1875, For. Clav. Száb. Schichten p. 62, t. 7, fig. 4.
»	globosa	Karrer 1878, Foram. Luzon; Bolet. Comis. Mapa geol. Esp. 7. 2, p. 21, t. F, fig. 6.
Syn.	Uvigerina paucicosta	Costa, 1854, Pal. Nap. 2, p. 268, t. 22, fig. 7.
»	eocæna	Gumb., 1868, Nordalp. Eocän.; K. Bayr. Ak. Wiss. Abh. 1. 10. 2, p. 645, t. 2, fig. 78.
»	gemmæformis, nitidula, crassicostata	Schwag., 1866, Foss. For. Kar.-Nikob.; Novara Reise, geol. Th. 2. 2, p. 247—249, t. 7, figg. 92—94.
»	striatella	Rss., 1851, Tert. Sch. Oberschles.; Zeitschr. deutsch. geol. Ges. p. 159, t. 8, fig. 7.
»	rugulosa	Rss., 1863, Crag. d'Anvers; Bull. Ac. Belg. (2) 15, p. 153, t. 3, fig. 43.

a. β) forma »Sagrina»:

Uvigerina nodosa   Parker & Jones 1865, Northatl. and Arct. Oceans; Phil. Transact. 155, 1, t. 18, fig. 15.

Uvigerina (Sagrina) Raphanus Park. and Jones, ibid. t. 18, fig. 16—17.

?Dimorphina striata   Schwag., 1866, Foss. For. Kar.-Nikob.; Novara Reise, geol. Th. 2. 2, p. 251, t. 7, fig. 99.

?   »   elegans   Hken., 1875, Clav. Száb. Sch. p. 63, t. 7, fig. 9.

b) semiornata:

Uvigerina semiornata, urnula d'Orb., 1846, For. Bass. tert. p. 95, t. 4, figg. 21—24.

»   »   Ego., 1857, Miocän. Ortenburg; Leonh. u. Bronns Jhrb. 1857, p. 285, t. 11, figg. 17—18.

Uvigerina cochlearis, Brunnensis, Parkeri KARR., 1877, Hochqu. Wasserl.; Österr. geol. Reichsanst. Abh. 9, p. 385, t. 16, figg. 48—50.
„ pygmæa var. PARK. and JONES, 1865, Northatl. and Arct. Oceans; Phil. Trans. 155. 1, p. 363, t. 13, figg. 53—57.

b. β) Sagrinæformis:

Sagr. pulchella   D'ORB., 1839, Cuba p. 150, t. 1, figg. 23—24; 1846, For. Bass. tert. Vienne p. 252, t. 21, figg. 48—49 (textulariæformis).

c) angulosa:

Uvigerina angulosa   WILLIAMS., 1858, Brit. rec. forf. p. 67, fig. 140.
„ pygmæa var. angulosa PARK. and JONES, 1865, North. Atl. and arct. Oc.; Phil. Transact. 155. 1, p. 364, t. 13, fig. 58.
„ trigona   SEG., 1862, Rhizop. foss. Catania p. 26, t. 2, fig. 1; Acad. Gioenia Att. (2) 18.
„ cristata   MARSS., 1876, Rüg. Schreibekr.; Greifsw. Nat. Verein. Mitth. 1877—78, p. 150, t. 3, fig. 20.

Uvigerina Auberiana D'ORB.

Tab. IV, figg. 71—75.

Our form is often more smooth and more slender than D'ORBIGNY'S — also from the West Indies. *Uvigerina gracilis* Rss. from the »Septaria«-clay at Berlin is prickly, but seems newertheless to belong to this species, as also does *Uvig. proboscidea* SCHWAG. and *Uvig. farinosa* HKEN.; probably also *Uvig. canariensis* D'ORB.

One would be inclined to consider this form as a starved variety of *Uvig. pygmæa*, but there is a remarkable difference between them in the fineness and arrangement of their pore-canals, for whilst Uvig. pygmæa has them nearly as fine and closely set as Nodosarina, this form has a somewhat coarser poration, resembling in this respect some of the Buliminæ.

Loxostomum aculeatum EHRENBG. is a biserial Uvigerina with a strong tendency to become uniserial (= *Heterostomella* Rss.). If a form with its sides somewhat produced in angles and coarse spines — not uncommon on the chalkbottom, and represented by fig. 75 — is identic with EHRENBERG'S form, it will be impossible to establish any specific distinction between our *Uvig. Auberiana* and this *Loxostomum* of EHRENBERG.

Fig. 71—73 the smooth *Uvig. Auberiana* from the chalkooze; fig. 74 more magnified.

Fig. 75—75 b the *Loxostomum* form (= *Heterostomella aculeata* PARK. and JONES).

a) spinosa aut rugosa:

Syn. **Uvigerina Auberiana**   D'ORB., 1839, Cuba p. 106, t. 2, figg. 23—24.
„ asperula, Orbignyana CZJZ., 1847, Foss. for. Wien. Beck.; Haid. nat. Abh. 2. 1, p. 146, t. 13, figg. 14—17 (an forma præcedentis).
„ „   Rss., 1867, Steinsalzablag. Wieliczka; Wien. Ak. Sitz.-Ber. 1. 55, p. 93, t. 4, figg. 6—9.

Syn. Uvigerina aculeata   D'ORB., 1846, For. tert. Vienne p. 191, t. 11, figg. 27—28.
   »   hispida   SCHWAG., 1866, For. Kar.-Nikobar; Novara Reise, geol. Th. 2. 2, p. 249, t. 7, fig. 95 (an forma præcedentia).
   »   gracilis   RSS., 1851, Sept. Thon Berlin; Ztschr. deutsch. geol. Ges. 3, p. 77, t. 5, fig. 39.

a. β) forma »Sagrina»:

Sagrina rugosa   D'ORB., 1839, For. Craie bl. Paris; Mem. Soc. geol. France (2) 4, p. 47, t. 4, figg. 31—32.
Heterostomella rugosa   RSS., Wien. Ak. Sitz.-Ber. 52, p. 448.
Uvigerina proboscidea   SCHWAG., 1866, For. Kar.-Nikobar; Novara Reise, geol. Th. 2. 2, p. 250 t. 7, fig. 96.

b) lævis:

Uvigerina nodosa var. β   D'ORB., 1826, An. Sc. Nat. 7, p. 269.
   »   farinosa   HIKEN., 1875, Clav. Scab. Sch. p. 62, t. 7, fig. 6.
   »   canariensis   D'ORB., 1844, Iles Canaries p. 138, t. 1, figg. 25—27.

c) »Loxostomum» EHRENB.:

Loxostomum tumens   EHRENB., 1854, Microgeol. t. 28, figg. 25—26.
     »   aculeatum   EHRENB., ibid. t. 27, figg. 21—22; t. 30, fig. 16.
Heterostomella aculeata   PARK. and JONES, 1872, Nomenclat.; An. Nat. H. (4), 9, 10.
Sagraina aspera   MARSS., 1878, Rügen. Schreibekreide; Greifsw. Nat. Verein. Mitth. 1877—78, p. 157, t. 3, fig. 26.

Appendix.

Uvigerina porrecta   BRADY, 1879, Qu. Journ. micr. Sc. (n. ser.) 75, p. 274, t. 8, figg. 15—16.

   »   interrupta BRADY, ibid. p. 274, t. 8, figg. 17—18.

Uvigerina (Heterostomella) lævis PARK. and JONES.

Tab. IV, fig. 76.

It may be that this form after all — according to the authority of Messrs. PARKER and JONES — ought to be considered as a variety of *Heterostomella aculeata* EHRENB.; but as there is a great difference in the structure of the test it seems reasonable to distinguish it as species. In transmitted light our species is amber-coloured, very delicate and without pores, so that one would be disposed to refer it to the Miliolina-group.

A single specimen only has been met with on the chalk-bottom, in a pigmy state.
Fig. 76 seen in transmitted light.
Fig. 76 b the same more enlarged.

Syn. Loxostomum longirostre EHRENB., 1854, Microgeol. t. 32, fig. 22.
Heterostomella aculeata β lævis PARK. and JONES, 1872, Nomenclature foramf.; A. M. N. H. (4) 9 and 10.

Uvigerina dimorpha Park. and Jones.
Tab IV, figg. 77—81.

Though the designation of »dimorpha« applied to a Sagrina, which genus has been founded on such a character, does not imply any specific distinction, we still retain Messrs. PARKERS and JONES' name for this form, being by no means inclined to enrich our nomenclature.

Its early uvigerina-stage is often reduced to a couple of chambers, and it would sometimes be hard to recognise the small egg-shaped bodies without any traces of septal marks as Uvigerina, if the somewhat prolonged mouth-necks did not betray its affinity to this genus.

Our form is highly agglutinant, constructing its shell of the finest chalkdebris and detritus. Its original form is mostly narrow cylindrical, but it seems to accumulate with age a thick deposit of loosely cemented detritus, so that it becomes egg-shaped with a somewhat rough and chalky surface.

It seems likely, that this species has been confounded by some authors with »Clavulina« forms. *Clavulina cylindrica* IKEN. and KARRER is probably identical with it, perhaps also *Glandulina rudis* of COSTA.

It is not uncommon on the chalkbottom and attains 3—4 mm. in length.

Figg. 77—78: the slender form.
Figg. 79—80: the eggshaped one.
Fig. 81 apertural side.

Syn. **Uvigerina dimorpha** (Sagrina) PARK. and JONES, 1865, Phil. trans. 155. 1, t. 18, fig. 18.
    Glandulina rudis   COSTA, 1855, Marna terz. Messina; Mem. Nap. 2, p. 142, t. 1, fig. 12.
    Clavulina cylindrica   HAL., 1875, For. Clav. Szab. Seb. p. 18, t. 1, fig. 8.
     »   »   KARR., 1877, k. k. österr. geol. Reichsanst. Abh. 9, p. 373, t. 16, fig. 4.
? **Haplophragmium verruculosum** GÜMB., 1871, Ulmer Cem. Mergel; Münch. Ak. Sitz.-Ber. 1, p. 63, t. 1, fig. 1.
? **Globulina fragaria**   GÜMB., ibid. p. 68, t. 1, fig. 16.

Appendix.

Sagrina virgula   BRAD., 1879, Notes on Ret. Rhizop. »Challeng.« Exp.; Qu. Journ. Micr. Sc. (n. Ser.) 75, p. 275, t. 8, figg. 19—21.

     »   **divaricata**   BRAD., ibid. p. 276, t. 8, figg. 22—24.

Bulimina pupoides D'ORB.
Tab. IV, figg. 82—94.

A very variable species, the small differences consisting in the chambers being more or less inflated and in the different degrees of overlapping, the chamber-wall being often very much lengthened out backwards so as to enclose a smaller or greater part of the preceding chambers. It is not compatible with a philosophical arrangement to attach to all these individual modifications varietal and even specific designations, as has been done by some authors.

Our form is remarkable for its extremely thin, glassy test. Owing to its extreme tenuity one or two of the last chambers often become detached from the rest, whence mature specimens in perfect condition are scarce. Sometimes the first chambers are provided with a few delicate folds in transmitted light looking as straight, bright streaks radiating from the primordial chamber.

Our specimens agree mostly with *Bul. pyrula*, *ovula* and *ovata* D'ORB.

The spinous form figg. 82—83 may more properly be referred to another species on account of its different poration, but being very young and scarce, there has been little chance of comparing and identifying it with other forms. It is nearly identical with *Polymorphina aculeata* EHRENBERG.

Bul. pupoides is not very common in the chalkooze.

Figg. 82—83 the aculeate form.
Fig. 82 b the same as 82 more enlarged.
Figg. 84—85: nearly the typical Bul. pupoides D'ORB.
Fig. 86, more blunt form approaching *Bul. pyrula* D'ORB.
Fig. 87: very small specimen, enlarged.
Fig. 88: with the chambers spirally set in a more regular row, approaching *Bul. arctica* D'ORB.; 88 b the same more magnified.
Fig. 89: small specimen.
Fig. 90: pigmy form with extenuated chambers, approaching the habitus of »*Virgulina*», and with radiating folds.
Figg. 91—93: very young specimens seen from above with radiating folds.
Fig. 94: slender form, between *Bul. pupoides* and *Bul.* (*Virgulina*) *squamosa* D'ORB.

Syn.	Bulimina	brevis	D'ORB., 1839, For. Craie bl. Paris; Mém. Soc. géol. France (2) 4. p. 41. t. 4, figg. 13—14.
	»	auriculata, turgida	BAILEY, 1850, Micr. Exam. of Soundings; Smiths. Contrib. 2, Art. 3, p. 12, fig. 25—30.
	»	pyrula	D'ORB., 1846, For. Bass. tert. Vienne p. 184, t. 11, figg. 9—10.
?	»	intermedia	RSS., 1845, Böhm. Kreide 1, p. 37, t. 13, fig. 71.
?	»	»	RSS., 1850, Kreidemerg. Lemberg; Haid. Nat. Abh. 4. 1, p. 39, t. 3, fig. 11.
	»	pustulosa	COSTA. 1854, Pal. Nap. 2, p. 264, t. 15, fig. 8.
	»	ovulum	RSS., 1845, Böhm. Kreidef. 1, p. 37, t. 8, fig. 37; t. 13, fig. 73.

Syn. **Bulimina ovulum** Rss., 1850, Kreidemerg. Lemberg; Haid. Nat. Abh. 4. 1, p. 38, t. 3, fig. 9.
» »   Alth., 1849, Umgeb. Lemb.; Haid. Nat. Abh. 3. 2, p. 264, t. 13, fig. 18.
» **Murchisoniana** d'Orb., 1839, For. Craie bl. Paris; Mem. Soc. geol. France (2) 4, p. 41, t. 4, figg. 15, 15'.
» »   Rss., 1845, Böhm. Kreide 1. p. 37, t. 8, figg. 69, 72, t. 13, fig. 70.
» **subsphaerica** Rss., ibid. 2. p. 109, t. 24, fig. 52.
» **imperatrix, incrassata** Karr., 1868, Mioc. For. Kostej; Wien. Ak. Sitz.Ber. 1. 58. p. 176, 177, t. 4, figg. 11—12.
» **socialis** Bornem., 1855, Sept. Thon Hermsdorf; Ztschr. deutsch. geol. Ges. 7. p. 342, t. 16, fig. 10.
» **pitocusana** Costa, 1854, Pal. Nap. 2, t. 15, fig. 5.
» **elipsoides** Costa, ibid. p. 265, t. 15, fig. 9.
» **Preslii** var. **pyrula** Park. and Jones, 1865, North. Atl. and Arct. Oc.; Phil. Trans. 155. 1, p. 372, t. 15, figg. 8—9.
» **caudigera** d'Orb., 1826, An. Sc. Nat. 7, p. 270, N:o 16. Mod. 68.
» **marginata** Park. and Jones, 1857, (partim) For. Norway; A. N. H. 19, t. 11, figg. 36—38.
» **buccinoides** Egger, 1857, Mioc. Ortenburg; Leonh. u. Bronn. Jhrb. 1857, p. 282, t. 10, figg. 9—11.
» **inconstans** Egger, ibid. p. 283, t. 12, figg. 1—3.
» **truncata**, d'Orbignyi Rss., 1845, Böhm. Kreide 1, p. 37, 38, t. 8, fig. 73, t. 13, fig. 74.
?**Pleurostomella brevis** Schwag., 1866, Foss. Foramf. Kar.-Nikobar; Nov. Reise, geol. Th. 2. 2, p. 239, t. 6, fig. 81.
Bulimina declivis Rss., 1863, Sept. Thon Offenbach; Wien. Ak. Sitz.-Ber. 1. 48, p. 55, t. 6, fig. 70; t. 7, fig. 71.
Robertina austriaca Rss., 1849, Neue Foramf.; Wien. Ak. Dkschr. 1. 1, p. 375, t. 47, fig. 15.
Bulimina ovulum d'Orb., 1839, Voy. Am. merid. 5, p. 50, t. 1, figg. 10—11.
» **ovata** d'Orb., 1846, For. Bass. tert. Vienne; p. 185, t. 11, figg. 13—14.
» »   Parker and Jones, 1865, North. Atl. and Arct. Oc.; Phil. Trans. 155. 1, p. 374, t. 17, fig. 67.
» »   Stache, 1865, tert. Merg. Whsingar. Haf.; Nov. Reise, geol. 1. 2, p. 266, t. 24, fig. 14.
» **pupula, aperta, propinqua** Stache, ibid. p. 265, 266, 267, t. 24, figg. 13, 15, 16.
» **pupoides** d'Orb., 1846, For. tert. Vienne, p. 185, t. 11, figg. 11, 12.
» »   Williams., 1858, Brit. rec. Foramf. p. 62, figg. 124—125.
» **pedunculata, mamillata** Costa, 1854, Pal. Nap. 2, p. 334, 335, t. 18, figg. 13, 16.
» **elongata** Iken., 1875, For. Clav. Szab. Sch., p. 61, t. 10, fig. 7.
» **elegans** d'Orb., 1826, Tabl. meth., Ann. Sc. Nat. 7, p. 270, Mod. 9.
» **obtusa** d'Orb., 1839, For. Craie blanche Paris; Mem. Soc. geol. Fr. 4, p. 39, t. 4, figg. 5—6.
» **affinis** d'Orb., 1839, Cuba. foramf. p. 105, t. 2, figg. 25—26.
? » **spec.** Schwag., 1863, Jurass. Seh. loc. cit. p. 136, t. 7, fig. 4.
? » **tortilis** Rss., 1861, Grünsand N. Jersey; Wien. Ak. Sitz.-Ber. 1. 44, p. 338, t. 8, fig. 3.
» **pupoides** var. **fusiformis** Williams., 1858, Rec. For. p. 63, figg. 129—130.
» **acuta, acicula** Costa 1854, Pal. Nap. 2, p. 336, t. 13, fig. 25, t. 22, figg. 6, 8.
» **tenera** Rss., 1867, Steinsalzablag. Wielicska; Wien. Ak. Sitz.-Ber. 1. 55, p. 94, t. 4, figg. 11—12.
» **acuta** Rss., 1850, Kreidem. Lemberg; Haid. Nat. Abh. 4. 1, p. 38, t. 3, fig. 8.
» **uva** Röm., 1838, Nordd. tert. Meeressand; Leonh. u. Bronn. Jhrb. 1838, p. 387, t. 3, fig. 43.
» **cylindrica** Röm., ibid. p. 387, t. 3, fig. 44. (an Bul. elongata d'Orb. vide Append. b).

Syn. Bulimina Puschi   Rss., 1850, Kreidem. Lemberg; Haid. Nat. Abh. 4. 1, p. 37, t. 3, fig. 6.
    »   imbricata   Rss., ibid. p. 38, t. 3, fig. 7.
    »   scabriuscula   Rss. 1860, For Crag. v. Antwerp.; Wien. Ak. Sitz.-Ber. 42, p. 360, t. 2, fig. 13.
    »   squamigera   d'Orb., 1844, Iles Canaries, p. 137, t. 1, figg. 22—24 (in »Virg.« squamosam transiens).

b) spinulosa:

Bulimina patagonica   d'Orb., 1839, Voy. Am. merid. 5, p. 50, t. 1, figg. 8—9.
    »   pupoides var. spinulosa Williams., 1858, Brit. rec. Forf. p. 62, fig. 128.
    »   aculeata   (Cajz.) Rss., 1849, Neue For. österr. tert. Beck.; Wien. Ak. Dkschr. 1. 1, p. 374, t. 47, fig. 13.
Polymorphina? aculeata   Ehrenb., 1854, Microgeol., t. 19, fig. 85.

c) marginata et spinose-marginata (an species distincta):

Bulimina marginata   d'Orb., 1826, Tabl. meth., Ann. Sc. Nat. 7, p. 269, t. 12, figg. 10—12.
    »   pupoides var. marginata Williams., 1858, Brit. rec. Forf. p. 62, figg. 126—127.
    »   marginata (part.) Park. and Jones, 1857, For. Coast. of Norway; An. Mag. Nat. Hist. 19, t. 11, figg. 39—40.
    »   Presli var. marginata, var. aculeata Park. and Jones, 1865, For. N. Atl. and Arct. Oc.; Phil. Trans. 155. 1, p. 372, 373, t. 15, figg. 10—11; t. 17, figg. 68—70.
    »   spinosa   Seg., 1862, Rhizopod. foss. d. Catania p. 23, t. 1, fig. 8 (sep. de Accad. Gioenia Atti (2) 18).
    »   etnea   Seg. ibid. p. 24, t. 1, fig. 9.
    »   acanthia   Costa, 1854, Pal. Nap. 2, p. 335, t. 13, figg. 35—36.
?   »   serrata   Bailey, 1850, Micr. Examin. of Soundings; Smithson. contrib. knowl. 2, Art. 3, p. 12, figg. 32—34.

e) carinata vel spinose alata:

Textul. echinata   d'Orb., 1826, Tabl. meth., Ann. Sc. Nat. 7, p. 263. N:o 24.
Bulimina trilobata   d'Orb., ibid. p. 269. N:o 6.
    »   aculeata   d'Orb., ibid. p. 269. N:o 7.

f) costata vel seminuda:

Bulimina inflata   Seg., 1862, Rhizopod. foss. Catan. p. 25, fig. 10 (Sep. Atti Accad. Gioenia (2) 18.
    »   »   Schwag., 1866, Kar.-Nikobar.; Novara Reise, geol. Th. 2. 2, p. 246. t. 7, fig. 91.
    »   Buchiana   Rss., 1867, Steinsalzablag. Wieliczka; Wien. Ak. Sitz.-Ber. 1. 55, p. 95, t. 4, fig. 10.
    »   Buchiana   d'Orb., 1846, For. tert. Vienne, p. 186, t. 11, figg. 15—18.
    »   Presli var. Buchiana Park. and Jones, 1865, North. Atl. and Arct. Oc.; Phil. Trans. 155. 1, p. 374, t. 17, fig. 71.
    »   truncana   Gümb., 1868, Nordalp. Eocän.; K. Bayr. Ak. Wiss. Abh. 1. 10. 2, p. 644, t. 1, fig. 77.
    »   »   Hken., 1875, For. Clav. Száb. Sch., p. 61, t. 7, fig. 5.

Appendix.

Plerumque agglutinans.

a) gibbosa:

Valvulina gibbosa   d'Orb., 1839, For. Craie bl. Paris; Mem. Soc. geol. Fr. (2) 4, p. 38, t. 4, figg. 1—2.
  » quadribullata v. Hagen, 1842, Rugen. Kreideverst., Leonh. u. Broun. Jhrb. 1842, p. 570.
Globigerina confluens v. Hagen, ibid. p. 571.
Bulimina obesa   Rss., 1850, Kreidemerg. Lemberg; Haid. Nat. Abh. 4. 1, p. 40, t. 3, fig. 12, t. 4, fig. 1.
Ataxophragmium globulare Rss., 1864, Oberoligocän.; Wien. Ak. Sitz.-Ber. 1. 50, p. 449, t. 1, fig. 2 (an B. variabilis d'Orb.).
  » arenaceum Karr., 1865, Wien. Sandstein; Wien. Ak. Sitz.-Ber. 52, p. 495, fig. 9.
  » Prestli Rss., 1845, Böhm. Kreide 1, p. 38, t. 13, fig. 72.
  » » Rss., 1850, Kreidemerg. Lemberg; Haid. Nat. Abh. 4. 1, p. 39, t. 3, fig. 10.
  » » Rss., 1862, Nordd. Hils u. Gault; Wien. Ak. Sitz.-Ber. 1. 46, p. 31.
?Bulimina rimosa   Marss., 1878, Rüg. Schreibekr.; Greifsw. Nat. Verein. Mitth. 1877—78, p. 153, t. 3, fig. 21 (forsan Lituola).

b) elongata:

Bulimina elongata   d'Orb., 1846, For. tert. Vienne, p. 187, t. 11, figg. 19—20.
Ataxophragmium oblongum Rss., 1865, Feuerstein-Kreide Kanara See; Wien. Ak. Sitz.-Ber. 52, p. 458, fig. 2.
  » magdalidiforme, subovale, laceratum Schwag., 1866, For. Kar.-Nikob.; Novara Reise, geol. Th. 2. 2, p. 193, 194, t. 4, figg. 1—3.

c) variabilis:

Bulimina variabilis   d'Orb., 1839, For. Craie bl. Par.; Mem. Soc. geol. Fr. (2) 4, p. 40, t. 4, figg. 9—12.
  » » Rss., 1845, Böhm. Kreide 1, p. 37, t. 8, figg. 56, 76, 77.
Ataxophragm. simile Karr., 1868, Mioc. For. Faun. Kostej; Wien. Ak. Sitz.-Ber. 1. 58, p. 126, t. 1, fig. 1.
  » humile Karr., 1878, Foramf. Luzon.; Bolet. Comis. Mapa del España. 7. 2, p. 11, t. E, fig. 3.

Bulimina elegantissima d'Orb.

Tab. IV, figg. 95—98.

I am unable to find any nearer type for our form than *Bul. elegantissima*, particularly its variety *Rob. arctica* d'Orb., though it does not quite agree with any of them. But it is either too young or too pygmean to be more accurately defined. The principal feature by which it is distinguished from Bul. pupoides is the extreme fineness and close arrangement of the pore-canals, in which respect it is scarcely surpassed by Nodosarinæ. The septal bands are generally very thick, somewhat amber-coloured in transmitted light.

Some of EHRENBERGS *Strophoconi* seem to be identical with our form.
It is not common in the chalk-ooze, seldom attaining more than 0,20 mm. in length.
Fig. 95: small specimen.
Fig. 96: the same seen in transmitted light.
Figg. 97—98: two other very small specimens.

Syn. Bulimina elegantissima D'ORB., 1839, Voy. Am. merid. 5, p 51, t. 7, figg. 13—14.
   »   »   WILLIAMS., 1858, Brit. rec. For. p. 64, figg. 134—135.
   »   Prosli var. elegantissima PARK. and JONES, 1865, N. Atl. and arct. Oc.; Phil. Transact. 155. 1, p. 375, t. 15, figg. 12—17.
   »   elegantissima var. BRADY, 1878, An. Mag. Nat. Hist. (5) 1, p. 436, t. 21. fig. 12.
   »   subteres   BRADY, 1881, Qu. Journ. micr. Sc. (n. s.) 21, p. 55.
Rotalina bulimoides   RSS., 1851. Sept. Thon Berlin; Ztschr. deutsch. geol. Ges. 3, p. 77, t. 5, fig. 38 (ad hanc pertinens sec. PARKER and JONES 1872.
Robertina arctica   D'ORB., 1846, For. Bass. tert. Vienne, p. 203, t. 21, figg. 37—38 (sec. PARKER and JONES).
?   »   obliqua   D'ORB., 1839, For. Craie blanc. Par.; Mem. Soc. geol. Fr. 4, p. 40, t. 4, figg. 7—8.

Bulimina (Virgulina) squamosa D'ORB.

Tab. IV, figg. 99—108.

I am not able to trace any sort of *essential* distinction between *Bul.* (*Virgulina*) *squamosa* D'ORB. and *Bul.* (*Virgulina*) *Schreibersiana* CZJZ. To judge by the representations of the latter given by different authors all agree in the shape and setting of the chambers, being not quite so regular as in *Bul. squamosa typica*, which seems to be more biserial in its growth, whilst the CZJZEKS form shews some tendency to a multiserial arrangement.

The boundary between this species and *Bul.* (*Bolivina*) *punctata* D'ORB. is far from being distinct. And yet Mr. D'ORBIGNY found himself compelled to distinguish these two species as two *genera*.

Bul. squamigera D'ORB. from Canary Islands comes very near to this species and may be more allied to this than to *Bul. pupoides* D'ORB.

The variation of *Bul. squamosa* consists chiefly in the greater or less flatness and breadth of the chambers and their greater or less elongation backwards. There is also a slight difference in the size and arrangement of the pores and in the transparency of the shell.

All our forms are from the chalk-bottom, where they are not unfrequent.

Figg. 99—103: comes next to *Virgulina Schreibersiana* CZJZ.; it is generally of a dusky hue, so that the pores are scarcely visible in transmitted light. It is not uncommon and attains a pretty good size.

Fig. 104: more textularia-formed, of the same dull hue in transmitted light as the preceding.

Fig. 105: approaching *Bul.* (*Boliv.*) *punctata* D'ORB.

Figg. 106—107: next to the typical *Virgulina squamosa* d'Orb. Our form is quite hyaline and very scantely provided with moderate sized pores. It is probably a pigmyform.

Fig. 108: broader, with the chambers less produced.

a) minus compressa, interdum fusiformis:

Syn. **Virgulina squamosa**   d'Orb., 1826, Tabl. meth., Ann. Sc. Nat. 7, p. 267, Nro 1, Mod. 64.
»   **punctata**   d'Orb., 1839, Cuba p. 139, t. 1, figg. 35—36.
»   **squamosa**   Röm., 1838, Nordd. tert. Meeress.; Leonh. u. Bronn. Jhrb. 1838, p. 386, t. 3, fig. 39.
Bulimina Preslii var. **Virg. squamosa** Park. and Jones, 1865, N. Atl. and Arct. Oc.; Phil. Trans. 155. 1, p. 375, t. 15, figg. 19—20.
Virgulina pertusa   Rss., 1860, Crag. Antwerp.; Wien. Ak. Sitz.-Ber. 42, p 362, t. 2, fig. 16.
»   »   Fric's Mod. 65.
»   **tegulata**   Rss., 1845, Böhm. Kreide 1, p. 40, t. 13, fig. 81.
»   **Schreibersiana** Czjz., 1847, For. Wien. Beck.; Haid. Nat. Abh. 2. 1, p. 147, t. 13, figg. 18—21.
Bulimina marginata var. **attenuata** Park. and Jones, 1857, For. Coast of Norw.; An. Nat. H. 19. t. 2, fig. 35.
»   **Preslii** var. **Schreibersii** Park. and Jones, 1865, N. Atl. and Arct. Oc.; Phil. Trans. 155. 1, p. 375, t. 15, fig. 18; t. 17, figg. 72—73.
»   **compressa**   Bail., 1850, Microsc. Exam. of Soundings; Smithson. Contrib. 2, figg. 35—37.
»   **cylindracea**   Costa, 1854, Pal. Nap. 2, t. 15, fig. 10.
»   **pupoides** var. **compressa** Williams., 1858, Brit. rec. forf. p. 63, fig. 131 (forma valde elongata).
Strophoconus nominib. variis Ehrenb., 1854, Mikrogeol. t. 20, figg. 2—4; t. 26, fig. 25; t. 28, fig. 27; t. 31, figg. 21, 23, 24, 25, 32—34.
Virgulina Schreibersi   Hken., 1875, Clav. Száb. Sch., p. 63, t. 7, fig. 15.

b) magis dilatata, cameris valde productis:

Strophoconus Hemprichii Ehrenb., 1854, Microgeol. t. 24, fig. 32.

c) magis compressa, Bolivinæformis h. e. textularioides (Buliminæ punctatæ valde propinqua):

Syn. **Virgulina Reussii**   Gein., Rss., 1845, Böhm. Kreide. 1, p. 40, t. 8, fig. 61.
»   »   Rss., 1865, Kreide am Kanara See; Wien. Ak. Sitz.-Ber. 52, t. 45, fig. 7.
Bolivina textilarioides   Rss., 1862, Nordd. Hils u. Gault; Wien. Ak. Sitz.-Ber. 1. 46, p. 81, t. 10, fig. 1.
»   **antiqua**   d'Orb., 1846, For. tert. Vienne, p. 240, t. 14, figg. 11—13.
»   **elongata**   Karr., 1878, For. Luzon; Bolet. Comis. Mapa geol. del España, 7. 2, p. 23, t. F, fig. 8.
»   »   Hken., 1875, For. Clav. Száb. Sch. p. 65, t. 7, fig. 14.
Polymorph. asparagus,   Grammost. macilentum Ehrenb., 1854, Microgeol. t. 27, figg. 14—16; t. 29, figg. 30—31
?Bolivina tenuis   Marsson, 1877, Rügen. Schreibekr.; Greifsw. Nat. Verein. Mitth. 1877—78, p. 156, t. 3, fig. 23 (an B. punctata).

Syn. **Bolivina tegulata**   Rss., 1850, Kreidemergel Lemberg; Heid. Nat. Abh. 4. 1, p. 65, t. 4, fig. 12.

d) striata:

Bolivina nobilis   Hken., 1875, For. Clav. Száb. Sch. p. 65, t. 15, fig. 4.
» **semistriata**   Hken., ibid. p. 65, t. 7, fig. 13.

Bulimina squamosa var. subsquamosa Egger.
Tab. IV, figg. 109—113.

This form, which is not to be identified with *Virg. subsquamosa* Egger without some hesitation, seems to occupy a position intermediate between d'Orbigny's genus *Bulimina* and his *Virgulina*; but it is more nearly allied to the latter than appears at first sight.

The generally slender and elongated *Virg. squamosa* becomes sometimes short and broad (see fig. 103) and then is hardly distinguishable from the variety in question.

Its shell-substance like the preceding has in transmitted light the same dusky hue, being, as it were, incorporated with fine dust, which almost hides the pores and presents a strong contrast to the clear, transparent shells of most of its nearest congeners. The pores are more wide apart than in *Bul. pupoides*.

The tendency of the early chambers to coil up is of no specific importance and is often wanting. Such broad forms resemble somewhat *Cassidulina oblonga* Rss. Williamson has described a *Bul. pupoides* var. *convoluta*, which may possibly belong to this variety (Brit. recent foramf. p. 63, figg. 132—133).

It is always of small size and not uncommon on the chalk-bottom.

Fig. 109: *a*. Textulariaformed; *b*. the same more enlarged.

Figg. 110—113: two somewhat coiled specimens.

Syn. **Virgulina subsquamosa**   Egger, 1857, Miocän. v. Ortenburg; Leonh. u. Bronn. Jhrb. 1857, p. 295, t. 12, figg. 19—21.
» **tenuis**   Seg., 1862, Rhizopod. foss. Catania p. 28, t. 2, fig. 2 (Accad. Gioenia Atti (2) 18).
Strophoconus? torotiuscula   Fourn, l. cit. p. 292, t. 12, figg. 30—32.
» **Hemprichii**   Ehrenb. (partim) t. 28, figg. 28—30; t. 29, fig. 38; t. 32, figg. 18—20?.
Grammostomum   Ehrenb., ibid. t. 24, figg. 28—23.

Bulimina (Bolivina) punctata d'Orb.
Tab. IV, figg. 114—126.

This is the most Textularialike of the Buliminæ. Its principal difference from *Bul. squamosa* should consist in the smaller degree of obliquity in its septa; of course a very vague mark of distinction among members of such a class as Rhizopodes.

Bolivina textularioides Rss., *Bol. elongata* Karr., *Bol. antiqua* d'Orb., *Virgul. Reussii* Geis. are all intermediate between *Bul. punctata* and *squamosa*.

The shape of the shell is liable to great variations according to the greater or less degree of convexity of the septa and marginal walls, the breadth of the chambers and its gradual or more rapid increase in size. Sometimes the surface is provided with faint hexagonal impressions like those found on Globigerinæ. Generally it has coarser pore-canals than its congeners, the pores equalling in size those of some Planorbulinæ.

The very faint longitudinal folds which some times adorn our form can scarcely be of any, even varietal, importance, being often wanting.

Figg. 114—115: the narrow form of *Bul. punctata*, sometimes provided with a few narrow folds. It is the same as *Grammostomum elegans* EHRENB., *Brizalina onariensis* COSTA, *Boliv. plicata* D'ORB. & MÖB. Generally this has finer pores than the var. *dilatata*. 115 b: the same more magnified.

Figg. 116—123: the commonest form of *Bul. punctata*.

Figg. 124—126: the broad form, called *dilatata* Rss.

It is very common on the chalk-bottom but it is of very small size.

a) minus dilatata:

Sys.	**Bolivina punctata**	D'ORB., 1843, Voy. Am. mer. for. p. 63, t. 8, figg. 10—12.
»	incrassata	Rss., 1850, Kreidemerg. Lemberg; Haid. Nat. 4. 1, p. 45, t. 4, fig 13.
»	catanensis	SEG., Rhizopod. Catania p. 29, t. 2, fig. 3; Accad. Gioenia Atti (2) 18.
»	punctata	BRADY, 1864, Rhizopod. Shetl.; Trans. Lin. Soc. 24, p. 468, t. 48, fig. 9.
»	antiqua	EGGER, 1857, Miocän. Ortenburg; Leonh. u. Bronn. Jhrb. 1857. p. 294, t. 12, figg. 22—26.
»	Presli var. punctata	PARK. and JONES, 1865, North. Atl. and Arct. Oc.; Phil. Transact. 155. 1, p. 376, t. 17, fig. 74.
»	punctata	PARK. and JONES, 1866, Crag. For.; Pal. Soc. 19, t. 3, figg. 3—4.
»	ligularia	SCHWAG., 1866, For. Kar.-Nikobar.; Novara Reise, geol. Th. 2. 2, p. 255, t. 7, fig. 102.
	Textil. jurassica	GÜMB., 1862, Streitenb. Schwammlag.; Württemb. Nat. Verein. Jhrhft. 21, p. 228, t. 4, fig. 17.
	Grammostomum laterale, polystigma, elegans, plica, aciculatum	EHRENS., 1854, Microgeol. t. 19, figg. 83—84; t. 20, fig. 7; t. 21, figg. 84, 85; t. 20, fig. 10.
	Proroporus argus	EHRENB., ibid. t. 20, fig. 8.
	Textul. linearis	EHRENB., 1854, Microgeol. t. 24, figg. 16—17.
	Nominib. variis	EHRENB., ibid. t. 25, figg. 16—20; t. 29, figg. 26—27.
	Grammost. cribrosum	EHRENB., ibid. t. 24, fig. 19.
	Brizalina œnariensis	COSTA, 1854, Pal. Nap. 2, p. 297, t. 15, figg. 1—2.
	Bolivina punctata	MÖB., 1880, Maur. u. Seychell. p. 94, t. 9, figg. 9—10.

b) magis dilatata:

	Bolivina dilatata	Rss., 1849, Neue For. Österr.; Wien. Ak. Dkschr. 1, *, p. 381, t. 48, fig. 15.
»	reticulata	HKEN., 1875, For. Clav. Stab. Sch. p. 65, t. 15, fig. 6.
»	linearis	MARSS., 1877, Rügen. Schreibekreide; Greifsw. Nat. Verein. Mitth. 1877—78, p. 155, t. 3, fig. 22.
	Grammost. nom. var.	EHRENB., 1854, Microgeol. t. 21, figg. 82, 86, 87; t.24, figg. 20—24; t. 27, figg. 13, 20; t. 29, fig. 23; t. 32, figg. 15—19.
	Bolivina thebaica	MÖB., 1880, Meeresfaun. Maurit. u. Scych. p. 95, t. 9, fig. 11.

c) striata vel costulata:

Syn. **Bolivina plicata**		D'ORB., 1843, Voy. Am. mer. 5, p. 62, t. 8, figg. 4—7.
»	»	MÖB., 1880, Beiträge z. Meeresfaun. Mauritius u. Seychell. p. 95, t. 9, figg. 12—13.
»	pusilla	SCHWAG., 1866, For. Kar.-Nikobar; Novara Reise, geol. Th. 2. 2, p. 254, t. 7, fig. 101.
? »	plicata	BRADY, 1870, Brack. water foram.; A. M. N. H. (4) 6, p. 302, t. 12, fig. 7 (as B. costata D'ORB.).
Grammost. sulcatum		EHRENB., 1854, Microgeol. t. 20, fig. 9.

Bulimina punctata var. decurrens EHRENB.

Tab. IV, fig. 127.

A handsome form not uncommon on the chalk-bottom and of pretty good size. It may be more allied to *Bul. squamosa* than to *punctata*.

Fig. 127: Bul. punctata var. decurrens; 127 b.: the same more magnified.

Syn. **Grammost. decurrens**		EHRENB., 1854, Microgeol. t. 30, fig. 17.
Bolivina decurrens		MARSS., 1877, Rügen. Schreibekr.; Greifsw. Nat. Verein. Mitth. 1877—1878, p. 156, t. 3. fig. 24.
»	**Beyrichi**	RSS., 1851, Sept. Thon Berlin; Zeitschr. deutsch. geol. Ges. 3, p. 83, t. 6, fig. 51.
? »	**Beyrichi**	HÆK., 1875, For. Clav. Szab. Sch. p. 64, t. 7, figg. 11—12.

Bulimina costata D'ORB.

Tab. IV, figg. 129—132.

Although our form exhibits some differences from *Bolivina costata* D'ORB. in being more closely ribbed and having the costæ often produced to short spines, particularly on the edges — as in »*Bulim. inflata*» SCHWAG. —, it cannot be entitled to rank of distinct species. It is more or less compressed; the pores are of the same size and scattered disposition as is often found in *Bul. punctata* D'ORB. In its outlines it often has some resemblance to *Sagrina pulchella* D'ORB. The aperture is very narrow and difficult to bring into view.

It is very common in the chalk-ooze, always of a pigmy size.

Fig. 129: very small specimen, highly magnified.
Fig. 130: more developed.
Fig. 131: edge view of the same; **132: apertural side.**

Syn. **Bolivina costata**		D'ORB., 1839, Voy. Amer. mer. p. 62, t. 8, figg 8—9; 1846, For. Bass. tert. Vienne p. 239, t. 21, figg. 44—45.
Bulimina Presli var. Boliv. costata		PARK. and JONES, 1865, N. Atl. and Arct. Oc.; Phil. Transact. 155. 1. p. 376, t. 17, fig. 75.
?**Bolivina subangularis**		BRADY, 1881, Notes on retic. Rhizopod.; Qu. Journ. Micr. Sc. (N. Ser.) 81. p. 59.

Textularia sagittula Defr.
Tab. IV, figg. 133—158.

The species of Textulariæ are not less difficult to define within proper boundaries than are Nodosarinæ. It is obvious that many gradations in the flatness or in the distention of the chambers will make the whole liable to numberless variations, from a compressed lanceolate to a quite conical shape with either straight or sinuous margins and contours.

The shellsubstance is also variable in character being sometimes more translucent and glossy, but it is usually agglutinated of calcareous or siliceous debris. In the whole range of known Textulariæ forms it is therefore not easy to distinguish besides the Gaudryina- and Verneuilina-forms more than 3 or 4 species; that is to say:

1. Textularia sagittula Defr. or agglutinans d'Orb., including such forms as: Textul. pygmæa, Mariæ, carinata, cuneiformis, Baudouiana, conica, caribœa, aciculata, agglutinans, Candeiana etc. d'Orb. and a long list of names from Reuss and others.
2. Textularia gibbosa d'Orb. should be another but, it is a very ill defined species; its chambers being more inflated.
3. A third species is Textularia trochus d'Orb.; this has some tendency to become »Cuneoline».
4. The fourth species is Textularia pennatula Batsch., apparently representing an intermediate form between the textularioid Bulininæ and the real Textulariæ.

All these species have their respective Bigenerinæ forms.

Whether »Gaudryina» and »Verneuilina» are to be considered as »varieties», or »species», is a question that we are not yet prepared to settle, as our collections are wanting in intermediate forms.

The transverse section of our form varies from narrow oval or pointed elliptical to nearly orbicular. The more »sagittular» form exhibits often raised bands along the sutures. In older specimens the surface is more chalky and uneven. All forms that we have met with are agglutinant; the shell being compactly built up of very fine chalk-debris and dust. Very young ones are semitransparent, presenting a deep brown tint in transmitted light; the fine granular texture of the shell concealing the pores. It appears from many instances in our collection, that whenever the Textularia-stadium becomes more developed, the Nodosarina growth is reduced to only one or two chambers; and on the other hand, whenever the Nodosarina-stadium has a high development the textularia-part is found to be stunted and often reduced to a few chambers. These fluctuations of development give rise to a number of varietal Bigenerina-forms. All our forms are composed solely of calcareous matter.

Figg. 133—136: intermediate form between d'Orbigny's Textul. agglutinans and Textul. sagittula, and provided with one »Nodosarina»-chamber, the first step towards forma »Bigenerina».

Figg. 137—139: the same more flattened and *sagittula*-like.

Figg. 140—143: is the typical Textul. agglutinans d'Orb.; it cannot properly be distinguished from Textul. sagittula Defr.

Figg. 144—146: a very compressed and often serrated form; it has received many names: *Textul. carinata, Maria, cuneiformis* d'Orb., *Plecanium serratum, spinulosum, pectinatum* etc. Rss. It is sometimes very much flattened out and has then again been loaded with a number of new names. The gradations between this and the conical form are many and altogether too insignificant to be distinguished from each another even by varietal-names.

Figg. 147—149: its first step towards the conical form.

Figg. 150—158: different gradations of Textul. sagittula into the conical form (= *Textul. cuneiformis* var. *conica* Williams.); sometimes with convex, another time with flat basis.

Figg. 150—151: small specimen.

Figg. 152—154: very developed with a chalky texture.

Figg. 155—156: smaller specimen with distended base, and nearly circular in transverse section.

Figg. 157—158: nearly of the same shape as the preceding.

a) pygmæa:

Syn. **Textularia pygmæa, aciculata** d'Orb., 1826, Tabl. meth.; Ann. Sc. Nat. 7, p. 263, t. 11, figg. 1—4, Mod. 7.

» **agglutinans** var. **pygmæa** Park. and Jones, 1865, Aret. and Northatl. Ocean; Phil. Trans. 155. 1, p. 370, t. 15, fig. 22; t. 17, fig. 78.

» **pygmæa** Rss., 1862, Nordd. Hils u. Gault; Wien. Ak. Sitz.-Ber. 1. 46, p. 80, t. 9, fig. 11.

» **Cariboæa** d'Orb., 1839, Cuba, p. 145, t. 1, figg. 28—29.

» **franconica** Gümb., 1862, Streitenberg. Schwammlager; Würtemb. Nat. Wiss. Ver. Jhrhft. 17 (1862), p. 229, t. 4, fig. 18.

» **ulmensis** Gümb., 1871, Ulmer Cementmergel; Münch. Ak. Sitz.-Ber. 1, p. 68, t. 1, fig. 17.

» **cognata** Rss., 1863, Sept. Thon Kreuznach; Wien. Ak. Sitz.-Ber. 1, 48, p. 68, t. 8, fig. 96.

» **bolivinoides** Rss., 1859, Westphäl. Kreidef.; Wien. Ak. Sitz.-Ber. 40, p. 335, t. 12, fig. 6.

» **tetraëdra, laminaris, mutata** Costa, 1854, Pal. Nap. 2, p. 288, t. 23, fig. 10, 15—17.

» **quadrilatera** Schwag., 1866, For. Kar.-Nikobar; Novara Reise, geol. Th. 2, 2, p. 253, t. 7, fig. 103.

» **triticum** Jones, 1850, Kings Monogr. Perm. foss, p. 18, t. 6, fig. 5 (== Brady).

» » Richt., 1855, Thüringer Zechstein; Zeitschr. deutsch. geol. Ges. 7, p. 532, t. 26, figg. 24—25; 1861, Grundz Dyas p. 122, t. 20, figg. 36—37.

» » Brady, 1877, Carbonif. and Perm. foramf.; Pal. Soc. 30, p. 134, t. 10, figg. 24—25 (au spec. distincta).

» **pusilla, pugiunculus** Schwag., 1863, Juras. Sch.; Würtemberg. Nat. Verein. Jhrhft 21, p. 140, t. 7, figg. 14, 16.

» **attenuata** Rss., 1863, Sept. Thon Offenbach; Wien. Ak. Sitz.-Ber. 1, 48, p. 59, t. 7, fig. 87.

» **variabilis**, γ. **lævigata** Williams., 1858, Brit. rec. For. p. 76, figg. 162—163; 168.

Syn. Textularia ovata, elliptica Röm., 1838, Nordd. tert. Meeress.; Leonh. u. Bronn. Jhrb. 1838, p. 384, t. 3, figg. 17—18.
» prælonga Schwag., 1866, For. Kar-Nikobar; Novara Reise, geol. Th. 2. 2, p. 252, t. 7, fig. 104.
» articulata Rss., 1850, Kreidemerg. Lemberg; Haid. nat. Abh. 4. 1, p. 45, t. 4, fig. 14.
» multilocularis Rss., 1861, Geinitz Dyas 1, p. 122, t. 20, fig. 38.
» » Brady, 1877, Carbon. and Perm. foramf.; Pal. Soc. 30, p. 135, t. 10, fig. 23.
Proroporus complanatus Rss., 1859, Westphäl. Kreide; Wien. Ak. Sitz.-Ber. 40, p. 231, t. 12, fig. 5.
» Schultzei Rss., 1862, Nordd Hils u. Gault; Wien. Ak. Sitz.-Ber. 1. 46, p. 80, t. 9, fig. 10.
» sp. Schwag., 1863, Jurass. Sch.; Würtemb. Nat. Verein. Jhrhft. 21, t. 7, fig. 19.
Textularia lævigata, nussdorfensis d'Orb., 1846, For. tert. Vienne, p. 243, t. 14, figg. 14—19.
Plecanium lanceolatum Karr., 1868, Mioc. Fauna Kostej; Wien. Ak. Sitz.-Ber. 1. 58, p. 129, t. 1, fig. 2.

b) margine obtuso s. rotundato:

Textularia agglutinans d'Orb., 1839, Cuba, p. 144, t. 1, figg. 17—18; 32—34.
» » Park. and Jones, 1865, North. Atl. and Arct. Oc.; Phil. Trans. 165, p. 369, t. 15, fig. 21.
» » Park. and Jones, 1866, Crag. Foramf.; Palæont. Soc. 19, t. 3, figg. 14—16 (esemeris divisis).
» » Seg., 1862, Rhizopod. foss. Catania p. 30, t. 2, fig. 4. Sep. Accad. Gioenia Atti (2) 18.
Plecanium agglutinans Rss., 1869, Oligocän. v. Gaas; Wien. Ak. Sitz.-Ber. 59, p. 452, t. 1, figg. 1—2.
Textularia Candeiana d'Orb., 1839 Cuba p. 143, t. 1, figg. 25—27.
» eximia (d'Eichwald) Brady, 1877, Carbonif. and Perm. forf.; Pal. Soc. 30, p. 132, t. 10, figg. 27—29.
» agglutinans var. abbreviata Park. and Jones, 1876, North. Atl. and Arct. Oc.; Phil. Trans. 155. 1, t. 17, fig. 76.
» conulus Rss., 1845, Böhm. Kreide 1, p. 38, t. 8, fig. 59, t. 13, fig. 75.
» » Rss., 1854, Kreidef. Ostalp.; Wien. Ak. Dkschr. 7, p. 72, t. 26, fig. 7.
» » Rss., 1859, Westph. Kreidef.; Wien. Ak. Sitz.-Ber. 40, p. 231, t. 13, fig. 3.
Plecanium concavum Karr., 1868, Mioc. For. faun. Kostej; Wien. Ak. Sitz.-Ber. 1. 58, p. 129, t. 1, fig. 3.
Textularia obtusangula Röm., 1841, Verstein. Nordd. Kreide, p. 97, t. 15, fig. 18.
» » Rss., 1845, Böhm. Kreide 1, p. 38, t. 8, fig. 58.
Plecanium Speieri Rss., 1864, Oligocän.; Wien. Ak. Sitz.-Ber. 1. 50, p. 447, t. 1, fig. 3.
Textularia concinna Rss., 1845, Böhm. Kreide 2, p. 109, t. 24, fig. 34.
» » Rss., 1854, Kreide. Ostalpen; Wien. Ak. Dkschr. 7, p. 71, t. 26, fig. 6.
» » Rss., 1859, Westphäl. Kreide; Wien. Ak. Sitz.-Ber. 40, p. 233, t. 13, fig. 1.
» budensis, elongata Hken., 1875, Clav. Száb. Sch., p. 67, t. 15, figg. 1, 3.
» globosa Hken., ibid. p. 67, t. 15, fig. 5.
» sagittula Costa, 1854, Pal. Nap. 2, p. 291, t. 23, fig. 11.
» fœda Rss., 1845, Böhm. Kreide 2, p. 109, t. 13, figg. 12—13.
? » minima Karr., 1865, Grünsandst. N. Zeel.; Novara Reise, geol. Th. 1. 2, p. 79, t. 16, fig. 9.
» convexa Karr., ibid. p. 78, t. 16, fig. 8.
» rotundata, granulata Costa, 1854, Pal. Nap. 2, t. 15, figg. 4, 6.
» rugosa Costa, ibid. t. 15, fig. 7.

Syn. **Textularia** proxima, elata, conuloides Costa, Pal. Nap. 2, t. 23, figg. 8, 9, 12.
» **Faujasi** Rss., 1861, Kreidetuff Maastricht; Wien. Ak. Sitz.-Ber. 1. 44, p. 320, t. 3, fig. 9.
» **Partschii** Rss., 1845, Böhm. Kreide 1, p. 39, t. 13, fig. 80; 1859, Westphäl. Kreidef.; Wien. Ak. Sitz.-Ber. 1. 40, p. 233 t. 13, fig. 6.
» **parallela** Rss., 1859, Westphäl. Kreidef.; ibid. p. 233, t. 12, fig. 7.
Plecanium parallelum Rss., 1862, Nordd. Hils u. Gault; Wien. Ak. Sitz.-Ber. 46. 1, p. 33.
» **cocœnum** Gümb., 1868, Nordalp. Eocän.; K. Bayr. Ak. Wiss. Abh. 1. 10. 2, p. 603, t. 1, fig. 3 bis.
» **Sturi** Karr., 1864, Leythakalk Wien. Beck.; Wien. Ak. Sitz.-Ber. 1. 50, p. 703, t. 1, fig. 1.
» **depravatum** Schwag., 1865, Jurass. Sch.; Würtemb. Nat. Verein. Jahresh. 21, p. 93, t. 2, fig. 3.
» **roscidum, foedum** Karr., 1870, Kreidef. Leitzendorf; Jhrb. k. k. österr. geol. Reichsanst. 20, p. 165, t. 10, figg. 2—3.
Textularia Hayi Karr., 1865, Grünsand. N. Zeeland; Novara Reise, geol. Th. 1. 2, p. 78, t. 16, fig. 7.

c) sagittula: magis anceps, interdum carinata et serrata:

Textularia sagittula (Defr.) d'Orb., 1826, Tab. Meth.; An. Sc. Nat. 7, p. 263, N:o 20.
» » Park. and Jones, 1857, For. Coast. of Norway; Ann. Mag. Nat. Hist. 19, p. 297, t. 11, figg. 44—45.
» » Park. and Jones, 1866, Crag. For.: Pal. Soc. 19, t. 3, figg. 7—9; 77.
» **agglutinans** var. **sagittula** Parker and Jones, 1865, North. Atl. and Arct. Oc.; Phil. Trans. 155. 1, p. 369, t. 17, fig. 77.
» **obsoleta** Rss., 1845, Böhm. Kreide 1. p. 39, t. 13, fig. 79; 1865, Kreide an Kanara See; Wien. Ak. Sitz.-Ber. 52, p. 455, fig. 8.
? » **lævis** Rss., 1841, Nordd. Kreidegeb. p. 97, t. 15, fig. 17.
» **deltoidea** Rss., 1849, Neue For. österr. tert. Beck.; Wien. Ak. Dkschr. 1. 1, p. 381, t. 49, fig. 4.
» **subrhombica** Stache, 1865, Tert. Merg. Whaingar. Hafen. Novara Reise, geol. Th. 1. 2, p. 271, t. 24, fig. 20.
» **flabelliformis** Gümb., 1868, Nordalp. Eoc.; K. Bayr. Ak. Wiss. Abh. 1. 10. 2, p. 649, t. 2, fig. 83.
» **subflabelliformis** Hkrn., 1875, For. Clavul. Szab. Sch.; p. 66, t. 15, fig. 2.
Plecanium laxatum Schwag., 1866, Foss. Foramf. Kar.-Nikobar; Nov. Reise, geol. Th. 2. 2, p. 195, t. 4. fig. 5.
Textularia subangulata, gramen, abbreviata, Hauerii d'Orb., 1846, For. tert. Vienne, p. 247, 249, 250; t. 15, figg. 1—15.
» **Bronniana, deperdita, Mayeriana, carinata, articulata** d'Orb., ibid. p. 244—250, t. 14, figg. 20—28, 32—34; t. 15, figg. 16—18.
» **compressa, gracilis, lanceolata, subangularis** Röm., 1838, Nordd. tert. Meerressand; Leonh. u. Bronn. Jhrb. 1838, p. 384, t. 3, figg. 13—16.
» **cuneiformis** d'Orb., 1839, Cuba, p. 147, t. 1, figg. 37—39.
» » Williams., 1859, Brit. rec. Foramf. p. 75, figg. 158—159.
» **prælonga** Czjz., 1847, For. Wien. Beck.; Haid. Nat. Abh. 2. 1, p. 149, t. 13, figg. 28—30.
» **sagittula** d'Orb., 1844, Iles Canaries p. 138, t. 1, fig. 19—21.
» **Baudouiana** d'Orb., 1839, Craie bl. Paris; Mem. Soc. géol. Fr. 4, p. 46, t. 4, figg. 29—30.
» **sagittula** Costa, 1855, For. foss. Marna blu' Vaticano; Mem. Nap. 2, p. 125, t. 1, fig. 16.

Syn. **Plecanium rugosum**　　Rss., 1869, Oligocaen. von Gass; Wien. Ak. Sitz.-Ber. 59, p. 453, t. 1, fig. 2.
　　Textularia anceps　　Rss., 1845, Böhm. Kreide 1, p. 39, t. 8, fig. 79; t. 13, fig. 78; 1859, Westphäl. Kreidef.; Wien. Ak. Sitz.-Ber. 40, p. 234, t. 13, fig. 2.
　　　　» **Saulcyana**　　d'Orb., 1839, Cuba p. 146, t. 1, figg. 21—22.
　　　　» **prælonga**　　Rss., 1845, Böhm. Kreide, 1, p. 39, t. 12, fig. 14; 1854, Ostalpen. Kreidef. Wien. Ak. Sitz.-Ber. 7, p. 72, t. 26, fig. 8.
　　　　» **agglutinans** var. **carinata** Park. and Jones, 1865, North. Atl. and Arct. Oc.; Phil. Trans. 155. 1, p. 570, t. 17, fig. 79.
　　　　» **attenuata, lacera** Rss., 1851, Sept. Thon Berlin; Zeitschr. deutsch. geol. Ges. 3, p. 84, t. 6, figg. 52, 54.
　　　　» **carinata**　　Hkes., 1875, For. Clav. Szab. Sch. p. 66, t. 7, fig. 8.
　　　　» **acuta**　　Rss., 1849, Neue Foramf.; Wien. Ak. Dkschr. 1. 1, p. 381, t. 49, fig. 1.
　　　　» **capitata, carinata** var. **antipodum**, var. **robusta** Stache, 1865, Tert. Mergel Whaingar. Hafen; Novara Reise, geol. Th. 1. 2, p. 270—272, t. 24, figg. 19, 21—22.
　　　　» **corrugata**　　Costa, 1855, For. Marea blu' d' Vaticano; Mem. Nap. 2, p. 125, t. 1, fig. 15.
　　Plecanium Lythostrotum, solitum Schwag., 1866, For. Kar.-Nikob.; Novara Reise, geol. Th. 2. 2. p. 194—195, t. 4, figg. 4, 6.
　　Textularia folium　　Parker and Jones, 1865, Phil. Transact. 155. 1, t. 18, fig. 19 (an spec. distincta);
　　　　»　　»　　Mob., 1881, Maurit. and Seychell. p. 92, t. 8, figg. 16—17.
　　　　» **cuneiformis**　　Jones, 1880, Kings Monogr. Perm. fossils p. 18, t. 6, fig. 6 (sec. Richter).
　　　　»　　»　　Richt., 1855, Zeitschr. deutsch. geol. Ges. 7, p. 532, t. 26, fig. 23.
　　　　»　　»　　Richt., 1861, Gein. Dyas p. 122, t. 20, fig. 34—35 (sec. Brady).
　　　　» **Jonesi**　　Brady, 1876, Carb. and Perm. foramin.; Pal. Soc. 30, p. 133, t. 10, figg. 20—22.
　　　　» **pala**　　Czjz., 1847, Foss. for. Wien. Beck.; Haid. nat. Abh. 2. 1, p. 148, t. 13, fig. 25.
　　　　» **dentata**　　Alth, 1849, Umgeb. Lemberg; Haid. Nat. Abh. 3. 2, p. 262, t. 13, fig. 13.
　　　　» **Mariæ**　　d'Orb., 1846, For. tert. Vienne, p. 246, t. 14, figg. 29—31.
　　Plecanium　　»　　var.　　Rss., 1867, Steinsalzablag. Wieliczka; Wien. Ak. Sitz.-Ber. 1. 55, p. 64, t. 1, figg. 5—7.
　　　　» **spinulosum, serratum** Rss., ibid. p. 66, t. 1, figg. 3—4.
　　　　» **Mariæ** var. **inerme** Gümb., 1868, Nordalp. Eocaen.; K. Bayr. Ak. Wiss. 10. 2, p. 603, t. 1, fig. 3 ter.
　　Textularia pectinata　　Rss., ibid. p. 98, t. 3, fig. 11.
　　　　»　　»　　Rss., 1849, Neue For. Wien. Beck.; Wien. Ak. Dkschr. 1. 1, p. 381, t. 49, figg. 2—3.
　　Textularia variabilis var. **spathulata, difformis** Will., 1858, Brit. rec. foramf. p. 76, 77, figg. 164—167.

d) conica:

Textularia conica　　d'Orb., 1839, Cuba p. 143, t. 1, figg. 19—20.
　　» **cuneiformis** var. **conica** Williams, 1858, Brit. rec. forf. p. 75, figg. 160—161.
　　» **turris**　　d'Orb., 1839, For. Craie blanche Paris; Mem. Soc. geol. Fr. 4, p. 46, t. 4, figg. 27—28.
　　»　　»　　Rss., 1845, Böhm. Kreide 1, p. 39, t. 13, fig. 76.

e) biformis (an species distincta):

Syn.	Spiroplecta rosula	EHRENB., 1854, Microgeol. t. 32, fig. 26.
»	Textularia biformis	BRADY, 1881, Österr. Ung. Nordpols-Exp.; Wien. Ak. Dkschr. 43. 2, p. 101.
»	» adnectens	PARK. and JONES, 1863, Nomenclature; A. M. N. H. (3), 11, p. 91.
»	» agglutinans var. biformis PARKER and JONES, 1865, North. Atl. and Arct. Oceans; Phil. Trans. 155. 1, p. 370, t. 15, figg. 23—24.
»	» complexa	BRADY, 1865, Trans. Northhumb. 1, p. 101, t. 12, fig. 6 (sec. PARKER and JONES).

Textularia sagittula forma bigenerina D'ORB.

Syn.	Bigenerina nodosaria	D'ORB., 1826, Tab. meth.; An. Sc. Nat. 7, p. 261, t. 11, figg. 9—12, Mod. 57.
»	»	FRICK' Mod. 12.
?	» subtilis	KARR., 1878, For. Luzon; Bolet. Comis. Mapa geol. d. España 7. 2, p. 13, t. E, fig. 6.
»	Textularia agglutinans var. Bigenerina nodosaria PARK. and JONES, 1865, North. Atl. and Arct. Oc.; Phil. Transact. 155. 1, p. 371, t. 15, fig. 25; t. 17. fig. 80.
»	Bigenerina pusilla	RÖM., 1838, Nordd. tert. Meeress.; Leonh. u. Bronn. Jhrb. 1838, p. 384, t. 3, fig. 20.
»	» agglutinans	D'ORB., 1846, For. Bass. tert. Vienne; p. 238, t. 14, figg. 8—10.
»	» torulosa	COSTA, 1854, Paleont. Nap. 2, p. 285, t. 15, fig. 12.
»	» annulata	COSTA, ibid. p. 284, t. 15, fig. 13.
»	Gemmulina digitata	D'ORB., 1826, Tabl. Meth.; Ann. Sc. Nat. 7, p. 262; Mod. 58.
»	Textularia agglutinans var. Bigen. digitata PARK. and JONES, 1865, North. Atl. and Arct. Oc.; Phil. Trans. 155, 1, p. 371, t. 17, fig. 81.
»	Bigenerina digitata	BRADY, 1864, Rhizop. Shetl.; Trans. Lin. Soc. 24, p. 468, t. 48, fig. 8.
»	» bifida	COSTA, 1854, Pal. Nap. 2, p. 287, t. 23, fig. 1.

Appendix.

Textularia spica, elongata COST., 1848, Nouv. foss. microsc.; Mem. Soc. geol. Fr. (2) 3, p. 258, t. 2, figg. 23—25.

Textularia gibbosa D'ORB.

Syn.	Textularia gibbosa, obtusa, lævigata D'ORB., 1826, An. Sc. Nat. 7, p. 262; Mod. 28.
»	» punctulata, tuberosa D'ORB., ibid. p. 262—263.
»	» gibbosa PARK. and JONES, 1865, Crag. foramf.; Pal. Soc. 19, t. 3, figg. 10—13.
»	» » BRADY, 1876, Carbon. and Perm. Forf.; Pal. Soc. 30, p. 131, t. 10, fig. 26.
»	» Ehrenbergii RÖM., 1841, Nordd. Kreidegeb. p. 97, t. 15, fig. 16.
»	» globulosa RSS., 1845, Böhm. Kreide 1, p. 39, t. 12, fig. 23.
»	» cordiformis SCHWAG., 1863, Joras. Sch.; Würtemb. Nat. Verein. Jhrshft. 21, p. 139, t. 7, fig. 15.
»	» globigera SCHWAG., 1866, For. Kar-Nikobar; Novara Reise, geol. Th. 2. 2, p. 252, t. 7, fig. 109.
»	» globifera Rss., 1859, Westphäl. Kreide; Wien. Ak. Sitz.-Ber. 40, p. 232, t. 13, figg. 7—8

Syn. **Textularia Partschii**   Czjz., 1847, Foramf. Wien. Beck.; Haid. Nat. Abh. 2. 1, p. 148, t. 13, figg. 22—24.
» **pupa**   Rss., 1859, Westphäl. Kreide; Wien. Ak. Sitz.-Ber. 40, p. 232, t. 13, figg. 4—5.
» **strombus, peocetia, clypeata, crassa** Costa 1854, Pal. Nap. 2, p. 293—296, t. 13, fig. 54, t. 23, figg. 4, 6, 7.
Plecanium Karreri, granosissimum, eurystoma Stache, 1865, Tert. Merg. Whainger. Hafen, Novara Reise, geol. Th. 1. 2, p. 179, t. 21, figg. 17—19.
Grammostomum depressum etc. Ehrenb., 1854, Microgeol., t. 19, fig. 82; t. 25, figg. 8—12; t. 28, fig. 31; t. 32, figg. 5, 9, 10.
Spiroplecta americana   Ehrenb., ibid. t. 32, fig. 25.

b) striata:

Textularia striato-punctata Egger, 1857, Micr. Ortenburg; Leonh. u. Bronn. Jhrb. 1857, p. 294, t. 12, figg. 27—29.
(Nominibus variis)   Ehrenb., 1854, Mikrogeol. t. 27, figg. 3—5.
Spiroplecta americana   Ehrenb., ibid. t. 32, figg. 13—14.

c) aculeata:

Textularia aculeata etc. Ehrenb., 1854, t. 29, fig. 20, a. b.

Forma bigenerina d'Orb.

Bigenerina lævigata   d'Orb., 1826, Tab. meth.; An. Sc. Nat. 7, p. 261.
» **ampla**   Karr., 1877, Hochquellenwasserleit.; Österr. geol. Reichsanst. Abh. 9, p. 371. t. 16, fig. 374.
» **patula**   Brady, 1876, Carb. and Perm. forf., Pal. Soc. 30, p. 136, t. 8, figg. 10—11. t. 10, figg. 30—31.

Textularia sagittula Defr. forma Bigenerina.

Tab. V, figg. 159—161.

Is liable to great variation in size, form and condition of its surface, depending on the greater or less development of the textularia-stage and on the coarseness or fineness of the constituents of the sea-bottom which have been agglutinated. It happens often that the textularia-stage is very atrophic and the chambers are difficult to trace. Our form from the chalk-bottom contains not seldom great many spongia spicula agglutinated with shell- and chalk-debris, so that de surface is quite bristly. The aperture is generally orbicular and central; but sometimes it is semilunar in shape. Among several representations given by different authors of »Bigenerinæ» we have not been able to find any, that fully agrees with our form. Bigenerina torulosa Costa is the nearest to our coarser specimens, but his is thicker.

It is very common in both coralline-gravel and chalk-ooze, and attains a length of 5—6 mm.

For the synonymy see under *Textul. sagittula*.

Fig. 159: a coarse form, which not unfrequently becomes still rougher and more shapeless, like a small piece of mortar.

Fig. 160: the bristly and more regularly made form; its Textularia-stage is often very attenuated with the chambers nearly obliterated; the different shape of the aperture is also represented.

Fig. 161: a pigmy-form with a nicely developed Textularia-stage. 161 b: the same more magnified. (The penultima-chamber of the Textularia-stage is wrongly represented with an aperture leading to the Nodosaria-stage.)

Textularia gibbosa D'ORB. forma Bigenerina.
Tab. V. figg. 162—164.

This form differs from the preceding by its Textularia-stage being more round or distended. Its whole appearance reminds one more of a «Clavulina» than a Bigenerina, but its early stage its plainly biserial and generally extremely short, without any external septal impressions or markings, its surface usually being polished and of yellowish tint. The Nodosaria-stage is generally more rough (not so smooth as is represented in the pictures).

The aperture is often replaced by a number of pores; sometimes triangular and provided with a tongue, nearly as in a Valvulina.

It is not uncommon in the coralline-gravel, of slender growth, generally of small size, but sometimes attaining a length of 7 mm.

Figg. 162—163: 2 specimens cut open, with a transvers section, fig. 164, of the Textularia-stage, shewing the biserial arrangement; the different forms of aperture are also represented

Textularia Pennatula BATSCH. var. aculeata EHRENB. forma Bigenerina.
Tab. V, figg. 165—166.

It is a pigmy with a thin, glassy shell, which soon becomes nodosarine in growth. This form may also be considered as a pigmyform of the preceding, *Textul. sagittula* forma *Bigenerina*, but not having met with transitory forms between the two we place it as a variety of *Textul. Pennatula*. REUSS has referred this form to his genus *Schizophora* and GÜMBEL to *Venilina*. It shews some affinity to «Bolivina» in the poration and the shell-substance.

It is sometimes provided with a few crescentshaped folds on each segment.

It is not common in the chalk-ooze.

Fig. 165: the textularia-stage.

Fig. 166 its bigenerinaform 0,42 mm. in length.

Textularia Trochus d'Orb.
Tab. V, figg. 167—170; Tab. VI, figg. 171—172.

In his wellknown treatise: *Mémoire sur les foraminifères de la craie blanche du Bassin de Paris*, Mem. Soc. géol. France 4, p. 45, t. 4, figg. 25—26, D'ORBIGNY has designated a young Textularia, that very much resembles, and is without doubt identical with our form.

Textularia cuneiformis var. *conica* WILLIAMS. has been referred by CARPENTER also to Textul. Trochus, but that form is rather a Textul. sagittula, to which also should be referred *Textul. conica* D'ORB. from Cuba.

In their admirable work upon the Crag-Foraminifera (Palæont. Soc. 19, tab. 3, figg. 14—16) Messrs PARKER, JONES and BRADY have represented a *Textul. agglutinans*, with the chambers divided nearly in the same manner as in the West Indian form, with which it also agrees in the shape of aperture and base, but its general shape and features are those of a common Textul. agglutinans.

The same Authors' *Textul. trochus* (Pal. Soc. 19, tab. 3, figg. 17—18) may be identical with our form, but may also prove to be a *Textul. sagittula*.

The Caribbean form is remarkable for its compressed and more or less spread out or fanlike shape, when of a more advanced age. The plane of this compression is quite contrary to that of the commonly known Textularia in as much as the zigzag boundary-lines, marking the septa are found on the edges. It agrees in this respect perfectly with D'ORBIGNY's *Cuneolina* from lower Cretaceous formation (For. Bass. tert. Vienne p. 253, t. 21, figg. 50—52) and is an intermediate form between that represented species and the common Textularia. It has sometimes the margins of its long fissure-like aperture here and there quite closely approached one to another and grown together, shewing thus a tendency to the same arrangement of a row of small apertures, as we find in Cuneolina.

Our form is very compact and thickwalled, tightly agglutinated of the finest debris of chalk; the surface is quite smooth and covered with fine pores. When laid open along the flat central space between the two rows of chambers, which space is formed by their apertures, the long chambers are exposed to view. They consist of, first a shallow vestibule occupying the whole breadth of the inner part of the shell; then at the back of the vestibule a row of a few deep impressions or shallow chambers, each of which has about four short channels leading out of it. These channels branch off into about the same number of short tubes and these again terminate in from 3 to 5 very fine porecanals. In this way a system of 4 different sets or orders of branching cavities and channels are produced. Each set of ramification is ordinarely arranged in pairs, one pair being placed above another. Such a regular arrangement as the mentioned is however far from invariable, for it happens sometimes, that the first ramification is only di- or trichotomous and the second and third may be variable in like manner. Occasionally too a part of a chamber or even a whole chamber is found to be destitute of one or other of the sets of channels.

The septa are thicker and more compact on the inner edge, their outer part being so taken up with channels, that they are absorbed, so to speak, in channelwalls.

The subdivisions of the chambers in the younger stages are more irregular and spongelike.

It is very common, both on the chalkbottom and in the coralline-gravel, and attains a length of 6 and a breadth of 4,5 mm.

Fig. 167: View of its flat side.
Fig. 168: » » » edge.
Fig. 169: » » » aperture-side.
Fig. 170: Vertical section in the flat median plane; in the background of the broad vestibules the first set of channels (or shallow chambers) shew their four ramifications, the upper couples being half hidden by the slanting septa.

Fig. 171, tab. VI: Vertical section through the median transverse plane; the interstices between the septa, the vestibules and the channels of sets N:ris 2 and 3 and the pore-canals are represented.

Fig. 172: A chamber, horizontally opened shewing the walls and subdivisions of the channels of the different sets.

Textularia pupoides d'Orb.
Tab. VI, figg. 173—180.

The close affinity between the genus *Gaudryina* d'Orb. and *Textularia* has long ago been proved by Messrs. Parker, Jones and Carpenter, and in fact there is no reason at all for their generic distinction. Indeed evidence may by and by be adduced to shew, that each Textularia-species has its Gaudryina-development, just as it has its Bigenerina form. But ad interim we must consider it as a distinct species, although there is no want of intermediate links, for sometimes the young tri- or multiserial stage is reduced nearly to nothing, and the biserial arrangement occupies almost the whole shell; as for instance in *Gaudr. chilostoma* Rss.

Our form comes next to *Gaudr. insecta* Stache, *Gaudr. rugosa* d'Orb. and *Gaudr. prolonga* Stache. It is often very irregular with small protuberances and wrinkles being nearly square in transverse section. Its early stage is often 3—5-serial. At other times it is quite regular, smooth and cylindrical with the multiserial stage reduced to 1—2 rows of chambers. Sometimes it is very slender and produced.

It is always agglutinated of the finest chalkdust, without siliceous sand. It occurs not very commonly both on the chalkbottom and in the coralline-gravel.

Figg. 173—174: the wrinkled form.
Figg. 175—176: transverse section of its 4—5 serial stage.
Fig. 177: smooth regular form.
Fig. 178: transverse section of the same.
Fig. 179: slender produced form.
Fig. 180: transverse section of its first stage.

a) Gaudryina rugosa, pupoides:

Gaudryina rugosa, pupoides D'ORB., 1839, For. craie bl. Paris; Mém. Soc. géol. Fr. 4, p. 44, t. 4, figg. 20—24.
» rugosa D'ORB., 1846, Bass. tert. Vienne, p. 197, t. 21, figg. 34—36
» » RSS., 1845, Böhm. Kreide 1, t. 12, figg. 15, 24; 1855, Tert. Sch. nördl. u. mittl. Deutschl.; Wien. Ak. Sitz.-Ber. 1. 18, p. 244, t. 6, fig. 61.
» » HKN., 1875, For. Clav. Szab. Sch. t. 1, fig. 4.
» pupa, subglabra GÜMB., 1868, Nordalp. Eocän.; K. Bayr. Ak. Wiss. Abh. 1, 10. 2, p. 602, t. 1, fig. 3—4.
» pupoides FRIČ Mod. 11.
» subrotundata SCHWAG., 1866, Kar.-Nikobar.; Novara Reise, geol. Th. 2. 2, p. 198. t. 4, fig. 9.
» prælonga KARR., 1877, Hochquellenwasserleit.; k. k. österr. geol. Reichsanst. Abh. 9, p. 374, t. 16, fig. 6.
Textularia chilostoma RSS., 1851, Tert. Sch. Oberschles.; Zeitschr. deutsch. geol. Ges. (2) 4, p. 18 (xylogr.).
Textularia labiata RSS., 1866, Crag. Antwerp.; Wien. Ak. Sitz.-Ber. 42, p. 362, t. 2, fig. 17.
Gaudryina chilostoma RSS., 1865, deutsch. Sept. Thon; Wien. Ak. Dkschr. 1. 25. 1, p. 120, t. 1, figg. 5—7 (Textilaria gibbosæ D'ORB. proxima, interdum vix distinguenda).
» oxycona RSS., 1859, Westph. Kreide; Wien. Ak. Sitz.-Ber. 40, p. 229, t. 12, fig. 3.
» textilaroides HKE., 1875, For. Clav. Szab. Schichten p. 15, t. 1, fig. 6.
» Reussi HKE., ibid. p. 14, t. 1, fig. 5.
» gyrophora GÜMB., 1871, Ulmer Cem. Mergel; Münch. Ak. Sitz.-Ber. 1, p. 64, t. 1, fig. 4.
» Draschei KARR., 1878, For. Luzon; Bolet. Comis. Mapa geol. del España, 7. 2, p. 12, t. E, fig. 5.
» badenensis RSS., 1849, Neue For. österr. Beck.; Wien. Ak. Sitz.-Ber. 1. 1, p. 374, t. 47, fig. 14.
» Reussi, obliquata, megastoma, novo Zelandica, capitata, insecta STACHE, 1865, Tert. Meeg. Whainger. Hafen; Novara Reise, geol. Th. 1. 2, p. 177, t. 21, figg. 11—16.
» crassa MARSSON, 1877, Rügen. Schreibekr.; Greifsw. Nat. Verein. Mitth. 1877—78, p. 158, t. 3, fig. 17.

b) magis bulloides:

Gaudryina globulifera RSS., 1851, Tert. Sch. Oberschl.; Ztschr. deutsch. geol. Ges. (2) 4, p. 18.
» baccata, uva SCHWAG., 1866, For. Kar.-Nikob.; Novara Reise, geol. Th. 2. 2, p. 200, 201, t. 4, figg. 12—13.
? » solida SCHWAG., ibid. p. 199, t. 4, fig. 11 (an Verneuilina?).
» irregularis HKN., 1875, Clav. Szab. Sch. p. 15, t. 1, fig. 7.
» crassa KARR., 1870, Kreidef. Leitzendorf; Jhrb. k. k. österr. geol. Reichsanst. 20, p. 166, t. 10, fig. 4.
» ulmensis GÜMB., 1871, Ulmer Cem. Mergel; Münch. Ak. Sitz.-Ber. 1, p. 64, t. 1, fig. 3.

c) forma bigenerina:

Gaudryina ruthenica RSS., 1850, Kreidem. Lemberg; Haid. Nat. Abh. 4. 1, p. 41, t. 4, fig. 4.
Plectina irregularis MARSS., 1872, Rügen, Schreibekr.; Greifsw. Nat. Ver. Mittheil. 1877—78, p. 160, t. 3, fig. 28.

Syn. Gaudryina pavicula	Schwag., 1866, For. Kar.-Nikobar; Novara Reise, geol. Th. 2. 2, p. 198, t. 4, fig. 10.
Plectina clava	Marss., 1877, Rügen. Schreibkreide; Greifsw. Nat. Verein. Mitth. 1877—78, p. 160, t. 3, fig. 29.
?Clavulina robusta	Stache, 1865, Tert. Merg. Whaingaz. Hafen; Novara Reise, geol. Th. 1. 2, p. 169, t. 21, figg. 9—10.
?Gaudryina siphonella	Rss., 1851, Sept. Thon Berlin; Ztschr. deutsch. geol. Ges. 3, p. 78, t. 5, figg. 40—42.
? » »	Hken., 1875, Clav. Száb. Sch. p. 14, t. I, fig. 3.

Textularia pupoides var. conica n.

Tab. VI, figg. 181—182.

This variety, which resembles somewhat *Gaudryina oxycona* Rss. differs from the type-species in being very pointed with a square or trigonal early stage and conical-round textularia-stage. It is very tightly built with scarcely any external visible traces of septal impressions or lines. Sometimes it is still more slender and produced than is represented by fig. 181.

It has been found only in the coralline-gravel.

Fig. 182: apertural side.

Textularia triquetra v. Münst.

Tab, VI, figg. 183—184.

This species, known as *Verneuilina tricarinata* d'Orb., has been even generically distinguished from *Text. pupoides* by d'Orbigny; and yet it is nearly impossible to draw a clear line of specific distinction between the two. Both have their young stage constructed after the same plan, both are dimorphous; the more developed form of *T. triquetra* is commonly referred to *Clavulina*.

It is besides somewhat remarkable, that Text. triquetra and T. pupoides sometimes, when from the same bottom, get exactly the same accidental feature of the shell surface; as for instance *Verneuilina cretacea* Karr. from the chalk at Letzerdorf which is provided with the same sort of tubercles all over its surface, as *Gaudryina crassa* Karr. from the same place. Whether this external likeness is the result of an extremely close relation between the two or an adaptation to local circumstances is in this case difficult to decide about.

Our form is in its young stage nearly transparent, with an amber tinge in transmitted light; the pores are fine and pretty close. The sides are sometimes scooped out a little, so that the edges become quite sharp; the mouth reminds one somewhat of the aperture in Valvulina or Miliolina.

It is identical with *Verneuilina spinulosa* Rss. from the tertiary formation of Austria.

It is scarce in the coralline-gravel. »*Tritaxia*« Rss. is nothing but an incipient »Bigenerina« of Text. triquetra. This developed form occurs also in the coralline-gravel. It is generally twice as large as the »Verneuilina« stage of the fully developed Bigenerina form.

Fig. 183: represents the flat side of Text. triquetra.
Fig. 184: the apertural side.

Syn.	Textularia triquetra	(v. Münst.). Röm., 1838, Nordd. tert. Meeress.; Leonh. u. Bronn. Jhrb. 1838, p. 384, t. 3, fig. 19.
»	»	Rss., 1845, Böhm. Kreide 1, p. 39, t. 13, fig. 77.
	Verneuilina Münsteri	Rss., 1854, Kreide Ostalp.; Wien. Ak. Dkschr. 7, p. 71, t. 26, fig. 5.
»	Bronni	Rss., 1845, Böhm. Kreide 1, p. 38, t. 12, fig. 5; 1855, Kreidem. Lemberg; Haid. Nat. Abh. 4. 1, p. 40, t. 4, fig. 2.
»	tricarinata	d'Orb., 1839, For. Craie bl. Paris; Mem. Soc. geol. France 4. p. 39, t. 4, figg. 3—4.
»	»	d'Orb., 1846, For. Bass. tert. Vienne p. 182, t. 21, figg. 26—27.
»	oberburgensis	Rss., 1863, Oberb. in Steiermark; Wien. Ak. Dkschr. 1. 23. 1, p. 6, t. 1, fig. 2.
»	cognata	Rss., 1864, Oberoligocän.; Wien. Ak. Sitz.-Ber. 1. 50, p. 448, t. 1, fig. 1.
»	spinulosa	Rss., 1849, Neue For. Wien. Beck.; Wien. Ak. Dkschr. 1. 1, p. 374. t. 47, fig. 12.
»	»	Egger, 1857, Miorän. v. Ortenburg; Leonh. u. Bronn. Jhrb. 1857, p. 292, t. 9, figg. 17—18.
»	cretacea	Karr., 1870, Kreidef. in Leitzerdorf; Jhrb. k. k. österr. geol. Reichsanst. 20, p. 164, t. 10, fig. 1.
?Textularia atlantica		Bailey, 1850, Examin. of Soundings; Smithson. Contrib. of knowledge 2, Art. 3, p. 12, figg. 38—43.
Grammost. aculeatum		Ehrenb., 1854, Microgeol. t. 28, fig. 17.

b) forma Tritaxia (Bigenerinæ incipienti æqualis):

Textularia tricarinata	Rss., 1845, Böhm. Kreide 1, p. 39, t. 8, fig. 60.
Uvigerina tricarinata	d'Orb., 1839, For. Craie bl. Par.; Mem. Soc. geol. Fr. (2) 4, p. 42, t. 4, figg. 16—17.
Tritaxia pyramidata	Rss., 1862, Nordd. Hils u. Gault; Wien. Ak. Sitz.-Ber. 1. 46, p. 32, t. 1, fig. 9.
Verneuilina dubia	Rss., 1854, Kreidemerg. Lemberg; Haid. Nat. Abh. 4. 1, p. 41, t. 4, fig. 3.
Tritaxia tricarinata	Rss., 1859, Westphäl. Kreidef.; Wien. Ak. Sitz.-Ber. 40, p. 228, t. 12, figg. 1-2.
» foveolata, minuta	Marss., 1877, Rügen. Schreibkr.; Greifsw. Nat. Verein. Mitth. 1877—78, p. 161, t. 3, figg. 30—31.
? » ulmensis	Gümb., 1871, Ulmer Cement. Mergel; Münch. Ak. Sitz.-Ber. 1, p. 63, t. 1, fig. 2.

c) forma Bigenerina completa:

Verneuilina communis	Park. and Jones, 1866, Crag. For.; Pal. Soc. 19, t. 3, fig. 19.
Clavulina irregularis	(Münst.) Röm., 1838, Nordd. tert. Meeress.; Leonh. u. Bronn. Jhrb. 1838, p. 387, t. 3, fig. 40.
» elegans	Karr., 1865, For. Grünsandst. N. Zeeland; Novara Reise, geol. Th. 1. 2, p. 80, t. 16, fig. 11.

Syn. **Clavulina antipodum** STACHE, 1865, Tert. Mergel Whaingar. Hafen; Novara Reise, geol. Th. 1. 2, p. 167, t. 21, figg. 3—8.
? » **variabilis** SCHWAG., 1866, Foss. For. Kar.-Nikobar.; Novara Reise, geol. Th. 2. 2, p. 197, t. 4, fig. 8.

Appendix.

Verneuilina polystropha PARK. and JONES, 1865. N. Atl. and Arct. Oc.; Phil. Trans. 155. 1, p. 371, t. 15, fig. 26.
»   » BRADY, Arct. Exped. 1875—76; A. M. N. H. (5) 1, p. 436, t. 20, fig. 9.

Huc a PARKER et JONES relatæ sunt:

Bulimina polystropha   RSS., 1845, Böhm. Kreide. 2, p. 109, t. 24, fig. 53.
?   »   scabra   ALTH, 1850, Umgeb. Lemberg; Haid. Nat. Abh. 3. 2, p. 265, t. 13, fig. 19.
»   »   WILLIAMS., 1858, Brit. rec. For. p. 65, figg. 136—137.
?   »   tuberculata   EGG., 1857, Miocän. Ortenburg; Leonh. u. Bronns Jhrb. 1857, p. 284, t. 12, figg. 4—7.
»   pygmæa   EGG., ibid. p. 284, t. 12, figg. 10—11.
Guttulina aculeata, turrita EHRENB., 1854, Microgeol. t. 27, figg. 35—36.

Vernouilina rotundata   KARRER 1878, Foram. Luzon; Bolet. Comis. Mapa geol. del Esp. 7. 2, p. 10, t. F, fig. 2 (an Gaudryina).

Textularia triquetra Bigenerina (alias Clavulina).
Tab. VI, figg. 185—186.

It is not an easy task to decide from the representations of »Clavulinæ» by the different authors which properly should be referred to *Text. triquetra* and which to *Valvulina* genus. Our list of synonyms will therefore be less satisfactory

Our form ressembles somewhat the Bigenerina form of Text. sagittula and is easily overlooked, when found mixed with the latter from the same locality. The shell is rough and bristly with spongeneedles, which are copiously incorporated with the chalkdebris, of which the shell is agglutinated. The aperture is often pouting, round or somewhat crescentshaped.

The »Verneuilina»-stage is very short and with scarcely any traces of outer septal-furrows or marks, obtuse trigonal.

It is not common either on the chalkbottom or in the coralline-gravel.

Fig. 185: Text. triquetra adulta.

Fig. 186: transverse section of the »Vernouilina» stage.

For the synonymy see under the preceding c).

Valvulina triangularis D'ORB., forma Clavulina angularis D'ORB.
Tab. XI, fig. 387—389.

Our form seems to be identical with *Clavulina tricarinata* D'ORB. from the West-Indies; but it is much larger, sometimes attaining 3 mm. in length. The trigonal circumference is not at all a constant feature in this form, for *Clavulina nodosaria* D'ORB. from the same locality is unquestionably a *Valvulina* but of cylindrical shape and not distinct from the tricarinate form.

I am far from being able with any satisfactory degree of certainty to identify all of D'ORBIGNY's *Clavulina* species, but most of them display an arrangement of their 3 or 4 serial stage more in accordance with the plan of growth of *Valvulina* than of the more regular type of *Text. triquetra*. In our form the septal impressions are ordinarily very strongly marked, particularly on the flat sides, where they become changed into broad semilunar transverse furrows. The angles of the chambers are often somewhat produced. The shell-substance is finely agglutinated of chalk-matter. It is not common in the coralline-gravel.

Fig. 387: the edge side; 389: the flat side; 389: the aperture.

a) rotaliæformis, plus minusve conica:

syn.	Valvulina triangularis		D'ORB., 1826, Tab. meth.; An. Sc. Nat. 7, p. 270. Mod. N:o 25.
	»	»	FRIES Mod. N:o 5.
	»	»	PARK. and JONES, 1857, For. Coast. of Norway; An. Mag. Nat. Hist. (2) 19, p. 209, t. 11, figg. 15—16.
	»	»	CARPENTER, 1860, Introd. t. 11, figg. 15—16.
	Rotalina fusca		WILLIAMS., 1858, Brit. rec. forf. p. 55, figg. 114—115 (sec. CARPENTER).
	Valvulina austriaca		D'ORB., 1846, For. Bass. tert. p. 181, t. 11, figg. 7—8.
	»	triangularis	var. conica PARK. and JONES, 1865, North. Atl. and Arct. Oc.; Phil. Trans. 155. 1, p. 406, t. 15, fig. 27.
?	»	allomorphinoides	RSS., 1859, Westph. Kreidef.; Wien. Ak. Sitz.-Ber. 40, p. 223, t. 11, fig. 6.
?	»	bulloides	BRADY, 1876, Carbonif. and Perm. foramf.; Pal. Soc. 30, p. 89, t. 4, figg. 12—15.
?	»	plicata	BRADY, ibid. p. 88, t. 4, fig. 10.
?	»	rudis	BRADY, ibid. p. 90, t. 3, figg. 19—20.

b) buliminæformis:

		CARPENT., Introd. t. 11, figg. 19, 25.
Valvulina gibbosa		D'ORB., 1839, For. Craie blanc. Par.; Mém. Soc. géol. Fr. 4, p. 3, t. 4, figg. 1—2.
»	parvula	v. MÜNST., globularis v. MÜNST. 1838, RÖM., Tert. Meeress. N. Deutschl.; Leonh. u. Bronn. Jhrb. 1838, p. 387, t. 3, figg. 41—42.
»	Oviedoana	D'ORB., 1839, Cuba p. 103, t. 2, figg. 21—22.
»	spicula	RSS., 1845, Böhm. Kreide 1, p. 37, t. 13, fig. 69.

c) Clavulina communis:

?Nautilus	radicula	Montagu, 1803, Test. Brit. p. 197, t. 14, fig. 6.
Clavulina	communis	d'Orb., 1826, Tab. meth.; An. Sc. Nat. 7, p. 268. Parés Mod. No 10.
»	»	d'Orb., 1846, For. Rass. tert. Vienne, p. 196, t. 12, figg. 1—2.
»	irregularis, communis Costa, 1854, Pal. Nap. 2, p. 270, t. 22—23, figg. 1—3; fig. 2.

d) Clav. angularis:

»	triquetra	Rss., 1869, Oberburg; Wien. Ak. Dkschr. 1. 23. 1, p. 6, t. 1, fig. 1.
»	triploura	Rss., 1865, Fenerstein-Kreide an. Kassra Sec; Wien. Ak. Sitz.-Ber. 52, p. 448, t. 1, fig. 1.
»	Szábói	Hatn., 1875, For. Clav. Száb. Sch. p. 15, t. 1, fig. 9.
»	Philippinica	Karr., 1878, Foramf. Luzon; Bolet. Comis. Mapa geol. del España, 7. 2, p. 11, t. E, fig. 4.
Clavulina	parisiensis	d'Orb., 1826, Tab. meth.; Acad. Sc. Nat. 7, p. 268, Mod. 66.
»	nodosaria	d'Orb., 1839, Cuba p. 110, t. 2, figg. 19—20.
Orthocerina	clavulus	d'Orb., 1826, Tab. meth.; An. Sc. Nat. 7, p. 255, Mod. 2 (sec. Parr. and Jones).
Clavulina	angularis	d'Orb., 1826, Tabl. Meth.; Ann. Sc. Nat. 7, p. 268, t. 12, fig. 7.
»	tricarinata	d'Orb., 1839, Cuba p. 111, t. 2, figg. 16—18.
		Czjz., Introduct. t. 11, figg. 17, 18.

Valvulina triangularis d'Orb. var. polyphragma n.

Tab. XI, figg. 390—400.

It is somewhat surprising, that this »Clavulina«, which is one of the most frequent rhizopodes on our chalk-bottom, has escaped the notice of our many and industrious scrutinizers of the different tertiary strata, amongst the constituents of which this species also may be anticipated. The loosely agglutinated structure of its shell may have prevented its more extensive preservation during the ages.

Its Valvulina-stage proper, is ordinarely very short and owing to its strongly agglutinant power the limits and arrangement of its chambers are nearly perfectly masked. This early stage seems sometimes to belong to the rotaline form of *Valvulina*. Sometimes, but not so frequently, it has a more produced (buliminoid) shape. The most remarkable feature by our form is the high development of its uniserial stage with its regular, handsome lituolina-like, radial subdivisions of the chambers. These subdivisions vary in number from 5 to 10 or rather from 10 to 20, each being subdivided into two branches. The aperture is usually closed by a thin cribriform lamina. The surface of the shell, even in the young, is often studded with knobs and coarse spines of accumulated chalkdebris.

The shape of the whole varies from cylindric and clavate to ovoid, and globular. The older ones assume ordinarely the ovoidform, resulting from the thick deposit of debris, which render the outer layers soft, like white-chalk. It is devoid of siliceous sand; but from the Atlantic Prof. Smitt and D:r Ljungman have braught home large specimens somewhat admixed with real and coarse sandy particles.

As far as I know, there is not on record any Valvulina with subdivided chambers but *Valv. Youngi* BRAD. from the lower carboniferous limestone in Scotland and England (Palæogr. Soc. 30, p. 86, t. 4, figg. 6—9).

Fig. 390: clavate, smooth and hard specimen, with produced valvuline stage.

Fig. 391: stout form with thick deposit of chalk.

Fig. 392: median section of the same.

Fig. 393: longitudinal section of a better defined specimen displaying the ovoid or uterus-shaped central space of the chambers, their radiating, bifid divisions, and the very short triserial stage.

Fig. 394: transverse section through the earlier stage, exhibiting the triserial arrangement.

Fig. 395: section at the commencement of the uniserial stage.

Fig. 396: section through the more advanced stage.

Fig. 397: young clavate form cut longitudinally.

Fig. 398: young ovoidal form.

Fig. 399: still younger form, nearly globular.

Fig. 400: longitudinal cut of a very young specimen, only 1.1 mm.

Valvulina triangularis var. eocæna GÜMB.

Tab. XI, figg. 401—403.

The multiserial stage is so very little developed as often to be wanting, and the specimen may be taken for a *Lituolina*; or at the best the early stage is reduced to a few chambers, rendered extremely indistinct or masked by the agglutinated coarse sandgrains. Unquestionably our form ought to be placed quite near to »*Clavulina communis*» D'ORB.

The shell of our form is tightly built of coarse sandgrains mixed with a greath many sponge-needles. Its shape varies from a more slender, to a stout pupoid form, which latter is prevalent. The aperture is generally very narrow, not unfrequently poreformed, sometimes obsoletely triangular. The chambers are ordinarely undivided, but occasionally there are at nearly regular intervals a few sandgrains projecting from the walls, representing rudimentary partitions.

From the northalpine Eocæn Mr. GÜMBEL has designated a variety of *Clavulina*, that seems nearly identical with our form (*Clavulina eocæna* GÜMB. 1868, K. Bay. Ak. Wiss. Abh. I. 10. 2, p. 601, t. I, fig. 2). It is not unfrequently met with in the coralline-gravel and chalk-ooze, attaining a length of 3 mm.

Figg. 401—402: thicker and narrower specimens, the first one with scarcely a valvulina-stage.

Fig. 403: the aperture

Candeina nitida d'Orb.
Tab. VI, figg. 187—189.

This distinguished form was considered by D'ORBIGNY as being in near affinity to Globigerina merely on account of its globular chambers. The same relationship is also attributed to it by Mr. BRADY (Notes on retic. Rhizop. Challeng. exped.; Quart. Journ. microsc. Sc. 75, p. 292). Professors PARKER and JONES again place it in the closest relation to the threeserial Textulariæ. The poration, which is extremely fine and exactly resembles that of the vitreous Textularia triquetra, as well as its plan of growth would seem to afford some support to this latter suggestion.

It is very scarce in the chalk-ooze, always of a pigmy size. According to BRADY its habits seem to be pelagic.

Fig. 187: the spiral side.
Fig. 188: sideview.
Fig. 189: basal-side.

Syn. **Candeina nitida**   D'ORB., 1839, Cuba p. 108, t. 2, figg. 27—28; 1846, For. Bass. tert. Vienne, p. 192, t. 21, fig. 28.

Sphæroidina bulloides d'Orb.
Tab. VI, figg. 190—193.

Our form differs sometimes from the typical one in having its aperture more regular and symmetrically placed in the midst of the septal suture of the last chamber. The apertural tongue is not seldom wanting and the mouth becomes of the same shape as in Globigerina. The poration is just as fine and delicate as in Candeina.

It occurs not frequently in the chalk-ooze, and is of small size.

Syn. **Sphæroidina bulloides**		D'ORB., 1826, Tab. meth.; An. Sc. Nat. 7, p. 267.
»	»	PARK. and JONES, 1854, Phil. Trans. 155, 1, p. 369, t. 16, figg. 52.
»	**austriaca**	D'ORB., 1846, Bass. tert. Vienne, p. 284, t. 20, figg. 19—21.
»	»	RSS., 1849, Neue For. österr. tert. Beck.; Wien. Ak. Dkschr. N 1, p. 387, t. 51, fig. 3—19.
»	»	EGGER, 1857, Miocän. Ortenburg; Leonh. u. Bronn. Jhrb. 1857, p. 273, t. 6, figg. 19—20.
»	»	HKEN., 1875, For. Clav. Szab. Seb. p. 62, t. 10, fig. 4.
»	»	SCHWAG., 1866, For. Kar.-Nikobar.; Novara Reise, geol. Th. 2, 2, p. 250, t. 7, fig. 98.
»	**variabilis**	RSS., 1851, Sept. Thon Berlin; Zeitschr. deutsch. geol. Ges. 3, p. 88, t. 7, figg. 61—64.
? »	**variabilis** var. **conica**	RSS., 1863, Sept. Thon Offenbach; Wien. Ak. Sitz.-Ber. 1, 48, p. 58, t. 7, fig. 86.

Globigerina universa d'Orb.
Tab. VI, fig. 194.

This species has received a smaller number of names than most of the other species of this class, owing to its simple and nearly uniform structure in all seas and in those geological strata, where it has appeared.

Orbulina Neojurensis Karr. from the secondary strata of Austria is distinguished by a strongly reticulated surface, but this feature is common within the whole genus, and is not a mark of essential importance.

A twinform is sometimes met with, which has been identified with *Glob. bilobata* d'Orb. from the tertiary strata at Vienna. But d'Orbigny's form is provided with a lateral aperture like that in the ordinary Glob. bulloides. Our twinform is destitute of such an orifice, in place of which it is provided with the usual large pores, scattered between the finer ones.

Globigerina bipartita Rss., from the Antwerpen.-Crag may belong to this form.

Globigerina universa of different sizes and thinness of shell is very common on both sorts of bottom at our localities.

The twinform, fig. 194, is very rare in the coralline-gravel.

Syn.	Orbulina universa	d'Orb., 1839, Cuba p. 3, t. 1, fig. 1; 1846, Iles Canaries p. 122, t. 1. fig 1; For. tert. Vienne p. 22, t. I, fig. 1.
"	"	Bail., 1850, Microsc. Exam. of Soundings; Smithson. Contrib. 2 , p. 9 fig. 1.
"	"	Costa, 1854, Pal. Nap. 2, t. 11, fig. 5.
"	tuberculata, granulata	Costa, ibid. fig. 1—2; t. 15, fig. 14.
"	granulata β impressa, γ areolata	ibid. t. 11, figg. 3—4.
"	universa	Williams, 1858, Brit. ree. Forf. p. 2, fig. 4 (=arenacea-).
"	Neojurensis	Karr., 1867, For. Ostert.; Wien. Ak. Sitz.-Ber. 1. 55, p 368, t. 3, fig. 10.
"	universa	Wallich, 1876, Deepsea Researches fig. 13.
Globigerina universa		Brad., 1879, Notes on Ret. Rhizop. »Challeng.« Exp.; Qu. Journ. Micr. Sc. (n. Ser.) 75, p. 289.

Globigerina bulloides d'Orb.
Tab. VI, figg. 195—207.

As with most other species of this class Glob. bulloides also has its tiny pigmy-form, that in some respect deviates from the type. It is usually of more regular growth; the first chambers are extremely small (about 0.02 mm.) and with 5 or 6 in each convolution; the pores are generally finer than in the larger and coarser form. It was distinguished by d'Orbigny as *Glob. cretacea* and *Glob. Dutertrei; Glob. dubia* Egger.

The stoutly developed form of *Glob. bulloides* commences its life with much larger and fewer chambers in each convolution. It is often very irregular, the chambers being more or less loosely connected, whence arises the difference in the number of visible apertures; not unfrequently the shell appears as if broken through by the immense apertures, which look like large defects in the chamber-walls. The shape of the chambers varies from globiform and oval to compressed thumb-like and even beak-formed.

The surface of the shell and the size of the pores are also liable to some variation, but even such features seem in this species to be only of an accidental character.

The most distinct character is found in the variety called *Glob. hirsuta* D'ORBIGNY, which has its chambers regularly coiled up in a nautiloid way, with the last ones generally unattached to the preceding coil. The aperture in this variety is situated on the inner (or lower) side of the last chamber. It is a mediate form between the pigmy and the typical forms. Notwithstanding all such peculiar features, we do not consider it in accordance with the usual conception of *varietal* distinction to mark this form with a separate designation.

The thick-walled, sometimes very coarse form with several outer apertures, by D'ORB. distinguished as *Glob. rubra*, is one of the commonest on our bottoms and has usually a reddish tint.

Mr. H. BRADY in his valuable paper »*Notes on some of the Reticularian Rhizopoda of the »Challenger» Expedition*« in Quart. Journ. Microscop. Science (new ser.) 75, p. 284. distinguishes the following varieties of Globigerina bulloides:

Globigerina dubia EGGER.
» *cretacea* D'ORB.
» *æquilateralis* D'ORB.
» *digitata* BRAD.
» *inflata* D'ORB.
» *Dutertrei* D'ORB.
» *rubra* D'ORB.
» *conglobata* BRAD.
» *saccudifera* BRAD.
» *helicina* D'ORB.

Fig. 195: a form near to REUSS' and others' *Glob. trilobata*, with the chambers highly developed from the first and with 1 or 2 apertures; seldom met with on the coralline-gravel.

Fig. 196: a coarse, thickshelled form with large chambers and several apertures; it comes near to *Glob. rubra* D'ORB. and may be identical with *Glob. conglobata* BRAD.; from the coralline-gravel.

Figg. 197—199: with large and loosely connected chambers, large apertures, and with the last chamber approaching to the thumbform. The pores are of middle size sunk in the bottom of the usual hexagonal impressions (fig. 199); from the coralline-gravel.

Fig. 200: the same form with still wider apertures; the latest chamber has a compressed beakform and is quite open underneath; from the chalk-ooze.

Fig. 201—202 the nautiloid form; from the chalk-ooze.

Fig. 203: the pigmyform: *Glob. cretacea* D'ORB., 203 b: the same more magnified from the chalk-ooze.

Figg. 204—207: the same form highly magnified with pores variable in size; viewed in transmitted light; from the chalk-ooze.

c) cameris conglomeratis:

Syn.	**Globigerina inflata**	D'ORB., 1844, Iles Canaries, p. 134, t. 1. figg. 7—9.
»	**bulloides** var. **inflata**	PARK. and JONES, 1865, N. Atl. and Arct. Oc.; Phil. Trans. 155, 1, p. 367, t. 16, figg. 16—17.
»	**bulloides**	D'ORB., 1826, Tabl. meth.; An. Sc. Nat. 7, p. 277, N:o 1, Mod. 17 et 76.
»	»	D'ORB., 1844, Iles Canaries p. 132, t. 2, figg. 1—3; 28.
»	»	RÖM., 1838, Nordd. tert. Meeressand, Leonh. u. Bronn. Jhrb. 1838, 4. 3, fig. 42 a.
»	»	D'ORB., 1846, For. tert. Vienne, p. 163, t. 9, figg. 4—6.
»	»	WILLIAMS., 1858, Brit. rec. Forf. p. 56, figg. 116—118.
»	»	PARK. and JONES, 1865, North. Atl. and Arct. Oc.; Phil. Transact. 155, 1, p. 365, t. 16, fig. 15.
»	»	GÜMB., 1868, Nordalp, Eocän; K. Bayr. Ak. Wiss. Abh. 1. 10. 2, p. 664, t. 2, fig. 106.
»	»	HKES., 1875, For. Clav. Szab. Seh. p. 69, t. 8, fig. 2.
»	*f borealis*	BRADY, 1881, Österr. Ung. Nordpols-Exp.; Wien. Ak. Dkschr. 13. 2. p. 101; An. Mag. Nat. Hist. (5) 1, t. 21, fig. 10.
»	**regularis**	D'ORB., 1846, For. tert. Vienne p. 162, t. 9, figg. 1—3.
»	**helicina**	D'ORB., 1826, Tab. meth.; An. Sc. Nat. 7, p. 277, N:o 5.
»	**globularis**	D'ORB., ibid. p. 277, N:o 3.
»	»	RÖM., 1838, Nordd. tert. Meeressand, Leonh. u. Bronn Jhrb. 1838, t. 3, fig. 57.
»	**trilocularis**	D'ORB., 1826, An. Sc. Nat. 7, p. 277, N:o 2.
»	»	RÖM., 1838, Nordd. tert. Meeressand; Leonh. u. Bronn. Jhrb. 1838, t. 3, fig. 41 a.
»	**bilobata**	D'ORB., 1846, For. tert. Vienne, p. 164, t. 9, figg. 11—14.
»	**quadrilobata**	D'ORB., ibid. p. 164, t. 9, figg. 7—10.
»	»	COSTA, 1854, Pal. Nap. 2, t. 21, fig. 5—6; p. 240.
»	**alpigena, asperula**	GÜMB., 1868, Nordalp. Eocan.; K. Bayr. Ak. Wiss. Abh. 1. 10. 2. t. 2, fig. 107—108.
»	**regularis**	COSTA, 1854, Pal. Nap. 2, p. 240, t. 21, fig. 3.
»	**triloba**	RSS., 1849, Neue For. österr. Beck.; Wien. Ak. Dkschr. 1. 1. p. 374, t. 47, fig. 11.
»	»	HKES., 1875, For. Clav. Szab. Seh., p. 69, t. 8, fig. 1.
»	**siphonifera**	D'ORB., 1839, Cuba, p. 83, t. 4, figg. 15—18.
»	**rubra**	D'ORB., ibid. p. 82, t. 4, figg. 12—14.
»	»	BAILEY, 1850, Micr. Exam. of Soundings; Smiths. Contrib. 2, Art. 3, p. 11, fig. 20—24.
»	**elevata**	D'ORB., 1839, For. Craie bl. Paris; Mém. Soc. géol. Fr. 4, p. 34, t. 3, figg. 15—16.
»	**reticulata**	STACHE, 1865, Tert. Merg. Whaingar. Haf.; Novara Reise, geol. Th. 1. 2, p. 287, t. 24, fig. 37

syn **Globigerina angipora**   Stache, 1865, Tert. Mergel Whaingar. Hafen; Novara Reise, geol. Th. 1. 2, p. 287, t. 24, fig. 36.
 »   seminulina   Schwag., 1866, Kar. Nikobar; Novara Reise, geol. Th. 2. 2, t. 7, fig. 112.
 »   conglomerata Schwag., ibid. p. 255, t. 7, fig. 113.
? »   bipartita   Rss., 1862, Crag. d'Anvers; Bull. Ac. Belg. (2) 15, p. 156, t. 3, fig. 46.
 »   (Rhynchospira) glomerata Karr., 1877, Hochquell. Wasserl.; geol. Reichsanst. Abh. 9, p. 387, t. 16, fig. 53.
?**Cassidulina globulosa**   Egg., 1857, Mioc. Ortenburg; Leonh. u. Bronn. Jhrb. 1857, p. 296, t. 10, figg. 4—6.

b) magis regularis helicoidea vel subhelicoidea; var. cretacea d'Orb.

Globigerina hirsuta   d'Orb., 1844, Iles Canaries p. 133, t. 2, figg. 1—6.
 »   concinna   Rss., 1849, Neue For. österr. tert. Beck.; Wien Ak. Dkschr. 1. 1. p. 373, t. 47, fig. 8.
 »   diplostoma Rss., ibid. p. 373, t. 47, figg. 9—10; t. 48, fig. 1.
 »   regularis   Rss., ibid. p. 373, t. 47, fig. 7.
 »   ooemna   Gümb., 1868, Nordalp. Foram.; K. Bayr. Ak. Wiss. 1. 10. 2. p. 662, t. 2, fig. 109.
 »   cretacea   d'Orb., 1839, For. Craie bl. Paris; Mem. Soc. geol. France 4, p. 34, t. 3, figg. 12—14.
 »   »   Rss., 1845, Böhm. Kreide 1, p. 36, t. 8, fig. 55.
 »   Dutertrei   d'Orb., 1839, Cuba, p. 84, t. 4, figg. 19—21.
 »   dubia   Egg., 1857, Miocän. Ortenburg; Leonh. u. Bronns Jhrb. 1857, p. 281, t. 9, figg. 7—9.
 »   Carteri   Karr., 1878, Foramf. Luzon.; Bolet. Comis. Mapa geol. del España 7. 2, p. 25, t. F, fig. 9.
 »   spirata   Hornes, 1855, Sept. Thon Hermsdorf; Ztschr. deutsch. geol. Ges. 7, p. 342, t. 16, fig. 9.

c) magis planata, rotaliformis; marginata Rss.:

Rotalina hirsuta   d'Orb., 1844, Iles Canaries p. 134, t. 1, figg. 37—39.
Rosalina marginata   Rss., 1845, Böhm. Kreide 1, p. 36, t. 8, figg. 54, 74, t. 13, fig. 68.
 »   »   Rss., 1854, Kreide Ostalp., Wien. Ak. Dkschr. 7, p. 69, t. 26, fig. 1.
 »   canaliculata Rss., ibid. t. 26, fig. 4.
 »   Linneiana   d'Orb., 1839, Cuba, p. 101, t. 5, figg. 10—12 (nec Park. et Jones).

d) trochoides sive Rhynchospira Ehrbg.:

Globigerina canariensis d'Orb., 1844, Iles Canaries, p. 133, t. 2, figg. 10—12.
 »   trochoides Rss., 1845, Böhm. Kreidef. 1, p. 36, t. 12, fig. 22.
 »   »   Rss., 1860, Kreidemerg. Lemberg; Naid. Nat. Abh. 4. 1, p. 37, t. 3, fig. 5.
?**Rhynchospira abnormis** Hkn., 1875, For. Clav. Szab. Sch. p. 69, t. 7, figg. 17—19 (Vermeulinæ-formis).

Carpenteria balaniformis Gray var. proteiformis n.

Tab. VI, figg. 208—214; Tab. VII, figg. 215—219.

In general our form agrees in structure with Carpenteria balaniformis from the Pacific (Carpenter Introduction t. 21); but it appears to be of a higher development than the latter. It is a Proteus without its equal in this class. Its original structure is regularly rotaline, but owing to its strong propensity to propagate additional chambers, particularly from its upper, i. e. apertural side and from the chamber-walls also issuing strong tubes, out of which new chambers are developed, the greatest variety of forms and alienation from the parent-type is the result. At one time the shell has its balaniform shape carrying on its top a cluster of ovoid or globular chambers. At another time this cluster appears detached from its parent shell, of which nothing is traceable. Sometimes the whole assumes the shape of a somewhat irregular Nodosarina. When this becomes ramified, the whole resembles some forms of Polytrema, to which genus Mr. Carter not improperly has referred this species (Carter, »On the Polytremata», A. M. N. H. (4) 17. 1876. p. 185). This variety is often of a roseo-coloured tinge; its chambers are generally of smaller size and more closely fitted and irregularly triserially arranged, the whole structure somewhat resembling a Ceriopora cribrosa Goldf., but not so regularly built as that. Its surface is often provided with coarse scattered impressions beside the channelpores.

Again it is developed in a free and unattached state into the shape of a large Globigerina or Bulimina. The chambers are sometimes of an extraordinary size — 3 or 4 mm. The pore-canals are large, pretty regularly and closely arranged in the thick walls.

Carpenteria Rhaphidodendron Mœbs., 1880, Maurit. u. Seychell. p. 81, t. 5, figg. 6—10, t. 6, figg. 1—6 seems not essentially to differ from the Philippine form.

Rupertia stabilis Wallich, A. M. N. H. (4) 19 (1877) p. 501, t. 20 seems to belong to this genus, and may be a pigmy form of this species notwithstanding its fissurelike and differently placed aperture. Its near affinity to Carpenteria is also indicated by Mr. Wallich.

Sphæroidina dehiscens Park. and Jones, from India (Philos. Trans. 155. 1. t. 19, fig. 5, seems also to come nearer to Carpenteria than to any other genus.

It is not rare in the coralline-gravel and also in the chalk-ooze; it grows not seldom to a hight of 10 mm. with long varicous branches.

Fig. 208 is the regular balaniform-rotaline, attached form; a new chamber shooting forth from the apertural part.

Fig. 209: a thin section of the walls, showing a network of pores very densely arranged.

Fig. 210: a tranverse section at the base, showing an entirely rotaline structure.

Fig. 211: another form with aulostomas-tubes on the latest segment.

Fig. 212; Nodosarina- or Virgulinaformed.

Fig. 213: rotaliform with a cluster of extra chambers.
Fig. 214: a single detached chamber with 3 eferent and 1 afferent tubes.
Fig. 215—216: free, globigerine form, with fissure like aperture.
Fig. 217: mediane section of the same.
Fig. 218: Polytremaformed, uniserial.
Fig. 219: Bulininaformed.

Syn. **Carpenteria balaniformis** Gray, 1858, On Carpenteria etc.; Proceed. Zool. Soc. 1858. 26, p. 266.
     Cart., 1862, Introduct. p. 186, t. 21.
  » **monticularis** Cart., 1877, A. M. N. H. (4) 19, p. 209, t. 13, ff. 9—15; Ibidem 20, p. 68.
Polytrema balaniforme Cart., 1876, A. M. N. H. (4) 17, p. 198, t. 13, figg. 7—10.

Planorbulina farcta Ficht. and Moll.

Tab. VII, figg. 220—225.

Our form has sometimes a subnautiloid shape with both sides nearly alike indicating an independent life, but in general it is »truncatuline.» This nautiloid form is hardly to be distinguished from *Plan. tuberosa* Ficht. and Moll. The early stage of growth is not distinguishable from the young of *Plan. vulgaris* d'Orb.

It is scarcely within our power to identify the many »species» referred to the genera *Truncatulina, Anomalina, Rosalina* etc.; which have been somewhat uncritically instituted by the different authors. Our list of synonyms, to a great deal founded on the able suggestions and unparalleled experience of Messrs. Parker and Jones, may still be liable to some errors in the disposition of the »species».

This cosmopolite is not uncommon, particularly in the chalk-ooze, but it seldom attains fully 1 mm. in diameter.

Figg. 220—222; 223—225: two specimens viewed from different sides; the one more »Anomalina» formed than the other.

Syn **Nautilus farctus**   Ficht. and Moll., 1803, Test. microsc. p. 64, t. 9, figg. g, h, i.

  a) irregularis: vulgaris d'Orb.

Webbina lœvis, tuberculata Sollas, 1877, Geol. Mag. Dec. 2: 4, N:o 1, p. 103, t. 6, figg. 1—3.
Truncatulina variabilis d'Orb., 1844, Iles Canaries p. 135, t. 1, fig. 29.
  »   »   Rss., 1864, Oberburg; Wien. Ak. Ditschr. 1. 23. 1, p. 10, t. 1, fig. 15.
  »   **innormalis** Costa, 1854, Pal Nap. 2, t. 21, fig. 11.
Planorb. truncata Ess., 1857, Mioc. Ortenb.; Leonh. u. Bronn. Jhrb. 1857, p. 280, t. 10, figg. 16—17.
Acervulina crotœ   Marss., 1877, Rügen. Schreibkreide; Greifsw. Nat. Verein. Mitth. 1877—78, p. 169, t. 5, fig. 39.
Anomalina anomala Ess., 1857, Mioc. Ortenb.; Leonh. u. Bronn. Jhrb. 1857, p. 280, t. 9, figg. 10—13.
Truncatulina tumescens Ess., ibid. p. 279, t. 9, figg. 14—16 (in Pl. tuberosam transgrediens)

Syn. **Truncatulina variabilis** d'Orb., 1826, Tabl. meth.; Ann. Sc. Nat. 7, p. 279 (= Pl. tuberosa sec. Parker et Jones).
Planorb. mediterranensis d'Orb., 1826, Tab. meth.; An. Sc. Nat. 7, p. 280. Mod. 79; 1846, Bas. tert. Vienne, p. 166, t. 9, figg. 15—17.
» **vulgaris** d'Orb., 1839, Cuba p. 85, t. 6, fig. 11—15; 1844, Iles Canaries p. 34, t. 2, fig. 30.
» » Williams., 1858, Brit. rec. Foramf., p. 57, figg. 119—120.
» **difformis** v. Münst.; Römer, 1838, Nordd. tert. Moerassande; Leonh. u. Bronn. Jhrb. 1838, p. 390, t. 3, fig. 59.
» **farcta** var. **mediterranensis** Park. et Jones, 1865, N. atl. and Aret. Oc., Phil. Trans. 155, 1, p. 383, t. 16, fig. 21.
» **retinaculata** Park. et Jones, 1862, Carp. Introd. p. 209; Phil. transact. 155, p. 421, t. 19, fig. 2.
» **larvata** Park. et Jones, 1865, ibid. t. 19, fig. 3; A. M. N. H. (3) 5, p. 68.
» » Carter, 1877, On for. found in and about Tubipora musica; A. M. N. H (4) 19, p. 214.
Nominib. variis Ehrenb., 1854, Microgeol. t. 25, fig. 42—43.

b) magis regularis: farcta Ficht. and Moll.:

Nautilus lobatulus Walk. and Jac., 1784, Test. min. rar. fig. 69. } sec. Park.
Serpula lobata Montagu, 1803, Test. Brit. Suppl. p. 515, fig. II. a. } et Jones.
Planorb. nitida d'Orb., 1826, Tab. meth.; An. Sc. Nat. 7, p. 280, Mod. 78.
Truncatulina tuberculata, Planulina incerta d'Orb., ibid. p. 279, 280, Mod. 37.
» **laevigata** Röm., Russ' Böhm. Kreide 1, p. 37, t. 13, fig. 47.
» **lobatula** Williams., 1858, Brit. rec. For. p. 59, figg. 121—123.
» » , **alternans** Costa, 1854, Pal. Nap. 2, p. 249, t. 14, fig. 7; t. 20, fig. 12.
Rosalina inaequalis Costa, ibid. t. 14, fig. 8.
Truncatulina carbonifera Brady, 1876, Carbonif. and Perm. foramf.; Pal. Soc. 30, p 138, t. 6, fig. 10.
Nominibus variis Ehrenb., 1854, Microgeol. t. 19, fig. 87, t. 25, figg. 27—28, 35—38; t. 26, figg. 32—36.
Truncatulina Beaumontiana d'Orb., 1839, For. Craie bl. Paris; Mém. Soc. geol. France 4, t. 3. figg. 17—19.
» **lobata** d'Orb., 1844, Iles Canaries, p. 134, t. 2, figg. 22—24.
» **lobatula** d'Orb., 1846, For. tert. Vienne p. 168, t. 9, figg. 18—23.
? » **Boueana, Anomalina variolata** d'Orb., ibid. p. 169, 170, t. 9, figg. 24—26, 27—29.
» **Boueana** Brady, 1876, Carb. and Perm. foramf.; Pal. Soc. p 138, t. 6, fig. 10.
» **lobatula** Park. et Jones, 1857, For. Coast. of Norway; An. Mag. Nat. Hist. 19, p. 293, t. 10, figg. 17—21.
Planorb. farcta var. **lobatula** Park. et Jones, 1865, North. Atl. and Arct. Oc.; Phil. Trans 155, 1, p. 381, t. 14, figg. 5—6; t. 16, figg. 18—20.
Truncatulina lobatula Park. et Jones, 1866, Crag. For.; Pal. Soc. 19, t. 2, figg. 4—10; 19.
» **convexa** Rss., 1854, Kreidemerg. Lemberg; Haid. Nat. Abh. 4. 1, p. 36, t. 3, fig. 4.
Rotalina sulcata Rss., 1862, Nordd. Hils u. Gault; Wien. Ak. Sitz.-Ber. 4. 46, p. 85, t. 11 fig. 2 (Obs. Rot. sulcata Rom. incerta est).
Rosalina rudis Rss., ibid. p. 87, t. 11, fig. 7.
» **nitens** Rss., ibid. p. 86, t. 11, fig. 4.

Syn. Truncatulina sublobatula, Bot. ammophila, macrocephala Gümb., 1868, Nordalp. Foram.; K.
         Bayr. Ak. Wiss. Abh. 1. 10. 2, p. 659, 652, t. 2, fig 103; figg. 90—91
         (in Pl. Ungerianam truncicus).
  Anomalina explanata   Costa, 1854, Pal. Nap. 2, p. 252, t. 14, fig. 4.
  ?Soldania hexagona   Costa, ibid. p. 248, t. 20, fig. 6.
  Truncatulina magnifica Costa, ibid. t. 14, fig. 3.
  Rotalia deplanata   Rss., 1855, Kreidegeb. Meklenburg; Zeitschr. deutsch. geol. Ges. 7, t. 11,
                         fig. 3.
  Truncatulina concinna Rss., ibid. p. 285, t. 11, fig. 4.
       »   Dekayi   Rss., 1861, Grünsand, New Jersey; Wien. Ak. Sitz.-Ber. 1. 44, p. 338, t. 7,
                         fig. 6.
       »   horrida   Karr., 1870, Kreidef. Leitzendorf; Österr. geol. Reichsanst. Jhrb. 20, p. 183,
                         t. 11, fig. 14.
  Rotalina pusilla   Schwag., 1863, Juras. Sch.; Würtemb. Nat. Verein. Jhrhft. 21, p. 141, t. 7,
                         fig. 20.
  Rosalina galiciana   Alth, 1850, Umgeb. Lemberg; Haid. Nat. Abh. 3. 2, p. 265, t. 13, fig. 20.
  Truncatulina lobatula Marss., 1877, Rüg. Schreibekr.; Greifsw. Nat. Verein. Mittheil. 1877—78,
                         p. 167, t. 5, fig. 38.
       »   advena   d'Orb., 1839, Cuba p. 87, t. 6, figg. 3—5.
  ?   »   communis   Rss., 1855, Tert. Schicht. nordl. u. mittl. Deutschl.; Wien. Ak. Sitz.-Ber.
                         1. 18, p. 242, t. 5, fig. 50.
       »   oblongata   Rss., 1863, For. Crag. d'Anvers; Bull. Ac. Belg. (2). 15, p. 155, t. 3,
                         fig. 45.
       »   Candei   d'Orb., 1839, Cuba p. 88, t. 3, figg. 6—8.
  Rosalina Bosqueti   Rss., 1861, Kreidetuff. Maastr.; Wien. Ak. Sitz.-Ber. 1. 44, p. 316, t. 3,
                         fig. 1.
  Rosalina Edwardsiana   d'Orb., 1839, Cuba, p. 101, t. 1, figg. 8—10.

Planorbulina fareta var. vulgaris d'Orb.

Tab. VII, figg. 226—227.

If one should venture to dispose the Planorbulina forms into species, instead of using the more philosophical way of arrangement initiated by Messrs. Parker and Jones, 3 or at the most 4 forms might be distinguished by somewhat specific characters. This genus is next to Nodosarina the clearest example of the advantage of the nomenclatural system adopted by those eminent naturalists.

Some or perhaps all of these species have a free and an attached form, whence it will be obvious, that a number of varieties may result from the different modes of life. The attached forms have a great propensity towards irregular growth, and forms like *Truncatulina variabilis* d'Orb, *Webbina lævis* and *tuberculata* Sollas, *Plan. vulgaris* d'Orb., *Acervulina* W Schultze are originated. In other instances the same attached species adopts a more regular growth, such as *Truncatulina lobatula* Walk. or the typical *Plan. fareta* Ficht. and Moll., and when it passes its life in a free condition, its shape may be more or less nautiloid.

It may for this reason be proper to arrange Planorb. vulgaris as a variety under *Plan. fareta* and take *Plan. lobatula* as quite synonymous with the typical *fareta*, maintaining the latter name for the species, notwithstanding the priority of *lobatula*.

A second species, but rather too closely allied to *farcta* to claim the rank of species, would be *Plan. tuberosa* FICHT. and MOLL., seemingly identical with *Rosalina ammonoides* Rss., *Plan. angulata* v. HAGEN, *Plan. coronata* PARK. and JONES. Many forms belonging to this group (*»Anomalinas* D'ORB.) may after a closer examination be recognised as the detached form of *Plan. farcta*, as is also suggested by Mr. CARPENTER (Introd. p. 208). *Planorbulina Ariminensis* D'ORB. is too closely allied both to *Plan. tuberosa* and *farcta* to be distinguished as a species.

Plan. Ungeriana D'ORB. which cannot be distinguished from *Plan. Haidingeri*, and oth., would be a third species. It has a more finished structure and is provided with finer pore-canals.

A fourth species is *Plan. reticulata* CZJZ.

Plan. farcta β vulgaris does not attain any larger size either on the coralline- or chalk-bottom; its pigmy form is not unfrequent. The early chambers have generally a reddish or orange tint.

Fig. 226: the developed form of *Plan. farcta vulgaris;* nearly of the same habitus as *Planorb. larvata* PARK. and JONES, with a narrow mouth on each of the outer chambers.

Fig. 227: pigmy form.

For the synonymy see under the preceding.

Planorbulina tuberosa FICHT. and MOLL. var. Ariminensis D'ORB.

Tab. VII, figg. 228—233.

It may be more consistent with natural affinity to rank this variety with *Plan. farcta*. But if Plan. tuberosa is to comprise the principal forms of the nautiloid and subnautiloid Planorbulina, this variety would be the first to take a place under this species on account of its decided and completely nautiloid plan of growth. Our form is often rough or wrinkled, with somewhat raised and sinuous septal lines and a truncated or even grooved margin, the edges of which are often crenulate or spinous (figg. 228—230).

Another form is smoother and has not a squared margin but is single-edged (figg. 231—233). It comes near to *Anomal. rotula* D'ORB.

The variety *Ariminensis* has generally a greater number of chambers in each convolution (7—10) than *Plan. farcta*. Its close affinity to this is shown by its coarse pores and the yellowish or reddish tint of its early chambers.

It is very common in the chalk-ooze, but its diameter is seldom greater than 0,5 mm.

a) tuberosa sive ammonoides:

Syn. Rotalina cryptomphala	Rss., 1849, Neue For. Wien. Beck.; Wien. Ak. Dkschr. 1. 1, p. 371, t. 47, fig. 2.
» »	Lūger, 1857, Mioc. Ortenburg; Leonh. u. Bronn, Jhrb. 1857, p. 277, t. 9, figg. 4—6.
Rosalina inflata	Rss., 1862. Nordd. Hils u. Gault; Wien. Ak. Sitz-Ber. 1. 46, p. 87, t. 11, fig. 6.
» simplex	d'Orb., 1846, For. test. Vienne p. 178, t. 10, figg. 25—27.
» »	Egger, 1857, Miocaen. v. Ortenburg; Leonh. u. Bronn. Jhrb. 1857, p. 278, t. 10, figg. 4—6.
Truncatulina granosa,	Pulv. similis Rkss., 1875, For. Clav. Szab. Sch., p. 71, 78, t. 10, figg. 2, 5
Rotalina depressa	Altii, 1849, Umgeb. Lemberg; Haid. Nat. Abh. 3. 2, p. 266, t. 13, fig. 21.
Anomalina rotula	d'Orb. 1846. Bass. tert. Vienne, p. 172, t. 10, figg. 10—12 (ab »Anom.» austriaca vix diversa).
» subæqualis	Rss., 1855, Tert. Sch. nordl. u. mittl. Deutschl.; Wien. Ak. Sitz.-Ber. 1. 18, p. 244, t. 5, fig. 59.
» complanata	Costa, 1854, Paleont. Nap. 2, t. 20, fig. 16.
» »	Rss., 1850, Kreidemerg. Lemberg; Haid. Nat. Abh. 4. 1, p. 36, t 3, fig. 3.
Rosalina complanata	Rss., 1862, Nordd. Hils u. Gault, Wien. Ak. Sitz.-Ber. 1. 46, p. 86, t. 11, fig. 3.
Anomalina tenuissima	Rss., 1855, Tert. Schicht. nordl. u. mittl. Deutschl.; Wien. Ak. Sitz-Ber. 1. 18, p. 244, t. 5, fig. 60.
Truncatulina tenuissima	Rss., 1861, Kreidetuff. Maastr. Wien. Ak. Sitz-Ber. 1. 44, p. 317, t. 3, fig. 2.
Truncatulina costata	Hann, 1875, Clav. Szab. Sch. p. 73, t. 9, fig. 2 (in Planorb. acumineasem vergens).
Nautilus tuberosus	Ficht. et Moll., 1803, Test. micr. p. 111, t. 20, figg. g—k.
Rosalina ammonoides	Rss., 1845, Böhm. Kreide 1, p. 36, t. 8, fig. 53; t. 13, fig. 66.
» » .	Rss., 1850, Kreidem. Lemberg, Haid. nat. Abh. 4. 1, p. 36, t. 3, fig. 2.
Truncatulina stella, inæqualis Karr., 1868, Mioc. Kostej.; Wien. Ak. Sitz.-Ber. 1. 58, p. 182, t. 4, fig. 13—14.	
Planorbulina angulata	v. Hagen., 1842, Rügen. Kreide; Leonh. u. Bronn. Jhrb. 1842, p. 571, t. 9, fig. 23.
Rotalina constricta	v. Hagen, ibid.: Rss., 1861, Kreide v. Rugen; Wien. Ak. Sitz.-Ber. 1. 44, p. 329, t. 6, fig. 7, t. 7, fig. 1.
Rosalina moniliformis	Rss., 1845, Böhm. Kreide. 2, p. 36, t. 12, fig 30, t. 13, fig. 67.
Anomalina Svessi	Karr., 1861, Marin Teg. Wien. Beck.; Wien. Ak. Sitz.-Ber. 1. 44, p. 447, t. 2, fig. 2.
Rosalina Kochi	Rss., 1855, Kreidegeb. Meklenburg; Zeitschr. deutsch. geol. Ges. 7, p. 274, t. 9, fig. 3.
» Weinkauffi	Rss., 1863, Sept. Thon Kreuznach; Wien. Ak. Sitz.-Ber. 1. 48, p. 68, t. 8, fig. 97.
Truncat. »	R—, 1866, deut. Sept. Thon; Wien. Ak. Dkschr. 25. p. 160.
Rotalia capitata, Rosalina rudis Gümb., 1868, Nordalp. Eocän.; K. Bayr. Ak. Wiss. Abh. 1. 10. 2, p. 653, 657, t. 2, figg. 92, 99.	

b) in Planorb. farctam vergens (a qua vix distinguenda):

Anomalina punctulata	d'Orb., 1826, Tabl. meth.; Ann. Sc. Nat. 7, p. 282, t. 15, figg. 1—3 bis.
Rosalina Lorneiana	d'Orb., 1839, For. Craie bl. Paris.; Mem. Soc. geol. Fr. 4, p. 36, t. 3, figg. 20—22.

Truncatulina grosserugosa Gümb., 1868, Nordalp. Eocän.; K. Bayr. Ak. Wiss. Abh. 1. 10. 2, p. 660, t. 2. fig. 104.
" " Hren., 1875, Clav. Száb. Sch. p. 74, t. 9, fig. 6.
Anomalina polymorpha Costa, 1854, Pal. Nap. 2, p. 252, t. 22, figg. 7—9.
" **badenensis, austriaca** d'Orb., 1846, Ros. tert. Vienne, p. 171, 172, t. 10, figg. 1—9.

c) »coronatas: nautiloidea, tumida:

Anomalina coronata   Parker et Jones, 1858, For. Coast. of Norway; A. M. N. H. (2) 19, p. 294, t. 10, figg. 15—16.
" "   Parker et Jones, 1865, North. Atl. and Arct. Oceans; Phil. Trans. 155. 1, p. 383, t. 14, figg. 7—11.
" "   Brady, 1864, Rhizop. Shetl.; Trans. Lin. Soc. 24, p. 469, t. 48, fig. 13.
Rotalia cochleata   Gümb., 1868, Nordalp. Eoc.; K. Bayr. Ak. Wiss. 1, 10. 2, p. 654, t. 2, fig. 94
Truncatulina cristata   Gümb., ibid. p. 660, t 2, fig. 105.
Rosalina Calymene   Gümb., ibid. p. 658, t. 2, fig. 100.
" **fasciata, maorica, latifrons** Stache, 1865, tert. Mergel. Whaingar. Haf.; Novara Reise, geol. Th. 1. 2, p. 282, 284, t. 24, figg. 31—33.
Rotalia speciosa   Karr., 1864, Leythakalk; Wien. Ak. Sitz.-Ber. 1. 50, p. 709, t. 2, fig. 12.
" **nonionina**   Rss., 1862, Nordd. Hils u. Gault; Wien. Ak. Sitz.-Ber. 1. 46, p. 81, t. 10, fig. 2.

d) »Ariminensis«: nautiloidea, compressa:

Planulina Ariminensis   d'Orb., 1826, Tab. meth.; An. Sc. Nat. 7, p. 280, t. 14, figg. 1—3 bis. Mod. 49.
" **Soldanii**   d'Orb., ibid. p. 280.
? " **Osnabrügensis** Röm., 1838, Nordd. tert. Meeres.; Leonh. u. Bronn Jhrb. 1838, p. 390, t. 3, fig. 58.
Rosalina Osnabrugensis Rss. 1855, Tert. Sch. nordl. u. mittl. Deutschl.; Wien. Ak. Sitz.-Ber. 1. 18, p. 243, t. 5, fig. 58.
Truncatulina compressa Hren., 1875, For. Clav. Szab Sch. p. 72, t. 8, fig. 8.
" **osnabr.**   Hren., ibid. p. 73, t. 9, fig. 4.

Planorbulina Ungeriana d'Orb.

Tab. VII, figg. 234—236.

Our form has the more distended shape of *Plan. Haidingeri* d'Orb. but in all other respects it falls in with *Plan. Ungeriana* of the same author. Sometimes it approaches the subnautiloid form, but its most common shape is that of a bi- or plano-convex, somewhat thick, lens with a blunt edge and rotaline arranged chambers.

It plainly exhibits the very vague and faint distinction between the »*Anomalines*« and *Planorbuline* types. Sometimes the shell is quite conical the aboral face being flat, the other raised conically. The central bosses are often granulated, not seldom spreading over a great portion of the shell around the centre and hiding the convolutions and septal lines, which often are somewhat raised (limbate). At another times the bosses are reduced to small specks of clear shell-substance.

The pores of the adult are finer and closer set than in Plan. farcta; in young specimens the pores are of variable size, often coars and scattered. The surface is of high finish without being quite polished.

It is one of the most common rhizopodes in deep water, both in the cretaceous ooze and on the coralline-gravel, attaining a horizontal diameter of 1,5 mm.

Fig. 234: the aboral side of *Plan. Ungeriana* with large and somewhat granulated central boss.

Fig. 235: side view.

Fig. 236: the apertural side with defectively grown umbilical boss.

a) magis convexa:

Syn. Rotalina	**Haidingeri**	D'ORB., 1846, For. tert. Vienne, p. 154, t. 8, figg. 7—9.
»	**rosea**	D'ORB., 1826, Tabl. meth.; Ann. Sc. Nat. 7, p. 272; Mod. 35.
»	»	D'ORB., 1839, Cuba p. 72, t. 3, figg. 9—11.
? »	**Ehrenbergii**	BAILEY, 1850, Examin. of Soundings; Smithson. Contrib. of knowledge 2, Art. 3, p. 10, figg. 11—13.
Planorb.	**Haidingeri**	BRADY, 1864, Rhizopod. Shetl.; Trans. Lin. Soc. 24, p. 469, t. 48, fig. 11.
»	farcta var. **Haidingeri** PARK. et JONES, 1865, North. Atl. and Arct. Oc.; Phil. Transact. 155. 1, p. 382, t. 16, fig. 22.	
»	**Haidingeri**	PARK. et JONES, 1866, Crag. Foramf.; Palæont. Soc. 19, t. 4, fig. 18.
Rotalina	**lenticula**	RSS., 1845, Böhm. Kreide 1, p. 35, t. 12, fig. 17
»	**grata**	RSS., 1865, deutsch. Sept. Thon; Wien. Ak. Dkschr. 1. 25. 1, p. 163, t. 4, fig. 17.
»	**Dutemplei**	EGGER, 1857, Mioc. Ortenburg; Leonh. u. Bronn. Jhrb. 1857, p. 274, t. 7, fig. 8—10.
»	**orthorapha**	EGG., ibid. p. 275, t. 10, figg. 1—3.
»	**discigera, anomphala** EGG., ibid. p. 275, t. 8, figg. 5—10.	
»	**propinqua**	EGG., ibid. p. 275, t. 7, figg. 14—17.
»	**Kalembergensis** EGG., ibid. p. 278, t. 9, figg. 21—23.	
Truncat.	**kallomphalia**	GÜMB., 1868, Nordalp. Eocän.; K. Bayr. Ak. Wiss. Abh. 1. 10. 2, p. 650, t. 2, fig. 102.
Rotalia	**oocœna**	GÜMB., ibid. p. 650, t. 2, fig. 87.
»	**pteromphala, mogomphala** GÜMB., ibid. p. 651, 655; t. 2, fig. 88, t. 2, fig. 94 bis.	
»	**truncana**	GÜMB., ibid. p. 653, , t. 2, fig. 93 (in b) transiens).
Rosalina	**subumbonata**	GÜMB., ibid. p. 657, t. 2, fig. 98.
Rotalina	**Akneriana** var.	BORNEM., 1855, Sept. Thon Hermsdorf; Ztschr. deutsch. geol. Ges. 7, p. 340, t. 16, fig. 7.
»	**Ungeriana** var.	BORNEM., ibid. p. 341, t. 16, fig. 5.
?Truncat.	**propinqua**	RSS., 1855, Tert. Sch. nordl. u. mittl. Deutschl.; Wien. Ak. Sitz.-Ber. 1. 18, p. 241, t. 4, fig. 53.
? »	»	HXES., 1875, Clav. Száb. Sch. p. 71, t. 8, fig. 9.
Pulvinulina	**Haidingeri**	HXES., 1875, For. Clav. Száb. Sch., p. 77, t. 15, fig. 10.
»	**umbilicata**	HXES., ibid. t. 15, fig. 9.
Rotalia	**peraffinis**	COSTA, 1855, Pal. Nap. 2, t. 22, fig. 17.
»	**Brücknerí**	RSS., 1855, Kreidegeb. Mcklenburg; Zeitschr. deutsch. geol. Ges. 7, p. 273, t. 9, fig. 7.
»	**hemisphærica**	RSS., 1861, Kreidetuff Maastricht; Wien. Ak. Sitz.-Ber. 1, 44, p. 314. t. 2, fig. 5.

Syn. ? **Rotalia præcincta**		Karr., 1868, Mioc. For. fauna Kostej; Wien. Ak. Sitz.-Ber. 1. 58, p. 189, t. 5, fig. 7 (Polv. eleganti similis).
»	**tenuimargo**	Rss., 1866, Crag. Antwerp.; Wien. Ak. Sitz.-Ber. 42, p. 359, t. 1, fig. 11.
»	**franconica**	Gümb., 1862, streitb Schwamm.; Würtemb. Nat. Ver. Jbrbft. 1862, p. 229, t. 4, fig. 9 (in b) transiens).
»	**semipunctata**	Bail., 1850, Researches on the Virg. forf.; Smithson. Contrib. 1850. 2, Art. 3, p. 11, figg. 17—19 (in b) transiens).
? »	**Siemensis**	d'Orb., 1826, Tabl. meth.: Ann. Sc. Nat. 7, p. 275.
? **Rosalina Clementiana**		d'Orb., 1839, For. Craie bl. Paris; Mém. Soc. geol. France 4, p. 37, t. 3, figg. 23—25 (= Planorb. tuberosa sec. Park. et Jones).
Rotalina scutellaris		Karr., 1864, Leythakalk Wien. Beck.; Wien. Ak. Sitz.-Ber. 1. 50, p. 709, t. 2, fig. 13.
»	**Voltziana**	d'Orb., 1839, For. Craie bl. Paris, Mem. Soc. geol. France 4. p. 31, t. 2, figg. 32—34.

b) magis compressa, interdum carinata (ab a non distincta):

Rotalina Ungeriana		d'Orb., 1846, For. Rss. tert. Vienne, p. 157, t. 8, figg. 16—18.
Planorb. farcta var.		Ungeriana Park. et Jones, 1865, North. Atl. and Arct. Ocean; Phil. Trans. 155. 1, p. 382, t. 16, figg. 23—25; Pl. Culter t. 19, fig. 1.
»	**Ungeriana**	Park. et Jones, 1866, Crag. For.; Pal. Soc. 19, t. 2, figg. 11—12.
Truncat. Ungeriana		Hken., 1875, Clav. Szab. Sch. p. 72, t. 8, fig. 7.
Planorb. Ungeriana		Brady, 1864, Rhizop. Shetl., Trans. Lin. Soc. 24, p. 469, t. 48, fig. 12.
Rotalia Mortoni		Rss., 1861, Grünsand N. Yersey; Wien. Ak. Sul.-Ber. 1. 44, p. 337, t. 8, fig. 1 (ab a) non distincta).
»	**tuberculifera**	Rss., 1861, Kreidetuff Maastricht.; Wien. Ak. Sitz.-Ber. 1. 44, p. 313, t. 2, fig. 2.
»	**granosa**	Rss., 1851, Sept. Thon Berlin; Ztschr. deutsch. geol. Ges. 3, p. 75, t. 5, fig. 36.
»	**umbonella**	Rss., 1859, Westph. Kreide; Wien. Ak. Sitz.-Ber. 40, p. 221, t. 11, fig. 5.
»	**Römeri**	Rss., 1855, Tert. Schicht. nördl. u. mittl. Deutschl.; Wien. Ak. Sitz.-Ber. 1. 18, p. 240, t. 4, figg. 52.
»	**involuta** var.	Rss., 1861, Kreidetuff Maastricht; Wien. Ak. Sitz.-Ber. 1. 44, p. 313, t. 2, fig. 4.
Rosalina crenata		Rss., 1855, Tert. Schicht. n. u. m. Deutschl.; Wien. Ak. Sitz.-Ber. 1. 18, p. 243, t. 5, fig. 57.

c) convexo-plana (forsan adnata) in Planorb. tuberosam et farctam Ficht & Moll. transiens:

Anomalina Wüllerstorfi		Schwag., 1866, For. Kar-Nikobar; Nov. Reise, geol. Th. 2, 2, p. 258, t. 7, figg. 105—107.
Rosalina Schlönbachi		Rss., 1862, Nordd. Hils u. Gault; Wien. Ak. Sitz.-Ber. 1. 46, p. 84, t. 10, fig. 5, t. 11, fig. 5.
»	**Kalembergensis**	d'Orb., 1846, For. Bass. tert. Vienne, p. 151, t. 7, figg. 19—21.
»	**Akneriana, Dutemplei**	d'Orb., 1826, ibid. p. 156, 157, t. 8, figg. 13—15, 19—21.
»	**lenticula**	Rss., 1862, Nordd. Hils u. Gault; Wien. Ak. Sitz.-Ber. 1. 46, p. 82, t. 10, fig. 3.
»	**affinis**	Czjz., 1847, Foss. for. Wien. Beck.; Haid. nat. Abh. 2. 1, p. 144, t. 12. figg. 36—38.
Rotalina involuta, polyrraphes		Rss., 1845, Böhm. Kreidef. 1, p. 35, t. 12, fig. 18; 1850, Kreidemergel Lemberg; Haid. Nat. Abh. 4. 1, p. 35, t. 2, fig. 14; t. 3, fig. 1.
Truncat. cryptomphala		Hken., 1875, Clav. Szab. Sch. p. 73, t. 9, fig. 1.
? »	**insignis**	Rss., 1869, Oligocän. v. Gaas; Wien. Ak. Sitz.-Ber. 1. 59, p. 461, t. 2. fig. 2.

Syn. Truncat. varians	Rss. 1860, For. Crag. v. Antwerp.; Wien. Ak. Sitz.-Ber. 42, p. 359, t. 2, fig. 12.
» lucida	Rss., 1865, Deutsch. Septarienthon; Wien. Ak. Dkschr. 1. 25. 1, p. 160, t. 4, fig. 15.
» Duteraplei	Rss., ibid. p. 160, t. 4, fig. 16.
» »	Hxx., 1875, For. Clav. Száb. Schichten p. 157, t. 8, figg 19—21.
» tenella	Rss., 1864, Oberoligocän; Wien. Ak. Sitz.-Ber. 1. 50, p. 477, t. 5, fig 6.
Rosalina patella	Egger, 1857, Mioc. Ortenb.; Leonh. u. Bronn. Jhrb. 1857, p. 278, t. 10, figg. 12—14.

Planorbulina Ungeriana var. affixa n.
Tab. VII, figg. 237—241.

Notwithstanding its finer pores and its other deviation from the type, the texture, surface of the shell and the arrangement of the chambers, this form bear too close an affinity to Plan. Ungeriana not to be ranged under this species. Its upper side is often scooped out in an irregular manner, and the much flattened shell is somewhat undulated with irregular sinuous edges, indicating an attached life. The central boss on this side is sometimes wanting, but never on the opposite (apertural) side.

It is not very common in the coralline-gravel.

Fig. 237: represents a transverse section near the attached side.

Fig. 238: edge view of the same specimen.

Fig. 239: another specimen; its upper hollowed out side.

Fig. 240: the edge view, showing the shell as if bent in its diameter, the upper side being concave, the apertural side convex.

Fig. 241: the apertural side.

Planorbulina reticulata Czjz.
Tab. VII, figg. 242—244.

This remarkable species was first described in 1847 as occuring in the tertiary strata of Austria by Czjzek. Its close affinity to the genus Planorbulina has been asserted by Messrs Parker and Jones. One side is generally smooth the other wrinkled or coarsely striated. The pores are coarse and often stand closer together at the central part of the shell. Its broad marginal keel is transversely costated and seems to be a constant appendage. Some pigmy forms have their chambers arranged in a very imperfect coil; the primordial chamber not being placed in the centre.

It occurs not uncommonly both in the chalk-ooze and in the coralline-gravel.

Fig. 242: the striated side.

Fig. 243: a younger specimen seen in transmitted light.

Fig. 244: pigmy form in transmitted light, magnified.

Syn. Rotalina reticulata	Czjz., 1847, For. foss. Wien. Beck.; Haid. Nat. Abh. 2. 1, p. 145, t. 13, figg. 7—9.
Siphonina fimbriata	Rss., 1849, Neue for. bsterr. tert. Becken; Wien. Ak. Dkschr. 1. 1, p. 372, t. 47, fig. 6
» puteolana	Costa, 1854, Psi Nap., t. 27, fig. 22.

Tinoporus vesicularis Park. and Jones.

Tab. VII, figg. 245—247.

Our form with its much flattened shape, and the form and arrangement of its chambers suggests at once its affinity to *Planorbulina;* an affinity almost too close to afford sufficient reason for a generic distinction. The surface is somewhat foveolate-reticulated with faintly marked septal lines, and of a light-brown colour. A remarkable feature is the slight differentiation of the chambers in the median plane, which are somewhat larger than those of the other layers, this arrangement in some degree approaching the structure of Orbitoides.

It is not common on the coralline-gravel.

Fig. 245: Tinoporus vesicularis with its areolated surface.

Fig. 246: a vertical section in the median plane.

Fig. 247: Section through or near the horizontal middle-plane.

Syn. Orbitulina vesicularis, congesta, lævis Park. et Jones, 1863, Nomenclature — Lamarck —; A. M. N. H. (3) 5, p. 285, et seqv.
Tinoporus lævis   Carpenter, 1862, Introd., p. 224, t. 15, figg. 1—4.
"   "   Brady, 1864, Rhizop. Shetland; Trans. Lin. Soc. 24, p. 470, t. 48, fig. 17.

Pullenia sphæroides d'Orb.

Tab. VIII, figg. 248—250.

This little thickwalled, highly polished, milkwhite rhizopode attains seldom a a greater diameter than 0,50 mm. Its shape is often subglobose, but somewhat compressed forms also occur. It is frequently somewhat unsymmetrical; the aperture being placed somewhat to one side. The form called *Pullenia obliqueloculata* Park. and Jones is such a variety with a more conspicuous lack of symmetry.

It is not uncommon in the coralline-gravel.

Fig. 248—249: the compressed form of *Pullenia sphæroides.*

Fig. 250: nearly globose, with slightly unsymmetrical whorls.

Syn. Nonion. sphæroides   d'Orb., 1826, Tabl. Méth.; Ann. Sc. Nat. 7, p. 293, N:o 1, Mod. 33.
"   bulloides   d'Orb., 1846, For. foss. tert. Vienne, p. 107, t. 5, figg. 9—10.
"   "   var.   Costa, 1854, Pal. Nap. 2, t. 17, fig. 13.
"   "   Bornemann, 1855, Sept. Thon Hermsdorf; Zeitschr. deutsch. geol. Ges. 7, p. 339, t. 16, figg. 1—3.
"   "   Park. et Jones, 1859, For. Coast. of Norway; Ann. Mag. Nat. Hist. (2) 19, p. 287, t. 11, figg. 9—10.
Pullenia sphæroides   Park. et Jones, 1865, North. Atl. and Arct. Oc.; Phil. Trans. 15, 1, p. 368, t. 14, fig. 43, t. 17, fig. 53.
"   "   Park. et Jones, 1866, Crag. For.; Pal. Soc. 19, t. 2, figg. 31—32.
"   "   Carpenter, 1862, Introd. p. 184, t. 12, fig. 12.

Syn. **Pullenia bulloides**   Hken., 1875, Clav. Scab. Sch., p. 59, t. 10, fig. 9.
  »   **obliqueloculata** Park. and Jones, 1865, Arct. and Northatl. Ocean; Phil. Trans. 155. 1, t. 19, fig. 4.

b) magis compressa:

Nonion. quaternaria   Rss., 1850, Kreidemerg. Lemberg; Haid. nat. Abh. 4. 1, p. 34, t. 2, fig. 13.
  »   **quinqueloba**   Rss., 1851, Sept. Thon v. Berlin; Zeitschr. deutsch. geol. Ges. 3, p. 72, t. 5, fig. 31.
Pullenia compressiuscula ⚥ **quadriloba** Rss., 1867, Steinsalzablager. Wieliczka; Wien. Ak. Sitz.-Ber. 1. 55, p. 87. t. 3, fig. 8.

Discorbina rosacea d'Orb.
Tab. VIII, figg. 251—257.

Our form is generally of pigmy size; it comes near to *Asterigerina planorbis* d'Orb. and Egger (from the tertiary strata) and is also nearly identical in shape with *Ros. Auberii* d'Orb. from the West Indies. Its most striking feature is its semilunar, long chambers, and their restricted number in each convolution. It has a yellowish hue in transmitted light.

The scantiness of our supply of Discorbinae and the uncritical method of specific distinction and representation of the forms adopted by the different authors make us unable to make a satisfactory disposition of the forms in their natural places, notwithstanding the very sagacious hints in regard to this matter given by Messrs. Parker and Jones.

The difference between *Discorb. rosacea* and *valvulata* is very slight.

It is not uncommon, but always in a pigmy-state, (0,25 mm.) in the chalk-ooze.

Figg. 251—253; *Discorbina rosacea;* 251 b: the same more enlarged, in transmitted light.

Figg. 254—255: another specimen, spiral and apertural sides.

Figg. 256—257: young small specimens; it has sometimes a clouded appearance in transmitted light.

Syn. **Rotalia rosacea**   d'Orb., 1826, Tab. meth.; An. Sc. Nat. 7, p. 273, N:o 15, Mod. 39.
Discorbina turbo var. **rosacea** Park. et Jones, 1865, North. Atl. and Arct. Oc.; Phil. Transact. 155. 1, p. 385, t. 16, fig. 28.
  »   **rosacea**   Park. et Jones, 1866, Crag. For.; Pal. Soc. 19, t. 4, fig. 17
Rotalia Mamilla, ochracea Williams., 1858, Brit. rec. forf. p. 54, 55, figg. 109—113
Asterigerina planorbis   d'Orb., 1846, For. tert. Vienne p. 205, t. 11, figg. 1—3.
  »   »   Egger, 1857, Mioc. Ortenburg; Leouh. u. Bronn. Jhrb. 1857, p. 281, t. 11, figg. 8—10.
Rosalina Auberii   d'Orb., 1839, Cuba, p. 94, t. 4, figg. 5—8.
Truncat. flos   Karr., 1868, Mioc. For. faun. Kostej; Wien. Ak. Sitz.-Ber. 1. 58, p. 182, t. 4, fig. 15.

Syn. ?**Discorbina baconica, elegans** Hken., 1875, Clav. Szab. Seh. p. 76, t. 10, fig. 3, t. 9, fig. 3, t. 15, fig. 7,
» **oximia** Hken., ibid. p. 76, t. 15, fig. 8.

Discorbina turbo d'Orb. et multæ aliæ trochiformes auctorum a **rosacea** forsan non sunt distinctæ.

Discorbina valvulata d'Orb.
Tab. VIII, figg. 258—261.

Although this form has been placed as a variety under *Discorb. vesicularis* Lmck, by Messrs Parker and Jones, it may be proper to distinguish it as a species in virtue of its peculiarly formed shell. It is identical with *Rosalina Binkhorsti* Rss. from the Maestrich-chalk, and is remarkable for the fewness and the large size of its chambers, its hollowed apertural side, which is of simpler structure than usually, not being complicated with additional »asterigerine« flaps, having no more than a narrow valvular strip on the upper margin of the aperture.

It attains a pretty good size, occurring only in the coralline-gravel.

Figg. 258—259: the spiral side.
Fig. 260: apertural side.
Fig. 261: edge-view.

Syn. **Rosalina valvulata**	d'Orb., 1826, Tabl. meth. Ann. Sc. Nat. 7, p. 271.
» »	d'Orb., 1839 Cuba p. 96, t. 3, figg. 21—23.
» **Binkhorsti**	Rss., 1861, Kreidetuff Maastricht; Wien. Ak. Sitz.-Ber. 1. 44, p. 317, t. 2, fig. 3.
?**Rotalina patella**	Rss., 1849, Neue For. Wien. Beck.; Wien. Ak. Dkschr. 1. 1, p. 371, t. 46, fig. 3 (an D. Berthelotiana).
Discorb. stellata, squamula	Rss., 1867, Steinsalzablag. Wieliczka; Wien. Ak. Sitz.-Ber. 1. 55, p. 101, t. 5, figg. 1—2 (an D. rosacea).

Discorbina bulloides d'Orb.
Tab. VIII, fig. 262—263.

I am not able to find any satisfactory reason for a generic nay even for specific distinction between Discorbina rosacea and this form, which has been referred to the genus *Cymbalopora* (Hagenow) by Messrs Parker, Jones and Carpenter.

This however seems to have very small affinity to our form — if any at all. (See also Schwager in Bütchli's Klassen und Ordnungen des Thierreichs 1881, p. 256.)

Prof. Mobius has carried the separation from its natural relations still further by assigning it a place in a new genus, *Tretomphalus*; (Meeresfauna Mauritius und Seychellen; foramf. p. 98, t. 10, figg. 6—9). The pores of various sizes on the last segment should not be regarded as a mark of generic nor of specific distinction. If this globular chamber is detached, the rest will hardly be distinguished from D. rosacea.

From *Discorbina globigerinoides* Park. and Jones it may be difficult to keep our form distinct. (Phil. trans. 155. 1, t. 19, fig. 7).

Fig. 262: Discorbina (Rosalina) bulloides d'Orb.
Fig. 263 b: The same more magnified.
Fig. 263: side-view.

Syn. **Rosalina bulloides** d'Orb., 1839, Cuba p. 98, t. 3, figg. 2—5.
Cymbalopora bulloides Carpent., Introd. 1862, p. 216.
Trotomphalus bulloides Mök., 1880, Meeresfaun. Maurit. v. Seych. p. 98, t. 10, figg. 6—9.

Discorbina Poeyi d'Orb.

Tab. VIII, figg. 264—265.

This remarkable form seems just as little entitled to generic distinction from Discorbina as the preceding. It is densely covered with ribs or knobs on its spire-side, the apertural face being more scarce provided but with somewhat larger tubercles.

It is more seldom met with on the chalk-bottom. According to Mr. d'Orbigny who found his specimens in great abundance among sea-weed, its true home seems to be in the littoral zone.

Fig. 264: apertural side.
Fig. 265, side-view

Syn. **Rosalina Poeyi** d'Orb., 1839, Cuba p. 92, t. 3, figg. 18—20.
 » **squamosa** d'Orb., ibid, p. 91, t. 3, figg. 12—14.
Cymbolopora Poeyi Carpent., Introd. p. 215; Möbs., Maurit. et Seych. p. 97, t. 10, figg. 1—5.
Rosalina granulosa Karr., 1864, Leythakalk Wien, Beck.; Wien. Ak. Sitz.-Ber. 1. so, p. 710, t. 2, fig. 14.

Discorbina Berthelotiana d'Orb.

Tab. VIII. figg. 266—268.

This tiny species may be a pigmy only to a more developed form. It is extremely thin, quite hyaline with very small and closely set pores. It is devoid of that yellowish tint, so common with this genus. The shape is sometimes flat and scale-like but often convex on the upper side: the hollowed apertural side with its prominent riblike septal sutures are its most conspicuous characteristic. Sometimes those ribs are sunken in septal furrows between the somewhat bulged chamberwalls.

It is the fineness of the pores only which seems to distinguish this form from some Planorbulina; f. instance, *Planorb. Bosqueti* Rss. (from Maestricht-chalk) being nearly isomorphous with this species.

In »Microgeology« by EHRENBERG t. 35, B, fig. 7 there is represented a young form called *Spiropleurites nebulosus*, which probably belongs to this species. From *Discorb. vesiculata* it differs only in closer and finer poration, not yellowish shell and its pigmy size.

Fig. 266: spire-side.
Fig. 267: side-view; 268: apertural side.

Syn. **Rosalina Berthelotiana** D'ORB., 1844, Hist. Iles Canaries for., p. 135, t. 1, figg. 28—30.
Discorbina Bertheloti REUSS, 1864, Rhizop. Shell.; Trans. Lin. Soc. 24, p. 469, t. 48, fig. 10.
» **Parisiensis** var. **Berthelotiana** PARK. et JONES, 1865, North. Atl. and Arct. Oc.; Phil. Trans. 155. 1, p. 387, t. 16, figg. 26—27.
?**Rosalina concava** Russ., 1854, Kreide. Ostalpen; Wien. Ak. Dkschr. 7, p. 70, t. 26, fg. 3.

Discorbina vesicularis LMK. var. elegans D'ORB.
Tab. VIII, figg. 269—271.

On the authority of Messrs PARKER and JONES we consider this form as identical with *Rosalina complanata* D'ORB. (For. Bass. tert. Vienne p. 176, t. 10, figg. 13—15) notwithstanding this, as also *Ros. complanata* Rss. (Neue For. österreich. tert. Beck.; Wien. Akad. Dkschr. 1. 1, p. 373, t. 47, fig. 5) has its spire less invested by the last convolution. Our form is remarkable for the great symmetry of both its sides, which are hardly distinguishable from each another; both being provided with a deep and narrow umbilicus. The aperturale fissure is very inconspicuous. The »valves« or »astral lobes« are represented by 2 or 3 small scalelike outgrowths partly covering the opening of the umbilicus; the shell surface is somewhat polished.

Where is not for the yellowish tint of the shell-substance in transmitted light and for the characteristic size and disposition of the pore-canals one would hardly be able to recognize this form as a Discorbina, but would rather refer it to Planorbulina.

It is not common in the chalk-ooze, and is always found in a pigmy state.

Fig. 269: spire-side.
Fig. 270: side-view.
Fig. 271: apertural-side.

Syn. **Anomalina elegans** D'ORB., 1826, Tabl. meth., Ann. Sc. Nat. 7, p. 282; Mod. N:o 42.

Spirillina vivipara EHRENB.
Tab. VII, fig. 272.

The pores of this very simple rhizopode are variable in closeness of arrangement. Fullgrown specimens have them pretty close and of the same size as *Planorbulina Ungeriana*. Very small ones are not easily distinguishable from young Trochamminæ incertæ.

It is very common; particularly in the chalk-ooze, seldom attaining in diameter more than 0,20 mm.

Syn. Spirillina vivipara	EHRENB., 1841, Verbreit. u. Einfluss des miktroskopischen Lebens in Süd- u. Nord-Amerika; Berl. Kön. Wiss. Akad. Abhandl. 1841, t. 3, fig. 41; ibid. 1847, t. 2, fig. 82.
Cornuspira perforata	M. SCHULTZE, 1854, Organ. Polythalam. p. 41, t. 2, fig. 22.
Spirillina vivipara	WILLIAMS., 1858, Brit. rec. For. p. 92, fig. 202.
Spirillina »	PARK. et JONES, 1854; An. Mag. Nat. Hist. 19, p. 12, t. 11, fig. 46.
» »	PARK. et JONES, 1865, North. Atl. and Arct. Oc.; Phil. Transact. 155. 1, p. 397, t. 15, fig. 28.
» »	PARK. et JONES, 1866, Crag. foramf.; Pal. Soc. 19, t. 3, figg. 20—22.
?Cyclolina impressa	EGGER, 1857, Mioc. Ortenburg; Leonh. u. Bronn. Jhrb. 1857, p. 304, t. 8, figg. 7—8.
?Spirillina polygyrata, ?tenuissima GÜMB., 1862, Streitenb. Schwammlag.; Wurtemb. Nat. Verein. Jhrhft. 1862, p. 214, t. 4, figg. 11—12.	
» margaritifera	WILLIAMS., 1858, Brit. rec. Foramf. p. 93, fig. 204.

Appendix.

Spirillina inæqualis	BRADY, 1879, Notes on retic. Rhiz.; Quart. Journ. micr. Sc. p. 278, t. 8, figg. 25, a, b.
» limbata	BRADY, ibid. p. 278, t. 8, figg. 26, a, b.
» obconica	BRADY, ibid. p. 279, t. 8, figg. 27, a, b.
» tuberculata	BRADY, ibid. p. 279, t. 8, figg. 28, a, b.

Pulvinulina auricula FICHT. and MOLL.

Tab. VIII, figg. 273—275.

This handsome, generally hyaline, species resembles very much *Nodosarina crepidula*. Although it seems to be one of the best defined species in the whole class, still intermediate forms are found with a nearly round, rotaline shape (as for instance *Rot. Haueri* D'ORB. from the tertiary strata at Vienna).

It is not uncommon both in the coralline-gravel and in the chalk-ooze, but attains a higher development in the former.

For clearing up the intricate synonymy of this genus we are indebted to Messrs PARKERS' and JONES' elaborate and careful inquiries, recorded in their lucid and admirable treatises »On foramf. from North Atlantic and Arctic Oceans 1865, and »On the foramf. of the Family Rotalinæ (CARPENTER) found in the cretaceous formations etc. in Qu. Journ. geol. Soc. 1872. 28, p. 103.

Fig. 273: frontal view;
Fig. 274: spire-side.
Fig. 275: pigmy, broad form.

Syn. Nautilus Auricula	FICHT. et MOLL., 1803, Test. micr. p. 108, t. 20, figg. a—f.
Valvulina oblonga	D'ORB., 1844, Iles Canaries p. 136, t. 1, figg. 40—42.
» excavata	D'ORB., ibid. p. 137, t. 1, figg. 43—45.
Rotalina oblonga	WILLIAMS., 1858, Brit. rec. forf. p. 51, figg. 98—100.

Syn. Valvulina auris, inæqualis d'Orb., 1845, Voy. Amer. merid. 5. 5, t. 2, figg. 15—17; t. 7, figg. 10—12.
Rotalina scaphoidea   Rss., 1849, Neue For. österr Beck.; Wien. Ak. Dkschr. 1. 1, p. 372, t. 47, fig. 3.
» deformis, Sagra d'Orb., 1839, Cuba, p. 77, t. 5, figg. 13—15.
Pulv. auricula   Park. et Jones, 1866, Crag. For.; Pal. Soc. 19, t. 2, figg. 33—35.
Valvulina cordiformis   Costa, 1854, Pal. Nap. 2, p. 262, t. 21, fig. 10.
Pulv. cordiformis   Rss., 1867, Steinsalzablag. Wieliczka; Wien. Ak. Sitz.-Ber. 1. 55, p. 103, t. 5, fig. 3.
Rotalia cristellarioides   Rss., 1863, For. Crag. d'Anvers; Bull. Ac. Belg. (2), 15, p. 154, t. 3, figg. 44.
» contraria   Rss., 1851, Sept. Thon. v. Berlin; Ztschr. deutsch. geol. Ges. 3, p. 76, t. 5, fig. 37.
» Brongniartii   d'Orb., 1826, Tabl. Meth.; Ann. Sc. Nat. 7, p. 273.
« »   d'Orb., 1846, For. tert. Vienne p. 158, t. 8, figg. 22—24 (valde porosa quasi Planorbulina fere).
» »   Ehrb., 1857, Micr. Ortenb.; Leonh. u. Bronn Jhrb. 1857, p. 274, t. 7, figg. 5—7.
« Haueri   d'Orb., 1846, For. tert. Vienne, p. 151, t. 7, figg. 22—24 (minus oblonga).
Discorb. inæqualis   Mob., 1880, Beitr. z. Meeresfaun. Mauritius u. Seychell. p. 97, t. 9, fig. 19.

Pulvinulina repanda Ficht. and Moll.

Tab. VIII, figg. 276—282.

Our form comes next to *Rotalina caribaea* d'Orb. or *Rot. pulchella* d'Orb. Its shape is generally inflated biconvex, but the younger specimens are often planoconvex or subconical with the spiral side quite flat. It is sometimes slightly marginated.

It has been found in the coralline-gravel only, attaining a diameter of 1,5 mm.

Figg. 276—277: the apertural-side and the edge-side of *Pulv. repanda* Ficht. and Moll.

Fig. 278: spiral-side, nearly flat, of a younger individual.

Fig. 279: a transverse section near the horizontal, median plane.

Fig. 280: section near the spiral side of a very young specimen.

Fig. 281: the side-view of the same.

Fig. 282: side-view of another young specimen, nearly biconvex.

Syn. Nautilus repandus   Ficht. et Moll., 1803, Test. micr. p. 35, t. 3, figg. a—d.
» sinuatus   Ficht. et Moll., ibid. p. 65, t. 10, fig. a—d.
Pulvin. repanda   Park. et Jones, 1866, Crag. For.; Pal. Soc. 19, t. 2, figg. 22—24.
? Rosalina Mediterranensis d'Orb., 1826, Tab. meth.; An. Sc. Nat. 7, p. 271, N:o 2.
Rotalia communis   d'Orb., ibid. p. 273, N:o 29 (an P. auricula).
» pulchella   d'Orb., ibid. p. 274, N:o 32; Mod. N:o 74.
» Caribæa   d'Orb., 1839, Cuba p. 74, t. 5, figg. 1—3.
Pulvin. pulchella   Park. et Jones, 1866, Crag. For.; Pal. Soc. 19, t. 2, figg. 25—27.
Rotalina Bouéana   d'Orb., 1846, For. tert. Vienne, p. 152, t. 7, figg. 25—27.
Pulvin. Bouéana   Rss., 1865, deutsch. Sept. Thon: Wien. Ak. Dkschr. 1. 25, 1, p. 161, t. 4, fig. 14.

Syn. (Nomina varia)	Ehrenb., 1854, Mikrogeol. t. 29, fig. 15; t. 30, fig. 28.
Rotalia punctulata	d'Orb., 1826, Tab. Meth.; An. Sc. Nat. 7, p. 273, N:o 25; Mod. No 12 (Pulvin. Schreibersi propinqua).
? » antillarum	d'Orb., 1839, Cuba, p. 75, t. 5, figg. 4—6 (Pulvin. Schreibersi valde propinqua).
Pulvin. repanda var. punctulata	Park. et Jones, 1865, North. Atl. and Arct. Or.; Phil. Trans. 155. 1, p. 394, t. 14, figg. 12—13.
» pygmæa	Hken., 1875, For. Clav. Saab. Sch. p. 78, t. 10, fig. 8.
» affinis	Hken., ibid. p. 78, t. 10, fig. 6.
Planorb. vermiculata	d'Orb., 1826, Tabl. meth., Ann. Sc. Nat. 7, p. 280, N:o 3.
Pulvin. »	Carpent., 1860, Introduct. p. 211, t. 13, figg. 4—6.

Pulvinulina elegans d'Orb.

Tab. VIII, figg. 283—285.

Comes very near to *Pulv. repanda*, its chief characteristic being its somewhat raised or thickened septal band on the appertural side.

Our form is nearly identical with *Rotalina Carpenteri* Rss., *Gyroidina caracolla* Rom., *Rot. Partschiana* d'Orb.

It has often a nearly hyaline, biconvex, and very symmetrical shell; often its both sides are umbonated and then it resembles Nodosarina calcar, so that it is easily overlooked, when associated with this.

It is not frequent in the coralline-gravel.

Fig. 283: the apertural side.

Fig. 284: cut open to show the spiral-side from underneath.

Fig. 285: edge-view.

Syn.	Rotalia	elegans	d'Orb., 1826, Tab. meth.; An. Sc. Nat. 7, p. 276. N:o 54.
	»	»	Park. et Jones, 1860, For. Chellast.; Qu. Journ. geol. Soc. 16, p. 455, t. 20, fig. 46.
	»	Partschiana	d'Orb., 1846, For. tert. Vienne, p. 153, t. 7, figg. 28—30; t. 8, figg. 1—3.
	»	»	Bornem., 1855, Sept. Thon Hermsdorf; Zeitschr. deutsch. geol. Ges 7, t. 16, fig. 6.
	»	reticulata	Rss., 1862, Nordd. Hils u. Gault; Wien. Ak. Sitz.-Ber. 1. 46, p. 83, t. 10, fig. 4.
	Gyroidina caracolla		Rom., 1841, Verstein. Nordd. Kreideg., p. 97, t. 15, fig. 22.
	Rotalia	»	Rss., 1862, Nordd. Hils u. Gault; Wien. Ak. Sitz.-Ber. 1. 46, p. 84, t. 10, fig. 6.
	»	spinulifera	Rss., ibid. p. 93, t. 13, figg. 3—5.
	»	Carpenteri	Rss., ibid. p. 94, t. 13, fig. 6.
	Anomal. Bengalensis		Schwag., 1866, For. Kar.-Nikobar.; Novara Reise, geol. Th. 2. v, p. 259, t. 7, figg. 111.
	Lenticulina pachyderma et nominibus aliis		Ehrenb., 1854, Microgeol., t. 29, fig. 14—14; t. 31, fig. 54.
	Rotalina stelligera		Rss., 1859, Kreideg. Ostalp.; Wien. Akad. Sitz.-Ber. 7, p. 69, t. 25, fig. 15.
	»	Bertheloitiana	d'Orb., 1844, Iles Canaries p. 130, t. 1, figg. 31—33.
	Pulvin. concentrica		Brady, 1865, Rhizop. Shetl.; Trans. Lin. Soc. 24, p. 470, t. 48, fig. 14.

Pulvin. sacculata		Park. et Jones, 1876, For. English Channel; A. N. H. (4) 17, p. 284, figg. 1—3.
Rotalina concamerata		Will., 1858, (partim) Brit. rec. foramf. p. 62, figg. 101—103.
»	infundibulum	Costa, 1854, Pal. Nap. 2, p. 237, t. 14, fig. 9.
»	repanda var. elegans	Park. et Jones, 1865, North. Atl. and Arct. Oceans.; Phil. Trans. 155, 1, p. 397, t. 16, figg. 44—46.
»	badensis	Czjz., 1847, Foramf. Wien. Beck.; Haid. Nat. Abh. 2. 1, p. 144, t. 13, figg. 1—3 (a Pulvin. Schreibersi d'Orb. vix diversa).
»	Cordieriana	d'Orb., 1839, Craie bl. Paris; Mem. Soc. geol. Fr. 4, p. 33, t. 3, figg. 9—11.
»	semigloboss	Rss., 1862, Nordd. Hils u. Gault; Wien. Ak. Sitz.-Ber. 1. 46., p. 85, t. 10 fig. 7, t. 11, fig. 1 (Pulvin. Michelianæ d'Orb. propinqua).
»	flosculiformis	Schwag., 1866, For. Kar.-Nikobar; Novara Reise, geol. Th. 2. 2, p. 262, t. 7. fig. 109.
Pulvin. prominens		Rss., 1860, Oligocän. von Gaas; Wien. Ak. Sitz.-Ber. 59, p. 463, t. 3, fig. 2.
»	Broeckiana	Brady, 1876, Carb. and Perm. foris; Pal. Soc. 30, p. 140, t. 6, fig. 12

Pulvinulina elegans var. trochus Röm.

Tab. VIII, figg. 286—288.

This form is remarkable for its strongly developed umbo, which as a solid, highly polished, porcellaneous cupola so covers nearly the entire spiral-side, that the margina part only of the 2 or 3 latest segments are visible. On the opposite side the umbilical boss is very small or is absorbed in the raised septal lines or in starlike exogenous shell-substance. It is slightly marginated.

It is very common on the chalk-bottom, but much developed specimens are scarce.

Fig. 286: apertural side with its starlike rays of thickened septal marks.
Fig. 287: the spire-side with its cupola.
Fig. 288: edge-view.

Syn. Rotalia trochus		(Münst.) Röm., 1838, Nordd. tert. Meeress.; Leonh. u. Bronn. Jhrb. 1838, p. 388, t. 3, fig. 47.
?	» mammillata	Röm., ibid. p. 388, t. 4, fig. 48.
	» trochus	Rss., 1855, Tert. Schicht. nördl. u. mittl. Deutschl.; Wien. Ak. Sitz.-Ber. 1. 18, p. 242. t. 5, fig. 55.

Pulvinulina Menardii d'Orb.

Tab. VIII, figg. 289—295.

The more conspicuous features of this elegant rhizopode are its flatness, its broad keel, its large and few chambers and its crenulated or jagged apertural lip, which is often produced into a sort of valve. The margin of the young individuals is often laciniated. As is the case with the whole class, its vertical diameter is liable to some variation in its proportion to the horizontal one and thus distended forms sometimes present themselves somewhat diverging from the flat type. Intermediate forms between *P. Menardii* und *repanda* and also *P. Micheliniana* D'ORB. are occasionally met with.

This species is next to *Globigerina bulloides* and *universa* the most common rhizopode in deep water and attains a diameter of 1,50 mm. and more.

The most beautiful and exact delineation of this species ever given is to be found in Prof. WYWILLE TOMSONS great work The »Challengers» Exped., *the Atlantic*, 1, p. 218, fig. 48.

Figg. 289—291: the flat form of *Pulv. Menardii* D'ORB.
Figg. 292—294: more distended form.
Fig. 295: very young.

Syn. Rotalia Monardii		D'ORB., 1826, Tab. meth.; An. Sc. Nat. 7, p. 273, N:o 26; Mod. 10.
Pulvin. repanda	var.	PARK. et JONES, 1865, North. Atl. and Arct. Oc.; Phil. Trans. 155. 1, p. 394, t. 16, figg. 35—37.
»	» var.	Monardii, subvar. pauperata PARK. et JONES, ibidem p. 395, t. 16, figg. 50—51.
?Rotalina spinimargo		RSS., 1849, Neue For. österr. tert. Beck.; Wien. Ak. Dkschr. 1. 1. p. 371, t. 47, fig. 1.
»	cultrata	D'ORB., 1839, Cuba, p. 76, t. 5, figg. 7—9.
»	»	BAILEY, 1850, Micr. Exam. of Soundings; Smiths. Contr. Knowl. 2, Art. 3, p. 11, figg. 14—16.
Rosalina asterites		GÜMB., 1868, For. nordalp. Eocän.; K. Bayr. Ak. Wiss. 1. 10. 2, p. 658, t. 2, fig. 101.
Discorb. saccharata		SCHWAG., 1866, Kar.-Nikobar., Novara Reise, geol. Th. 2. 2, p. 257. t. 7, fig. 106.
Rotalia paupercula		STACHE, 1865, Tert. Merg. Whainger. Hafen; Novara Reise, geol. Th. 1. 2, p. 277, t. 24, fig. 27.
»	canariensis	D'ORB., 1844, Iles Canaries p. 130, t. 1, figg. 34—36.
?Truncat budensis		HANS., 1875, For. Clav. Szab. Sch. p. 75, t. 8, fig. 6.
Pulvin. orinacea		KARR., 1868, Micr. Fauna Kostej; Wien. Ak. Sitz.-Ber. 1. 58, p. 187, t. 5, fig. 6.

b) in Pulvin. Michelinianam D'ORB. transgrediens:

Pulvin. repanda var. Monardii subvar. canariensis	PARK. et JONES, 1865, North. Atl. and Arct. Oc.; Phil. Trans. 155. 1, p. 395, t. 16, figg. 47—49.
Rotalina dubia	D'ORB., 1839, Cuba, p. 78, t. 2, figg. 29—30.
» crassa	D'ORB., 1839, For. Craie bl. Paris; Mém. Soc. géol. France 4, p. 32, t. 3, figg. 7—8.
» bimammata, campanella	GÜMB., 1868, Nordalp. Eoc.; K. Bayr. Ak. Wiss. Abh. 1. 10. 1, p. 649—650, t. 2, figg. 85—86 (an Pulv. Schreibersi var.).

c) in Pulvin. repandam FICHT. et MOLL. transgrediens:

Rotalina umbonata	RSS., 1851, Sept. Thon Berlin.; Zeitschr. deutsch. geol. Ges. 3, p. 75, t. 5, fig. 35.
Pulvin. »	HANS., 1875, Clav. Szab. Sch., p. 77, t. 9, fig. 8.
» formosa	RSS., 1864, Olmützerg; Wien. Ak. Dkschr. 1. 23, t. 1, fig. 14; 1869, Oligoc. v. Gaas; Wien. Ak. Sitz.-Ber. 1. 59, p. 464, t. 3, fig. 1

Pulvinulina Micheliniana d'Orb.
Tab. VIII, figg. 296—298.

Our ordinary form comes close to *Rotalia truncatulinoides* d'Orb. from the Canary Islands. Its prominent characteristics are its conical form, restricted number of chambers, deep umbilicus and deep incisions between the umbilical prolongations of the chambers. The chamberwalls are often nearly plain or so very little bent, that the flat spiral side becomes obtusely angulous. The pores are not quite as fine as in its congeners in general.

It has been met with principally in the coralline-gravel, where it is common.

Fig. 296: the spiral side seen in transmitted light.
Fig. 297: sideview.
Fig. 298: apertural side.

Syn. **Rotalia Micheliniana**	d'Orb., 1839, For. Craié bl. Paris; Mem. Soc. geol. Fr. 4, p. 31, t. 3, figg. 1—3	
» nitida	Rss., 1845, Böhm. Kreide, 1, p. 35, t. 12, figg. 8, 20, 31, t. 8, fig. 52.	
» truncatulinoides	d'Orb., 1844, Iles Canaries p. 132, t. 2, figg. 25—27.	
(Nom. varia)	Ehrenb., 1854, Microgeol. t. 27, figg. 48, 51, 52; t. 28, fig. 53.	
Pulv. repanda var. **Menardii**, subvar. **Micheliniana** Park. et Jones, 1865, North. Atl. and Arct Oc.; Phil. Transact. 155, p. 396, t. 14, fig. 16; t. 16, figg. 41—43.		
» **Normanni**	Karrer 1878, For. Luzon; Bolet. Comis. Mapa geol. d. España 7, 2, p. 24, t. F. fig. 10.	

Polystomella crassula Walk. var. Scapha Ficht. & Moll.
Tab. VIII, figg. 299—300.

Our form is usually very much compressed and starved. The aperture is narrow and not easely discoverable.

It is unfrequently met with in the chalk-ooze.

Syn. **Nautilus Scapha**	Ficht. et Moll., 1803, Test. microscop. p. 105, t. 19, figg. d—f.	
Nonionina Grateloupi	d'Orb., 1839, Cuba, p. 46, t. 6, figg. 6—7.	
» **Sloanii**	d'Orb., ibid. p. 46, t. 6, figg. 18—18bis.	
» **Brownii**	d'Orb., ibid. p. 45, t. 7, figg. 22—23.	
» **communis**	d'Orb., 1846, Bass. tert. Vienne, p. 106, t. 5, figg. 7—8.	
» »	Park. et Jones, 1857, For. Coast. of Norway; An. Mag. Nat. Hist. (2) 19, p. 287, t. 11, figg. 7—8.	
Pallenia communis	Hken., 1875, For. Clav. Száb. Sch. p. 59, t. 10, fig. 10.	
Nonionina Franzana	Gümb., 1862, Streitenberg. Schwammlager; Würtemb. Nat. Wiss. Ver. Jhrbft. 1862, p. 233, t. 4, fig. 5.	
» **communis**	(partim) Egg., 1857, Misc. Ortenburg; Leonh. u. Bronn. Jhrb. 1857, p. 298, t. 14, figg. 11—13.	
» **Labradorica**	Daws., 1860, Canad. Geol. et Nat. 5, p. 192, fig. 4.	

Syn. **Nonion.** Scapha var. labradorica DAWS., 1870, For. Gulf and Riv. St. Laur.; A. M. N. Hist. (4) 7, p. 86, fig. 5.
Polystomella crispa var. Scapha PARK. et JONES, 1865, North. Atl. and Arct. Ocean.; Phil. Trans. 155. 1, p. 404, t. 14, figg. 37—38; t. 17, figg. 55—56.
Nonionina Labradorica PARK. et JONES, 1866, Crag. For.; Pal. Soc. 19, t. 2, figg. 44—45.
» **Scapha** PARK. et JONES, ibid. t. 2, figg. 36—37.
Rotalina turgida WILLIAMS., 1858, Brit. rec. Foramf., p. 50, figg. 95—97.
Polystom. crispa var. **Non. turgida** PARK. et JONES, 1865, N. atl. and Arct. Oc., Phil. Trans. 155. 1, p. 405, t. 17, fig. 57.

Appendix.

Nautilus crassulus	WALK. Test. min. rar. 17–4, figg. 68, 70 (sec. PARK. et JONES).	
Syn **Nonion. crassula**	WILLIAMS., 1858, Brit. rec. For. p. 38, figg. 70—71.	
Nonion. Boueana	D'ORB., 1846, Bas. tert. Vienne p. 108, t. 5, figg. 11—12.	
» »	RSS., 1863, Crag. d'Anvers; Bull. Ac. Belg. (2) 15, p. 156, t. 3, figg. 47, 48 (in Scapham transiens).	
Polystom. crispa var. **umbilicatula** PARK. et JONES, 1865, N. Atl. and Arct. Oc.; Phil. Trans. 155. 1, p. 405, t. 14, fig. 42, t. 17, figg. 58—59.		
Nonion. punctata	D'ORB., 1846, For. tert. Vienne, p. 111, t. 5, figg. 21—22.	
» affinis	RSS., 1851, Sept. Thon Berlin; Zeitschr. deutsch. geol. Ges. 3, p. 72, t. 5, fig. 32.	
? » perforata	D'ORB., 1846, Bass. tert. Vienne p. 110, t. 5, figg. 17—18.	
» bathyomphala	RSS., 1862, Nordd. Hils u. Gault; Wien. Ak. Sitz.-Ber. I. 46, p. 95, t. 13, fig. 1.	
? » rudis	COSTA, 1854, Pal. Nap. 2, p. 205, t. 20, fig. 2.	
» communis	(partim) EGG., 1857, Miocän. Ortenburg; Leonh. u. Bronns Jhrb. 1857, p. 298, t. 14, figg. 14—15.	
Dendr. lævis	COSTA, 1854, Pal. Nap. 2, t. 20, fig. 4.	
Nonion. dense-punctata	EGG., 1857, Mioc. Ortenb.; Leonh. u. Bronn. Jhrb. 1857, p. 299, t. 14, figg. 22—23.	
» pauper	EGG., ibid. p. 300, t. 14, figg. 26—27.	
» simplex	KARR., 1865, Grunsandst. N. Zeel.; Novara Reise, geol. Th. 1. 2, p. 83, t. 16, fig. 17.	
» Soldanii	D'ORB., 1846, Bass. tert. Vienne p. 109, t. 5, figg. 15—16.	
» »	COSTA, 1854, Pal. Nap. 2, p. 201, t. 17, fig. 11.	
» **Melo**	D'ORB., 1826, Tab. meth.; An. Sc. Nat. 7, p. 293, N:o 4.	
» umbilicata	D'ORB., Mod. 86.	

b) umbonata aut granulata:

Nautilus crassulus	MONTAGU, 1803, Test. Brit. p. 191; 1808. Suppl. p. 79, t. 18, fig. 2.	
» umbilicatulus	MONTAGU, ibid. t. 18, fig. 1.	
» pompilioides	FICHT. et MOLL., 1803, Test. microscop. p. 31, t. 2, figg. a—c.	
Nonion. umbilicata	D'ORB., 1826, Tab. meth.; An. Sc. Nat. 7, p. 294, N:o 5; t. 15, figg. 10—12.	
» falx	CZJZ., 1847, For. Wien. Beck.; Haid. Nat. Abh. 2. 1. p. 142, t. 12, figg. 30—31.	
» attenuata	COSTA, 1854, Pal. Nap. 2, p. 202, t. 17, fig. 10.	
» Barleana	WILLIAMS., 1858, Brit. rec. Forf. p. 32, fig. 68—69.	

Syn. **Nonion.** crassula		PARK. et JONES, 1857, For. Norway; A. M. N. Hist. (2) 19, p. 286, t. 11, figg. 5—6.
»	glabra	RÖM., 1838, Nordd. tert. Meeressand; Leonh. u. Bronn. Jhrb. 1838, p. 392, t. 3, fig. 66.
»	compressa	Ress., 1845, Böhm. Kreide 1, p. 35, t. 8, fig. 51.
»	lævis	D'ORB., 1826, An. Sc. Nat. 7, p. 294, N:o 11; Mod. 46.
»	subcarinata	SEG., 1862, Rhizopod. Catania; Accad. Gioena Atti (2) 18, p. 15, t. 1, fig. 3, (sep.)
?**Robulina Planciana**		D'ORB., 1826, Tabl. meth.; Ann. Sc. Nat. 7, p. 290, N:o 20.
Nonion. helicina		COSTA, 1855, For. foss. Marna blu' Vaticano; Mem. Nap. 2, p. 123, t. 1, fig. 18; t. 14, fig. 13.
»	ornata	COSTA, 1854, Pal. Nap. 2, p. 203, t. 17, fig. 17.
Nautilus incrassatus		FICHT. et MOLL., 1803, Test. microscop. p. 38, t. 4, figg. a—c.
Nonion. punctulata		COSTA, 1854, Pal. Nap. 2, t. 19, fig. 9.
»	tuberculata	D'ORB., 1846, Bass. tert. Vienne, p. 108, t. 5, figg. 13—14.
»	granosa	D'ORB., ibid. p. 110, t. 5, figg. 19—20.
»	subgranosa	EGGER, 1857, Miocän. Ortenburg; Leonh. u. Bronn. Jhrb. 1857, p. 299, t. 14, figg. 16—18.
? »	macromphalus	GÜMB., 1862, Streitberg. Schwammlag.; Würtemb. Nat. Verein. Jhrb. 1862, p. 232, t. 4, fig. 4 (au Nodosarina).

c) striata:

Nonion. striolata, ornata		COSTA, 1854, Pal. Nap. 2, p. 203, t. 17, fig. 12, t. 19, fig. 8 (in Pol. striato-punctatam transiens).

d) asterisans:

Nautilus asterizans		FICHT. et MOLL., 1803, Test. microsc. p. 37, t. 3, figg. c—h.
?**Nonion.** costata		ROMER, 1838, Nordd. tert. Meeress.; Leonh. u. Bronn. Jhrb. 1838, p. 392, t. 3, fig. 67.
»	limba	D'ORB., 1826, Tab. meth.; A. Sc. N. 7, p. 294, N:o 14, Mod. N:o 11
»	stelligera	D'ORB., 1844, Iles Canaries, p. 128, t. 3, figg. 1—2.
»	asterisans	PARK. et JONES, 1857, For. Norway; A. M. N. H. (2) 19, p. 287, t. 11, figg. 20—21.
Polystom. crispa var. **deprossula**		PARK. et JONES, 1865, North. Atl. and Arct. Ocean.; Phil Trans 155. 1, p. 403, t. 14, fig. 39.
Polystomella crispa var. **stelligera**		PARK. et JONES, 1865, North. Atl. and Arct. Oc.; Phil. Transact. 155. 1, p. 404, t. 14, fig. 40.
» »	var. **asterisans**	PARK. et JONES, 1865, ibid. p. 403, t. 14, fig. 35, t. 17, fig. 54.
Nonion. stelligera		BRADY, 1864, Rhizop. Shetl.; Trans. Lin. Soc. 24, p. 471, t. 48, fig. 19.
»	loo	KARR., 1868, Mioc. Kostej; Wien. Ak. Sitz.-Ber. 1. 58, p. 190, t. 5, fig. 8.

Polystomella crispa LIN. var. Poëyana D'ORB.

Tab. VIII, figg. 301—302.

It may be unnecessary to keep this form distinct from *Polyst. umbilicata* (WALK.) WILLIAMS., their chief differens consisting in the arrangement of the apertural pores. Our form seems also identical with *Polyst. articulata* D'ORB., and *Polyst. rugosa obtusa, Fickteliana* etc. D'ORB., *Polyst. Ortenburgensis, angulata, subcarinata* EGGER.

Owing to the scarcity of our supply of specimens we are not able to make an even approximately correct and critical survey of the several (about 40) described species of *Polyst. crispa* but refer the student to the able and interesting arrangement of this genus devised by Messrs PARKER and JONES in their admirable treatise on Foraminf. of North Atlantic and Arctic Oceans; Phil. Trans. 155. 1, p. 400.

It has been met with in the chalkooze only.

Heterostegina depressa D'ORB. var. simplex D'ORB.

Tab. VIII. figg. 303.

This form comes next to *Heterostegina curva* MÖB. (from Mauritius), which is a weak form of *Heterost. depressa* with few and large chamberlets. Our form is very thin and gives at first sight the impression of a starved and miscarried Amphistegina, with which as to shell-substance and pores it has much in common.

It is very seldom met with, but reaches a pretty good size on both the coralline-gravel and the chalk-bottom.

Fig. 303: viewed in transmitted light.

a) Septis secundariis paucis:

Syn. Heterosteg. simplex		D'ORB., 1846, For. tert. Vienne, p. 211, t. 12, figg. 12—14.
»	curva	MÖB., 1880, Maur. u. Seychell. p. 105, t. 13, figg. 1—5.

b) Septis secundariis numerosis:

Heterosteg. depressa		D'ORB., 1826, Tab. meth., An. Sc. Nat. 7, p. 305, Mod. 99; t. 17, figg. 5—7.
»	Antillarum	D'ORB., 1839, Cuba, p. 122, t. 7, figg. 24—25.
»	costata	D'ORB., 1846, For. tert. Vienne, p. 212, t. 12, figg. 15—17.
»	»	PARS Mod. 100.
»	reticulata	(RÜTIM.) HANT., 1875, For. Clav. Szab. Sch. p. 81, t. 12, fig. 3
Gen. indef.		COSTA, 1854, Pal. Nap. 2, t. 20, fig. 15.
?Heterosteg. Grotriani		REUSS, 1865, Deutsch. Septarienthon, Wien. Ak. Dkschr. 1. 25. p. 164, t. 4, fig. 18 (an *Operculina complanata* DEFR.).

Amphistegina vulgaris D'ORB.

Is very common in the coralline-gravel and attains a diameter of 3 mm. and more, with many gradations in the relation between the length of the vertical and horizontal diameters. It seems on our bottom to substitute genus *Nummulina*, of which no trace has appeared, even in the shape of *Operculina*.

Syn. **Amphistegina vulgaris**, Lessonii D'Orb., 1826, Tabl. meth., Ann. Sc. Nat. 7, p. 304, 305; Mod. 40, 98; t. 17, figg. 1—4.
» **gibbosa** D'Orb., 1839, Cuba, p. 120, t. 8. figg. 1—3.
» **Hauerina**, mamillata, rugosa D'Orb., 1846, For. tert. Vienne, p. 186, t. 12, figg 3—11.
» **vulgaris** Parker et Jones et Brady, 1866, Crag. For.; Pal. Soc. 19, t. 2, figg. 46—48.
» **minuta** Brady, 1876, Carbonif. and Perm. foramif.; Pal. Soc. 30, p. 146, t. 11, fig. 7.
» **Campbelli, Aucklandica** Karr., 1865, For. Grünsandst. N. Zeeland., Novara Reise, geol. Th. 1. 2, p. 84—85, t. 16, figg. 19.
? » **ornatissima** Karr., 1865, Grünsandst. N. Zeel.; Novara Reise, geol. Th. 1. 2, p. 85, t. 16, fig. 20.

Orbiculina adunca Fichr. et Moll.

Tab. IX, figg. 304—307.

This handsome and variable species presents itself in deep water promiscuously in both its *adunca-* and *orbicula-*forms. The latter is for the most part flattened out to a singlefloored thin disc, that often shows a few broad radiating impressions on both its sides. These impressed bands are occupied by somewhat wider subdivisions or »chamberlets«.

A *Peneropli-*form variety is also met with in company with the common forms. It is impossible to distinguish it from some forms designated as *Peneroplis proteus* D'Orb. from the West Indies, *Peneropl. prisca* Rss. from the tertiary strata and *Peneropl. planatus* var. *lævigatus* Karr., also from the tertiary formation.

Since no other true distinction between *Orbiculina* and *Peneroplis* has been stated than the striation or plication of the surface of the latter, it would be inconsistent with the notion of *genus* and even of *species* to distinguish forms, which cannot duly be entitled higher than as to rank of varieties.

D'Orbigny himself admits that »les Orbiculines, pour nous, ne sont que des *Peneroples* à loges divisées« (Hist. d. l'Ile de Cuba Foraminif. p. 64).« On this account it seems justifiable to range »*Peneroplis*« as a variety under *Orbiculina* or vice versa, as the latter may be regarded as a higher developed Peneroplis.

The striated form, in no way but in this feature differing from young *Orbiculinæ*, are also met with, but always scanty and in a pigmy state.

Orbiculina adunca is very common also in deep water, particularly its orbiculaform, which attains a diameter of 6 mm.

The *simple* and unstriated form is more rarely met with.

By examing several specimens whole and in horizontal section I have satisfied myself that the outer chamberwalls are *perforated* with veritable pores of a middle size, now pretty closely arranged and now more scattered.

Figg. 304—305: quite young specimens.

Figg. 306—307: peneropliform, unstriated Orbiculina adunca.

a) striata s. costulata, simplex, compressa (Peneroplis MONTF.), plus minusve nautiloidea:

Syn. Nautilus planatus   FICHT. et MOLL., 1803, Test. micr. p. 91, t. 16, figg. a—i.
    Spirol. depressa   D'ORB., 1826, Tabl. meth.; Ann. Sc. Nat. 7, p. 287, N:o 3.
    Peneroplis planatus   D'ORB., ibid. p. 285, N:o 1; Mod. 16.
    »   »   WILLIAMS., 1858, Brit. rec. Forf. p. 45, figg. 83—85.
    CARP., 1862, Introduct. t. 7, figg. 16, 18.

b) striata simplex rotulata, crassa, apertura ramosa (Dentritina D'ORB.) aut porosa:

Dendritina arbuscula   D'ORB., 1826, Tabl. meth.; Ann. Sc. Nat. 7, p. 285, N:o 1, Mod. 21, t. 15, fig. 6—7bis.
    »   Antillarum   D'ORB., ibid. N:o 3; 1839, Cuba p. 58, t. 7, figg. 3—6.
    »   Haueri, Juleana, elegans D'ORB., 1846, For. tert. Vienne, p. 134—135, t. 7, figg. 1—6.
Peneroplis elegans   D'ORB., 1839, Cuba, p. 61, t. 7, figg. 1—2.
    CARP., 1862, t. 7, figg. 13—15, 17, 19.

c) striata, lituiformis (Spirolinites LMCK.):

Nautilus arietinus   BATSCH, 1791, t. 6, figg. 15 d—f. (see. PARK. et JONES); D'ORB. Mod. 48.
Spirolina cylindracea   (LMK.) D'ORB., 1826, Tabl. meth.; Ann. Sc. Nat. 7, p. 286, Mod. 24.
    »   austriaca   D'ORB., 1846, For. tert. Vienne, p. 137, t. 7, figg. 7—9.
    »   »   FRIES' Modell, 25.
    »   longissima   COSTA, 1854, Palæont. Nap. 2, p. 225, t. 20, fig. 11.
Peneroplis Laubei   KARR., 1868, Mioc. For. Kostej.; Wien. Ak. Sitz.-Ber. 1. 58, p. 154, t. 3, fig. 8.

d) lævis simplex:

Peneroplis proteus   D'ORB., 1839, Cuba p. 60, t. 7, figg. 7—11.
    »   dubius   D'ORB. ibid. p. 62, t. 6, figg. 21—22.
    »   prisca   Rss., 1863, Oberburg. Steiermark; Wien. Ak. Dkschr. 1. 23. 1, p. 9, t. 1, fig. 7.
    »   planatus var. lævigatus KARRER, Mioc. For. Kostej; Wien. Ak. Sitz.-Ber. 1. 58, p. 153, t. 3, fig. 7.
Dendritina arbuscula   PARK. et JONES, BRADY, 1866, Crag. For., Pal. Soc. 19, t. 3, figg. 48—49.
Peneroplis aspergilla   KARR., 1868, Mioc. For. Kostej; Wien. Ak. Sitz. Ber. 1. 58, p. 154, t. 3, fig. 9.

e) cameris divisis (Orbiculina LMCK.):

Nautilus aduncus   FICHT. et MOLL., 1803, Test. micr. p. 115, t. 23.
    »   angulatus, orbiculus FICHT. et MOLL., ibid. p. 112—113, t. 21, 22.
Orbic. Numismalis   (LMCK.) D'ORB., 1826, Tabl. Méth.; Ann. Sc. Nat. 7, p. 305, Mod. 20, t. 17, figg. 8—10.
    »   compressa, adunca D'ORB., 1839, Cuba p. 66, t. 8, figg. 4—16.
    CARPENTER, 1862, Introd., t. 8, figg. 1—12.
    »   Rotella   D'ORB., 1846, Rass. tert. Vienne p. 142, t. 7, figg. 13—14 (as »Dendritina»).

Cornuspira foliacea PHIL.

Tab. IX, figg. 308—310.

This widely diffused form attains a pretty high development on the chalk-bottom. Its shape is very variable, according to the more or less rapid increase of the breadth of its convolutions. Some of the more marked striæ, which like septal-lines closely adorn the surface, look very much like septa when viewed in transmitted light.

It is not uncommon on the chalk-bottom. It seems to reach its highest development in the arctic seas, where it occurs in shallow water sometimes in good numbers.

Fig. 308: a halfgrown specimen with more numerous and narrow convolutions.
Fig. 309: large specimen with unusually sudden increase of the last convolution.
Fig. 310: the edge with the aperture.

Syn. Orbis foliaceus   PHIL., 1844, Enumer. Mollusc. Sicil. 2, p. 147, t. 24, fig. 26.
Operculina striata, plicata CZJZ., 1847, Foss. for. Wien. Beck.; Haid. nat. Abh. 2, 1, p. 146, t. 12, figg. 10—11; t. 13, figg. 12—13.
Spirillina foliacea   WILLIAMS., 1858, Brit. rec. for. p. 91, figg. 199—201.
Cornusp. rugulosa   RSS., 1855, Tert. Sch. nordl. u. mittl. Deutschl.; Wien. Ak. Sitz.-Ber. 1, 18, p. 222, t. 1, fig. 1.
Operculina carinata, ammonitiformis COSTA, 1856, Pal. Nap. 2, p. 209, t. 17, figg. 15—16.
Cornuspira planorbis   SCHULTZE, 1854, Org. Polythal. p. 40, t. 2, fig. 21.
    »   Bornemanni   RSS., 1863, Sept. Thon Offenbach. Wien. Ak. Sitz.-Ber. 1, 48, p. 39, t. 1, fig. 3.
    »   Reussi   (BORNEM.) RSS., 1865, Deutsch. Septarienthon; Wien. Ak. Dkschr. 1, 25, 1, p. 121, t. 1, fig. 10.
    »   foliacea   PARKER et JONES, 1865, North. Atl. and Arct. Oceans, Phil. Trans. 155, 1, p. 408, t. 15, fig. 33.
    »   »   PARK. et JONES, BRADY, 1866, Crag. For.; Pal. Soc. 19, p. 3, t. 3, figg. 52—54.
Operculina involvens   RSS., 1849, Neue For. Wien. Beck.; Wien. Ak. Dkschr. 1, 1, p. 370, t. 46, fig. 20.
Cornuspira involvens   RSS., 1863, Sept. Thon. Offenbach; Wien. Ak. Sitz.-Ber. 1, 48, p. 39, t. 1, fig. 2.
    »   »   HKRN., 1875, Clav. Szab. Sch. p. 19, t. 1, fig. 2
    »   oligogyra   HKRN., ibid. p. 20, t. 1, fig. 10.
    »   tenuissima   SCHWAG., 1863, Juras. Sch.; Wurtemb. Nat. Verein Jhrhft. 21, p. 94, t. 2, fig. 6.
?   »   pachygyra   GÜMB., 1869, Cassian u. Raibl. Schicht., Österr. geol. Reichsanst. Jhrb. 19, p. 178, t. 5, figg. 9—10.
Operculina angigyra   RSS., 1849, Neue for. österr. tert. Becken, Wien. Ak. Dkschr. 1, 1, p. 370, t. 46, fig. 19.
Cornuspira polygyra   RSS., 1863, Sept. Thon Offenbach; Wien. Ak. Sitz.-Ber. 1, 48, p. 39, t. 1, fig. 1.
    »   »   HKRN., ibid. p. 19, t. 1, fig. 11; t. 2, fig. 1
    »   nummulitica   GÜMB., 1868, Nordalp. Eocän; K. Bayr. Ak. Wiss. Abh. I. 10, 2, p. 604, t. 1, fig. 5.
    »   Archimedis, elliptica STACHE, 1865, Tert. Mergel Whaingar. Hafen; Novara Reise, geol. Th. 1, 2, p. 180—181, t. 22, figg. 1—2.

Vertebralina conicoarticulata BATSCH.
Tab. IX, figg. 311—318.

This species includes a great number of forms with such an inconstancy of characters that it would be wasted time and labour, and not only so, but inconsistent with a philosophical notion of designation, to range them even as distinct varieties. It has one stout, highly developed, and one pigmy form. Its most singular form is that in which the primordial chamber is flaskformed and the subsequent chamber developes itself from the top of its neck and so on, one chamber after the other in Nodosarina fashion; thus its usual *Miliolina* formed stage is passed over altogether.

The *peneropliform* variety, recorded by CARPENTER, we have not met with. This species is not unfrequent both in the chalk-ooze and in the coralline-gravel, and attains a higher development on the latter.

Figg. 311—313: broad, stout forms, designed by D'ORBIGNY as *Vertebr. cassis* and *striata*; *Articulina Sagra* D'ORB. etc.

Figg. 314—315: sections in the medial plane, exhibiting the young Milioline stage included in the succeeding flattened chamber of the Nodosarina growth.

Fig. 316: pigmy form from the chalk-ooze.

Fig. 317: rodformed »*Articulina nitida*» D'ORB., a primordial highly developed chamber taking the place of the early Miliolina-stage.

Fig. 317 b: the same more magnified.

Fig. 318: Very young Vertebralina, about 0,11 mm. in length.

a) tenuis, articulata, striata:

Syn. Nautilus conico-articulatus BATSCH, 1791, Sechs Kupfertafeln etc. t. 3, fig. 11 (see. PARK. et JONES).
    Articulina nitida   D'ORB., Tabl. meth.; An. Sc. nat. 7. p. 300; Mod. N:o 22.
    » Sagra   D'ORB., 1839, Cuba p. 183, t. 9, figg. 23—26.
    » gibbosula   D'ORB., 1846, For. tert. Vienne, p. 282, t. 20, figg. 16—18
    Vertebralina elongata   KARR., 1868, Mioc. For. fauna Kostej; Wien. Ak. Sitz-Ber. 1. 58, p. 155, t. 3, fig. 10.
    » striata var. CARPENTER, 1862, Introd. t. 5, fig. 23.

β) tenuis, articulata, lævis v. sublævis:

Vertebralina striata var. CARPENTER, 1862, Introd. t. 5, figg. 19. 24.
    » sarmatica   KARR., 1877, Hochqu. Wasserleit.; Österr. geol. Reichsanst. Abh. 9, p. 376, t. 16, fig 12.

b) magis dilatata, striata:

Vertebralina striata   D'ORB., 1826, Tabl. meth.; Ann. Sc. Nat. 7, p. 283, N:o 1; Mod. N:o 81.
    » cassis, mucronata D'ORB., 1839, Cuba p. 51, 52, t. 7, figg. 14—15., 1846, Foss. tert. Vienne p. 120, t. 21, figg. 18—19.
Articulina sulcata   REUSS, 1849, Neue For. österr. tert. Beck.; Wien. Ak. Dkschr. 1. 1, p. 383 t. 49, figg. 13—17.

Vertobralina sulcata   Rss., 1863, Oberburg in Steiermark; Wien. Ak. Dkschr. 1. 23. 1, p. 9, figg. 2—6.
Articulina compressa   Rss., 1863, Mainzer Becken; Leonh. u. Broun. Jhrb. 1853, p. 673, t. 9, fig. 3.
Vertobralina striata   Williams., 1858, Rec. Brit. For. p. 90, figg. 197—198.
   » »   Carpenter, 1862, Introd. t. 5, figg. 17—22, 25.
?Spidostomella globulifera Costa 1854, Pal. Nap. 2, t. 27, fig. 27 (as Miliolina).

Miliolina seminulum Lin.
Tab. IX, figg. 319—355; Tab. X, figg. 356—360.

As the type for this species, — the varied forms of which have been ranged in a bewildering assemblage of species, founded even on the most trifling and inconstant differences —, could properly be chosen the oblong, more or less compressed, usually smooth form. The relation of the length of the different diameters to each another is subject to an infinity of variations, whence a mass of varietal modifications originates (besides all those, resulting from different arrangement of the chambers) from produced oblong to the disciform *Triloc. orbicularis* Röm. The shape of the mouth is also very variable: if the last chamber is provided with a long tubiform neck, the mouth is round with a very reduced tongue, while a flat and broad neck usually has a narrow, produced mouth with a flat, often raised tongue; the thick inflated forms have broad mouth and valvelike tongue somewhat resembling that of *Mil. ringens*. It is often finely agglutinant, and is one of the commonest rhizopodes in the chalk-ooze, particularly its pigmyforms, *Triloc. oblonga* Montag. and d'Orbigny.

1. Var. *scapha* d'Orb. This variety has a fine porcellaneous lustre and a nearly semilunar aperture. It seems in some way closely allied to *Mil. ringens*. It has a a lenticular, somewhat marginated shape. When the edge of an older chamber occasionally becomes turned outside on the flat side of the shell, its shape approaches to *triangularis* d'Orb. Such a form has been designated as *Quinqueloculina Lamarckiana* d'Orbigny.

It is common both in the coralline-gravel and the chalk-ooze.

2. Var. *triangularis* d'Orb. is scarcely deserving to be ranked as a distinct variety, since its features seem to be quite accidental and inconstant. It is not seldom 3 to 4 keeled or even winged as in *Quinqueloculina Candeiana* d'Orb. When the edges or the keels and ridges become truncate, the form has been called *Ferusaci*, *quadrilatera* d'Orb. It is often finely agglutinated.

Occurs chiefly in the coralline-gravel.

3. Var. *trigonula* Lmck. seems to be a more distinct form; Prof. Williamson has also ranked it as a distinct species. Our form is quite trigonal, sometimes with sharp edges and flat sides. It has a porcellaneous lustre, but its intimate shellstructure is not homogeneous, either because of some slight admixture of agglutinated particles or because of a spongious texture.

It is unfrequently met with on our terrain.

4. Var. *agglutinans* D'ORB. We retain this name, notwithstanding it is not properly applied in a group of forms through which this feature is so commonly distributed. It comes near to the typical form, but its *aperture being furnished with marginal teeth* — which feature seems to be of some constancy — there is a reason for ranking it as a distinct variety. The tongue of the mouth is generally forked. It is finely agglutinant (h. e. composed of finest chalkdebris) and attains on the chalk-bottom a larger size than any other of these varieties.

5. Var. *pulchella* D'ORB. On the experienced authority of Mr. BRADY we refer to this variety all longitudinally plicated forms of *Mil. seminulum*. It may be, that the designation of *bicornis* WALK., should have the preference as older. Our form is not a typical *pulchella*, but irregularly and scantely plicated, generally longnecked and a little agglutinant. It is found very rarely in coralline-gravel.

6. Var. *Brogniartii* D'ORB. A finestriated Mil. seminulum, usually of the same shape as *Mil. oblonga* MONT.

It would, no doubt, be more conformable to a natural arangement of the varieties of this species to assign to the striated and ribbed forms a place under their respective corresponding smooth forms; for it seems as if those varieties had originated directly from each of the principal smooth ones. Nevertheless we have provisionnally brought together in our synoptical list of synonyms all *striate* and *costate* forms under one head.

Figg. 319—320: the typical or nearly typical *Mil. seminulum* somewhat agglutinant; from the chalk-bottom.

Figg. 321—329: pigmyforms and young of *Mil. seminulum*; from 0,07 to 0,20 mm. in length.

Figg. 330—334: var. *scapha* D'ORB.; 330: endview; 331: edgeview; 332: sideview; the aperture resembling that of *Mil. ringens*; 333—334: transverse and longitudinal sections of the same.

Figg. 335—345: transitional forms to flat *triangularis* form (porcellaneous); from chalk-ooze.

Figg. 346—354: carinate forms of *triangularis* D'ORB.; slightly agglutinant, not quite porcellaneous; from the coralline-gravel.

Fig. 355: transverse section of *trigonular*, highly magnified; of porcellaneous lustre; from the coralline-gravel.

Figg. 356—358, tab. X: »*pulchella*» with few and irregular folds, slightly agglutinant; from the coralline-gravel.

Figg. 359—360: the typical »*agglutinans*» D'ORB.; 360 shows the closely toothed mouthedge and the produced forked tongue.

a) lævis, oblonga, interdum tumida:

Syn. **Vermiculum oblongum** Montagu, 1808, Testac. Brit. p. 522, t. 14, fig. 9.
    Trilocul. oblonga   d'Orb., 1826, Tabl. méth.; An. Sc. Nat. 7, p. 300, Mod. 95.
    »   »   Röm., 1838, Nordd. tert. Meeress.; Leonh. u. Bronn. Jhrb. 1838, p. 393, t. 3, fig. 70.
    »   **oblonga, oburnea** d'Orb., 1839, Cuba, p. 175, 180 t. 10, figg. 3—5; 21—23.
    »   »   Park. et Jones, 1866, Crag. Foramf.; Pal. Soc. 19, p. 7, t. 3, figg. 31—32.
    Miliola oblonga   Park. et Jones, 1865, North. Atl. and Arct. Oc.; Phil. Trans. 155 1, p. 411, t. 15, figg. 34, 41, t. 17, figg. 85, 86.
    Triloculina Chemnitziana d'Orb., 1844, Iles Canaries p. 141, t. 3, figg. 19—21.
    »   **nitida**   d'Orb., ibid. p. 141, t. 3, figg. 22—24.
    Quinqueloc. lævigata d'Orb., ibid. t. 3, figg. 31—33.
    Triloculina consobrina d'Orb., 1846, For. tert. Vienne p. 277, t. 17, figg. 10—12.
    Miliolina seminulum var. **oblonga** Williams., 1858, Brit. rec. Foramf. p. 86, figg. 186—187.
    Triloculina nitens, microdon Rss., 1849, Neue For. österr. Beck.; Wien. Ak. Dkschr. 1. 1, p. 383, t. 49, figg. 9—11.
    »   **carinata, angusta** Purt., 1843, Tert. Verstein. nordw. Deutschl. t. 1, figg. 36, 40.
    Quinqueloc. angusta   Rss., 1855, Tert. Schicht. nördl. u. mittl. Deutschl.; Wien. Ak. Sitz.-Ber. 1. 18, p. 253, t. 9, fig. 20.
    Triloculina æmulans, acutangula Rss., 1864, Oberoligocän.; Wien. Ak. Sitz.-Ber. 1. 50, p. 451, t. 1, figg. 5—6.
    »   **Raibliana**   Gümb., 1869, St. Cassian-Raibl. Sch.; k. k. österr. geol. Reichsanst. Jhrb. 19, p. 182, t. 6, fig. 34.
    Miliolina consobrina   Egger, 1857, Mioc. Ortenburg; Leonh. u. Bronn. Jhrb. 1857, p. 271, t. 6, figg. 7—9.
    »   **prælonga**   Egg., ibid. p. 273, t. 6, figg. 16—18.
    ?**Quinquelocul. lyra, longirostra** d'Orb., 1826, Tabl. meth., Ann. Sc. Nat. 7, p. 303, N:o 45; Mod. 8.
    »   **Bosciana** d'Orb., 1839, Cuba p. 191, t. 11, figg. 22—24.
    »   **angustissima, concinna, pygmæa, tenuis**, Rss., 1849, Neue For. Wien. Becken; Wien. Ak. Dkschr. 1. 1, p. p. 384—385, t. 49, fig. 18, t. 50, figg. 2—3, 8.
    Quinquelocul. tenuis   Czjz., 1847, For. foss. Wien. Beck.; Haid. Nat. Abh. 2. 1, p. 149, t. 13. figg. 31—34. (in Spiroloculinam vergens).
    »   »   Rss., 1851, Sept. Thon v. Berlin; Zeitschr. deutsch. geol. Ges. 3, p. 87, t. 7, fig. 60.
    Miliolina tenuis   Park. et Jones, 1865, Arct. and Northatl. Ocean; Phil. Trans. 155. 1, p. 411, t. 17, figg. 84.
    Quinquelocul. gracilis   Karr., 1867, For. Faun. Österr.; Wien. Ak. Sitz.-Ber. 1. 55, p. 361, t. 3. fig. 2.
    »   **Philippi, oblonga** Rss., 1855, Tert. Schicht. nordl u. mittl. Deutschl.; Wien. Ak. Sitz.-Ber. 1. 18, p. 252, t. 9, figg. 87, 89.
    »   **Ludwigi**   Rss., 1865, Sept. Thon Deutschland; Wien. Ak. Dkschr. 1. 25. 1, p. 126, t. 1, fig. 12.
    Triloc. lucida   Karrer 1868, Mioc. Kostej; Wien. Ak. 8. Ber. 1. 58, p. 139, t. 2, f. 7.

b) ovalis et dilatata

Triloculina inflata, ovalis, Quinquelocul. ovata, Röm., 1838, Nordd. tert. Meeressand, Leonh. u. Bronn. Jhrb. 1838, p. 393—394, t. 5, figg. 72, 73, 78.
Quinquelocul. aspera   d'Orb., 1826, Tab. meth; An. Sc. Nat. 7, p. 301. N:o 11.
Miliolina agglutinans   Park. et Jones, 1865, North. Atl and Arct. Oc.; Phil. Trans. 155. 1, p. 410, t. 15, fig. 37.

Syn. **Miliolina sominulum** WILLIAM. 1858, Brit. rec. Foramf. p. 86, figg. 183—185.
  Quinquelocul. foeda Rss., 1849, Neue For. österr. Beck.; Wien. Ak. Dkschr. 1. 1, p. 384, t. 50 figg. 5—6.
  » **seminulum** PARKER et JONES, 1858, For. Coast. of Norway; A. M N. H. (2) 19 p. 300, t. 10, figg. 34—36.
  Triloculina scapha, oculina, Quinqueloc. pauperata, Haueriana, Mayeriana, Bronniana, Akneriana D'ORB., 1846, Bass. tert. Vienne, p. 276, 278 etc., t. 17, figg. 4—9, 22—27; t. 18, figg. 1—6, 16—21.
  Quinquelocul. rotundata COSTA, 1854, Pal. Nap. 2, t. 26, fig. 10.
  Quinquelocul. transsilvanica KARR., 1864, Leythakalk Wien. Beck.; Wien. Ak. Sitz.-Ber. 1. 50, p. 701, t. 1, fig. 4.
  Triloculina moguntiaca Rss., 1853, Mainzerbeck.; Leonh. u. Bronn. Jhrb. 1853, p. 672, t. 9, fig. 5.
  » **cuneata** KARR., 1867, For. Faun. Osterr.; Wien. Ak. Sitz.-Ber. 1. 55, p. 359, t. 2, fig. 8 (var. secanti approximans).
  orbicularis, rotundata ROM., 1838, Nordd. tert. Meeressand, Leonh. u. Bronn. Jhrb. 1838, p. 393, t. 3, figg. 74, 79 (var. triangulari propinqua).
  » » Rss., 1855, Tert. Sch. nördl. u. mitl. Deutschl.; Wien. Ak. Sitz.-Ber. 1. 18, p. 251, t. 8, fig. 85.
  » **vitrea** KARR., 1870, Kreidef. Leitzendorf; Jhrb. k. k. österr. geol. Reichsanst. 20, p. 167, t. 10, fig. 5.
  » **Seleue** KARR., 1868, Mioc. For. faun. Kostej; Wien. Ak. Sitz.-Ber. 1. 58, p. 138, t. 1. fig. 12.
  Quinquelocul. seccans KARRER 1878, Foram. Luvon; Bolet. Comis. Mapa geol. del Esp. 7. 2, p. 14, t. E, fig. 7.
  Triloculina lævissima COSTA, 1854, Pal. Nap. 2, t. 25, fig. 8.
  » **subinflata, exilis** Rss., 1869, Oligocän. v. Gaas; Wien. Ak Sitz.-Ber. 1. 59, p. 454, 455, t. 1. figg. 4—5.
  » **obotritica** BOLL., Ostseeländer p. 127, t. 2, fig. 11.
  Quinquelocul. Brauni, Klipsteini Rss., 1853, Mainzer Beck.; Leonh. u. Bronn. Jhrb. 1853, p. 674, t. 9, figg. 4, 6.
  Triloc. anceps, Qu. lenticularis, suturalis Rss., 1849, Neue For. österr. tert. Beck.; Wien. Ak. Dkschr. 1. 1, p. 383 385, t. 49, f. 11; t. 50, figg. 4, 9.
  Miliolina Haidingeri EGGER, 1857, Mioc. Ortenburg; Leonh. u. Bronn. Jhrb. 1857, p. 272, t. 6, figg. 10—12.
  Quinquelocul. confusa Rss., 1863, Sept. Thon Offenbach; Wien. Ak. Sitz.-Ber. 1. 48, p. 42, t. 2, fig. 8 (ad triangularem adiens).
  » **lamellidens** Rss., ibid. p. 41, t. 1, fig. 7.
  » **obliqua, suturalis** Rss., 1867, Steinsalzablager. Wieliczka; Wien. Ak. Sitz.-Ber. 1. 55, p. 75, 76, t. 2, figg. 6—7, t. 3, fig. 1.
  » **rugosa** KARR., 1866, Grünsandst. Orakay Bay N. Zeeland; Novara Reise, geol. Th. 2. 2, p. 203, t. 4, fig. 16.
  » **subrotunda** PARK. et JONES, 1865, North. Atl. and Arct. Ocean; Phil. Trans. 155. 1, p. 411, t. 15, fig. 38.
  » » PARK. et JONES, BRADY 1866, Crag. For.; Pal. Soc. 19, p. 11.
  » **dilatata** D'ORB., 1839, Cuba, p. 192, t. 11, figg. 28—30.
  » **labiosa** D'ORB., ibid. p. 178, t. 10, figg. 12—14.

f) magis inflata:
  » **seminulum** PARK. et JONES, BRADY, 1866, Crag. For.; Pal Soc. 19, p. 9, t. 3, figg. 35—36.
  » **impressa** Rss., 1851, Sept. Thon Berlin; Zeitschr. deutsch. geol. Ges. 3, p. 87, t. 7, fig. 59.

Sya. **Quinqueloeul. sarmatica** KARR., 1877, Hochquell. Wasserleit.; k. k. österr. geol. Reichsanst. Abh. 9, p. 375, t. 16, fig. 11.
» **ovula** KARR., 1868, Mioc. Kostej; Wien, Ak. S. Ber. 1. 58, p. 147, t. 2, fig. 8.
» **lævigata** BORNEM., 1855, Sept. Thon Hermsdorf; Ztschr. deutsch. geol. Ges. 7, p. 350, t. 19, fig. 5.
» **cognata, impressa, ovalis** BORNEM., ibid. p. 350, t. 19, figg. 7—9.
» **impressa** RSS., 1865, deutsch. Sept. Thon; Wien. Ak. Dkschr. 1. 25. 1, p. 124
» **regularis** RSS., 1849, Neue For. österr. tert. Beck.; Wien. Ak. Dkschr. 1. 1, p. 384, t. 50, fig. 1.
Triloculina Martiana D'ORB., 1841, Iles Canaries p. 141, t. 3, figg. 16 - 18.
» **Schreibersiana** D'ORB., 1839, Cuba p. 174, t. 9, figg. 20—22 (in M. ringentem transiens).
» **inflata, inornata** D'ORB., 1846, Bass. tert. Vienne. p. 278, 279, t. 17, figg. 13—18.
» **pyrula** KARR., 1862, For. Faun. Österr.; Wien. Ak. Sitz.-Ber. 1. 55, p. 350, t. 2, fig. 7.
» **decipiens** RSS., 1849, Neue For. Wien Beck.; Wien. Ak. Dkschr. 1. 1, p. 382, t. 49, fig. 8.
Adelosina lævigata D'ORB., 1826, Tabl. Meth.; An. Sc. Nat. 7, p. 304; For. tert. Vienne p. 302, t. 20, figg. 22—24.
» **cretacea** RSS., 1850, Kreidem. Lemberg; Haid. nat. Abh. 1. 1, p. 16, t. 1, fig. 15

Miliola cribrosa EGGER, 1857, Miocan. v. Ortenburg; Leonh. u. Bronn. Jhrb. 1857, p. 273, t. 6, figg. 13—15.
Sexloculina Haueri CZJZ., 1847, Haid. Nat. Abh. 2, 1, p. 149, t. 13, fig. 35—38.
?**Triloculina cryptella, sphæra** D'ORB., 1845, Voy. Amer. merid. 5. t. 9, figg. 4—5; t. 8, figg. 13—16.
» » PARK. et JONES, 1865, North. Atl. and Arct. Oc.; Phil. Trans. 155. 1, p. 410, t. 15, fig. 39 (an M. ringens var.).
» **truncata** KARR., 1864, Leythakalk Wien. Beck.; Wien. Ak. Sitz.-Ber. 1. 50, p. 704, t. 1, fig. 2.
» **valvularis** RSS., 1851, Sept. Thon Berlin; Ztschr. deutsch. geol. Ges. 3, p. 85, t. 7, fig. 56 (ad Mil. ringentem vergens).
» **turgida** RSS., ibid. p. 86, t. 7, fig. 58.
Triloculina austriaca D'ORB., 1846, For. tert. Vienne p. 275, t. 16, figg. 25—27 (ad Mil. ringentem vergens).
Miliola austriaca EGGER, 1857, Mioc. Ortenb.; Leonh. u. Bronn Jhrb. 1857, p. 271, t. 6, figg. 4—6.
Triloculina trigonula var. RSS., 1864, Oberburg, Steiermark, Wien. Ak. Dkschr. 1. 23. 1, p. 8, t. 1, fig. 12.

c) trigonula:

Miliolites trigonula LMCK., 1804, 1816, Encycl. meth. t. 469, fig. 2.
Triloculina trigonula D'ORB., 1826, Tabl. Meth.; Ann. Sc. Nat. 7, p. 293, t. 16, figg. 5—9, Mod. 93.
» » ROEMER, 1838, Nordd. tert. Meeress.; Leonh. u. Bronn Jhb. 1838, p. 393, t. 3, fig. 71
Miliolina trigonula WILLIAMS., 1858, Brit. rec. forf. p. 84, figg. 180—182.
Triloculina tricarinata D'ORB., 1826, Tabl. meth. Ann. Sc. Nat. 7, Mod. 94.
» **gibba** D'ORB., ibid., 1846, For. tert. Vienne, p. 274, t. 16, figg. 22—24.
» » var. RSS., 1864, Oberoligoc.; Wien. Ak. Sitz.-Ber. 1. 50, p. 450, t. 1, fig. 4.
» » EGGER, 1857, Mioc. Ortenburg; Leonh. u. Bronn. Jhrb. 1857, p. 271, t. 6, figg. 1—3.

Syn. **Triloculina gibba** Harn., 1875, For. Clav. Szab. Sch., p. 21, t. 12, fig. 10.
  » trigonula, angulosa Costa, 1854, Pal. Nap. 2, p. 314, 315, t. 24, figg. 8, 14—15.
  » tricarinata Brady, 1864, Rhizop. Shetl.; Trans. Lin. Soc. 24, p. 466, t. 48, fig. 3
Miliolina tricarinata Park. et Jones, 1865, North. Atl. and Arct. Oc.; Phil. Transact. 155, 1, p. 409, t. 15, fig. 40.
Mil.-Triloculina-tricarinata Park. et Jones, Brady, 1866, Crag. foramf.; Pal. Soc. 19, p. 7, t. 3, figg. 33—34.
Triloculina tricarinata Rss., 1867, Steinsalzablag. Wieliczka; Wien. Ak. Sitz.-Ber. 1. 55, p. 71, t. 2, fig. 4.
Cruciloculina triangularis d'Orb., 1846, For. tert. Vienne, p. 280, t. 21, fig. 57.
  » Czjzanczam, 1862, Introd., t. 6, fig. 15.

d) angularis: ab a) vix diversa; lateribus interdum truncatis (Qu. Fernasci d'Orb.):

Quinqueloculi. triangularis d'Orb., 1826, Tab. meth.; An. Sc. Nat. 7, p. 302. N:o 34.
  » » d'Orb., 1846, For. tert. Vienne p. 288, t. 18, figg. 7—9.
  » » Park. et Jones, Brady, 1866, Crag. For.; Pal. Soc. 19, t. 4, fig. 1.
  » peregrina, Partschii d'Orb., 1846, For. tert. Vienne p. 292—293, t. 19, figg. 1—6.
Miliolina sominulum Park. et Jones, 1865, North. Atl. and Arct. Oceans.; Phil. Trans. 155, 1, p. 410, t. 15, fig. 35.
Quinqueloculi. Ermani Bornem., 1855, Sept. Thon Hermsdorf; Ztschr. deutsch. geol. Ges. 7, p. 351, t. 19, fig. 6.
Triloculina decipiens, exigua, Quinqueloculi. lobata, Buchiana Costa, 1854, Pal. Nap. 2, t. 24, figg. 13—17, t. 26, figg. 2, 7.
Quinqueloculi. semiplana Rss., 1855, Kreidegeb. Meklenburg; Zeitsch. deutsch. geol. Ges. 7, p. 275, t. 10, fig. 1.
  » ovata Rss., 1855, Tert. Schicht. nordl. u. mittl. Deutschl.; Wien. Ak. Sitz.-Ber. 1. 18, p. 252, t. 9, fig. 88.
  » Biondi, tubulosa Seg., 1862, Rhizopod. Catan. p. 35, t. 2, fig. 7, 8. Accad. Gioenia Atti (2) 18.
Triloculina Kochi Rss. (partim) 1855, Kreideg. Meklenb.; Ztschr. deutsch. geol. Ges. 7, p. 289, t. 11, fig. 6.
Quinqueloculi. inæqualis d'Orb., 1841, Iles Canaries, p. 142, t. 3, figg. 28—30.
  » **Lamarckiana, Cuvieriana, Auberiana** d'Orb., 1839, Cuba p. 189, 190, 193, t. 11, figg. 14—15, 19—21; t. 12, figg. 1—3.
  » **bicostata, Candeiana** d'Orb., ibid. p. 195, 199, t. 12, figg. 8—10, 24—26.
  » **planciana** d'Orb., ibid. p. 186, t. 11, figg. 4—6.
  » **Gualteriana** d'Orb., ibid. p. 186, t. 11, figg. 1—3. (transversim plicata).
  » **Buchiana, Ungeriana, longirostra** d'Orb., 1846, For. tert. Vienne p. 289, 291, t. 18, figg. 10—12, 22—27.
  » **punctata** Rss., 1853, Mainzer Becken; Leonh. u. Bronn. Jhrb. 1853, p. 675, t. 9, fig. 8.
  » **eborea** Schwag., 1866, For. Kar.-Nikobar.; Novara Reise, geol. Th. 2. 2, p. 204, t. 5, fig. 18
  » **signata** Rss., 1849, Neue For.; Wien Ak. Dkschr. 1. 1, p. 385, t. 50, fig. 11.
  » **venusta** Karr., 1868, Mioc. For. Faun. Kostej; Wien. Ak. Sitz.-Ber. 1. 58, p. 147, t. 2, fig. 6.
Triloculina intermedia, sulcata Karr., ibid. p. 139, t. 1, figg. 11, 13.
  » **angulata, nodosa** Karr., 1867, For. Faun. Österr.; Wien. Ak. Sitz.-Ber. 55, p. 359, t. 2, f. 6.
Quinqueloculi. bicarinella Rss., 1869, Oligoc. Gass.; Wien. Ak. Sitz.-Ber. 1. 59, p. 461, t. 3, fig. 1
  » **latidorsata, Grintzingensis, concava** Rss., 1849, Neue For. österr. tert. Beck. p. 385—386, t. 50, fig. 12, t. 51, figg. 1—2.

Sys. ??**Triloculina nodosaroides** KARR., 1867, For. Faun. Österr.; Wien. Ak. Sitz.-Ber. I. 55, p. 360, t. 2, fig. 9.
    Triloculina quadrilatera D'ORB., 1839, Cuba, p. 173, t. 9, figg. 14—16.
      »   **bicarinata**, Qu. **polygona** D'ORB., ibid. p. 180, t. 10, figg. 18—20; t. 12, figg. 21—23.
    Quinqueloсul. Sagra, Antillarum D'ORB., ibid. p. 188, 194, t. 11, figg. 16—18; t. 12, figg. 4—6.
        (transversim plicata).
      »   **Ferussacii** D'ORB., 1826, Tabl. méth., Ann. Sc. Nat. 7, p. 304, N:o 18, Mod. 32.
Adelosina pulchella   D'ORB., 1846, For. tert. Vienne, p. 303, t. 20, figg. 25—30.
Miliolina bicornis var. **angulata** WILLIAMS., 1858, Brit. rec. For. p. 88, fig. 196.
    »   **Ferussci**   PARK. et JONES, 1865, North. Atl. and Arct. Ocean; Phil. Trans. 155. 1, p. 411, t. 15, fig. 36.
    »   »   PARK. et JONES, BRADY, 1866, Crag. For.; Pal. Soc. 19, p. 12, t. 4, fig. 4.
Quinqueloсul. Juleana, contorta, Rodolphina, Badenensis, Mariæ D'ORB., 1846, For. tert. Vienne, p. 298—300, t. 20, figg. 1—15.

    β) agglutinans et rugosa:

Quinqueloсul. agglutinans D'ORB., 1839, Cuba p. 195, t. 12, fig. 11—13.
    »   **enoplostoma, bidentata** D'ORB., ibid. p. 196, t. 12, figg. 14—20.
    »   **Bertholetiana** D'ORB., 1844, Iles Canaries p. 142, t. 3, figg. 25—27.
    »   **opaca**   Rss., 1862, Sept. Thon. Offenbach; Wien. Ak. Sitz.-Ber. I. 48, p. 42, t. 2, fig. 9.
    »   **Atropos, Kostejana, excavata** KARR., 1868, For. Kostej; Wien. Ak. Sitz.-Ber. I. 58, p. 148, 152, t. 3, figg. 4, 6; t. 2, fig. 9.
    »   **sclerotica** KARR., ibid. p. 152, t. 3, fig. 5.
    »   **asperula** SEG., 1862, Rhizopod. foss. Catania p. 36, t. 2, fig. 6 (Accad. Gioenia Atti (2) 18).

Appendix.

    e) transversim plicata:

Quinqueloсul. secans   D'ORB., 1826, Tab. meth.; An. Sc. Nat. 7, p. 303, N:o 43, Mod. 96.
    »   »   ROEM., 1838, Nordd. tert. Meerres.; Leonh. u. Bronn. Jhrb. 1838, p. 393, t. 3, fig. 77.
Miliolina seminulum var. **disciformis** WILLIAMS., 1858, Brit. rec. Forf. figg. 188—189.
Quinqueloсul. Haidingeri D'ORB., 1846, For. tert. Vienne, p. 289, t. 18, figg. 13—15.
    »   **denticulata, corrugata, transversa** COSTA, 1854, Pal. Nap. 2, p. 324, 325, t. 25, figg. 6, 14, t. 26, fig. 9.
    »   **notata**   Rss., 1849, Neue For. österr. tert. Becken; Wien. Ak. Dkschr. I. 1, p. 385, t. 5, fig. 7.
    »   **ornatissima** KARR., 1868, Mior. Kostej. Wien Ak. Sitz.-Ber. I. 58, p. 151, t. 3, fig. 2.
Triloculina dilatata   KARR., ibid. p. 139, t. 2, fig. 1.
Quinqueloсul. falcifera   KARR., ibid. p. 151, t. 3, fig. 3.
?   »   **fabularoides** KARR., 1864, Leythakalk; Wien. Ak. Sitz. Ber. I. 50, p. 704, t. 1, fig. 3. (apertura cribriformis).
    »   **acidula**   KARR., 1867, For. Faun. Österr.; Wien. Ak. Sitz.-Ber. I. 55, p. 361, t. 3, fig. 1.

    f) angularis:

    »   **Sandbergeri** Rss., 1853, Mainzer Beck.; Leonh. u. Bronn. Jhrb. 1853, p. 674, t. 9, fig. 7.

Syn. Quinqueloeul. speciosa   Rss., 1855, Tert. Seh. nordl. u. mittl. Deutschl.; Wien. Ak. Sitz.-Ber. 1. 18.
p. 251, t. 8, fig. 86.
»   plicatula Rss., 1867, Steinsalzablag. Wieliczka; Wien. Ak. Sitz.-Ber. 1. 55, p. 74,
t. 3, fig. 2.
»   Clotho   Karr., 1868, Mioc. Kostej; Wien. Ak. Sitz.-Ber. 1. 58, p. 151, t. 2, fig. 5.
»   Lachesis Karr., ibid. p. 146, t. 2, fig. 4.
»   Ungeriana var. stenostoma Karr., ibid. p. 141, t. 2, fig. 3.
»   undosa   Karr., 1867, For. Faun. Österr.; Wien. Ak. Sitz.-Ber. 1. 55, p. 361, t. 3,
fig. 3.

f) longitud. plicata sive costata (Qu. pulchella d'Orb.):

Adelosina Soldanii   d'Orb., 1826, Tab. meth.; An. Sc. Nat. 7, p. 304; N:o 4.
Triloculina tricostata, Quinquelocul. Soldanii d'Orb., ibid. p. 300, 303; N:ris 21, 48.
Quinquelocul. pulchella d'Orb., ibid. p. 303; N:o 42.
»   »   Brady, 1864, Rhizop. Sheti.; Trans. Lin. Soc. 24, p. 466, t. 48, fig. 1.
»   »   Parr. et Jones, Brady, 1866, Crag. For.; Pal. Soc. 19, p. 13, t. 4, fig. 3.
»   trisulcata, sulcifera Röm., 1838, Nordd. tert. Meeress.; Leonh. u. Bronn. Jhrb. 1838,
p. 393, t. 3, figg. 75—76.
»   Verneuiliana, Schreibersii, Josephina d'Orb., 1846, For. tert. Vienne, p. 296, 297,
t. 19, figg. 19—27.
Uniloculina indica   d'Orb., ibid. p. 261, t. 21, figg. 53—54.
Triloculina pulchella   d'Orb., ibid. t. 17, figg. 19—21.
Quinquelocul. tricarinata d'Orb., 1839, Cuba p. 187, t. 11, figg. 7—9, 13.
»   plicosa, Josephina Costa, 1855, Pal. Nap. 2, p. 321, 322, t. 25, figg. 2, 4.
?   »   nobilis Karr., 1868, Mioc. For. Kostej; Wien. Ak. Sitz.-Ber. 1. 58, p. 149, t. 2,
fig. 11 (ad d) forsan pertinens).
Miliolina bicornis   Williamson, 1858, Brit. rec. For. p. 88, figg. 190—194.
Quinquelocul. Bousana, Dutemplei, nussdorfensis d'Orb., 1846, For. Bass. tert. Vienne p. 293 et
seqq. t. 19, figg. 7—15.
Triloculina Linneiana   d'Orb., 1839, Cuba p. 172, t. 9, figg. 11—13.
Quinquelocul. Pooyiana   d'Orb., ibid. p. 191, t. 11, figg. 25—27.
Miliolina bicornis var. elegans Williams., 1858, Brit. rec. Forf. p. 98, fig. 195.
Triloculina dichotoma   Rss., 1849, Neue For. österr. tert. Beck.; Wien. Ak. Dkschr. 1. 1, p. 383,
t. 49, fig. 12.
»   porvaensis Hkn., 1875, Clav. Száb. Sch. p. 21, t. 13, fig. 3.
Miliola Schreibersii   Blake, 1876, Yorkshire Lias p. 451, t. 18, fig. 2 (an Vertebralina).

g) striata, a præcedente vix distinguenda:

Adelosina striata   d'Orb., 1826, Tabl. meth.; Ann. Sc. Nat. 7, p. 304, Mod. 18, 97.
Quinquelocul. seminulum d'Orb. partim, ibid. p. 303; N:o 44.
Triloculina Brongniartii d'Orb., 1826, Tabl. meth.; Ann. Sc. Nat. 7, p. 300; N:o 23.
»   Brogniartiana d'Orb., 1839, Cuba; For. p. 176, t. 10, figg. 6—8.
»   Gualteriana, Fichteliana, suborbicularis d'Orb., ibid. p. 170, 171, t. 9, figg. 5—10;
t. 10, figg. 9—11.
»   Planciana d'Orb., ibid. p. 173, t. 9, figg. 17—19.
Quinquelocul. gracilis   d'Orb., ibid. p. 181, t. 11, figg. 10—12.
Triloculina Webbiana, Quinqueloc. Guanche d'Orb., 1844, Iles Canaries, p. 140, 143, t. 3, figg.
13—15, 34—36.

Syn. Quinqueloeul. Brongniartii Park. et Jones, Brady, 1865, Crag. For.; Pal. Soc. 19, p. 14, t. 3, fig. 41, t. 4, fig. 2.
Triloculina Brogniartiana Bailey, 1850, Examin. of Soundings; Smithson. Contrib. 2, Art. 3, p. 13, figg. 44—45.
» striatella Karr., 1868, Mioc. Kostej; Wien. Ak. Sitz.-Ber. 1. 58, p. 140, t. 2, fig. 2.
Quinqueloeul. seminuda Rss., 1865, For. deutsch. Sept. Thon; Wien. Ak. Dkschr. 1. 25. 1 p. 125, t. 1, fig. 11 (d) angulari par).
» triedra, obsoleta, striatella, Boueana, affinis, nussdorfensis Costa, 1854, Pal. Nap. 2, p. 326—329, t. 25, figg. 11, 13, 15; t. 26, figg. 3, 4, 6 (var. angulari par).
» longicollis, gracillis Costa, ibid. t. 25, fig. 3, t. 26, fig. 1.
Quinqueloeul. hiantula Rss., 1863, Oberburg. Steiermark; Wien. Ak. Dkschr. 1. 23. 1, t. 8, fig. 11.
» striolata Rss., 1849, Neue For. österr. tert. Beck.; Wien. Ak. Dkschr. 1. 1, p. 385, t. 50, fig. 10.
» costata Karr., 1867, For. faun. Österr.; Wien. Ak. Sitz.-Ber. 1. 55, p. 362, t. 3, fig. 4.
» paucisulcata Rss., 1864, Oberoligocän.; Wien. Ak. Sitz.-Ber. 1. 50, p. 452, t. 1, fig. 7.
» Eos Rss., 1869, Oligocän. von Gaas; Wien. Ak. Sitz.-Ber. 59, p. 457, t. 1, fig. 7.
» incrassata, Schroekingerii, vermicularis Karr., 1868, Mioc. Kostej; Wien. Ak. Sitz.-Ber. 1. 58, p. 148—150, t. 2, figg. 10, 12, t. 3, fig. 1.
» Carp. Introd. t. 6, fig. 3.

h) serratim lineata:

Quinqueloeul. zigzag d'Orb., 1846, For. tert. Vienne p. 295, t. 19, figg. 16—18.

i) ordine punctata:

Quinqueloeul. saxorum (Lmck.) d'Orb., 1826, Tab. méth.; An. Sc. Nat. 7, p. 301, t. 16, figg. 10—14 Mod. 33.
Miliola saxorum Egger, 1857, Mioc. Ortenb.; Leonh. u. Bronn. Jhrb. 1857, p. 272, t. 10, figg. 18—20.
Quinqueloeul. striatopunctata Karr., 1867, For. Österr.; Wien. Ak. Sitz.-Ber. 1. 55, p. 362, t. 3, fig. 5.
» lacunosa Karr., ibid. p. 362, t. 3, fig. 6.
Triloculina carinata d'Orb., 1839, Cuba p. 179, t. 10, figg. 15—17.
» granulata Rss., 1863, Oberburg, Steiermark; Wien. Ak. Dkschr. 1. 23. 1, p. 8, t. 1, fig. 13.

k) reticulata:

Triloculina reticulata d'Orb., 1826, Tab. méth.; An. Sc. Nat. 7, p. 299; N:o 9 (var secanti affinis).
Quinqueloeul. reticulata Karr., 1861, Marin. Teg. Wien. Beck.; Wien. Ak. Sitz.-Ber. 1. 44, p. 449, t. 2, fig. 5.
» Carp. Introduct. t. 6, fig. 13.

Miliolina ringens Lмк.

Tab. X, figg. 361—386.

The form which usually occurs on our bottom is identical with *Biloculina bulloides* D'Orb. with its more or less broad, often carinated and inclined shelf, produced by the excess of the last chamber beyond the preceding. The modification with lobate limb — *Bil. caudata* Bornem., *Bil. appendiculata* Rss. — are often met with, but such trifling features are too accidental to entitle to any separate designation whatever. *Biloc. sphæra* Brady or *Bil. globulus* Bornem. is ordinarily distinguished by higher lustre and absence of limb, the sutural mark being quite faint; the shell nearly globular and the last chamber much larger than and overlapping the preceding one. It is found associated with the typical form.

Triloculina enoplostoma Rss. from the »Septaria»-clay at Berlin, is a »triloculine» form, which also occurs on our bottom, but is very rare. Its glossy porcellaneous lustre and the shape of its aperture betray its close kindred to *Mil. ringens*. Some of D'Orbigny's *Triloculinæ* may also be referred to this variety, as *Triloc. Schreibersiana, austriaca* D'Orb. etc. also *Triloc. circularis* Bornem.; *Triloc. valvularis* Rss. From the Atlantic ocean off the Azores Prof. Smitt and Ljungman brought home in 1868 an extensive series of highly developed *Miliolina ringens*, elucidating the indistinct demarcation between it and *Mil. seminulum*. Some delineations of a few examples from this valuable collection will illustrate this gradational transition.

The form with tubulated round aperture recorded by Lamarck as *Miliolit. ringens* and by Costa as *Biloc. tubulosa* has not been met with on our bottom. But in deep water in the Atlantic it seems to be common.

The form »contraria» D'Orb. has not occurred.

The typical form is sometimes finely striate — figg. 370—371. A handsome *costulate triloculine* form is sometimes met with on our bottom, figg. 384—385.

Figg. 361—362: the typical *Mil. ringens*, from chalk-bottom; the limb being thick and uneven with folds.

Figg. 363—365: oblong, cyclostome form (*Biloc. tubulosa* Costa); from the Atlantic off the Azores, 790 fathoms, Smitt and Ljungman.

Figg. 366—367: depressed form (*Bil. carinata, depressa* D'Orb.) with nearly tubular mouth; from the same locality as the preceding, 550 fathoms.

Figg. 368—369: the *spheroidal* variety; the last chamber being much larger than the preceding; from the chalk-bottom.

Figg. 370—371: finely striate form; from the Atlantic, 790 fathoms, Smitt and Ljungman.

Figg. 372—373: *triloculine* variety, from the coralline-gravel off the Virgin Islands.

Figg. 374—375: irregular, *triloculine* form of high development, from the Atlantic, off the Azores, 600 fathoms, Smitt and Ljungman.

Figg. 376—378: *quadriloculine*, tubulated form, from the same place, Smitt and Ljungman.

Figg. 379—381: *quinqueloculine* form, associated with the preceding.
Figg. 382—383: *triloculine*, tubulated variety; with the preceding.
Figg. 384—385: *costulate, triloculine* form of Mil. ringens; from the chalk-bottom.
Fig. 386: young or pigmy, with very thin shell, viewed in transmitted light.

Syn. **Miliolites ringens**   Lmck., 1804, Ann. du Mus. 5, p. 351, N:o 1; IX, t. 17, fig. 1.

a) sphærica vel subsphærica, interdum carinata:

Biloculina bulloides, ringens d'Orb., 1826, Tab. meth.; An. Sc. Nat. 7, p. 297, N:o 1, 2.
» subsphærica d'Orb., 1839, Cuba, p. 162, t. 8, figg. 25—27.
» sphæra Brady, 1864, Rhizop. Shetland; Trans. Lin. Soc. 24, p. 466, t. 48, fig. 1.
» simplex d'Orb., 1846, For. tert. Vienne, p. 264, t. 15, figg. 25—27.
» bulloides, simplex, inornata, æquivoca, circumclausa Costa, 1854, Pal. Nap. 2, t. 24, figg. 1, 3—6.
» globulus Bornem., 1855, Sept. Thon Hermsdorf; Ztschr. deutsch. geol. Ges. 7, p. 349, t. 19, fig. 3.
» » Rss., 1863, Sept. Thon Offenbach, Wien. Ak. Sitz.-Ber. 1. 48, p. 40, t. 1, fig. 4.
» globiformis, antiqua Karr., 1867, For. Fauna Österr.; Wien. Ak. Sitz.-Ber. 1. 55, p. 357, 365, t. 2, fig. 1, t. 3, fig. 7.
» obesa Rss., 1864, Oberoligocän.; Wien. Ak. Sitz.-Ber. 1. 50, p. 450, t. 5, fg. 7.
» ringens Park. et Jones, 1857, For. Coast. of Norway; An. Mag. Nat. Hist. (2) 19, p. 298, t. 10, figg. 28—33.
» lucernula Schwag., 1866, Kar.-Nikobar.; Novara Reise, geol. Tb. 2. 2, p. 202, t. 4, fig. 17.
» amphiconica var. Rss., 1867, Steinsalzablag. Wieliczka; Wien. Ak. Sitz.-Ber. 1. 55, p. 67, t. 1, fig. 8.
» bulloides var. calostoma, anodonta Karr., 1868, Mioc. For. Kostej.; Wien. Ak. Sitz.-Ber. 1. 58, p. 133, t. 1, figg. 4, 6.
» turgida Rss., 1851, Sept. Thon Berlin; Zeitschr. deutsch. geol. Ges. 3, p. 85, t. 7, fig. 55.
» appendiculata Rss., 1863, Crag. d'Anvers; Bull. Ac. Belg. (2) 15, p. 137, t. 1, fig. 1.
» Murrhina Schwag., 1866, For. Kar.-Nikobar.; Novara Reise, geol. Tb. 2. 2, p. 203, t. 4, fig. 15.

b) magis ovalis:

Biloculina bulloides d'Orb., 1826, An. Sc. Nat. 7, t. 16, figg. 1—4; Mod. 90.
Miliola (Biloculina) ringens Park et Jones, 1865, North. Atl. and Arct. Oc.; Phil. Trans. 155. 1, p. 409, t. 15, figg. 42—43.
Biloculina canariensis d'Orb., 1844, Iles Canaries p. 139, t. 3, figg. 10—12.
» peruviana d'Orb., 1845, Voy. Am. mér. 5, p. 65, t. 9, figg. 1—3.
» patagonica d'Orb., ibid. p. 65, t. 3, figg. 15—17.
» clypeata, affinis, inornata d'Orb., 1846, For. tert. Vienne, p. 263, 266, t. 15, figg. 19—21, t. 16, figg. 1—3, 7—9.
» cyclostoma Rss., 1849, Neue For. Wien. Beck.; Wien. Ak. Dkschr. 1. 1, p. 382, t. 49, fig. 6.
» lobata Rss., 1863, Sept. Thon Offenbach; Wien. Ak. Sitz.-Ber. 1. 48, p. 40, t. 1, figg. 5—6.
» oblonga d'Orb., 1839, Cuba, p. 163, t. 8, figg. 21—23.

Sys. Biloculina ringens   Williams., 1858, Brit. rec. Forf. p. 79, figg. 169—171, 175—176.
    »   ventricosa, bulloides var. larvata Rss., 1867, Steinsalzablag. Wieliczka; Wien. Ak. Sitz.-
                            Ber. 1. 55, p. 68, 69, t. 1, fig. 9; t. 2, figg. 1—3.
    »   constricta   Costa, 1854, Paleont. Nap. 2, p. 301, t. 24, fig. 2.
    »   Grinzingensis Karr., 1877, Hochquellenwasserleit.; Jhrb. Österr. geol. Reichsanst. Abh. 9,
                            p. 375, t. 16, fig. 8.
    »   caudata   Bornem., 1855, Sept. Thon Hermsdorf; Zeitschr. deutsch. geol. Ges. 7, p.
                            348, t. 19, fig. 2.
    »   elongata   d'Orb., 1826, Tabl. méth.; An. Sc. Nat. 7, p. 298; N:o 4.
    »   »   Park. et Jones, 1865, North. Atl. and Arct. Ocean.; Phil. Trans 155,
                            p. 402, t. 17.
    »   tenuis   Karr., 1868, Mioc. For. Kostej; Wien. Ak. Sitz.-Ber. 1. 58, p. 133, t. 1,
                            fig. 5.
    »   Carp. introduct. tab. 6, fig. 7.

c) angulata:

Biloculina aculeata   d'Orb., 1826, Tabl. meth.; Ann. Sc. Nat. 7, p. 296, Mod. 31.

d) depressa:

Biloculina depressa   d'Orb., 1826, Tab. méth.; An. Sc. Nat. 7, p. 298, N:o 7, Mod. 91.
    »   »   Park. et Jones, 1865, North. Atl. and Arct. Oc.; Phil. Trans. 155, 1, p. 409,
                           t. 17, fig. 89; 1866, Crag. For.; Pal. Soc. 19, p. 6, t. 3, figg. 29—30.
    »   carinata   d'Orb., 1839, Cuba p. 164, t. 8, fig. 24, t. 9, fig. 1—2.
    »   lunula   d'Orb., 1846, For. tert. Vienne p. 264, t. 15, fig. 22—24.
    »   ringens var. carinata Williams., 1858, Brit. rec. Foramf., p. 79, figg. 172—174.
    »   amphiconica Rss., 1849, Neue for. österr. tert. Becken; Wien. Ak. Dkschr. 1. 1, p. 382,
                           t. 49, fig. 5.
    »   scutella   Karr., 1868, Mioc. Kostej; Wien. Ak. Sitz.-Ber. 1. 58, p. 134, t. 1, fig. 7.
    »   plana   Karr., 1877, Hochquellen-Wasserleitung; Österr. geol. Reichsanst. Abh. 9,
                           p. 375, t. 16, fig. 9.

e) apertura subrotunda:

Biloculina applanata   Gümb., 1862, Streitenberg Schwammlager; Würtemb. Nat. Wiss. Ver. Jhrhft.
                           1862, p. 233, t. 4, fig. 16.
    »   tubulosa   Costa, 1854, Pal. Nap. 2, t. 24, fig. 7.

f) compressa:

Biloculina contraria   d'Orb., 1846, For. tert. Vienne, p. 266, t. 16, figg. 4—6.
    »   »   Brady, 1864, Rhizop. Shetl.; Trans. Lin. Soc. 24, p. 466, t. 48, fig. 2.
    »   »   Rss., 1867, Steinsalzablag. Wieliczka; Wien. Ak. Sitz.-Ber. 1. 55, p. 70,
                           t. 1, fig. 10.
Nummoloculina   Steinmann, 1881, Leonh. u. Bronn. Jhrb. 1881, p. 31, t. 2.

g) in seminulam transiens:

Syn. **Biloculina lucernula** var. Schwag., 1866, Kar. Nikobar; Novara Reise, geol. Th. 2. 2, p. 202, t. 4, fig. 14.
    Triloculina enoplostoma Rss., 1851, Sept. Thon Berlin.; Zeitschr. deutsch. geol. Ges. 3, p. 86, t. 7, fig. 57; 1867, Steinsalzablag. Wieliczka; Wien. Ak. Sitz.-Ber. 1. 55, p. 72, t. 2, fig. 5.
    »   **circularis**   Bornem., 1855, Sept. Thon Hermsdorf; Ztschr. deutsch. geol. Ges. 7, p. 349, t. 19, fig. 4.
? »   **bipartita**   d'Orb., 1846, For. tert. Vienne, p. 275, t. 17, figg. 1—3.
    (Cfr. p. 126).

Miliolina planulata Lмск.

The usual form on the chalk-bottom is *Spiroloculina canaliculata* d'Orb., which cannot claim particular designation. It is met with less frequently than either *Mil. seminulum* or *ringens*.

Syn. **Miliolites planulata**   Lmk., 1804, Ann. Mus. 5, p. 352, N:o 4.
    Spiroloculina depressa, perforata d'Orb., 1826, Tabl. meth.; Ann. Sc. Nat. 7, p. 298, N:o 12, Mod. 92.
    »   **nitida**   d'Orb., ibid. p. 298, N:o 4.
    »   **badenensis** d'Orb., 1846, For. tert. Vienne, p. 270, t. 16, figg. 13—15.
    »   **dilatata**   d'Orb., ibid. p. 271, t. 16, figg. 16—18.
    »   **excavata**   d'Orb., ibid. p. 271, t. 16, figg. 19—21.
    »   **depressa** var. **rotundata** Williams., 1858, Brit. rec. Forf. p. 82, fig. 178.
    Miliola-Spiroloculina-planulata Parker et Jones et Brady, 1866, Crag. For.; Pal. Soc. 19, p. 15, t. 3, figg. 37—38.
    Miliola planulata   Park. et Jones, 1865, North. Atl. and Arct. Oc.; Phil. Transact. 155. 1, p. 408, t. 17, fig. 82.
    Spiroloculina excavata Costa, 1854, Pal. Nap. 2, p. 311, t. 24, fig. 11.
    »   **Sandbergeri** Rss., 1853, Mainzerbecken; Leonh. u. Bronn. Jhrb. 1853, p. 671, t. 9, fig. 2.
    »   **Freyeri**   Rss., 1863, Oberburg. Steiermark; Wien. Ak. Dkschr. 1. 23. 1, p. 7, t. 1, fig. 9.
    »   **tenuissima** Rss., 1867, Steinsalzablag. Wieliczka; Wien. Ak. Sitz.-Ber. 1. 55, p. 71 t. 1, fig. 11.
    »   **Lapugyensis** Karr., 1867, For. Fenn. Österr.; Wien. Ak. Sitz.-Ber. 1. 55, p. 357, t. 2, fig. 1.
    »   **compressiuscula** Karr., ibid. p. 358, t. 2, fig. 4.
    »   **tenuirostra** Karr., ibid. p. 358, t. 2, fig. 5.
    »   **panda**   Schwag., 1863, Jurass. Sch.; Würtemb. Nat. Verein. Jhrhft. 17, p. 95, t. 2, fig. 6.
    »   **Carp.** Introd. t. 6, fig. 1.

b) limbata:

Spiroloculina limbata   d'Orb., 1826, Tab. meth.; An. Sc. Nat. 7, p. 299, N:o 12.
Miliola limbata   Park. et Jones, 1865, North. Atl. and Arct. Oc.; Phil. Trans 155. 1, p. 409, t. 17, fig. 83.

Syn. Spiroloculina dorsata		Rss., 1865, Deutsch. Septarienthon; Wien. Ak. Dkschr. 1. 25. 1, p. 123, t. , fig. 83.
»	limbata	Bornem., 1855, Sept. Thon Hermsdorf; Zeitschr. deutsch. geol. Ges. 7, p. 348, t. 19, fig. 1.
»	»	Rss., 1863, Sept. Thon Kreuznach; Wien. Ak. Sitz.-Ber. 1. 48, p. 64, t. 8, fig. 89.
»	»	Hken., 1875, For. Clav. Szab. Sch. p. 20, t. 13, fig. 2.
»	depressa	Williams., 1858, Brit. rec. for. p. 82, figg. 177.
»	canaliculata	d'Orb., 1846, For. tert. Vienne, p. 269, t. 16, figg. 10—12.
»	»	Costa, 1854, Pal. Nap. 2, t. 24, figg. 9—10.
»	»	Parr. et Jones, Brady, 1866, Crag. For.; Pal. Soc. 19, p. 16, t. 3, figg. 39—40.
»	alata	Rss., 1853, Mainzer Becken; Leonh. u. Bronns. Jhrb. 1853, p. 671, t. 9, fig. 1.
»	ovalis	Röm., 1838, Nordd. tert. Meeressand; Leonh. u. Bronn. Jhrb. 1838, p. 392, t. 3, fig. 68.
»	dubia	Röm., ibid. p. 392, t. 3, fig. 69.
»	ornata	d'Orb., 1839, Cuba, p. 167, t. 12, figg. 7, 7'.
»	cymbium	d'Orb., 1844, Iles Canaries, p. 140, t. 3, figg. 5—6.
»	cretacea	Rss., 1855, Kreide. Ostalpen; Wien. Ak. Dkschr. 7, p. 72, t. 26, fig. 9.
»	rostrata	Rss., 1849, Neue For. österr. tert. Beck.; Wien. Ak. Dkschr. 1. 1, p. 382, t. 49, fig. 7.
»	Morloti	Rss., 1863, Oberburg in Steiermark; Wien. Ak. Dkschr. 1. 23. 1, p. 7, t. 1, fig. 10.
»	cavernosa	Karr., 1867, For. Faun. Österr.; Wien. Ak. Sitz.-Ber. 1. 55, p. 358, t. 2, fig. 3.
»	Berchtoldsdorfensis Karr., 1877, Hochquellen-Wasserleit.; Jhrb. Österr. geol. Reichsanstalt Abh. 9, p. 375, t. 16, fig. 10.	
»	depressa var. Cymbium Williams., 1858, Brit. rec. For. p. 82, fig. 179.	
»	Carp. Introd. t. 6, f. 2.	

c) crenata:

Spiroloculina plicata		d'Orb., 1826, Tab. méth.; A. Sc. N. 7, p. 299, N:o 15.
»	speciosa	Karr., 1868, Mioc. Fauna Kostej; Wien. Ak. Sitz.-Ber. 1. 58, p. 135, t. 1, fig. 8.
»	crenata	Karr., ibid. p. 135, t. 1, fig. 9.

d) striata aut aspera:

Spiroloculina Poeyiana		d'Orb., 1839, Cuba p. 168, t. 10, figg. 1—2.
»	antillarum	d'Orb., ibid. p. 166, t. 9, figg. 3—4.
»	striatella	Rss., 1863, Oberburg in Steiermark; Wien. Ak. Dkschr. 1. 23. 1, p. 7, t. 1, fig. 8.
»	asperula	Karr., 1868, Mioc. Kostej; Wien. Ak. Sitz.-Ber. 1. 58, p. 137, t. 1, fig. 10.
»	celata	Costa, 1854, Pal. Nap. 2, t. 26, fig. 5.
»	»	Costa, 1855, For. foss. Marna blu' Vaticano; Mem. Nap. 2, p. 126, t. 1. fig. 14.

Trochammina incerta d'Orb.

Tab. XI, figg. 404—405.

This form is one of the smoothest amongst the arenaceous group of this class, being composed of the finest siliceous particles and probably a large quantity of secreted or precipitated cementing siliceous matter, the lime being quite absent; a rusty colouring matter renders the shell yellowish brown. It is very regularly formed, somewhat biconcave. The aperture is a very narrow crescent placed on the inner part of the last convolution. It is sparsedly met with on the chalk-bottom, attaining a diameter of 2 to 3 m. m.

Fig. 404: side-view of *Trochammina incerta*.
Fig. 405: edge-view.

Syn.	Operculina incerta	d'Orb., 1839, Cuba, p. 49, t. 6, figg. 16—17.
»	cretacea	Rss., 1845, Böhm. Kreide 1, p. 35, t. 13, figg. 64—65 (sec. Park. et Jones).
?	» punctata	Rss., 1849, Neue Foramf. österr. tert. Becken; Wien. Ak. Dkschr. 1. 1, p. 370, t. 46, fig. 21.
	Orbis infimus	Strickland, 1846, Microsc. Shells found in the Lias; Qu. Journ. geol. Soc. 2 p. 30, fig. a.
	Spirillina arenacea	Williams., 1858, Brit. rec. for. p. 93, fig. 203.
	Trochamnina squamata	var. incerta Carp., 1860, Introduct. p. 141, 312, t. 11, fig. 2.
»	incerta	Park. et Jones, 1869, The perm. Troch. pusilla etc.; A. M. N. H. (4) 4, p. 388, t. 13, fig. 1.
»	»	Brady, 1876, Carbonif. and Perm. foramf.; Pal. Soc. 30, p. 71, t. 2, figg. 10—14.
	Ammodiscus	Rss., 1861, Entwurf einer systematischen Zusammenstellung etc.; Wien. Ak. Sitz.-Ber. 44, p. 365.
	Serpula Roesleri	Schmid, 1867, Leonh. u. Bronn. Jhrb. 1867, p. 583, t. 6, figg. 46—47.
	Ammodiscus infimus	Bornem., 1874, Ueber Involutina; Zeitschr. deutsch. geol. Ges. 26, p. 725, t. 8, figg. 4—7; t. 9, fig. 8.
»	miocenicus	Karr., 1877, Hochquellenwasserleitung; Osterr. geol. Reichsanst. Abh. 9. p. 372, t. 16, fig. 2.
?	Cornuspira Hörnesi	Karr., 1865, Wien. Sandstein.; Wien. Ak. Sitz.-Ber. 52, p. 495, figg. 10—11.
»	granulosa, infraoolithica, silicea, aspera	Terquem. (sec. Brady l. cit. p. 72).
»	oolithica	Schwag., 1867 (see. Brady l. cit. p. 72).
»	infima	Blake, 1876, Yorkshire Lias p. 451, t. 18, fig. 2. (Vide etiam Brady, Carbonif. and Perm. foramf.; Pal. Soc. 30, p. 71—72)

Lituolina scorpiurus Mtfrt.

Tab. XI, figg. 406—409.

A great deal of confusion has been brought into the designation and definition of the genus Lituolina; and of late the dissociation of its closely allied forms even into new genera, based upon very trifling and inconstant characters, has scarcely contributed to advance our knowledge as to the real relation between its different forms

It has been repeatedly noticed and stated, that the mode of life, in a free or attached state, amongst this class does not afford sufficient characteristics even for specific, much less for generic, distinction; and no greater importance seems to be attributable to the feature of the chambers being subdivided or not.

Our form commences its early growth with a thin, slender, somewhat angular, half transparent, horny nodosarina-stage of a few produced chambers, the apex of which always seems to be broken off. From this condition in connection with rare instances of very young — twochambered — specimens being attached endwise to shells of larger rhizopodes its ordinary mode of life — at least in its youth — may be inferred.

Its young state ressembles very much *Reophax spiculifera* BRADY. The increase in size of the consecutive chambers are somewhat rapid; its agglutinating power is very strong, large pieces of broken shells and some sponge-needles, but no grains of sand, being used for the fabric. The aperture is usually reniform, a feature on which the genus *Hippocrepina* DAWS. et PARK. has been founded. It is one of the most abundant rhizopodes chiefly on the chalk-bottom.

Figg. 406—407: Two specimens of *Lit. scorpiurus* with part of their slender early stage.

Fig. 408: the apertural end.

Fig. 409: Longitudinal section through the medial plane.

Syn.	**Reophax scorpiurus**	MONTF., 1808, Conchyliol. syst. 1, Genre 83, p. 330.
	Dentalina Scorpionus	D'ORB., 1826, Tabl. meth., Ann. Sc. Nat. 7, p. 255, N:o 40.
	?Margin. hirsuta	D'ORB., ibid. p. 259, N:o 5.
	Lituola scorpiurus	BRADY, 1864, Rhizop. Shetl.; Trans. Lin. Soc. 24, p. 467, t. 48, fig. 5.
»	**nautiloides** var. **scorpiurus**	PARK. et JONES, 1865, North. Atl. and Arct. Oc.; Phil. Transact. 155. 1, p. 407, t. 15, fig. 48.
»	**scorpiurus** var.	DAWS., 1870, For. Gulf and Riv. St. Laur.; A. M. N. Hist. (4) 7, (1871) p. 86, fig. 4 (fr. Canadian Naturalist 1870).
»	**Soldanii**	CARPENT., 1862, Introduct. t. 6, fig. 43.
	Proteonina fusiformis, pseudospiralis	WILLIAMS., 1858, Brit. rec. For. p. 1—2, figg. 1—3.
	Rhoophax fusiformis	BRADY, 1882, Ret. Rhizopod., Österr. Ungar. Exped. Wien. Ak. Dkschr. 43. 2, p. 99.

Lituolina scorpiurus var. ammophila n.

Tab. XII, fig. 410—414.

The shell of Lituolina scorpiurus when solely depending on siliceous sand for its construction becomes sometimes very much enlarged, with immense, thick walls. Such is the case with our form, which is built of loosely coherent grains of sand and sponge-needles. This deficiency in the coherence of the structure, particularly in aged specimens, is seldom met with in this class and indicates a lack of cementing secretion or precipitation by the animal. Young specimens have a firmer construction with a great many sponge-needles entering into the building-materials, rendering its surface quite bristly. The earliest stage seems to be of the same slender form as in the preceding. The septal impressions are very indistinct; the aperture does not exhibit that decided semilunar form as the preceding, being rounder or of undecided form, owing to the looseness and coarseness of the texture. The chambers are on their inside lined throughout with bright rust-coloured reddish sand.

It is not common either on the chalk or in the coralline-gravel, attaining 10 mm. in length and about 3 mm. in diameter.

Fig. 410: *Lit. scorpiurus* var. *ammophila*.
Fig. 411: Section through the median plane.
Fig. 412: apertural end.
Figg. 413—414: young individuals.

Litnolina foedissima Reuss.

Tab. XII, figg. 415—418.

Notwithstanding the more compact and homogeneous texture of this form than the foregoing and its striking difference I am not quite convinced of its specific distinctness from *Lit. scorpiurus*. It is no doubt identical with Reuss' species from the cretaceous formation, although his form is stated to be furnished with subdivided chambers, on which character he has based his new genus: *Haplostiche*.

The surface is very rough, but still the shell is agglutinated of fine chalk-particles and probably also a great deal of *precipitated* or *secreted* carbonate of lime. The chambers are somewhat roughly sketched out, often very irregular in size and shape, with impressed and quite distinct septal lines. The aperture is semilunar, often furnished with a small tongue.

It occurs chiefly in the coralline-gravel and grows to a length of 8 mm.

Fig. 415: Stout form, with sudden increase of the size of the chambers.
Fig. 416: A longitudinal section of the same.
Fig. 417: More pointed form.
Fig. 418: The aperture furnished with a tongue.

Syn.	Dentalina foedissima		Rss., 1859, Kreidef. Westphal.; Wien. Ak. Sitz.-Ber. 40, p. 189, t. 3, figg. 2—3.
	Haplostiche	»	Rss., Gesnitz' Elbthalgeb. Sachs., 1873, 2, p. 121, t. II. 24, figg. 1—3.
	»	»	Fričs' Modell. 2.
	?Nodosaria constricta		Rss., 1845, Böhm. Kreide. 1, p. 26, t. 13, figg. 12—13.
	?Haplostiche		Rss., 1873, Gesnitz Elbthalgeb. Sachs. 2, p. 122, t. II. 24, figg. 9—12.
	»	dentalinoides, clavulina	Rss., ibid p. 121, t. II. 24, figg. 4—8.
	»	horrida	Schwag., 1863, Jaress. Sch.; Würtemb. nat. Verein. Jhrhft. 21, t. 2, fig. 2. (an *Lit. scorpiurus* var.).

Lituolina irregularis Röm.
Tab. XII, figg. 419—420.

As I am unable with any degree of certainty to identify *Lituolites deformis* (alias *difformis*) LMCK. (Encycl. meth. Moll. Test. t. 466, fig. 1; Ann. Mus. 8, t. 62, f. 13) on account of it being less satisfactorily delineated, ROEMERS designation must be applied to this form, which is of the same shape as *Haplophragmium crassum* REUSS, an inflated form of *Lit. canariensis* D'ORB., which is to be regarded as a juvenile form of Lit. irregularis.

Since the difference between this species and its variety, *Lit. nautiloidea* LMCK. consists only in the chambers of the latter being subdivided, it is not always possible to refer their different designations by various authors to their proper places in a list of synonyms.

Our form has a tolerably compactly built shell composed of coarse polished grains of siliceous sand. The aperture is narrow and sometimes replaced by a number of pores; the chambers undivided.

It is sparsely met with in the coralline-gravel.

A) libera:
  a) minus inflata:

Syn. Spirolina irregularis   Röm., 1841, Verstein. nordd. Kreidegeb. p. 98, t. 15, fig. 29.
    »   lagenalis   Röm., ibid. fig. 28.
    »   æqualis   Röm., ibid. fig. 27.
?Haplophrag. irregulare   Fries Modell. N:o 4 (an Lit. nautiloidea LMCK.).
Spirolina irregularis   Rss., 1845, Böhm. Kreide II, p. 35, t. 8, figg. 62—66, 75.
Haplophragm. irregulare   Rss., 1859, Westphäl. Kreidegeb.; Wien. Ak. Sitz.-Ber. 40, p. 219, t. 11, fig. 1.
    »   æquale   Rss., ibid. p. 218, t. 11, figg. 2—3; 1862, Nordd. Hils. u. Gault.; Wien. Ak. Sitz.-Ber. 1. 46, p. 29, t. 1, fig. 1—7.
Spirolina agglutinans   D'Orb., 1846, For. Bass. tert. Vienne, p. 137, t. 7, figg. 10—12.
Lituola nautiloidea var.   Park. et Jones, 1860, For. Chellaston; Quart. Journ. geol. Soc. 16, p. 453, t. 20, fig. 47.
Spirolina grandis   Rss., 1854, Kreide Ostalp., Wien. Ak. Dkschr. 7, p. 69, t. 25, fig. 14.
    »   simplex   Rss., 1855, Tert. Schicht. nordl. u. mittl. Deutschl.; Wien. Ak. Sitz.-Ber. 1. 18, p. 232, t. 2, fig. 30.
Haplophragm. rectum   Brady, 1876, Carbonif. and Perm. Foram.; Pal. Soc. 30, p. 66, t. 8, figg. 8—9.
    »   suprajurassicum   Schwag., 1863, Jurass. Sch.; Württemb. Nat. Verein. Jhrhft. 1865, p. 92, t. 3, fig. 1.
    »   tuba   Gümb., 1868, For. nordalp. Eocän.; K. Bayr. Ak. Wiss. 1. 10. 2, p. 600, t. 1, fig. 1.
    »   lituus   Karr., 1861, Marin. Tegel Wien. Beck.; Wien. Ak. Sitz.-Ber. 1. 44, p. 450, t. 2, fig. 7.
Spirolina Humboldti   Rss., 1854, Sept. Thon v. Berlin; Zeitschr. deutsch. geol. Ges. 3, p. 65, t. 3, figg. 17—18.
Haplophragm. Humboldti   Rss., 1865, deutsch. Sept. Thon; Wien. Ak. Dkschr. 1. 25. 1, p. 119, t. 1, figg. 1—4.

Syn. Haplophragm. Humboldti Hken., 1875, Clav. Szab. Sch. p. 11, t. 2, figg. 3—4.
  Spirolina Sacheri   Rss., 1850, Kreidemergel Lemberg; Haid. Nat. Abh. 4. 1, p. 31, t. 2, figg. 3—4.
  Nonionina canariensis   d'Orb., 1844, Iles Canaries p. 128, t. 2, figg. 33—34.
  Placopsilina canariensis Parker et Jones, 1858, Fos. Coast. of Norway; A. M. N. H. (2) 19, p. 301, t. 10, figg. 13—14.
  Nonionina Jeffreysii   Williams., 1858, Brit. rec. Foramf. p. 34, figg. 72—73.
       »   placenta   Rss., 1851, Sept. Thon Berl.; Ztschr. d. geol. Gesellsch. 3. p. 72, t. 5, f. 33.
  Lituola canariensis   Carpent., 1862, Introduct. t. 6, figg. 39—40.
       »   nautiloidea var. canariensis Parker et Jones, 1865, North. Atl. and Arct. Oceans.; Phil. Trans. 155, 1, p. 406, t. 15, fig. 45; t. 17, figg. 92—95.
  Cristellaria aspera   Alth, 1849, Umgeb. Lemberg; Haid. Nat. Abh. 3. 2, p. 268, t. 13, fig. 24.
  Haplophragm. grande   Rss., 1865, Kanara See; Wien. Ak. Sitz.-Ber. 52, p. 446, fig. 3.
       »   inclsum, macricum Stache, 1865, Tert. Merg. Whainger. Hafen; Novara Reise, geol. Th. 1. 2, p. 166, t. 21, fig. 1—2.
       »   nonionoides Rss., 1862, Nordd. Hils u. Gault; Wien. Ak. Sitz.-Ber. 1. 46, p. 30, t. 1, fig. 8.
       »   acutidorsatum, rotundidorsatum Hken., 1875, Clav. Szab. Sch., p. 12, t. 1, fig. 1—2.
       »   crassum Rss., 1867, Steinsalzablager. Wieliczka; Wien. Ak. Sitz.-Ber. 1. 55, p. 62, t. 1, figg. 1—2.
       »   nanum   Brady, 1881, Austro-Hung. Exped.; A. M. N. Hist. (5) 8, p. 406, t. 21, figg. 1; Wien. Ak. Dkschr. 1. 43. 2, p. 99, t. 2, fig. 1.
  Nonionina latidorsata   Bornem., 1855, Sept. Thon Hermsdorf; Ztschr. deutsch. geol. Ges. 7, p. 339, t. 16, fig. 4.

  b) inflata:
  Orbignyna ovata   v. Hagen. Rügen. Schreibekr.; Leonh. u. Bronn. Jhrb. 1842, p. 573, t. 9, fig. 26.
  Haplophragm. ovatum   Rss., 1861, Kreide v. Rügen; Wien. Ak. Sitz.-Ber. 1. 44, p. 329, t. 5, figg. 8—9.
  Nonionina inflata   Alth, 1849, Umgeb. Lemberg; Haid. nat. Abh. 3. 2, p. 266, t. 13, f. 22.
  Lituola ovata   Marss 1877, Rüg. Schreibekr.; Greifsw. Mitth. Nat. Ver. p. 171, t. 5, f. 40.
  Spirolina inflata   Rss., 1850, Kreidem. Lemberg; Haid. nat. Abh. 4. 1, p. 32, t. 2, fig. 5.
  Haplophragm. inflatum   Karr., 1861, Mariu. Tegel Wien. Beck.; Wien. Ak. Sitz.-Ber. 1. 44, p. 449, t. 2, fig. 6.
       »   »   Fries Modell, N:o 3.
  ?   »   subglobosum   (Sars) Brady 1882, Österr. Ung. Exped.; Wien. Ak. Dkschr. 43. 2, p, 100.
  ?Cyclammina cancellata   Norm., 1876, Proc. Roy. Soc. 25, p. 214.

  B) adnata:
  Placopsilina irregularis, conomana, d'Orb., 1850, Prodrom. Paleontol. 2. p. 185.
       »   »   Fries, Modell, N:o 1.
       »   »   Rss., 1854, Kreide Ostalp.; Wien. Ak. Dkschr. 7, p. 71, t. 28, fig. 4—5.
                           »Oeufs de mollusques» Corn., 1848, Nouv. foss. micr. cret.; Mem. Soc. geol. France (2) 3, t. 2, fig. 36.
  Lituola conomana forma placopsilina Carpenter, 1862, Introd. t. 11, figg. 11—14.

Appendix.

Cameris compositis:
  Lituolites nautiloidea   Lmck., 1816, Tabl. Encyclop. meth.; Moll. test., tab. 465, fig. 6 et Ann. d. Mus. 8, t. 62, fig. 12.
  Spirolina nautiloides   d'Orb., 1826, Tab. meth.; An. Sc. Nat. 7, p. 287. N:o 6.

Syn.	Lituola nautiloides	d'Orb., 1839, For. Craie bl. Paris; Mém. Soc. géol. France 4, p. 29, t. 2, figg. 28—31.
	»	d'Orb., 1846, For. Bas. tert. Vienne p. 138, t. 21, figg. 20—21.
	»	Rss., 1859, Westphäl. Kreide; Wien. Ak. Sitz.-Ber. 40, p. 220, t. 10, figg. 5—8.
»	nautiloidea	Brady, 1876, Carbonif. and Perm. For.; Palæontogr. Soc. 30, p. 63, t. 8, fig. 7.
»	»	Carpent., Introduct. t. 6, fig. 44.

Lituolina irregularis var. compressa n.

Tab. XII, figg. 421—423.

This form seems nearly identical with *Haplophragmium acutidorsatum* Hantken from the Clavulina Szaboi strata in Hungary.

Compressed forms of Lituolinæ have seldom come under notice, but this surpasses in flatness all such described forms being probably a starved variety of the type. It is on both sides somewhat umbilicated; somewhat rough or scrobiculate, and appears as if felted together of siliceous needles and a smaller quantity of grains of sand, whence the surface presents a sericeo-tomentous aspect. The septal lines are very indistinct. The adult shows a tendency to become lituiform, the aperture being placed near the top of the last chamber, otherwise it has its ordinary Nonioninoid shape and place. Since the principal constituents of the shell are hyaline and colourless in themselves, it is evident that its rust-colour is not derived from any materials with colour of their own but from the partly precipitated and partly secreted, coloured cementing matter.

Raphidohelix elegans Mob., Mauritius p. 76, t. 2, fig. 2 seems to belong to this variety; perhaps also *Haplophragmium foliaceum* Brady, Qu. J. Micr. Sc. (N. S.) 81, p. 50.

It is scantily met with in the coralline-gravel.

Fig. 421: sideview.

Fig. 422: edgeview.

Fig. 423: Thin section showing the texture of the test and the faintly marked septa.

Lituolina irregularis var. globigerinæformis Park. and Jones.

Tab. XII, figg. 424—425.

Notwithstanding the suggestive assumption advanced by some most able and experienced investigators as to the true *Globigerine* nature of this form, its arrangement of chambers and apertures being so characteristic »as to leave no room for doubt that these forms are true Globigerinæ and not Lituolæ» (G. C. Wallich, M. D., Deep-sea-researches on the biology of Globigerina, Lond. 1876, p. 63), and although there is occasionally associated with it a *nautiloid* form with globular chambers exactly in conformity with that form of *Globigerina*, previously mentioned, I still provisionally and until further evidence has been adduced, place this form under *Lituolina*.

The shell is very thin, but firmly constructed of polished uniform grains of sand, rendering its surface in comparison with other sandstructures smooth and neat, and the septal lines nearly as distinct as in *Globigerina bulloides*.

It is not frequent, but occurs both in the coralline-gravel and chalk-ooze.

Fig. 424: outer form.

Fig. 425: Longitudinal section through the medial plane.

Syn. **Lituola nautiloides** var. **globigerinæformis** PARK. et JONES, 1865, North. Atl. and Arct. Oc.; Phil. Transact. 155, 1, p. 407, t. 15, figg. 46—47; t. 17, figg. 96—98.
    "   "   WALLICH, 1862, N. Atl. seabed. t. 6, figg. 22.
?   "   **glomerata**   BRADY, 1879, Retic. and Rad. of the Arctic Exp. 1875—76; A. N. H. (5) 1, p. 433, t. 20, figg. 1 a—c.

Haplophragmium globigerinæforme BRADY 1882. Österr. Ung. Exped., Wien. Ak. Dksche. 43, 2, p. 100.

Hyperammina elongata BRADY.
Tab. XII, figg. 426—429.

The generic separation of this form from the closely allied *Rhabdammina linearis* BRAD. and *Rh. abyssorum* SARS. seems uncalled for, and not quite appropriate from a systematical and biological point of view; for it is likely that *Hyperammina* should be regarded as a single-armed *Rhabdammina*. I still keep these forms asunder until further evidence of their unity may be produced.

Our form is usually a long, slender, seldom quite straight tube, constructed of siliceous sand and a large portion of sponge-needles, very brittle and with moderately thick walls. Sometimes it becomes so enlarged in the transverse direction as to approach a produced ovoid form.

It reaches a length of 15 mm. and is met with on the coralline-gravel and in the chalk-ooze.

Fig. 426: The common form of a halfgrown specimen.
Fig. 427: The same cut open.
Fig. 428: Aperture.
Fig. 429: Ovoidal form.

Syn. **Hyperammina elongata** BRADY, 1879, Retic. and Radiol. of the Arctic Exp. 1875—76; A. M. N. H. (5) 1, p. 433, t. 20, figg. 2 a, b.; A. M. N. H. (5) 1, p. 425, t. 20, f. 2.

Appendix.

Syn. **Hyperammina ramosa** BRADY, 1879, Retic. Rhizopod. Challenger-Exped.; Qu. Journ. micr. sc 73, p. 33, t. 3, figg. 14—15

Rhabdammina abyssorum Sars. var. robusta n.

Tab. XII, figg. 430—431.

As far as I am aware of, the type form has not been described except in a short notice in the last Edit. of GRIFFITHS and HENFREY's Micrograph. Dictionary, and in »Descript. Catalogue of objects from Deep-sea dredgings exhibited at the Soirée of the Roy. Microscop. Soc. Kings College 1870, by W. B. CARPENTER.»

Our form has a very brittle test, composed entirely of siliceous sandgrains. Its »body» displays at the roots of its 3 or 4 arms a tendency to swelling, corresponding to the swelling or bulb in the early stage of *Hyperammina*. The arms radiate in the same plane, tapering gradually at their ends, which are furnished with a central, narrow and round aperture.

It is scantily met with in the coralline-gravel attaining a length of 16 mm.

Fig. 430: Three-armed specimen.
Fig. 431: Four-armed.

Syn. **Rhabdammina abyssorum** SARS., 1868, Fortsatte Bemærkning over det dyriske Livs Udbredning i Havets Dybder; Christiania Vid. Selsk. Forhandl. 1868, p. 248 (nec descripta nec delineata).

Appendix.

Syn. **Rhabdammina linearis** BRADY, 1879, Retic. Rhizop. Challenger-Exp.; Quart. Journ. microsc. sc. 73, p. 37, t. 3, figg. 10—11.

Jaculella acuta BRADY.

Tab. XII, fig. 432.

Provisionally I refer our form to this species although not convinced either as to the true nature of these organisms or of their identity. Ours is slender with a very narrow channel, which here and there exhibits very faintly traces of septa.

It is not common in the coralline-gravel.

Syn. **Jaculella acuta** BRADY, 1879, Reticul. Rhizopod. Challenger-Exped.; Quart Journ. microsc. sc. 73, p. 35, t. 3, figg. 12—13.

APPENDIX.

To the lists of synonyms are to be added the following names adopted by Mrss. J. G. BORNEMANN and J. F. BLAKE in their valuable essays, resp. from 1854 and 1876, on the *Liasformation*, which have been partly omitted in this paper. There are also a few other omissions remarked.

Nodosarina radicula LIN. p. 12.

Syn. Glandulina rotundata, tenuis, major; Orthocerina pupoides BORNEMANN, 1854, Liasformat. Gottingen p. 31, t. 2, figg. 1—4; p. 35, t. 3, fig. 16.
" humilis, cuneiformis BLAKE, 1876, Yorkshire Lias p. 454, t. 18, figg. 11—12.
Dentalina tecta, nodosa BLAKE, l. c. p. 459, t. 18, figg. 25—26.
Frondicularia intumescens BLAKE, loc. cit. p. 468, t. 19, fig. 21 pertinet ad variet. in Nodos. complanatam transientem: d) p. 14; aut forsan ad Nodos. carinatam D'ORB.

Nodosarinæ radiculæ forma Orthocerina p. 14.

Syn. Orthocerina hœringensis, rhomboidalis BLAKE, 1876, Yorkshire Lias p. 469, 470, t. 17, figg. 29—30.

Nodosarina radicula var. monile SOLD. p. 14.

Syn. Nodosarina radicula   BLAKE, 1876, Yorkshire Lias p. 456, t. 18, fig. 17.
Glandulina laguncula   BORNEMANN, 1854, Liasformation Göttingen p. 32, t. 2, fig. 5 (forsan ad b typicam, p. 18, pertinens).
Dentalina oligostegia   BLAKE, loc. cit. p. 458, t. 18, fig. 21 (in Nodos. communem, d) p. 19, transiens).

Nodosarina radicula var. raphanus LIN. p. 21.

Syn. Glandulina quinquecostata, sexcostata, septangularis, melo, abbreviata, costata, Orthocerina multicostata BORNEMANN, 1854, Liasformation Göttingen p. 32—35, 39, t. 2, figg. 6—12; t. 3, figg. 14—15, 26.
Nodosarina raphanus, raphanistrum BLAKE, 1876, Yorkshire Lias p. 456, 457, t. 18, figg. 14—18.

Syn. **Glandulina paucicosta** BLAKE, loc. cit. p. 455, t. 18, fig. 13; t. 19, fig. 1—1 a
» **Dentalina burgundiæ, nummulina** BLAKE, loc. cit. p. 461, t. 18, figg. 29—30.
» **Lingulina tenera** BORNEMANN, loc. cit. p. 38, t. 3, fig. (21 ad var. d) p. 23 pertinens).
» » **tenera, striata** BLAKE, loc. cit. p. 455, t. 18, figg. 15—16 (eandem ad var. pertinentes).
» **Frondicularia nodosaria** BLAKE, loc. cit. p. 469, t. 17, fig. 44; t. 19, fig. 24; var. in Linguliuam transiens — Lingul. semiornata Rss., in p. 24 omissa.
» **Lingulina semiornata** Rss., 1862, Nordd. Hils u. Gault; Wien. Ak. Sitz.-Ber. 1, 46, p. 91, t. 12, fig. 11 (ad varietatem inter f) et g) p. 24 pertinens; — Nod. radicula var. raphanus in Nod. carinatam transiens).

Nodosarina communis D'ORB. p. 26.

Syn. **Dentalina brevis** BLAKE, 1876, Yorkshire Liass p. 459, t. 18, fig. 24; ad var. a p. 26 pertin.
» **monilis, pauperata** BLAKE, loc. cit. p. 458, 459, t. 18, figg. 23, 27; ad b p. 28 pertin.
» **planata** BLAKE, loc. cit. p. 458, t. 18, fig. 22, ad c p. 30 pertinens.
» **communis** BLAKE, loc. cit. p. 457, t. 18, fig. 19, ad var. d p. 30 pertinens.
» **subarcuata** WILLIAMS, 1858, Brit. rec. For. p. 18, fig. 40; ad eandem pertinens.

Nodosarina communis var. obliqua LIN. p. 31.

Syn. **Dentalina funiculosa** BLAKE, 1876, Yorkshire Liass p. 461, t. 18, fig. 28; ad a p. 31 pertinens.
» **rapa** BLAKE, loc. cit. p. 460, t. 19, fig. 3; ad b p. 32 pertinens.
» **obliquestriata** BLAKE, loc. cit. p. 460, t. 19, fig. 4; ad c p. 33 pertinens.

Nodosarina legumen LIN. p. 34.

Syn. **Margin. reversa, depressa, Crist. pauperata** BLAKE, 1876, Yorkshire Liass p. 464—465, t. 18, fig. 31, t. 19, figg. 9, 12; ad c p. 36 pertinentes.
Cristellaria protracta, Listi BORNEMANN, 1854, Liassformation Göttingen p. 39, 40, t. 4, figg. 27—28, ad c p. 36 pertinentes.
Planularia arguta BLAKE, loc. cit. p. 2, 64, t. 19, fig. 10; ad d p. 37 pertinens.
Vaginulina Hausmanni BORNEMANN, loc. cit. p. 38, t. 3, fig. 25; ad e p. 37 pertinens.
Margin. Römeri, Vagin. legumen BLAKE, loc. cit. p. 463, 464, t. 19, figg. 8, 11; ad e p. 37 pertinentes.

Nodosarina legumen var. linearis MONTAG. p. 39.

Syn. **Marginulina rugosa** BORNEMANN, 1854, Liassformation Göttingen p. 39, t. 3, fig. 26.
» **raphanus, picta** BLAKE, 1876, Yorkshire Liass p. 462, t. 19, figg. 5—6; ad a p. 39 pertinens.
» **inæquistriata** BLAKE, loc. cit. p. 462, t. 19, fig. 7; ad b p. 40 pertinens.

Nodosarina Crepidula Ficht. et Moll. p. 43.

Syn. **Cristellaria recta** Blake, 1876, Yorkshire Lias p. 465, t. 19, fig. 13; t. 17, fig. 24; ad var. α p. 43, aut ad Nod. legumen var. c p. 36 pertinens.
» **Bronnii** Blake, loc. cit. p. 466, t. 17, fig. 26; ad var. α p. 43 pertinens.
» **crepidula, major** Blake, loc. cit. p. 465, 466, t. 17, fig. 25; t. 19, figg. 14—15; forma typica p. 44.
» **globifera** Blake, loc. cit. p. 467, t. 19, fig. 17; typicæ forma inflata.
Flabellina rugosa Blake, loc. cit. p. 467, t. 19, fig. 19; ad formam c p. 46 pertinens.
Cristellaria varians Blake, loc. cit. p. 466, t. 17, fig. 27; t. 19, fig. 16, ad d p. 46 pertinens.
» **navis** Bornemann, 1855, Sept. Thon Hermsdorf; Zeitschr. deutsch. geol. Ges. 7, p. 338, t. 14, figg. 4—5; ad eandem d pertinens.

Nodosarina crepidula var. italica Defr. p. 47.

Syn. ? **Vaginulina anomala** Blake, 1876, Yorkshire Lias p. 464, t. 17, fig. 23.

Nodosarina calcar Lin. p. 50.

Syn. **Cristellaria rotulata** Blake, 1876, Yorkshire Lias p. 467, t. 19, fig. 18.
? » **lituoides, spirolina** Bornemann, 1854, Liasformation Göttingen p. 40, t. 4, figg. 29—30; ad var. g p. 55 forsan pertinentes.

Nodosarina complanata Defr. p. 56.

Syn. **Frondicularia complanata** Blake, 1876, Yorkshire Lias p. 468, t. 19, fig. 20.
» **brizæformis** Bornemann, 1854, Liasformation Göttingen p. 36, t. 3, figg. 17, 18, 20.

Nodosarina complanata var. striata d'Orb. p. 42.

Syn. **Frondicularia Terqvemi, sulcata** Blake, 1876, Yorkshire Lias p. 468, 469, t. 19, figg. 22—23.
» **lignaria** Blake, loc. cit. p. 468, t. 17, fig. 28; ad β. p. 42 pertinens.

Nodosarina carinata d'Orb. p. 58.

Syn. **Frondicularia intumescens, major** Bornemann, 1854, Liasformation Göttingen p. 36, t. 3, figg. 19, 21.

Bulimina pupoides D'ORB. p. 63.

Syn. ?Bulimina textilariformis, arcuata STACHE, 1865, Tert. Mergel Whaingar. Hafen; Novara Reise, geol.
Th. 1. 2, p. 268, 269, t. 24, figg. 17—18 (an Pleurostomella Rss. sedis incertæ).

Textularia sagittula DEFR. p. 72.

Syn. Textularia agglutinans BLAKE, 1876, Yorkshire Lias p. 472, t. 17, fig. 37.
Bigenerina mitrata TRAUTSCHOLD, 1879, Kalkbrüche v. Mjatschkowa; Nouv. Mem. Soc. impér. nat. Mosc. 14, p. 47, t. 6, figg. 6a—c; eadem ac B. patula BUSP.
p. 78 = Cribrostomum patulum v. MÖLLER 1880.

Textularia Pennatula BATSCH. p. 79.

a) typica:

Syn. Nautilus (Orthocer.) Pennatula BATSCH, 1791, Sechs Kupfertaf. etc. t. 4, figg. 13 a—c (sec. PARK. et JONES).
Vulvulina Capreolus D'ORB., 1826, Tabl. meth., Ann. Sc. Nat. 7, p. 264, N:o 1, t. 11, figg. 5—8.
» pupa D'ORB., ibid. N:o 2.
» ?subrhomboidalis, textilis SCHWAG., 1863, Jurass. Sch., Württemb. Nat. Ver. Jhshft. 21, p. 140, t. 7, figg. 17—18.
Grammostomum dilatatum RSS., 1851, Tert. Sch. Oberschles.; Zschr. deutsch. geol. Ges. 3, p. 162, t. 8, fig. 8.

b) marginato-aculeata vel marg.-lobulata:

Grammostomum aculeatum EHRENB., 1854, Microgeol. t. 35 B, fig. B: A. p.
» apiculatum EHRENB., ibid t. 26, fig. 7.
?Vulvulina alata SEG., 1862, Rhizopod. Catania; p. 31, t. 2, fig. 5. (Accad. Gioena Atti (2) 18).
» pectinata HRN., 1875, For. Clav. Szab. Sch. p. 68, t. 7, fig. 10.
?Bolivina draco MARSS., 1876, Rügen. Schreibekr.; Greifsw. Nat. Verein. Mitth. 1877—78, p. 157, t. 3, fig. 25.

c) cameris acuminatis, productis:

Vulvulina elegans D'ORB., 1826, Tabl. meth.; Ann. Sc. nat. 7, p. 264, N:o 3.
» gramen D'ORB., 1839, Cuba p. 148, t. 1, figg. 30—31; 1846, Bass. tert. Vienne p. 251, t. 21, figg. 46—47.
?Ehrenborgina serrata RSS., 1849, Neue Foramf. Wien. Beck.; Wien Ak. Dksehr. 1. t. p. 377, t. 48, fig. 7.

d) forma Bigenerinæ:

Schizophora Neugeboreni Rss., Frics Model. N:o 80.
  »   »   Karr., 1877, Hochquell. Wasserleitung; Österr. geol. Reichsanst. Abh. 9, p. 386, t. 16, fig. 51.
Venilina nummulina, hæringensis Gümb., 1868, Nordalp. Eocän.; K. Bayer. Ak. Wiss. 1. 10. 2, p. 648, 649, t. 2, figg. 84—84 bis.
Schizophora hæringensis Hken., 1875, Clav. Száb. Sch. p. 68. t. 7, fig. 3.

d. β) **cameris productis:**

Bigenerina nicobarica Schwag., 1867, For. Kar. Nikobar.; Novara Reise, geol. Th. 2. 2, p. 196, t. 4, fig. 7.

Corrigenda.

Pag. 14: **Frondicularia Stachei** KARR. is rather to be referred to e ß) p. 24.
- " 16: **Dentalina subnodosa** REV. is a **Pleurostomella** REV., Westphäl. Kreide; Wien. Ak. Sitz.-Ber. 40, p. 204, t. 8, fig. 2, as is also partly **Nodosaria nodosa** REV. p. 29.
- " 24: Under head e β) second line stands 15, should be 14.
- " 32: 11th line from below stands, t. 12, fig. 13, should be t. 4, fig. 6.
- " 45: **Cristellaria Cassis, Soldanii** D'ORB. should rather be referred to **Nodosaria crepidula** var. **Cassis** FICHT. et MOLL. p. 49.
- " 46: **Planularia pauperata** PARK. et JONES may perhaps more properly be ranged under d) p. 37.
- " 72: 2nd line stands Tab. IV, should be Tab. V.
- " 76: **Textularia Mariæ** D'ORB. and its proximate forms could possibly be ranged as separate variety under **Text. sagittula** DEFR.
- " 96: Some of the synonyms under **Planorbulina lobatula** WALK. may be more properly referred to the Truncatuline form of **Planorb. Ungeriana** D'ORB.
- " 103: 17th line: (apertural) should be cancelled.
- " " 21st line: upper also to be cancelled.
- " " 22d line: upper to be replaced by attached.
- " " 23d line: apertural should be free.
- " 107: **Discorbina Berthelotiana**: Our form has its pores quite as fine and closely set as a **Pulvinulina**. In their «Nomenclature of Foraminifera» Messrs. PARKER & JONES also have referred EHRENBERGS **Spiroplevrites nebulosus** to **Pulvinulina** (A. M. Nat. Hist. (4), 10) and notwithstanding its Discorbinalike habitus it may prove to be a distinct species of that genus.
- " 108: **Discorbina vesicularis** LMK. var. **elegans** D'ORB. may prove to be a starved **Polystomella crassula** WALK. var. **asterisans** FICHT. & MOLL. This species has its pores somewhat larger and more scattered than the most of this genus.
- " 111: **Pulvin. repanda** var. **punctulata** PARK. & JONES may prove to belong to another species.
- " 115: **Nonionina crassula** WILLIAMS. should be referred to d) **asterisans** p. 116 and replaced by **Non. Boueana** WILLIAMS. **N. umbilicata** D'ORB. and a few more of those synonyms placed under b) p. 115.

INDEX.

	Pag.
AMPHISTEGINA vulgaris	117
BULIMINA costata	71
» elegantissima	66
» punctata	69
» » var. decorticus	71
» pupoides	63
» squamosa	67
» » var. subsquamosa	69
CANDEINA nitida	89
CARPENTERIA balaniformis var. proteiformis	94
CORNUSPIRA foliacea	120
DISCORBINA Berthelotiana	107
» bulloides	104
» Poeyi	107
» rosacea	105
» valvulata	106
» vesicularis var. elegans	108
GLOBIGERINA bulloides	90
» universa	90
HETEROSTEGINA depressa var. simplex	117
HYPERAMMINA elongata	142
JACULELLA acuta	143
LAGENA distoma-polita	10
» lævis	10
» » var. desmophora	10
» » » marginata	10
» » » tetragona	10
» squamosa	10
LITUOLINA fœdissima	138
» irregularis	139
» » var. compressa	141
» » » globigeriniæformis	141
» scorpiurus	136
» » var. ammophila	137
MILIOLINA planciata	134
» ringens	131
» semisulum	122
NODOSARINA calcar	49
» carinata	58
» communis	26
» » var. obliqua	31
» complanata	56

Corrigenda.

Pag. 16: **Dentalina subnodosa** Rss. is a **Pleurostomella** Rss., Westphäl. Kreide, Wien. Ak. Sitz.-Ber. 40, p. 204, t. 8, fig. 2, as is also partly **Nodosaria nodosa** Rss. p. 29.
» 14: **Frondicularia Stachei** Karr. is rather to be referred to e,f) p. 24.
» 24: Under head e,? second line stands 15, should be 14.
» 32: 11th line from below stands, t. 12, fig. 13, should be t. 4, fig. 6.
» 45: **Cristellaria Cassis, Soldanii** d'Orb. should be referred rather to **Nodosaria crepidula** var. Cassis Ficht. et Moll. p. 49.
» 46: Planularia pauperata Park. et Jones may perhaps more properly be ranged under d) p. 37.
» 72: 2nd line stands Tab. IV, should be Tab. V.
» 76: **Textularia Mariae** d'Orb. and its proximate forms could possibly be ranged as separate variety under Text. sagittula Defr.
» 107: Discorbina Berthelotiana: Our form has its pores quite as fine and closely set as a **Pulvinulina**. In their »**Nomenclature of Foraminifera**« Messrs. Parker & Jones also have referred Ehrenbergs **Spiroplevrites nebulosus** to **Pulvinulina** (A. M. Nat. Hist. (4), 10) and Notwithstanding its Discorbinalike habitus it may prove to be a distinct species of that genus.
» 111: **Pulvin. repanda** var. punctulata Park. & Jones may prove to belong to another species.

INDEX.

	Pag.
AMPHISTEGINA vulgaris	117
BULIMINA costata	71
» elegantissima	66
» punctata	69
» » var. decurrens	71
» pupoides	63
» squamosa	67
» » var. subsquamosa	69
CANDEINA nitida	89
CARPENTERIA balaniformis var. proteiformis	94
CORNUSPIRA foliacea	120
DISCORBINA Berthelotiana	107
» bulloides	106
» Poeyi	107
» rosacea	105
» valvulata	106
» vesicularis var. elegans	108
GLOBIGERINA bulloides	90
» universa	90
HETEROSTEGINA depressa var. simplex	117
HYPERAMMINA elongata	142
JACULELLA acuta	143
LAGENA distoma-polita	10
» laevis	10
» » var. desmophora	10
» » » marginata	10
» » » tetragona	10
» squamosa	10
LITUOLINA foedissima	138
» irregularis	139
» » var. compressa	141
» » » globigerinaeformis	141
» scorpiurus	136
» » var. ammophila	137
MILIOLINA planulata	134
» ringens	131
» seminulum	122
NODOSARINA calcar	49
» carinata	58
» communis	26
» » var. obliqua	31
» complanata	50

		Pag.
NODOSARINA Crepidula		43
» » var. cassis		49
» » » italica		47
» legumen		34
» » var. linearis		39
» radicula		10
» » var. monile		15
» » » raphanus		20
» » » scalaris		21
ORBICULINA adunca		118
PLANORBULINA farcta		95
» » var. vulgaris		97
» » reticulata		103
» tuberosa var. Arimonensis		98
» Ungeriana		100
» » var. affixa		103
POLYSTOMELLA crassula var. Scapha		114
» crispa var. Počyana		116
PULLENIA sphæroides		104
PULVINULINA auricula		109
» elegans		111
» » var. trochus		112
» Menardii		112
» Micheliniana		114
RHABDAMMINA abyssorum var. robusta		143
SPHÆROIDINA bulloides		89
SPIRILLINA vivipara		108
TEXTULARIA gibbosa forma Bigenerina		79
» Pennatula var. aculeata forma Bigenerina		79, 147
» pupoides		81
» » var. conica		83
» sagitulla		72
» » forma Bigenerina		78
» triquetra		83
» » forma Bigenerina		85
» Trochus		80
TINOPORUS vesicularis		104
TROCHAMMINA incerta		136
UVIGERINA Auberiana		60
» dimorpha		62
» lævis		61
» pygmæa		59
VALVULINA triangularis forma Clavulina		86
» » var. polyphragma forma Clavulina		87
» » var. coccana forma Clavulina		88
VERTEBRALINA conicoarticulata		121

EXPLANATION OF THE PLATES.

(The meagre ciphers represent the length in millimeters.)

Plate I.

Fig. 1—2: Nodosarina radicula LIN. p. 10.
" 3—7: Nodosarina radicula var. monile SOLD. p. 15.
" 8: Nodosarina radicula var. scalaris BATSCH p. 21.
" 9—10: Nodosarina radicula var. raphanus LIN. p. 20.
" 11—16: Nodosarina communis D'ORB. p. 26.
" 17—19: Nodosarina communis var. obliqua LIN. p. 31.
" 65—67: Nodosarina carinata D'ORB. p. 58.

Plate II.

Fig. 20—31: Nodosarina legumen Lin. p. 34.
 " 32—35: Nodosarina legumen var. linearis Montag. p. 39.
 "   44: Nodosarina crepidula var. Ficht. & Moll. p. 43.

Plate III.

Fig. 36—43: Nodosarina crepidula FICHT. & MOLL. p. 43.
» 45—49: Nodosarina crepidula var. italica DEFR. p. 47.
» 50—51: Nodosarina crepidula var. cassis FICHT. & MOLL. p. 49.
» 52—61: Nodosarina calcar LIN. p. 49.
» 62—64: Nodosarina complanata DEFR. p. 56.

Plate IV.

Fig. 68—70: Uvigerina pygmæa D'ORB. p. 59.
» 71—75: Uvigerina Auberiana D'ORB. p. 60.
» 76: Uvigerina (Heterostomella) laevis PARK. & JONES p. 61.
» 77—81: Uvigerina dimorpha PARK. & JONES p. 62.
» 82—94: Bulimina pupoides D'ORB. p. 63.
» 95—98: Bulimina elegantissima D'ORB. p. 66.
» 99—108: Bulimina (Virgulina) squamosa D'ORB. p. 67.
» 109—113: Bulimina squamosa var. subsquamosa EGGER. p. 69.
» 114—126: Bulimina (Bolivina) punctata D'ORB. p. 69.
» 127: Bulimina punctata var. decurrens EHRENB. p. 71.
» 129—132: Bulimina costata D'ORB. p. 71.

Plate V.

Fig. 133—158: Textularia sagittula DEFR. p. 72.
» 159—161: Textularia sagittula forma Bigenerina p. 78.
» 162—164: Textularia gibbosa D'ORB. forma Bigenerina p. 79.
» 165—166: Textularia Pennatula BATSCH var. aculeata EHRENB. p. 79.
» 167—170: Textularia Trochus D'ORB. p. 80.

Plate VI.

Fig. 171—172: Textularia Trochus D'ORB. p. 80.
» 173—180: Textularia pupoides D'ORB. p. 81.
» 181—182: Textularia pupoides var. conica n.; p. 83.
» 183—184: Textularia triquetra v. MÜNSTER p. 83.
» 185—186: Textularia triquetra forma Bigenerina p. 85.
» 187—189: Candeina nitida D'ORB. p. 89.
» 190—193: Sphæroidina bulloides D'ORB. p. 89.
»   194: Globigerina universa var. D'ORB. p. 90.
» 195—207: Globigerina bulloides D'ORB. p. 90.
» 208—214: Carpenteria balaniformis GRAY, var. proteiformis n.; **p. 94.**

Plate VII.

Fig. 215—219: Carpenteria balaniformis GRAY var. proteiformis n.; p. 94.
» 220—225: Planorbulina farcta FICHT. & MOLL. p. 95.
» 226—227: Planorbulina farcta var. vulgaris D'ORB. p. 97.
» 228—233: Planorbulina tuberosa FICHT. & MOLL. var. Ariminensis D'ORB. p. 98.
» 234—236: Planorbulina Ungeriana D'ORB. p. 100.
» 237—241: Planorbulina Ungeriana var. affixa n.; p. 103.
» 242—244: Planorbulina reticulata CZJZ. p. 103.
» 245—247: Tinoporus vesicularis PARK. & JONES p. 104.
- 272: Spirillina vivipara EHRENB. p. 108.

Plate VIII.

Fig. 248—250: Pullenia sphæroides d'Orb. p. 104.
» 251—257: Discorbina rosacea d'Orb. p. 105.
» 258—261: Discorbina valvulata d'Orb. p. 106.
» 262—263: Discorbina bulloides d'Orb. p. 106.
» 264—265: Discorbina Poëyi d'Orb. p. 107.
» 266—268: Discorbina Berthelotiana d'Orb. p. 107.
» 269—271: Discorbina vesicularis var. elegans d'Orb. p. 108.
» 273—275: Pulvinulina auricula Ficht. & Moll. p. 109.
» 276—282: Pulvinulina repanda Ficht. & Moll. p. 110.
» 283—285: Pulvinulina elegans d'Orb. p. 111.
» 286—288: Pulvinulina elegans var. trochus Röm. p. 112.
» 289—295: Pulvinulina Menardii d'Orb. p. 112.
» 296—298: Pulvinulina Micheliniana d'Orb. p. 114.
» 299—300: Polystomella crassula Walk. var. Scapha Ficht. & Moll. p. 114.
» 301—302: Polystomella crispa Lin. var. Poëyana d'Orb. p. 116.
» 303: Heterostegina depressa d'Orb. var. simplex d'Orb. p. 117.

Plate IX.

Fig. 304—307: Orbiculina adunca FICHT. & MOLL. p. 118.
- 308—310: Cornuspira foliacea PHIL. p. 120.
- 311—318: Vertebralina conicoarticulata BATSCH. p. 121.
- 319—355: Miliolina semisulum LIN. p. 122.

Plate XII.

Fig. 410—414: **Lituolina** scorpiurus var. ammophila n.; p. 137.
- 415—418: Lituolina foedissima Reuss p. 138.
- 419—420: Lituolina irregularis Röm. p. 139.
- 421—423: Lituolina irregularis var. compressa n.; p. 141.
- 424—425: Lituolina irregularis var. globigerinæformis Parr. & Jones p. 141.
- 426—429: Hyperammina elongata Brady p. 142.
- 430—431: Rhabdammina abyssorum Sars var. robusta n.; p. 143.
- 432: Jaculella acuta Brady p. 143.

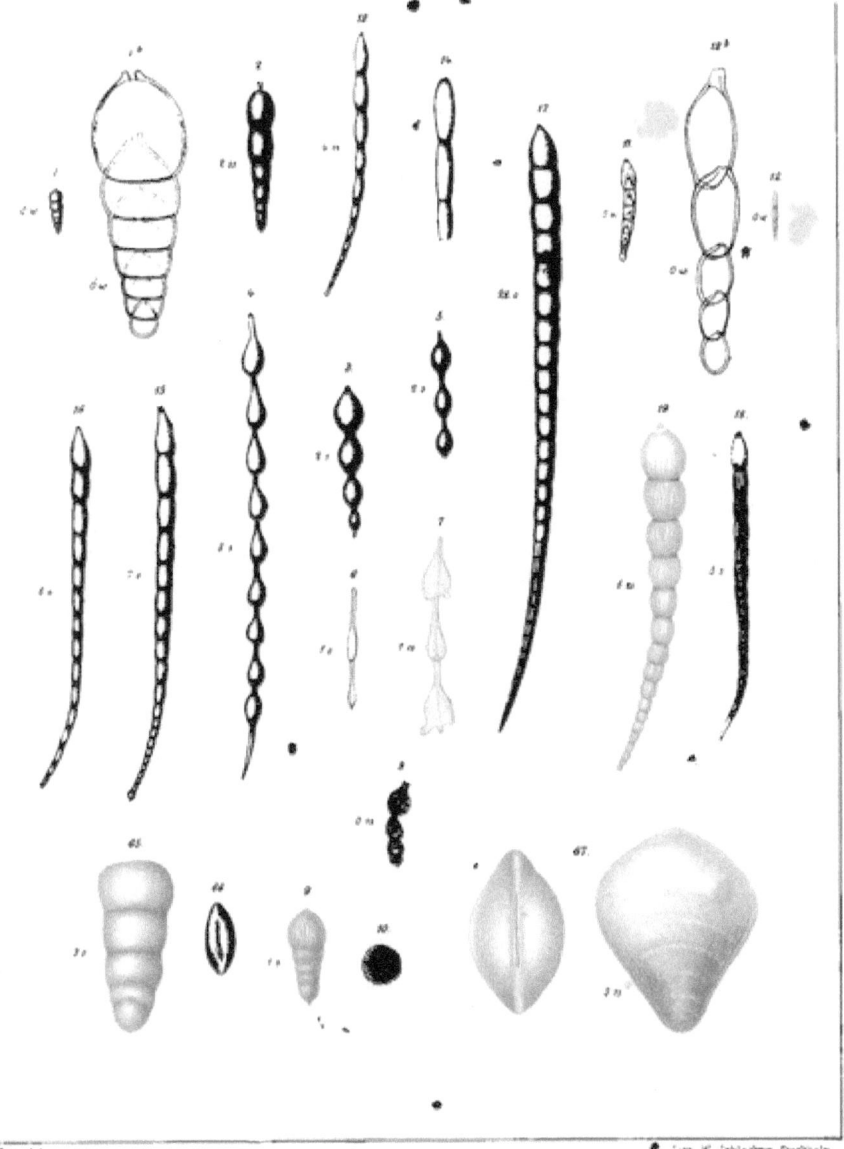

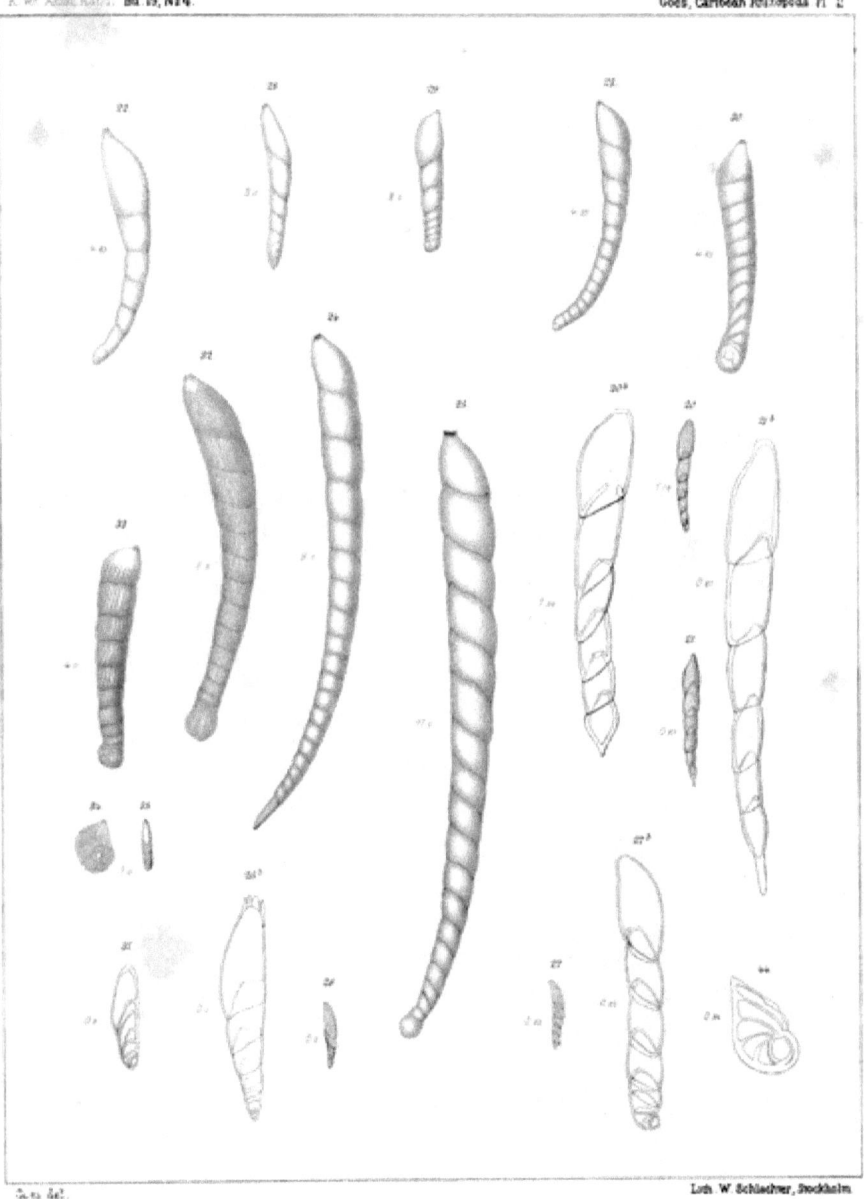

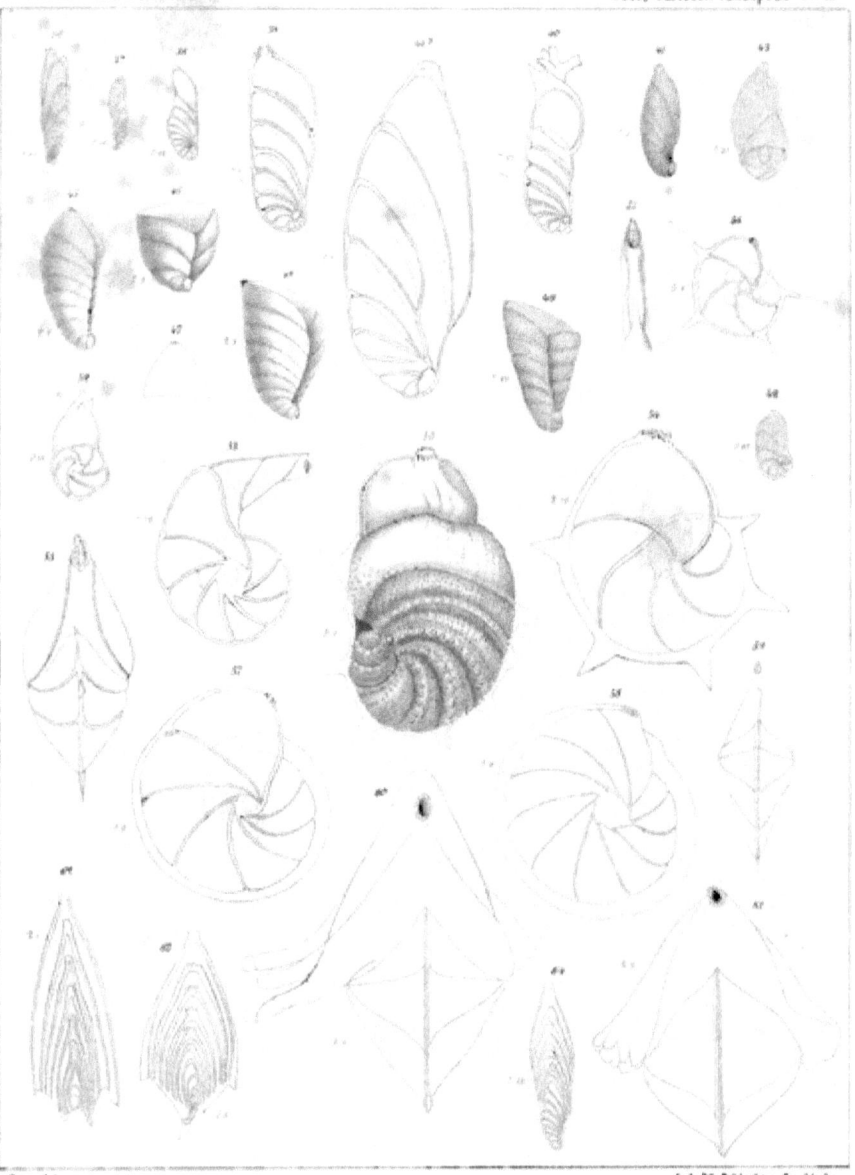

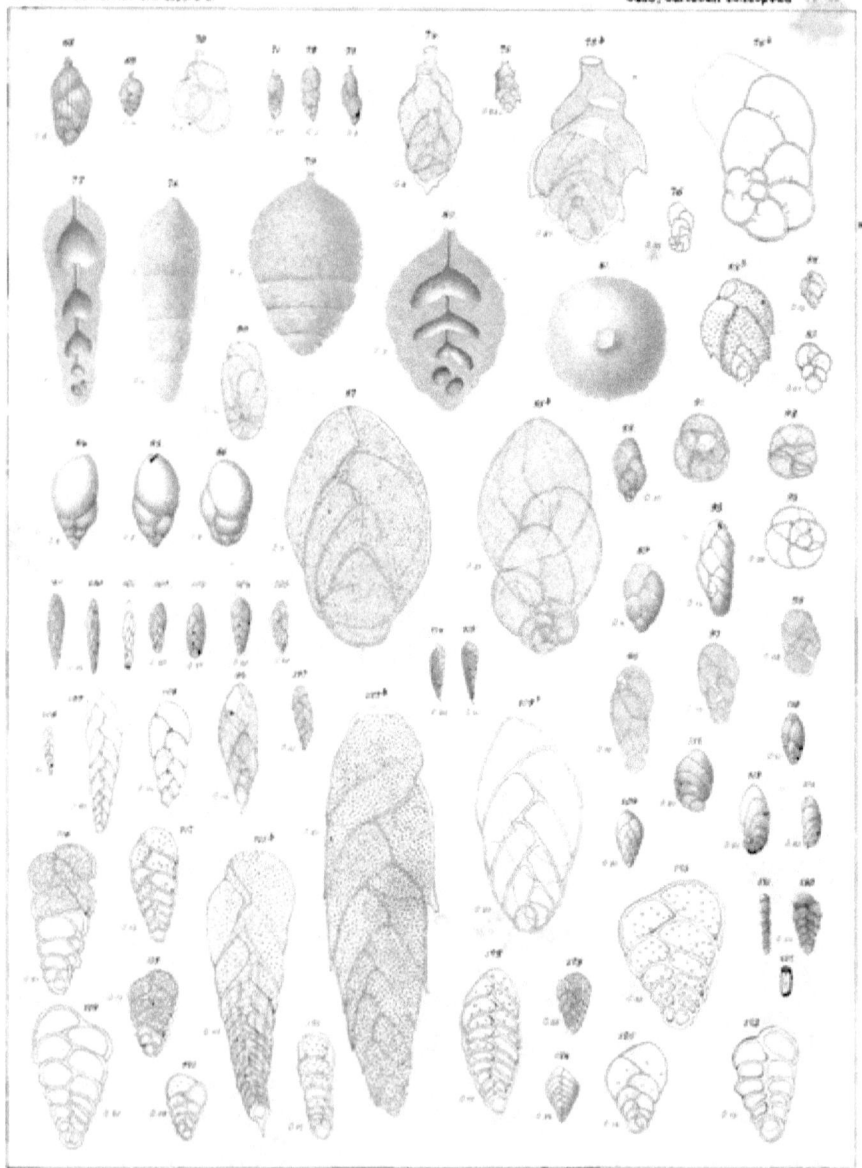

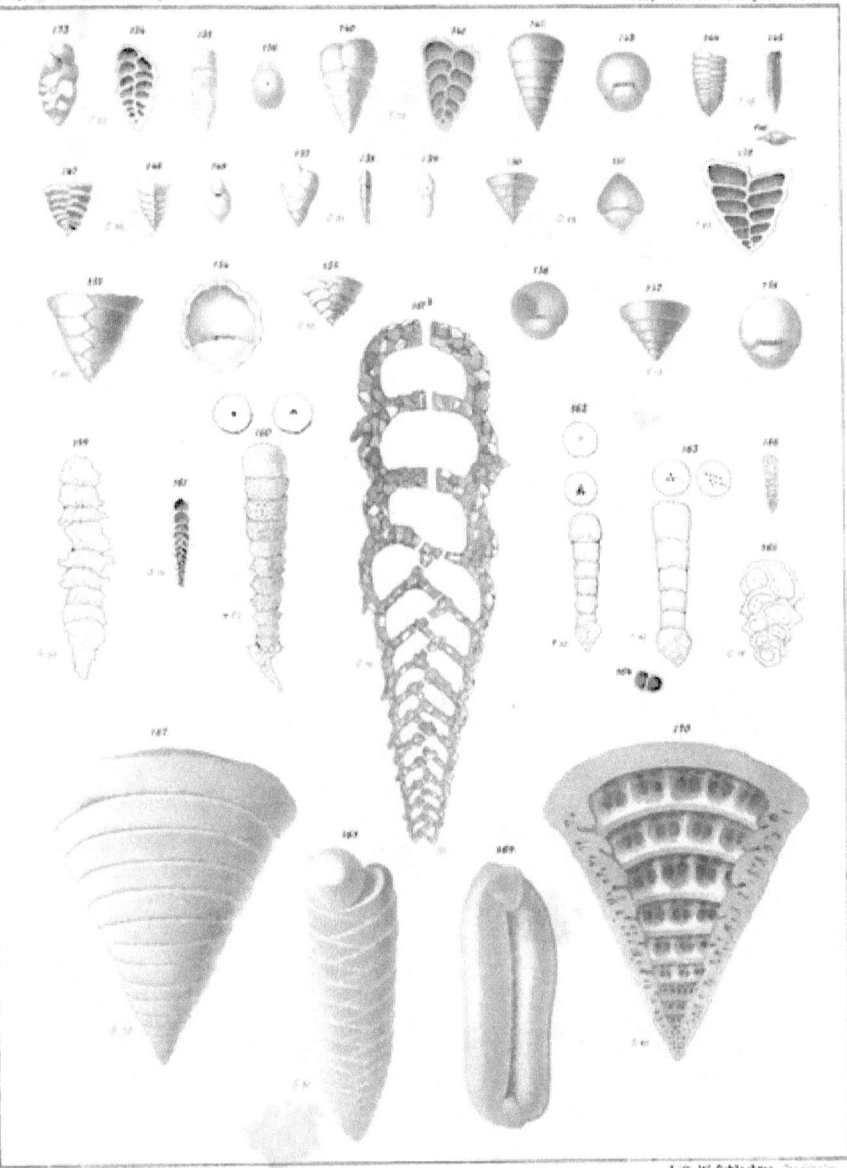

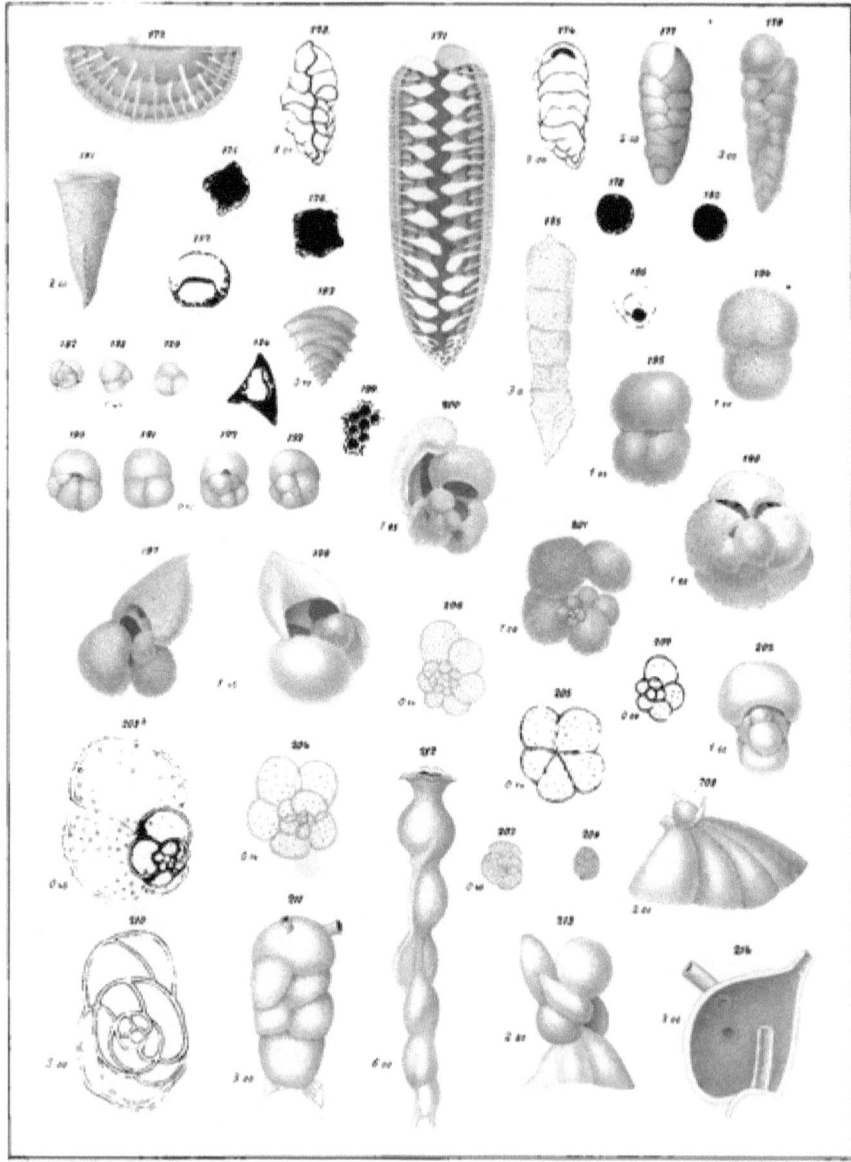

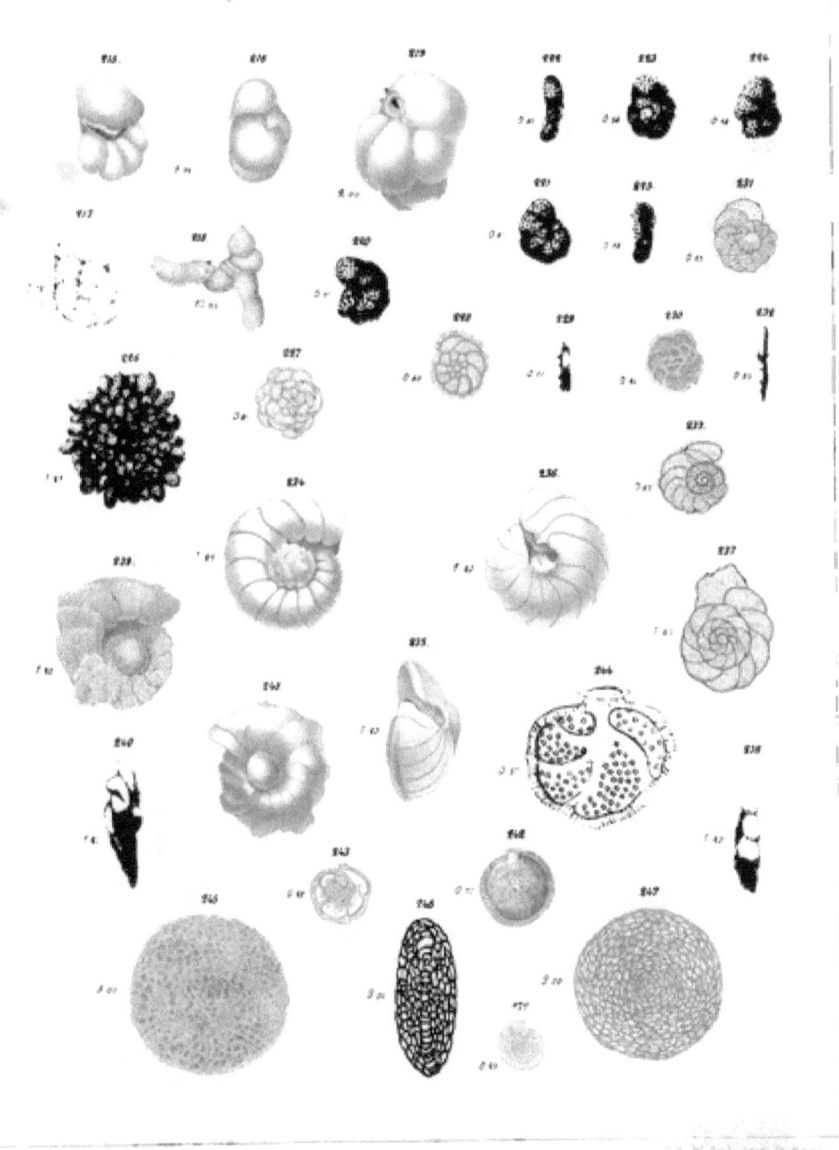

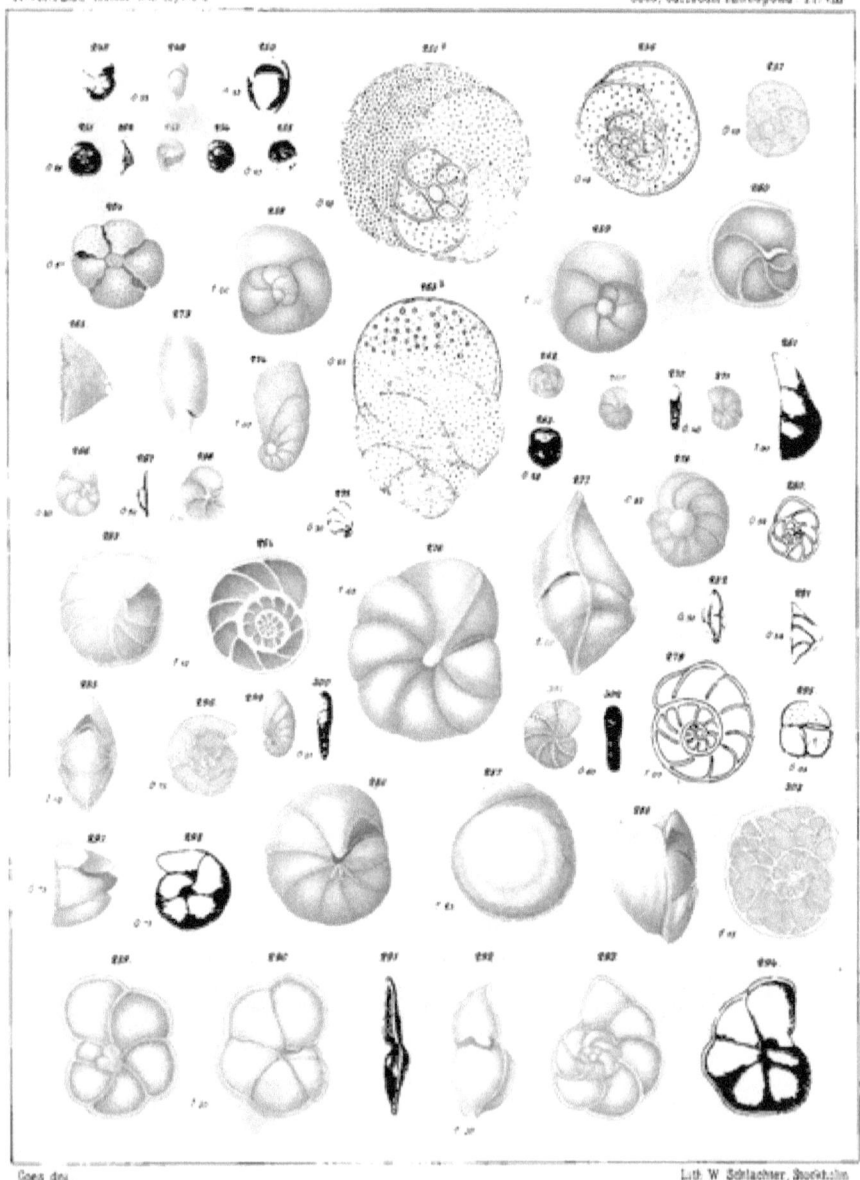

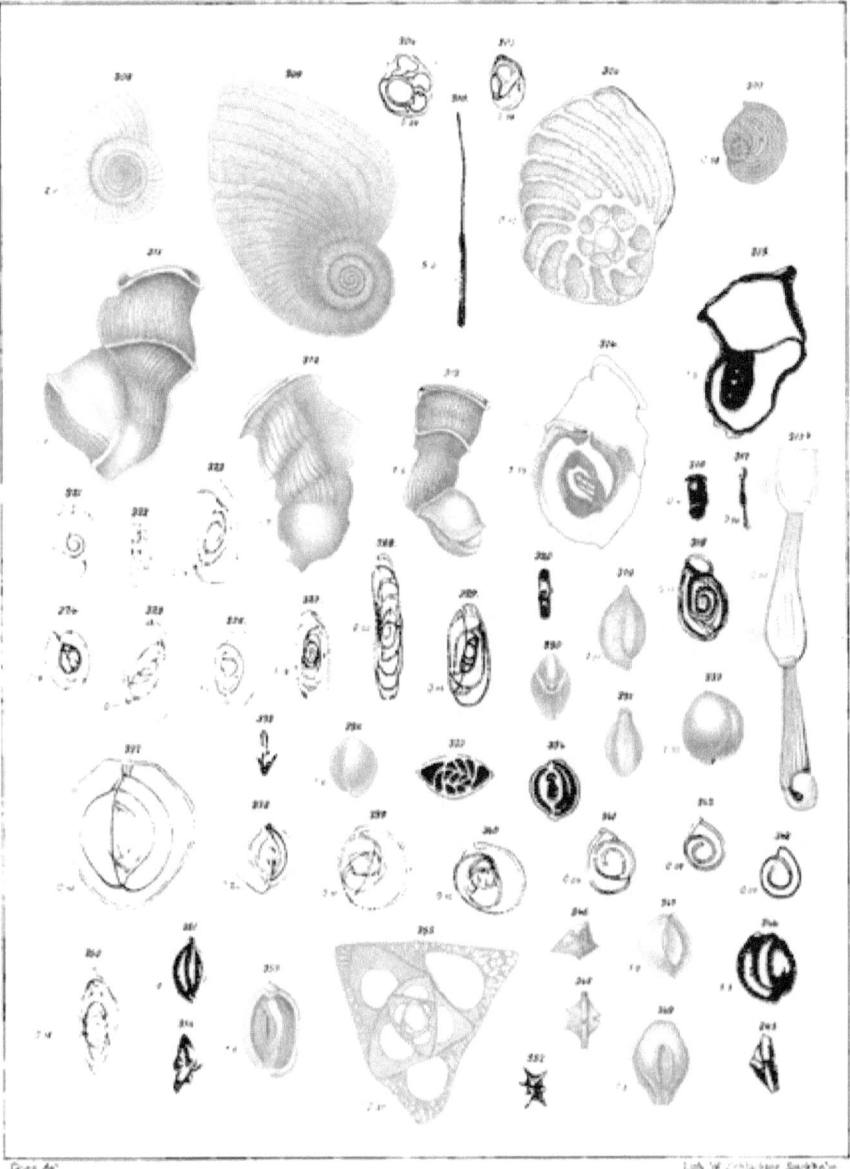

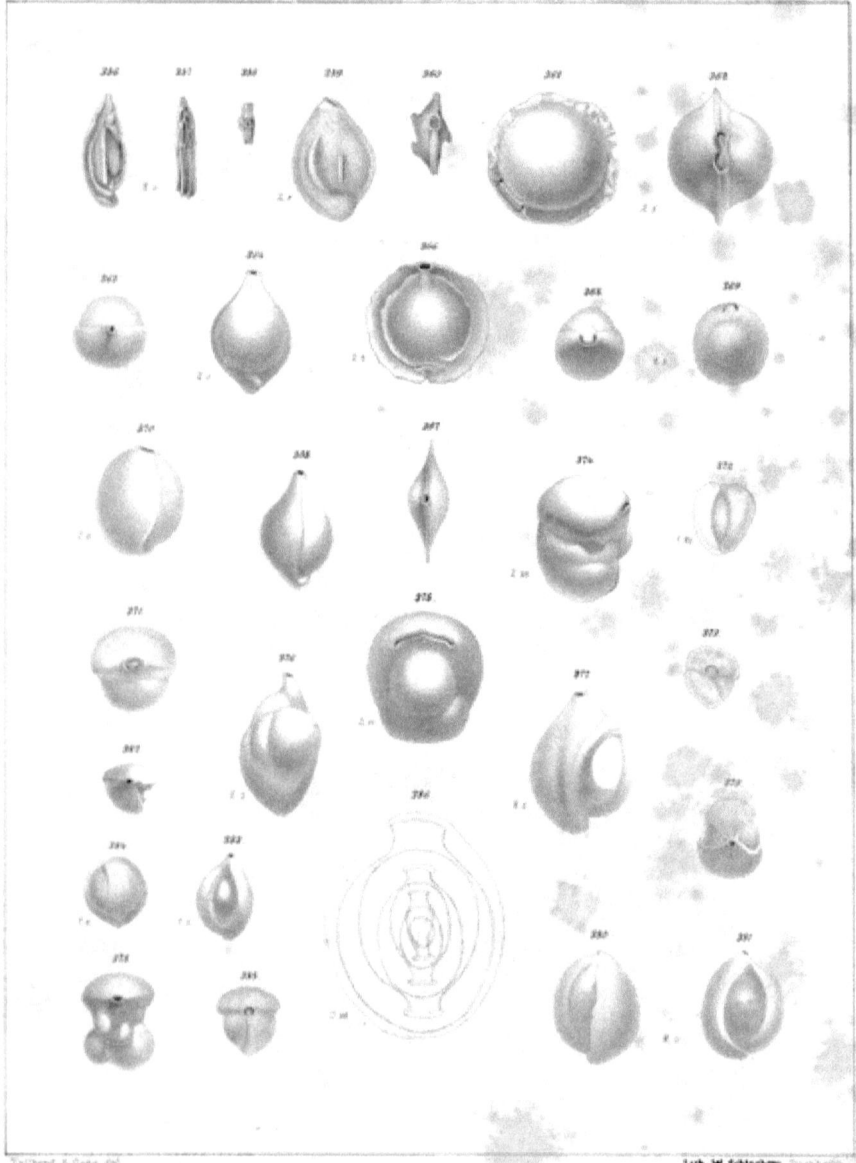

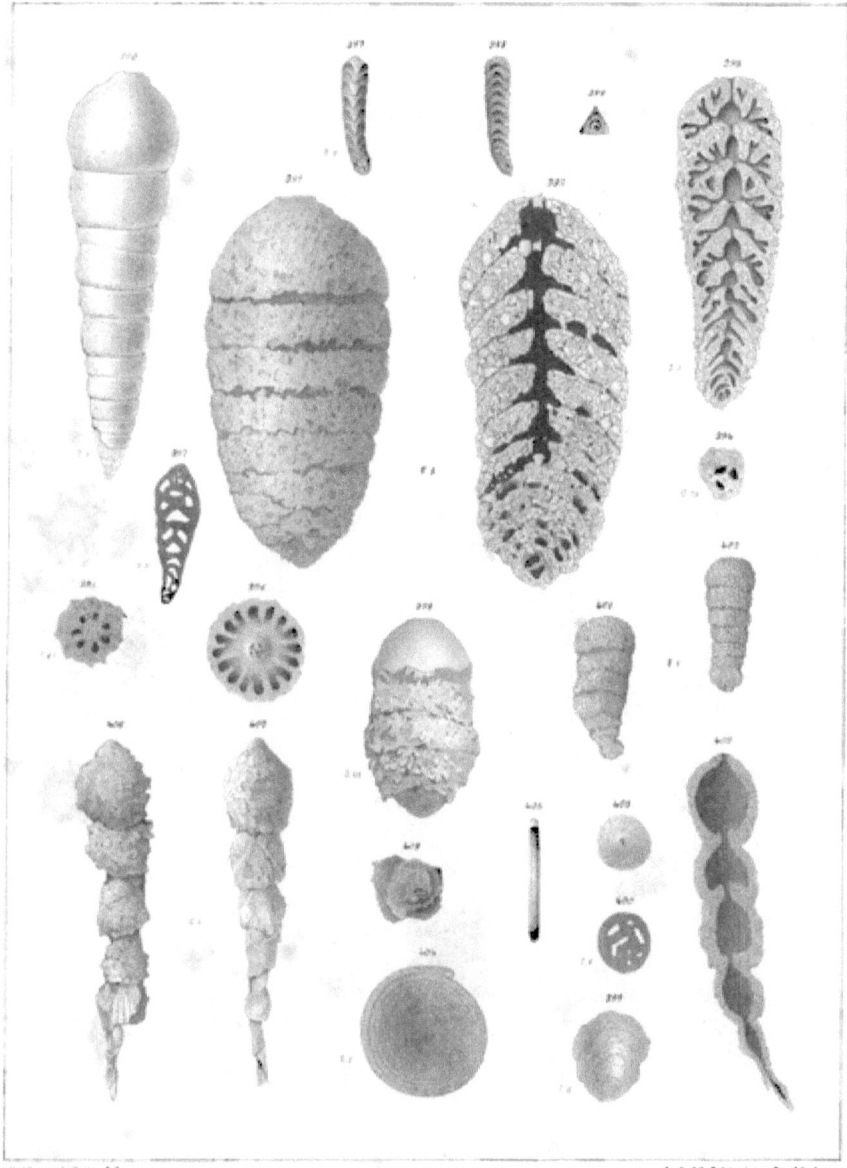

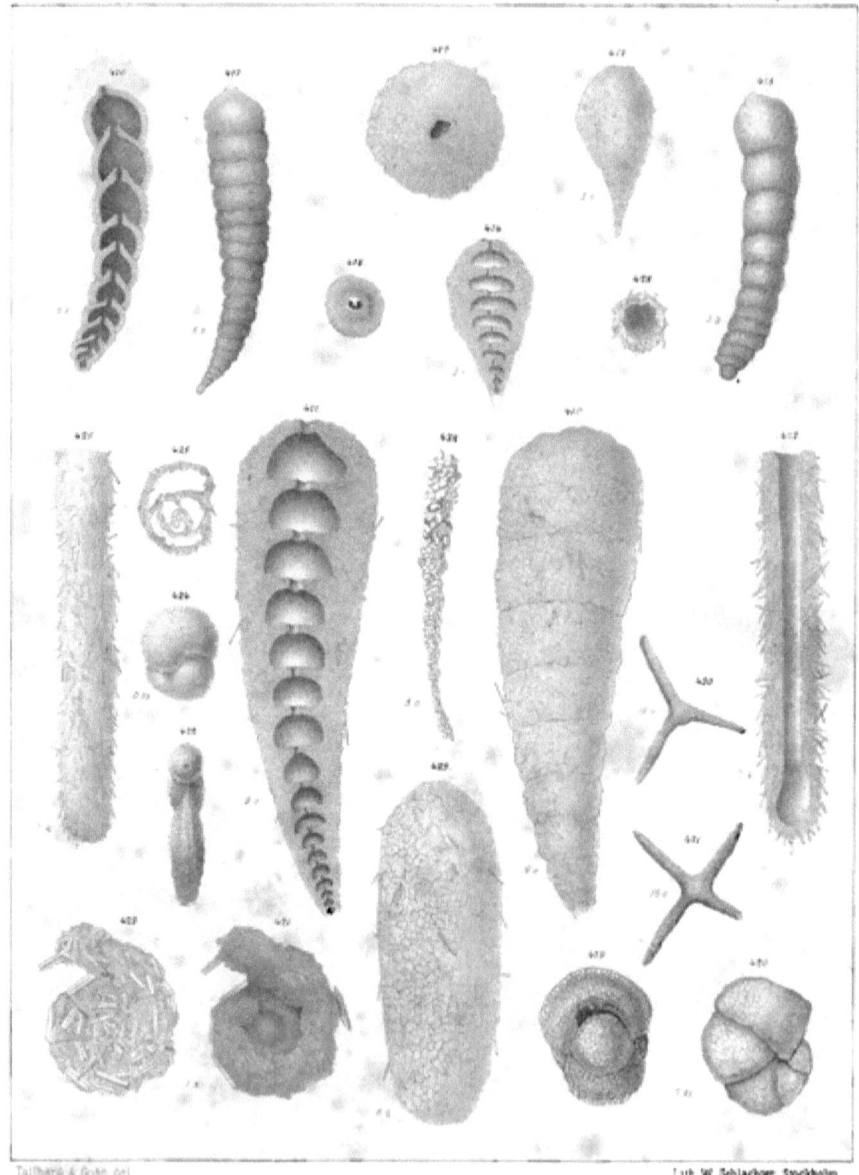

www.ingramcontent.com/pod-product-compliance
Lightning Source LLC
Chambersburg PA
CBHW020258170426
43202CB00008B/419